AGENTS OF THE INVISIBLE WORLD

Agents of the Invisible World explores an underappreciated aspect of the well-researched early modern witchcraft trials: children. In particular, this work analyses the various roles children played in English and New English witchcraft trials between 1589 and 1692, seeking to understand not only how children became involved in witchcraft trials but also why.

Using primary sources, including legal documents, pamphlets and hitherto overlooked archival materials, this book reveals that children were not always passive accusers who identified witches, but could be aggressive in their denunciations, sometimes even being accused of witchcraft themselves. By once again allowing these children to take centre stage, Northcott uncovers the haunting history behind children's pervasive involvement in witchcraft trials on both sides of the Atlantic. Readers are guided through thirty-six case studies from England and New England, making this the most detailed work on the role of children in England and New England to date. The main themes discussed include agency, motivation, influence and impact, incorporating multidisciplinary insights and principles from feminism, anthropology, history of emotion, social, cultural and religious studies.

This volume is a valuable resource for students, scholars and anyone interested in concepts of early modern witchcraft and magic, children and childhood, and social history.

Molly Northcott received her PhD at the University of New England, Australia. Her current research focuses on the different roles children played in early modern English and New English witchcraft trials in the sixteenth and seventeenth centuries. Ever since studying early modern witch-hunting as an undergraduate at UNE in 2017, Northcott has become fascinated by the subject. Her research interests focus on witchcraft trials in England and New England as well as issues and questions of youth, gender, motivation, agency and fraud.

Routledge Studies in the History of Witchcraft, Demonology and Magic

Magic, Witchcraft, and Ghosts in the Enlightenment
Edited by Michael R. Lynn

Witchcraft and Magic Beliefs in Italy between 1550 and 1850
Debora Moretti

An Anatomy of Witchcraft
Between Cognitive Sciences and History
Oscar Di Simplicio and Martina Di Simplicio

Science and Specters at Salem
Matt Goldish

The Construction of Witchcraft in Early Modern Denmark, 1536–1617
Louise Nyholm Kallestrup

Prophets and Witches
Witchcraft, Gender and Politics in Revolutionary England
Debra Parish

Agents of the Invisible World
Children and Witchcraft in England and New England, 1589–1692
Molly Northcott

For more information about this series, please visit: www.routledge.com/Routledge-Studies-in-the-History-of-Witchcraft-Demonology-and-Magic/book-series/RSHWDM

AGENTS OF THE INVISIBLE WORLD

Children and Witchcraft in England and New England, 1589–1692

Molly Northcott

Routledge
Taylor & Francis Group
LONDON AND NEW YORK

Designed cover image: Witchcraft at Salem Village. Engraving. The central figure in this 1876 illustration of the courtroom is usually identified as Mary Walcott. Source: GL Archive/ Alamy.

First published 2026
by Routledge
4 Park Square, Milton Park, Abingdon, Oxon OX14 4RN

and by Routledge
605 Third Avenue, New York, NY 10158

Routledge is an imprint of the Taylor & Francis Group, an informa business

British Library Cataloguing-in-Publication Data
A catalogue record for this book is available from the British Library

ISBN: 978-1-041-16580-4 (hbk)
ISBN: 978-1-041-16578-1 (pbk)
ISBN: 978-1-003-68531-9 (ebk)

DOI: 10.4324/9781003685319

Typeset in Sabon
by Newgen Publishing UK

For Professor Thomas A. Fudge
Who is known by many epithets and titles but my favourite ones will always be 'mentor' and 'friend'.

CONTENTS

MAPS

Children in English Witchcraft Trials: Key Sites

MAP 0.1 A map of England showing where children featured in English witchcraft trials, 1566–1716. Points are grouped georgraphically and do not follow the chronological order of Appendix A.

Number	Name	County
1	Orpington	Kent
2	Ashford	Kent
3	Faversham	Kent
4	Hadlow	Kent
5	Tunbridge	Kent
6	Westwell	Kent
7	Woolwich	Kent
8	Baildon	Yorkshire
9	Bishop Burton	Yorkshire
10	Burton Agnes	Yorkshire
11	Halifax	Yorkshire
12	Huddersfield	Yorkshire
13	Northowram	Yorkshire
14	Scarborough	Yorkshire
15	Sheffield	Yorkshire
16	Thorne	Yorkshire
17	Wakefield	Yorkshire
18	Warmfield	Yorkshire
19	West Riding	Yorkshire
20	Fewston	Yorkshire
21	Woolley	Yorkshire
22	Middleham	Yorkshire
23	Beckington	Somerset
24	Taunton Dean	Somerset
25	Milton Ernest	Bedfordshire
26	Bewdley	Worcestershire
27	Droitwich	Worcestershire
28	Bilson Brook	Staffordshire
29	Burton upon Trent	Staffordshire

MAP 0.1 (Continued)

30	Birchen Nook	Northumberland
31	Northumberland	Northumberland
32	Newcastle upon Tyne	Northumberland
33	Borough of Southwark	Surrey
34	London	Middlesex
35	Whitechapel	Middlesex
36	Wapping	Middlesex
37	Tyburn Tree (London executions site)	Middlesex
38	Shipyard near Temple-Bar	Middlesex
39	Edmonton	Middlesex
40	Stanmore	Middlesex
41	Isleworth (Thistleworth)	Middlesex
42	Kingswood	Gloucestershire
43	Bristol	Gloucestershire / Somerset
44	Bow	Devon
45	Exeter	Devon
46	Penzance	Cornwall
47	Trebitian (unclear spelling)	Cornwall
48	Honiton	Devon
49	Lyme Regis	Dorset
50	Bury St Edmunds	Suffolk
51	Dunwich	Suffolk
52	Herringswell	Suffolk
53	Stradbroke	Suffolk
54	Walsingham	Suffolk
55	Denham	Buckinghamshire
56	Ilkeston	Derbyshire
57	Ipswich (was Essex historically)	Essex
58	St. Osyth	Essex
59	Stisted	Essex

MAP 0.1 (Continued)

60	Upton	Essex
61	Great Bowden	Leicestershire
62	Husbands Bosworth	Leicestershire
63	Leicester	Leicestershire
64	Hertford	Hertfordshire
65	Little Gaddesden	Hertfordshire
66	Sarrett	Hertfordshire
67	Ware	Hertfordshire
68	Chester	Cheshire
69	Northwich	Cheshire
70	Huntingdon	Huntingdonshire
71	Warboys	Huntingdonshire
72	Isle of Ely	Cambridgeshire
73	Leyland	Lancashire
74	Ormskirk	Lancashire
75	Pendle Forest	Lancashire
76	Samlesbury	Lancashire
77	Surrey (general)	Surrey
78	Ewell (Yowel)	Surrey
79	Norfolk (general)	Norfolk
80	North Moreton	Berkshire
81	Windsor	Berkshire
82	Northamptonshire (general)	Northamptonshire
83	Nottingham	Nottinghamshire
84	Oxford	Oxfordshire
85	Rutland (general)	Rutland
86	Rye	Sussex
87	Warwick	Warwickshire

MAP 0.1 (Continued)

Children in New English Witchcraft Trials: Key Sites

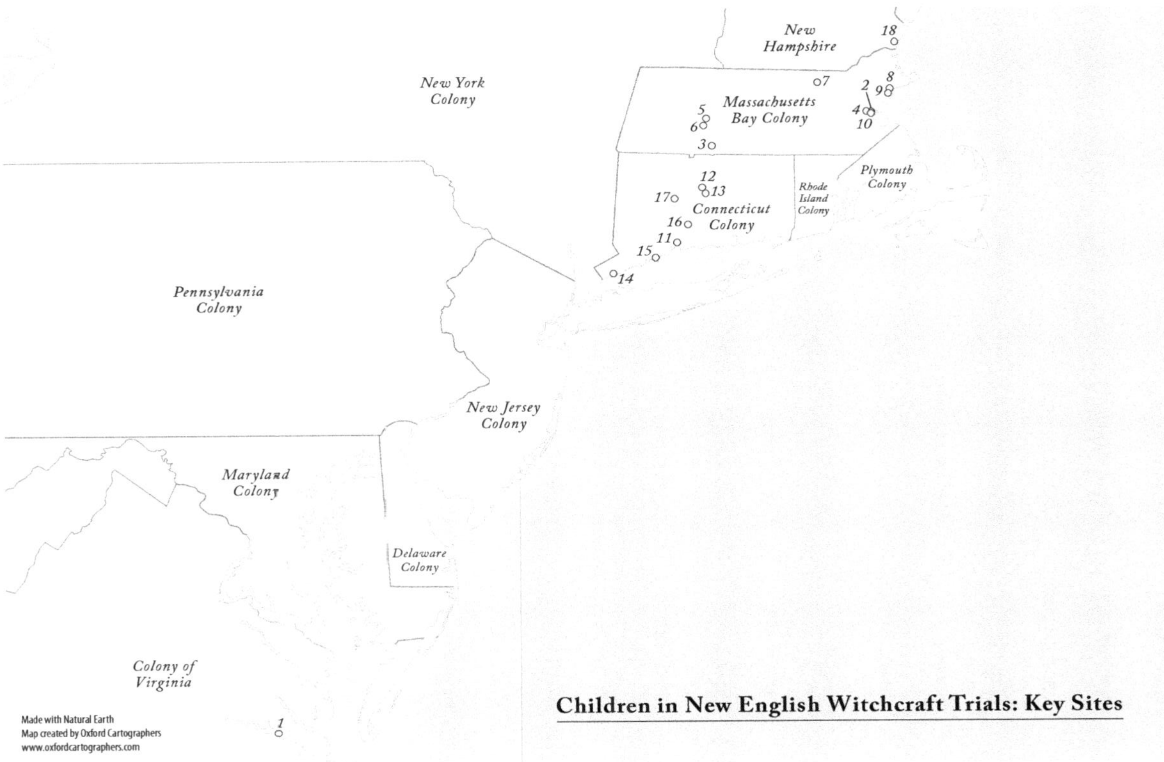

MAP 0.2 A map of New England showing where children featured in New English witchcraft trials, 1626–1768. Points are grouped geographically and do not follow the chronological order of Appendix B.

Number	Name	Colony
1	N/A	Virginia
2	Charlestown	Massachusetts
3	Springfield	Massachusetts
4	Cambridge	Massachusetts
5	Northampton	Massachusetts
6	Easthampton	Massachusetts
7	Groton	Massachusetts
8	Beverly	Massachusetts
9	Salem (Village)	Massachusetts
10	Boston	Massachusetts
11	New Haven	Connecticut
12	Hartford	Connecticut
13	Wethersfield	Connecticut
14	Stamford	Connecticut
15	Stratford	Connectict
16	Wallingford	Connecticut
17	Bristol	Connecticut
18	Hampton	New Hampshire

MAP 0.2 (Continued)

ACKNOWLEDGEMENTS

They say it takes a village to raise a child, and it certainly took an immense amount of support and encouragement to help complete this book. Firstly, I would like to thank the following institutions for allowing me access to vital archival documents: The British Library, The Bodleian Library, The National Archives (Kew), The Devonshire Record Office and The Gloucestershire Record Office. I also wish to sincerely thank Peter Boyce and Owain Vaughan from the Association of British Counties for their assistance with creating the maps used in this work. I would also like to thank the anonymous readers for the Press whose suggestions towards improvement were helpful, Brian Levack for advice and Gary K. Waite for his expert and thoughtful comments on the text. I want to acknowledge Richard Raiswell, Teresa van der Kraan and Vanessa Braganza for their assistance with accessing source documents. Lastly, I want to extend my deepfelt gratitude to Laura Pilsworth and Sneha Shiralagi for their commitment, patience and enthusiasm in helping me prepare this book for publication.

ABBREVIATIONS

AEEBO	American Early English Books Online.
ASSI	Records of Justices of Assize, Gaol Delivery, Oyer and Terminer and Nisi Prius.
BL	British Library
EEBO	Early English Books Online.
ESRO	East Sussex Record Office
Ewen, WD	Ewen. C. L'Estrange, *Witchcraft and Demonism Witchcraft and Demonism: A Concise Account Derived from Sworn Depositions and Confessions Obtained in the Courts of England and Wales*, London: Heath Cranton Limited, (1933)
Ewen, WH	Ewen. C. L'Estrange *Witch Hunting and Witch Trials*, London: Kegan Paul, Trench, Trubner and Co., (1929)
GRO	Gloucester Record Office
NLA	National Library of Australia
PRO	Public Record Office
STAC	Records of the Court of Star Chamber.

INTRODUCTION

Troublesome Children and the Trouble with Children

On a spring day in 1983, staff members at the McMartin Preschool in Manhattan Beach, California, found a young, shy boy who could barely speak.[1] After looking through his bag, they discovered his name was Matthew Johnson. He was two years old, and his mother, Judy Johnson, was recently told that the preschool was not accepting new enrolments. For whatever reason and without telling anyone, Judy simply dropped her son at the preschool, much to the anger of the preschool's owner, Virginia McMartin. When Virginia adamantly stated that Matthew would not be enrolled in the school, her daughter, Peggy Ann Buckey, implored her mother to be more understanding: 'we could be compassionate'.[2] Virginia conceded, and Matthew attended the McMartin Preschool for two days a week for around six weeks.

That summer, Judy Johnson became 'preoccupied' with the condition of her son's anus.[3] On 11 August 1983, Judy examined Matthew's anus before he left for the McMartin Preschool, believing it looked normal; however, when he returned home that afternoon, she found that Matthew's anus was red and irritated. Judy became suddenly convinced that McMartin's only male teacher, Ray Buckey, had sodomised her son. When Judy asked Matthew, he said nothing happened at the preschool. Judy repeated her question, phrasing it in terms of a game where the children pretended to be medical practitioners. At this, Matthew said that Ray 'took his temperature'; Judy concluded that the 'thermometer' must have been Ray's penis.[4] Judy swiftly took her son to the hospital and lodged a report with the police. Although the doctor at the hospital did not definitively diagnose sodomy, and investigator Jane Hoag could not get Matthew to admit anything, Judy insisted her son had been molested; the police, meanwhile, opened an investigation of Ray Buckey.

DOI: 10.4324/9781003685319-1

In September of 1983, a letter was circulated amongst two hundred families whose children attended or had attended the McMartin Preschool. The letter directed parents to:

> Please question your child to see if he or she has been a witness to any crime or if he or she had been a victim. Our investigation indicates that possible criminal acts include oral sex, fondling of genitals, buttock or chest area, and sodomy, possibly under the pretence of 'taking the child's temperature'.[5]

Panic ensued as anxious parents questioned their children about whether they had been molested. By the spring of 1984, it was claimed that 360 children had been abused. However, the techniques used by the Children's Institute International (CII) when interviewing the children were said to have been extremely suggestable, inviting the children to pretend or speculate about supposed events and even creating false memories.[6] As a consequence, the allegations from the children included seeing witches fly and testifying to 'orgies' that occurred at car washes.[7] Other children added Satanic elements to their stories, claiming that Ray Buckey had taken them to a Church where he sacrificed a rabbit on the altar and drank its blood.[8] In every single interview the CII conducted, they found sexual abuse.[9] The way in which the children were manipulated is aptly summed up by one of the children who, in 2005 as an adult, retracted allegations of abuse:

> anytime I would give them an answer they didn't like they would ask again and encourage me to give them the answer they were looking for ... I felt uncomfortable and a little ashamed that I was being dishonest but at the same time, being the type of person I was, whatever my parents wanted me to do, I would do.[10]

As a result of the accusations against him, Ray Buckey was held in gaol for five years without ever being convicted of committing any crime. What began as one mother's paranoia about her son's anus quickly turned into one of the most infamous cases regarding the ritual satanic abuse of children. The McMartin Preschool trials lasted for seven years and were, at the time, the longest and most expensive trial in U.S. history.[11] The trials resulted in no convictions, but their legacy meant that generations of parents remained suspicious of people and places that were supposed to keep their children safe.

The McMartin Preschool trial and other cases during the 'Satanic Panic' of the 1980s triggered an enormous amount of paranoia as parents, authorities and care givers struggled to discern between the truth and media sensationalism. The stakes were high; legally and socially speaking, children are unable to protect themselves; it is therefore the duty of the adult, as their guardians, to protect them. Notwithstanding, these trials also raised countless questions surrounding the veracity of children's testimony in court, their ability to remember and describe past events and whether they have any agency in the process or are simply pawns in a much larger, adult game. Relying primarily on stories from children, prosecutors in the McMartin case believed they were doing their civic duty in preventing the McMartin family from hurting another child again.

About 400 years earlier, in 1582, eight-year-old Thomas Rabbet also stood in a courtroom to provide evidence of his neglect against his own mother, Ursley Kempe. To our modern minds, the crime Thomas Rabbet accused his mother of appeared much less sinister, even impossible in nature. Thomas told the court that his mother had:

> four several spirits, the one called Tyffin, the other Tettey, the third Pigine and the fourth Jacke and being asked of what colours they were, saith that Tettey is like a little grey cat, Tyffin is like a white lamb, Pigine is black like a toad and Jacke is black like a cat.[12]

Thomas continued stating that his mother often fed these familiar spirits beer and loaves of bread. At night-time, Thomas stated that his mother let these familiars suck blood from her arm and other parts of her body. While these crimes appear benign compared to what Ray Buckey was accused of, Thomas Rabbet was outlining to the court his abuse: Ursley Kempe had become the inverse mother and care giver; instead of taking care of him, she had made a pact with Satan and embraced evil familiar spirits. Unlike the McMartin trial, Ursley Kempe confessed and confirmed her son's information. Due to this and other evidence (which also came largely from children) Kempe was executed as a witch. Of course, vital elements of the McMartin trials and Kempe's trial make these cases inescapably different. Yet, one theme evident in both cases transcends historical boundaries and reveals an important element of judicial and social control: the role of children in court cases, particularly regarding preternatural crimes and abuse.

The inclusion of children in court cases has always raised some level of scepticism amongst people who question the reliability of child witnesses. More recently, consideration has been given to the mental and emotional effects of asking children to recall and describe traumatic events.[13] Why, then, are children asked to give testimony despite what we know of the possible ramifications of their involvement? In lieu of a monocausal answer, one of the best explanations revolves around what sixteenth-century French jurist Jean Bodin called 'exceptional crimes' which included witchcraft.[14] In 1983, it is doubtful any accusation of 'witchcraft' in the McMartin trial would have been taken seriously; however, the inclusion of Satanic elements, interwoven with allegations of sexual abuse, was meant to be seen as 'the horror of horrors'.[15] Hence why the prosecutors in the McMartin case maintained such absurd testimony from children claiming that Ray Buckey ate dead babies and went grave-robbing with naked nuns.[16] Like Bodin's 'exceptional crimes' the prosecutors in the McMartin case permitted the children's stories because the nature of the crime (if committed) was so great, it was seen as necessary to transgress usual procedural norms that would otherwise exclude these children from giving evidence. In a similar way, Thomas Rabbet's testimony about his mother's familiar spirits was seen as evidence of a larger and abominable sixteenth-century crime: witchcraft. Whether the supernatural stories these children told were true is, in part, immaterial. The fact that they were believed and acted on in a court of law represents both a fascinating and troubling phenomenon: children's knowledge of and participation in invisible crimes.

With a particular focus on early modern England and New England, this book explores children's involvement in witchcraft trials, not just as witnesses to invisible crimes but also as victims and perpetrators of them. Through an in-depth analysis of primary sources, the following discussion reveals that children played an important and often pivotal role in witchcraft cases. While some children were consigned as victims, the evidence shows that children helped shape witchcraft discourse and held a unique position in this particularly *adult* cultural phenomenon. Other children demonstrated considerable autonomy, becoming magistrates of the invisible world which sometimes rivalled the adults' ability to control the courtroom. In this way, children were instrumental in gathering information from accused witches that adult prosecutors otherwise could not obtain. Of course, some children were either manipulated or engaged in fraud (or both), yet this often appeared to have little effect on their roles as decisive shapers of witchcraft trials.

The themes explored in the modern-day case of the McMartin Preschool transcend historical boundaries and reveal a deep-rooted human condition: fear for the safety of defenceless and innocent children. There is no shortage of examples in modern times. From the 'Satanic Panics' in the 1980s and 1990s, to Pizzagate and QAnon, the safety of our children is held as one of the highest paragons of our society, but these are not new ideas.[17] Although Lawrence Stone has argued that families in medieval and early modern times did not love their children in the same way we do now, the early modern witchcraft trials are a prime example that the safety of children has always been a high priority.[18] During the witch-hunts, the human instinct to protect children and punish their aggressors resulted in transgressing procedures that usually excluded children, for their own protection, as well as the protection of the accused adults. This instinct, unfortunately, resulted in the utter destruction of hundreds of innocent lives, adults and children alike. As Richard Kieckhefer rightly pointed out: 'history may teach few lessons clearly, but it does give dramatic evidence of vengeance against evil becoming itself a source of evil'.[19]

Conceptual Framework

At its core, this work demonstrates that children were active and instrumental participants that influenced witchcraft trials and witch-hunting discourse in England and New England, particularly during the years 1589–1692. Broadly speaking, children were seen as innocent in ways that adults were not. In a religious sense, children were viewed in a similar way to women, that is, that they were spiritually weak and in need of strict spiritual and moral guidance. Due to their inherent weakness, children, like women, were seen as prime targets for Satan. In a broader sense, concepts of 'children' and 'childhood' were not understood in the same ways we think of them today. Indeed, this has changed drastically over time depending heavily on religious identity, as well as social and class status; these themes will be explored throughout. What is significant to note here is that children had a unique status in society; usually they were to be seen and not heard, be bound as apprentices or servants, or be prepared for marriage and a life of motherhood and domesticity. They were also to be watched closely for any rising moral or spiritual abnormalities that would plague their soul into adulthood. It appears somewhat surprising, then, that in the realm of witch-hunting and witchcraft trials, children seemed to hold a singular and often powerful role as agents of the invisible world. In both physical and spiritual senses of the word, children were in a place of liminality and this helped allow them to exercise a level of active participation and influence in witchcraft trials.

During the witch-hunts, children frequently appeared as victims, accusers and sometimes even witches themselves. In England and New England, children featured so frequently almost all of the large-scale or well-known witchcraft cases in these two countries involved the active participation of at least one child. Indeed, the first and last documented early modern witchcraft trials in England and New England involved children. Children also played dominant roles in European trials, particularly in the Basque region of Spain, Germany, and in Sweden which will be the focus of Chapter 1. Yet, it appears that scholars have dedicated more attention to these European locations than to England and New England.[20] In recent scholarship, children were either not taken seriously by scholars (who relegate their role in witchcraft trials to that of passive or voiceless victims), or they are seen as simple tools (manipulated by adults), or scholars have ignored them completely.[21] Over the last decade, interest in the role of children in witchcraft proceedings has increased with important ideas and conclusions circulating.[22] However, even in these more recent works, historians have either chosen to focus on one trial/case, or their approach is too broad and not wholly engaged with the aspect of children.[23]

This book identifies at least 130 English and New English witchcraft cases that involved children in a meaningful sense.[24] The cases chosen for discussion in this book were determined by the following criteria: their case contained sufficient detail whereby viable speculations could be made, as well as whether or not the child (or children) had a unique or decisive influence in the shaping of witch-hunting discourse and/or witchcraft trials. This resulted in ten cases for New England and twenty-six cases for England.[25] From this, there is an important distinction to make between cases/trials and individual children. For example, there may be reference to the 'Witches of Warboys' or the case of the Throckmorton children, but there are distinctions made to the individual children in this case, being the five Throckmorton children. It is necessary, with an emphasis on children's agency, to allow these individuals to come to light – where the evidence allowed – as these children often played different and separate roles. Even though a collective approach can be useful, it is important to not always view these cases simply as hegemonic groups. Therefore, within the aforementioned cases, there are forty-three individual children in England and twenty-four in New England that had a meaningful impact on witchcraft trials and/or witch-hunting discourse. Included in this number are three cases in England which are best described as 'supernatural affairs', as the children involved in these events did not generate accusations of witchcraft per se. However, including the stories of Elizabeth Crofts, Anne Mylner and Thomas Lever are vital in establishing context that adds valuable information to the multifaceted role of children as preternatural agents. Furthermore, in the case of Mylner, even though no witch was named, cases of demonic possession permeated and influenced witch-hunting discourse. Indeed, eminent historian Keith Thomas stated that the terms 'possessed' and 'bewitched' came very near to being 'synonymous' in seventeenth-century England.[26] Therefore, it may be a false dichotomy to try to clearly separate demonic possession and witchcraft cases in England.

Through a close examination of these thirty-six cases, certain qualitative data became clear, allowing for fascinating interpretations which will be expanded on throughout the body of this work. For example, analysing the concept of 'age' reveals a fresh perspective regarding the diversity of children who participated in witch-hunting. Of the English cases in this book, age could be determined of all but four of the individual children.[27] Of these children, ages varied from four to twenty years old, the aggregate age being twelve. Of the New English children, age was determined of all but seven.[28] For New England, the age range varied between five and twenty-one years of age, the aggregate age being fourteen.[29]

This nature of this book is chronological, rather than a thematic, with regard to the cases of children explored herein. It is clear that the role of children in English witchcraft trials changed over time according to certain circumstances, ebbing and flowing with the political, religious and social turmoil of the time. In this way, children remained pervasive and important in witchcraft trials despite society's shifting priorities, which included ecclesiastical debates, the Civil War, as well as magisterial and clerical scepticism. Furthermore, this idea – with the necessary caveats given to time and population density – could be seen with regard to the role of children in New England, where the role of children quickly evolved from passive victims to active influencers. Hence, a chronological approach allowed for a comprehensive engagement with the role of children, whereby their influence can be traced over the sixteenth and seventeenth centuries. This also gave insight into how children may have learned from earlier cases, as well as seeing how they adjusted their role within the changing circumstances in which they lived.

Using the Term 'Children'

Questions surrounding early modern English and New English 'children' and 'childhood' will be explored more in-depth in Chapter 1, but it is essential to first outline the justification for adopting the term 'children'. Firstly, the fact that the aggregate age for England and New England is twelve and fourteen, respectively, it makes sense to refer to these people as children rather than adults. I have chosen the term 'children' over 'youth' or 'adolescents' as it is more encompassing, transcends historical bounds, and importantly, it is more impactful with regard to its symbolism and connotations.[30] Furthermore, 85% of English children and 76% of New English children used in this study are under the age of eighteen.[31] Therefore, by some of our legal and cultural standards, one could argue that the majority of the individuals identified as children would be classified as such by modern standards. However, it would be anachronistic to assume that early modern English and New English society did not have its own ways of defining childhood. To understand this properly, it may be necessary to move away from quantifiable data and analyse the primary documents. This assists in ascertaining how 'children' and 'childhood' were understood on both sides of the British Atlantic in the sixteenth and seventeenth centuries.

The evidence shows that children have long been intertwined with witchcraft discourse, trials and demonic possession. In light of this, even when a person's age is not explicitly stated, primary sources can illuminate how old they might be based on the ways in which they are spoken about as they will often fit into well-established roles of an accuser or demoniac. This idea fits in with the concept of a 'cultural phenomenon' which will be expanded on in Chapter 1. What is significant to note is that bewitchment and demonic possession seemed to be weapons wielded mostly by the young against adults. The reasons for this are many, but put simply, children's liminality in both a physical and spiritual sense was the main reason they were frequently seen as having a connection to the supernatural in ways that adults did not. This idea, of course, has exceptions: notably the thirty-year-old English demoniac Robert Brigges who was possessed in 1574 in London. While Brigges' symptoms were closely aligned with those that children manifested, Brigges' possession was culturally understood to be related to and informed by his experiences as an adult.[32]

Overall, the concept of age can be seen less as a numerical figure but more of a 'status' in early modern England and New England. This was undoubtedly influenced by gender, social status and wealth; in most cases, a person was no longer considered a child once they were married. This too fits with the idea of age as being a 'cultural phenomenon'. Often when people got older, became married and owned property and possessions, these concerned them more so than expressions of their spiritual vitality. Demonic possession and bewitchment, then, may have been dominated by children because it was thought to be within *their* centre of control, one of the only valid ways to express themselves. In this way, it becomes clearer why children often actively engaged with aspects of demonology and witchcraft. In legal terms, it is important to note that children under the age of fourteen were 'generally' not allowed to testify in court.[33] However, high-ranking members of society, including King James I and eminent judges such as Matthew Hale and Geoffrey Gilbert, all conceded that testimony from children under the age of fourteen was allowed in cases of witchcraft.[34] This was likely due to the 'exceptional' nature of the crime of witchcraft.

While age can be understood to be more of a 'status', considerations must be made for the children who had likely entered or had gone through puberty. For example, Ann Cole and Anne Gunter were both around twenty years of age at the time of their bewitchments. By twenty, one could assume they had both gone through puberty and had started menstruating. This is important, as historian Ursula Potter notes, because menstruating had certain connotations associated with it.[35] For example, in *The Midwives Book* (1671), Jane Sharp stated that 'maids will not be easily ruled' and 'lustful thoughts draw away their minds' when girls begin to menstruate.[36] Indeed, when Ann Cole suffered bewitchment in 1662, she expressed worry that witches would 'hinder' her marital prospects.[37] Menstruation was linked to an illness called 'green-sickness' and became widely discussed in medical texts throughout the seventeenth century.[38] 'Green-sickness' was associated with the effects of menarche on the virginal body and 'the dangers of retained menses of female seed once the girl had reached "ripeness"'.[39] One of the symptoms of 'green-sickness', according to Sharp, was that 'it was always almost attended with disgust and loathing of good nutriment and longing after hurtful things'.[40] Although it cannot be determined with certainty, many of the pubescent girls in this study exhibited symptoms that closely align with 'green-sickness', such as fatigue, weeping, irrational behaviour, depression and suicidal tendencies.[41] It is important to question how accessible information about 'green-sickness' was to ordinary people; however, Potter suggests that sixteenth- and seventeenth-century popular drama (as one example) can be seen as a purveyor of this contemporary medical knowledge.[42]

There appeared to be less anxiety around pubescent boys; Sharp simply noted that 'men about the same age change their faces and grow downy with hair and … change their notes and voices'.[43] Yet, it would be inaccurate to claim that puberty was not considered an important milestone for boys. For example, in 1716, Sarah Savage fretted over her fourteen-year-old son because he would not do as he was told in this 'critical time of life'.[44] While it is important to acknowledge the significance of puberty and its effect on children, it is equally important to assess how children were perceived by their society; this idea interplays with the important issue of gender.

Early modern witch-hunting has sometimes been characterised as 'gynocide' because of the disproportionately large number of women who were accused and executed.[45] In fact, Alan Macfarlane, in his research on witches in Essex, found that only twenty-three of the 291 accused witches were men.[46] Of these twenty-three, eleven were married to an accused witch or appeared in a joint indictment with a woman.[47] However, there is a finite amount of value that can be gained from viewing history as a collection of statistics; they help inform but cannot dictate conclusions. The fact that men were victims of witchcraft at all means that witch-hunting cannot wholly be considered woman-hunting.[48] The persistence of children in English and New English witchcraft trials adds an additional problem to the issue of gender and witch-hunting.[49] While most witch-hunting scholarship acknowledges 'gender' to some extent, only adult men and women are discussed.[50] With regard to the English children examined in this study, the gender split appears to be slightly more balanced than existing adult statistics with 70% girls and 30% boys. The New English context represented a greater disparity with 88% girls and 12% boys. One conclusion from these statistics is that girls were more predominant in both English and New English witchcraft trials than boys. Several theories – ranging from pathological hysteria to heightened sexual impulses – have been put forward to explain this phenomenon.[51] The answer to why girls appeared in more witchcraft cases than boys remains unclear. Popular beliefs in witchcraft did not inherently assume that witches were biologically female, but they did associate witchcraft as being maternal in nature.[52] Therefore, girls may have found it more socially acceptable than boys to participate in witchcraft trials as the crime itself was closely aligned with aspects of femininity. Furthermore, connotations with girls and 'green-sickness' may have made them more believable demoniacs over younger boys, who were rarely (if ever) portrayed as 'hysterical'. Yet, the fact that boys feature consistently throughout witch-hunting trials (especially in England) indicates that the phenomena cannot neatly be explained as a 'gender issue'.

Understanding children's prevalence in witchcraft trials adds to historians' knowledge about gender and witch-hunting more broadly. When an analysis of age/puberty is added to this, greater insights can be revealed. For example, younger children (both girls and boys) appeared to have less malicious motivations in their witchcraft accusations; their testimony often seemed to be born out of fear, fantasy or even fun.[53] Accusations from older, pubescent children often appeared more complex; their motivations were focused on themselves, as well as their growing wants and needs, such as not wanting to go to school or a desire to earn money.[54]

Chronological and Geographical Constraints

This book's examination begins in earnest in 1589 which starts with the famous witches of Warboys case, also known as the Throckmorton case in Huntingdonshire, England. It concludes in 1692 with the large-scale Salem witch-hunt in Massachusetts Bay Colony, New England. Both these trials marked pivotal moments regarding the role of children in witchcraft trials. In addition, nine earlier English cases (1564–1589) and seven later English and New English cases (1693–1768) are discussed, as these cases hold great significance in helping to clarify how the role of children was established and sustained over time.[55]

While the core focus of this book is on England and New England, Chapter 1 briefly explores the role of children in witchcraft trials in Germany, the Basque region in Spain and Sweden. This discussion assists in establishing context, as well as providing a helpful platform from which to compare the role of children in witchcraft trials on the Continent against England and New England. From this, analysing and comparing England and New England appears logical, as they share many legal, social and cultural elements.

In England, there was a substantial number of children involved in witchcraft trials in twenty-one counties. The most significant areas, in terms of the highest number of cases, were Essex and Yorkshire with eight, Lancashire with six, London with five and Hertfordshire with four.[56] With regard to New England, the highest predominance of children in witchcraft cases occurred in Massachusetts and Connecticut. Other research indicates that records for witchcraft trials in the southern colonies were either relatively non-existent or are now lost.[57] Endeavouring to understand the role of children in multiple trials across a larger geographic and chronological timeframe adds insight to the narrative of early modern witch-hunting. There is also inherent value added to the history of children and childhood and their place in early modern society.

'Out of the mouths of babes and sucklings': Interpreting Early Modern Sources

In order to better understand early modern witchcraft, it is necessary to highlight the nature of the sources that underpin this study. The most obvious challenge is the lack of substantial trial documents. Unlike the Salem witchcraft trials – where the sheer amount of trial documents provides a bounty of information for historians – the English Assize system has not yielded similar volumes of evidence. According to J. S. Cockburn, the Assize system in England had been well and truly cemented by 1558 although the 'essential elements' were much older.[58] For the purposes of understanding this study, as well as the deficit of trial documents, it is essential to briefly outline how the Assize circuits worked and the kind of sources they typically produced. Twice a year, in the Lent vacation during late February and March and the Trinity vacation during late July and August, two common law judges would travel around a circuit – usually one they did not reside in – to hear pleas and deliver gaols in county towns.[59] As of 1337 the six circuits were as follows:[60]

Home: Essex, Hertfordshire, Kent, Middlesex, Surry and Sussex
Midland: Derbyshire, Leicestershire, Lincolnshire, Nottinghamshire, *Northamptonshire*, Rutland and Warwickshire
Norfolk: Bedfordshire, Buckinghamshire, Cambridgeshire, Huntingdonshire, Norfolk and Suffolk
Oxford: Gloucestershire, Herefordshire, Shropshire, Staffordshire and Worcestershire
Northern: Cumberland, Lancashire, Northumberland, Westmoreland and Yorkshire
Western: Berkshire, Cornwall, Devon, Dorset, Hampshire, Oxfordshire, Somerset and Wiltshire

In his pioneering work, C. L'Estrange Ewen noted no major witchcraft trials in the Palatinate of Lancaster and Durham.[61] The Palatinate of Chester noted fifty 'wise men' accused of witchcraft, and eight of those were executed.[62] Unfortunately for the historian, the trial documents pertaining to the Assize records are at best patchy and at worst completely wiped from the historical record. For example, Tracey Boreman's research on the case of Margaret and Phillipa Flower from Rutland in 1619 was thwarted by a frustrating error of judgement:

> The papers from Margaret and Phillipa's trial probably survived until 1800, when the Midland circuit clerk declared that he saw no point in keeping the 'cart load' of records received from his predecessor and

> proposed to destroy everything when it was 60 years old. He evidently did so, for when most of surviving assize records were transferred to the national Archives in 1911, the earliest document from the Midland circuit was dated 1818.[63]

Other than lapses of judgement, the eroding nature of time itself is the main reason why English witchcraft trial records have not survived. The only circuit for which records survive in bulk is the Home circuit, but even these are not complete; about a quarter of Assize files for the Elizabethan and Stuart periods are missing.[64] Furthermore, the bulk of the records from the Home circuit are limited mainly to indictments, which can have limited value for the historian as they were used largely as quantitative insights for past law enforcers.[65] This creates a quandary for the historian, particularly one wanting statistical or quantifiable data. Without full and consistent trial documents, the early modern English witchcraft historian must turn to other sources of evidence, namely, pamphlets.

The first witchcraft pamphlet in England appears to have surfaced out of nowhere in 1566 and details the story of three accused witches.[66] Arriving with much of the lore and features of English witchcraft clearly established, this pamphlet seems to offer historians more questions than answers. Historians such as Marion Gibson have rightly pointed out the many limitations of relying on pamphlet literature.[67] Gibson argued that the sensational nature of pamphlets can lead to distortions or stereotypes of the 'truth' of the events. Although Gibson admitted that 'subjectivity is inevitable', her book sought to challenge previously held assumptions about the reliability of pamphlet literature.[68] However, this does not mean that historians should abandon them altogether or assume trial documents are not also flawed.

Unless one is a devout empiricist, one would have to conclude that, in some capacity, all historical documents are flawed, that is, that they have limitations. Understanding elements such as authorship, motivation and other contextual questions, such as, how was it written and when was it written, is essential to ask of *all* historical documents in order to tease out as much 'truth' as can be reliably given. It is true that pamphlet accounts are often trivialised and sensational, but even accounts that are wholly fictitious add something to our understanding, especially of the attitudes relating to early modern witch-hunting. As Diane Purkiss astutely noted: 'in psychoanalysis, a fantasy is a story in which people both express and relieve their unconscious (and sometimes their conscious) fears, conflicts and anxieties'.[69] Rather than being outwardly dismissed, accounts such as these should be analysed and interpreted so historians can probe deeper into why accounts that are wholly made up are thought of, written about and distributed. All sources have meaning and value regardless of whether they reflect real events or not. Of course, making this distinction is a noble and important feature of the historian's work, but one should not disregard historical sources based on this single feature alone.

The first two major challenges for historians working with English witchcraft trial records have already been noted: their lack of availability, and even where they are available, the trial documents are limited mainly to indictments which do not often allow a deep level of insight for historians. In two separate lines of inquiry, J.S. Cockburn noted that the occupation of the accused person, as well as their place of abode, was in most accounts 'entirely fallacious'.[70] Cockburn's studies led him to the conclusion that 'in taking assize indictments at their face value' historians can run the risk of 'seriously oversimplifying their possibilities as historical evidence'.[71] Other trial evidence, such as recognizances, depositions, examinations and confessions, frequently yields fascinating insights, yet the lack of complete data creates a climate of frustration for the historian.

Similarly, the availability of sources for New English witchcraft trials varies greatly. Firstly, there were significantly fewer witchcraft trials in New England. This can be attributed largely to quantifiable reasons such as the age of the colony and the size of its population relative to England. Therefore, this study noted only twenty-one witchcraft cases that had any significant or notable references to children in the years between 1626 and 1768.[72] Many of the sources for these cases are not formal court records but rather mentions in annals, lengthy tracts or letters. The exception to this rule are the 1692 Salem witchcraft trials where there are bountiful trial records, as well as other primary source documents in the forms of books and treatises.[73]

In addition to acknowledging the issues of bias in popular pamphlets, it is important to consider the evidence surrounding the distribution of pamphlets, as well as how this relates to children being able to learn and follow a 'cultural script'. It is suggested throughout this book that many bewitched/possessed children mimicked the behaviour of cases/children who preceded them after learning about them from pamphlets or word of mouth. There is explicit evidence of this occurring in some cases, for instance, where the child admits to having read or heard of a previous case of bewitchment or possession. For example, Agnes Briggs explained that after she saw Rachel Pindar exhibit fits, she thought to copy her, for reasons that remain unclear.[74] Thomas Darling also admitted to having read the infamous account of the Throckmorton children.[75] This is evident when Darling claimed that Alice Goodridge (the accused witch) wore a thrummed hat, the same kind of hat the Throckmorton girls saw Alice Samuels wore when she was first accused.[76] In 1604, Anne Gunter also admitted to having read the Throckmorton case to learn how to mimic their bewitchment symptoms.[77]

In many other cases, one must infer how and why the behaviour of bewitched children seemed similar across cases that traverse many years and locations. For these, there are three possible scenarios to consider. Firstly, the fact that children appeared to mimic one another in their bewitchment or possession cases was mere coincidence. Secondly, there really was an epidemic of Satanic assaults on early modern children, or thirdly, children learnt to copy the behaviour of other cases after learning about them from word of mouth or by other means of knowledge transfer. Based on the evidence available – where children admitted to copying one another – it would appear that the last option is the most likely. Of course, adults learnt how to perceive and decipher the behaviour of children who acted bewitched or possessed. Additionally, authors of pamphlets sometimes distorted or sensationalised events to replicate a bewitchment or possession trope in their account.[78] However, the agency of children in this exchange should not be downplayed. For example, when Agnes Briggs admitted to copying Rachel Pindar in her fits she declared that no one was 'privy' to it 'but herself'.[79] The influence of adults is important, especially as it may not be captured in the primary documents. Yet, evidence suggests that most children were able to 'act' bewitched or possessed outside of direct adult manipulation.[80] From this, it is imperative to ascertain how widely read/circulated pamphlet accounts of witchcraft trials were. This facilitates a greater understanding of how children may have come into contact with ideas and stories pertaining to bewitchment and possession.

Popular propaganda or pamphlets have been shown to be powerful spreaders of information. They were cheap, often mass-produced and captured society's attention with sensational stories that were relevant to them. Of course, one must consider how many people could read during this period. Though illiteracy was common, Margaret Spufford's work on popular fiction noted that scholars have too often portrayed a negative interpretation on the literacy statistics for early modern England, rather than taking a positive stance.[81] For example, in 1642 there was an 'absolute minimum' of 20% of men who could read in the *least* literate areas.[82] Therefore, Spufford states, there was a growing incentive for publishers to print materials, including pamphlets, sales of which were booming in the 1660s.[83]

The distribution of pamphlets came mostly from hawkers, pedlars and petty chapman, all of which had been common figures since the beginning of the sixteenth century. These men (and sometimes women) were an integral part of English society and a profitable source of revenue. For example, in 1697, an Act was passed whereby all pedlars, hawkers and petty chapman who travelled on foot had to apply for a licence to trade outside of market days. These licences cost four pounds each, for both the individual and their beast; by the end of the year, 2500 licences had been issued.[84] This trade seemed to be so profitable that in 1684, a group of booksellers petitioned the Stationers' Company, complaining that the great number of hawkers selling books both in London and at country markets was damaging the booksellers' retail trade.[85] While pamphlets were clearly important in English society, it would be a fallacy to assume that printed media was the major means of transmitting information. Historian Robert Scribner's work has rightfully noted that 'the profoundly oral nature of the culture was inescapable'.[86] Thus, the power of popular propaganda – in the form of pamphlets – combined with an oral tradition allowed for an almost seamless transmission of ideas.

While pamphlet accounts and trial records provide brief snapshots, they can still paint vivid pictures of children's lives during their brushes with witchcraft trials. After which, most children return to obscurity within the historical record. It is for these aforementioned reasons that this book uses both trial documents and pamphlet accounts. Other primary sources used in this work include sermons, genealogical records and censuses. Analysing, comparing and understanding the vast array of sources available helps to weave the tapestry of early modern English and New English witch-hunting. This balanced approach recognises the inherent limitations of all types of sources, but it also perceives the rich value that can be gleaned from understanding witch-hunting as the people who lived understood it, through the courts and through society itself. Thus, this study offers questions and tentative answers that have been arrived at after analysing an array of different sources that illuminate this neglected but important feature of early modern witch-hunting.[87]

Finally, it is important to note that the quantitative data outlined in this study has elements of subjectivity. This is due largely to the subjectivity of the sources themselves – what and how the recorder chose to include – as well as a general lack of complete information. Care has been taken to present this statistical information as accurately as possible. Minor flaws undoubtedly exist, and, where relevant, it is noted where the data is incomplete or missing. These issues have not been overly detrimental but are important to note. Nevertheless, this study paints a clear picture showing that children played a key role in shaping witchcraft trials and witch-hunting discourse.

Notes

1 Debbie Nathan and Michael Snedecker, *Satan's Silence: Ritual Abuse and the Making of a Modern American Witch Hunt* (Lincoln: Author's Choice Press, 1995), p. 68.
2 Paul Eberle and Shirley Eberle, *The Abuse of Innocence: The McMartin Preschool Trial* (New York: Prometheus Books, 1993), p. 28.
3 Debbie Nathan and Michael Snedecker, *Satan's Silence: Ritual Abuse and the Making of a Modern American Witch Hunt* (Lincoln: Author's Choice Press, 1995), p. 69.
4 Ronald C. Summit, 'The Dark Tunnels of McMartin', *Journal of Psychohistory* 21 (No. 4, 1994), note 4.
5 Manhattan Beach Police Department, letter to parents of former and current McMartin Preschool children, 8 September 1983, as cited in Debbie Nathan and

Michael Snedecker, *Satan's Silence: Ritual Abuse and the Making of a Modern American Witch Hunt* (Lincoln: Author's Choice Press, 1995), p. 72.

6 Nadja Schreiber, Lisa D. Bellah, Yolanda Martinez, Kristin A. McLaurin, Renata Strok, Sena Garven and James M. Wood, 'Suggestive Interviewing in the McMartin Preschool and Kelly Michaels Daycare Abuse Cases: A Case Study', *Social Influence* 1 (No. 1, 2006), p. 35.

7 Paul Eberle and Shirley Eberle, *The Abuse of Innocence: The McMartin Preschool Trial* (New York: Prometheus Books, 1993), pp. 42, 77–78 and 372; Reinhold, 'The Longest Trial…', n.p.

8 Paul Eberle and Shirley Eberle, *The Abuse of Innocence: The McMartin Preschool Trial* (New York: Prometheus Books, 1993), p. 171.

9 Debbie Nathan and Michael Snedecker, *Satan's Silence: Ritual Abuse and the Making of a Modern American Witch Hunt* (Lincoln: Author's Choice Press, 1995), p. 80.

10 Kylie Zirpolo, 'I'm Sorry: A Long-Delayed Apology from One of the Accusers in the Notorious McMartin Pre-School Molestation Cases', *Los Angeles Times Magazine*, October 2005, n.p.

11 Robert Reinhold, 'The Longest Trial – A Post-Mortem: Collapse of Child-Abuse Case: So Much Agony for So Little', *The New York Times*, January 24, 1990, n.p.

12 W. W., *A True and Just Recorde of the Information, Examination and Confession of all the Witches…* (London: Imprinted by Thomas Dawson, 1582), sig. A4v.

13 See for example Mary S. Tarsha and Darcia Narvaez, 'Effects of Adverse Childhood Experience of Physiological Regulation Are Moderated by Evolved Developmental Niche History', *Anxiety, Stress & Coping* 35 (No. 4, 2022), pp. 488–500.

14 Jean Bodin, *On the Demon-Mania of Witches*, trans. Randy A. Scott (Toronto: Centre for Reformation and Renaissance Studies, 2001), p. 187.

15 Paul Eberle and Shirley Eberle, *The Abuse of Innocence: The McMartin Preschool Trial* (New York: Prometheus Books, 1993), p. 339.

16 Paul Eberle and Shirley Eberle, *The Abuse of Innocence: The McMartin Preschool Trial* (New York: Prometheus Books, 1993), p. 227.

17 See for example Michael J. Cat, *QAnon & and the #Pizzagates of Hell: Unreal Tales of Occult Child Abuse by the CIA* (Walterville: Trine Day, 2022).

18 Lawrence Stone, *The Family, Sex and Marriage in England 1500-1800* (London: Weidenfeld and Nicolson, 1977); see for example pp. 70, 117 and 420.

19 Richard Kieckhefer, 'Avenging the Blood of Children: Anxiety over Child Victims and the Origins of the European Witch Trials' in *The Devil, Heresy and Witchcraft in the Middle Ages: Essays in Honor of Jeffrey B. Russell,* ed. Alberto Ferreiro (Koninklijke: Brill, 1998), p. 108.

20 See Chapter 2.

21 For example, see Paul Boyer and Stephen Nissenbaum, *Salem Possessed: The Social Origins of Witchcraft* (Cambridge and London: Harvard University Press, 1974), p., 35; Michael MacDonald, ed., *Witchcraft and Hysteria in Elizabethan London: Edward Jorden and the Mary Glover Case* (New York: Routledge, 1991), p. liii; and Richard Hite, *In the Shadow of Salem: The Andover Witch Hunt of 1692* (Yardley: Westholme Publishing, 2018), p. 214.

22 For example, see Anna French, *Children of Wrath: Possession, Prophecy and the Young in Early Modern England* (Oxford and New York: Routledge, 2016).

23 Diane Purkiss, 'Invasions: Prophecy and Bewitchment in the Case of Margaret Muschamp', *Tulsa Studies in Women's Literature* 17 (No. 2, 1998), pp. 235–253, and Brian P. Levack, *The Devil Within: Possession and Exorcism in the Christian West* (New Haven and London: Yale University Press, 2013), respectively.
24 See Appendix A: Catalogue of Children in English Witchcraft Trials and Appendix B: Catalogue of Children in New English Witchcraft Trials. There are doubtlessly more cases, especially for England, but the limitations of archival research prevented an exhaustive approach.
25 More trials are mentioned peripherally.
26 Keith Thomas, *Religion and the Decline of Magic: Studies in Popular Beliefs in Sixteenth- and Seventeenth-Century England* (Harmondsworth: Penguin Books, 1973), p. 570.
27 Elizabeth Noel, Elizabeth Parkson, Katherine Malpas and the younger of the unnamed Cony boys. The ages of these children are not mentioned in the sources.
28 An unnamed maid in the colony of Virginia, Rebekah Moxon, Martha Moxon, a child of Goodman Gennings, Hannah Goodyear, Sellevant Goodyear, Elizabeth Lamberton and a girl known only as 'Norton'. The ages of these children are not mentioned in the sources.
29 Children whose ages could not be verified is due to a lack of evidence.
30 On the definition and understanding of children and teenagers see Konrad Eisenbichler, ed., *The Premodern Teenager: Youth in Society 1150-1650* (Toronto: Centre for Reformation and Renaissance Studies, 2002), and Joanna M. Ferraro, 'Medieval and Early Childhood', in *The Routledge History of Childhood in the Western World*, ed. Paula Fass (New York: Routledge, 2013), pp. 61–77.
31 For quantifiable purposes, it is important to note that eleven of the sixty-seven children used in this study are of an unknown age. This is because their ages were not mentioned in the primary documents and attempts to determine their ages by other means have been unsuccessful.
32 Kathleen R. Sands, *Demonic Possession in Elizabethan England* (Westport: Praeger, 2004), pp. 57–59.
33 Orna Alyagon Darr, *Marks of an Absolute Witch: Evidentiary Dilemmas in Early Modern England* (Oxford and New York: Routledge, 2016), p. 199.
34 Orna Alyagon Darr, *Marks of an Absolute Witch: Evidentiary Dilemmas in Early Modern England* (Oxford and New York: Routledge, 2016).
35 Ursula Potter, 'Navigating the Dangers of Female Puberty in Renaissance Drama', *Studies in English Literature, 1500-1900* 53 (No. 2, 2013), pp. 421–422.
36 Jane Sharp, *The Midwives Book, or, The Whole Art of Midwifery Discovered…* (London: Printed for Simon Miller, 1671), p. 84.
37 John Whiting, 'Letter from John Whiting to Increase Mather' in *Collections of the Massachusetts Historical Society*, vol. 8, fourth series (Boston: published for the Society, 1868), p. 467.
38 Ursula Potter, 'Navigating the Dangers of Female Puberty in Renaissance Drama', *Studies in English Literature, 1500-1900* 53 (No. 2, 2013), p. 422.
39 Ursula Potter, 'Navigating the Dangers of Female Puberty in Renaissance Drama', *Studies in English Literature, 1500-1900* 53 (No. 2, 2013).
40 Jane Sharp, *The Midwives Book, or, The Whole Art of Midwifery Discovered…* (London: Printed for Simon Miller, 1671), p. 257. In modern times, many of

these symptoms are likened to a *forme fruste* of anorexia nervosa. Ursula Potter, 'Navigating the Dangers of Female Puberty in Renaissance Drama', *Studies in English Literature, 1500-1900* 53 (No. 2, 2013), p. 423.

41 Seefor example the cases of Agnes Briggs (aged 20) in Anon., *The disclosing of a late counterfeited possession by the devil in two maidens within the city of London...* (London: printed by Richard Watkins, 1574); Mildred Norrington (aged 17) in Reginald Scot, *The Discoverie of Witchcraft*, 1691 edn. (London: publisher unknown); Joan and Elizabeth Throckmorton (aged 15 and 13 respectively) in Anon., *The most strange and admirable discoverie of three Witches of Warboys...* (London: printed by the Widow Orwin for Thomas Man and John Winnington, 1593); Ann Cole (aged 21) in John Whiting, 'Letter from John Whiting to Increase Mather' in *Collections of the Massachusetts Historical Society*, vol. 8, fourth series (Boston: published for the Society, 1868); Elizabeth Knap (aged 16) in Samuel Willard, 'A Brief Account of a Strange and Unusual Providence of God Befallen to Elizabeth Knap of Groton' in Groton in *The Witchcraft Times*, ed. Samuel A. Green (Cambridge: John Wilson and Son, 1883); and Mary Warren (aged 20) in Bernard Rosenthal, ed., *Records of the Salem Witch-Hunt* (New York: Cambridge University Press, 2009).

42 Ursula Potter, 'Navigating the Dangers of Female Puberty in Renaissance Drama', *Studies in English Literature, 1500-1900* 53 (No. 2, 2013), p. 423.

43 Jane Sharp, *The Midwives Book, or, The Whole Art of Midwifery Discovered...* (London: Printed for Simon Miller, 1671), p. 85.

44 'Diary of Sarah Savage', *Bodleian Library*, MS Eng, misc. e 331 as quoted in Patricia Crawford, *Blood, Bodies and Families in Early Modern England* (London and New York: Routledge, 2004), p. 187.

45 See Andrea Dworkin, *Woman Hating* (New York: E. P. Dutton, 1974), p. 118. Brian Levack stated that in England, women made up 90% of all accused witches. See Brian Levack, *The Witch-Hunt in Early Modern Europe*, 4th edn. (London and New York: Routledge, 2016), p. 128.

46 Alan Macfarlane, *Witchcraft in Tudor and Stuart England: a regional and comparative study*, 2nd edn. (London: Routledge, 1999), p. 160.

47 Alan Macfarlane, *Witchcraft in Tudor and Stuart England: a regional and comparative study*, 2nd edn. (London: Routledge, 1999).

48 Christina Larner, *Enemies of God: The Witch-Hunt in Scotland* (Baltimore: The Johns Hopkins University Press, 1981), p. 3.

49 E. J. Kent, *Cases of Male Witchcraft in Old and New England, 1592-1692* (Turnhout: Brepols, 2013). This work does not include a discussion on children which limits its usefulness for this study.

50 See for example Robin Briggs, *Witches and Neighbours: The Social and Cultural Context of European Witchcraft,* 2nd edn. (Malden: Blackwell Publishing, 2002), pp. 217–219 and Alison Rowlands, 'Witchcraft and Gender in Early Modern Europe' in *The Oxford Handbook of Witchcraft in Early Modern Europe and Colonial America*, ed. Brian Levack (Oxford: Oxford University Press, 2014), pp. 449–468.

51 See for example Marion L. Starkey, *The Devil in Massachusetts: A Modern Enquiry into the Salem Witch Trials* (New York: Doubleday, 1949), pp. 13 and 18, and John Putnam Demos, *Entertaining Satan: Witchcraft and the Culture of Early New England* (New York: Oxford University Press, 2004), pp. 163–164.

52 Deborah Willis, *Malevolent Nurture: Witch-Hunting and Maternal Power in Early Modern England* (Ithaca and London: Cornell University Press, 1995), p. 33.
53 See for example Anon., *The Most Strange and Admirable Discoverie of Three Witches of Warboys...* (London: printed by the Widow Orwin for Thomas Man and John Winnington, 1593), sig. B5v.
54 See for example R. B., *The Boy of Bilson: or, A True Discovery of the Late Notorious Impostures of a Certain Romish Priests...* (London: Imprinted by Felix Kingston for William Barret, 1622), sig. Kv and STAC 8/32/13 f. 12r, q.14.
55 Chronological awareness will be maintained throughout as developing religious, legal, social and cultural changes undoubtedly influenced witch-hunting as a phenomenon.
56 See Appendix A: Catalogue of Children in English Witchcraft Trials.
57 David D. Hall, *Witch-Hunting in Seventeenth-Century New England: A Documentary History 1638-1693*, 2nd edn. (Boston: Northeastern University Press), p. 15.
58 J. S. Cockburn, *A History of English Assizes 1558-1714* (Cambridge: Cambridge University Press, 197), p. 15.
59 J. S. Cockburn, *A History of English Assizes 1558-1714* (Cambridge: Cambridge University Press, 197), pp. 21 and 23–24.
60 J. S. Cockburn, *A History of English Assizes 1558-1714* (Cambridge: Cambridge University Press, 197), p. 19; 'Deliver a gaol' was the right of judges to go to local jurisdictions and deliver prisoners from gaol and bring them to trial.
61 C. L'Estrange Ewen, *Witch Hunting and Witch Trials* (London: Kegan Paul, Trench, Trubner and Co., 1929), p. 111. A palatinate was an area ruled by a nobleman that had an exclusive administration of justice see C. L'Estrange Ewen, *Witchcraft and Demonism: A Concise Account Derived from Sworn Depositions and Confessions Obtained in the Courts of England and Wales* (London: Heath Cranton Limited, 1933), p. 407.
62 C. L'Estrange Ewen, *Witch Hunting and Witch Trials* (London: Kegan Paul, Trench, Trubner and Co., 1929), p. 111.
63 Tracy Borman, *Witches: A Tale of Sorcery, Scandal and Seduction* (London: Jonathan Cape, 2013), p. 17.
64 James Sharpe, *Witchcraft in Early Modern England* (London: Pearson Education, 2001), p. 24.
65 J. A. Sharpe, *Crime in Early Modern England 1550-1750*, 2nd edn. (Harlow and New York: Longman, 1984), p. 10.
66 Anon., *The Examination and Confession of Certain Witches at Chelmsford in the County of Essex...* (London: printed by William Powell, 1566).
67 Marion Gibson, *Reading Witchcraft: Stories of Early English Witches* (Oxford: Routledge, 1999), p. 4.
68 Marion Gibson, *Reading Witchcraft: Stories of Early English Witches* (Oxford: Routledge, 1999), pp. 4–5.
69 Diane Purkiss, *The Witch in History: Early Modern and Twentieth-Century Representations* (London and New York: Routledge, 1996), p. 93.
70 J. S. Cockburn, 'Early Modern Assize Records as Historical Evidence', *Journal of the Society of Archivists* 5 (No. 4, 1975), p. 224.
71 J. S. Cockburn, 'Early Modern Assize Records as Historical Evidence', *Journal of the Society of Archivists* 5 (No. 4, 1975), p. 215.

72 See Appendix B: Catalogue of Children in New English Witchcraft Trials.

73 Arguably, the most important source with regard to the Salem witchcraft trials is Bernard Rosenthal, ed., *Records of the Salem Witch-Hunt* (New York: Cambridge University Press, 2009). With regard to referencing the primary sources in *Records*, I used document numbers rather than page numbers, as this enabled a more precise reference regardless of edition used. Furthermore, I devised a method so one can distinguish between the trial documents and Rosenthal's informative comments and notes in *Records*. As the editor of this work, Rosenthal highlights several important details that the reader would otherwise be ignorant of. When referring to Rosenthal's notes, I will cite the page number in order to differentiate between the primary source and the secondary comments. With regard to the trial documents, I was not always able to specify the author as many of them are either not mentioned or lost to history. For consistency purposes, when referring to the trial documents, I will cite, for example, Bernard Rosenthal, ed., *Records of the Salem Witch-Hunt* (New York: Cambridge University Press, 2009), doc. 523, and when referring to Rosenthal's comments I will cite, for example, Bernard Rosenthal, ed., *Records of the Salem Witch-Hunt* (New York: Cambridge University Press, 2009), p. 833. It is important to note that in my use of pamphlets, some were unpaginated. Rather than stating this, as many pamphlets were made available through Early English Books Online (EEBO), I devised a system whereby I used the image number (im) as a replacement for page numbers.

74 Anon., *The disclosing of a late counterfeited possession by the devil in two maidens within the city of London...* (London: printed by Richard Watkins, 1574), im. 8v–8r.

75 Brendan C. Walsh, *The English Exorcist: John Darrell and the Shaping of Early Modern English Protest Demonology* (New York: Routledge, 2021), p. 78.

76 I. D., *The most wonderful and true storie of a certaine Witch named Alse Gooderige...* (London: printed for I.O., 1597), p. 4.

77 James Sharpe, *Instruments of Darkness: Witchcraft in Early Modern England* (Philadelphia: University of Pennsylvania Press, 1997), p. 192.

78 Marion Gibson demonstrates this neatly using the story of the 1612 Pendle Witches as an example. See Marion Gibson, *Reading Witchcraft: Stories of Early English Witches* (New York: Routledge, 1999), pp. 1–5.

79 Anon., *The disclosing of a Late Counterfeited Possession by the Devil in Two Maidens...* im. 9v.

80 Examples of children taking the initiative in their own bewitchment/possession narratives include (but are not limited to): Anon., *The Most Strange and Admirable Discoverie of Three Witches of Warboys...* (London: printed by the Widow Orwin for Thomas Man and John Winnington, 1593); Edward Jorden, *A Briefe Discourse of a Disease Called the Suffocation of the Mother* (London: publisher unknown, 1603); John Swan, *A True and Briefe Report of Mary Glovers Vexation, and of Her Deliverance by Fastings and Prayer* (London: publisher unknown, 1603); I. D., *The Most Wonderful and True Storie of a Certaine Witch Named Alse Gooderige...* (London: printed for I.O., 1597).

81 Margaret Spufford, *Small Books and Pleasant Histories: Popular Fiction and Its Readership in Seventeenth-Century England* (London: Methuen & Co., 1981), p. 22.

82 Margaret Spufford, *Small Books and Pleasant Histories: Popular Fiction and Its Readership in Seventeenth-Century England* (London: Methuen & Co., 1981). According to Spufford, the statistics for women are unknown as girls were not generally taught to read and write.
83 Margaret Spufford, *Small Books and Pleasant Histories: Popular Fiction and Its Readership in Seventeenth-Century England* (London: Methuen & Co., 1981).
84 Margaret Spufford, *Small Books and Pleasant Histories: Popular Fiction and Its Readership in Seventeenth-Century England* (London: Methuen & Co., 1981), p. 116.
85 Margaret Spufford, *Small Books and Pleasant Histories: Popular Fiction and Its Readership in Seventeenth-Century England* (London: Methuen & Co., 1981), p. 118.
86 R. W. Scribner, *For the Sake of Simple Folk: Popular Propaganda for the German Reformation*, 2nd edition (Oxford: Clarendon Press, 1994), p. xv. While Scriber was writing about Reformation Germany, it is valid to apply his ideas to early modern England and New England.
87 I decided to modernise the language and, where appropriate, grammar. This is to allow ease of reading and comprehension. Where relevant to include the original spelling and/or punctuation, these will appear in the endnotes.

1

UNDERSTANDING CONCEPTS OF THE 'CHILD', 'CHILDHOOD' AND THEIR ROLE IN WITCH-HUNTING MORE BROADLY

In Jaques' famous monologue from Shakespeare's *As You Like It,* he explained the seven stages a man goes through in life. First is the infant, 'mewling and puking in the nurse's arms'. Then the 'whining' schoolboy 'creeping like a snail'. The last stage of all, Jaques tells us, is 'second childness and mere oblivion: without teeth, without eyes, without taste, without anything'.[1] It is striking that Jaques' stages of man are cyclical in nature, but while Shakespeare has captured the hearts and minds of generations, locating the 'real' early modern child has confounded historians for decades. Questions of what it means to be a child have preoccupied us for centuries: when does childhood start? When does it end? Do children require different treatment or punishment to adults? These questions remain prominent even today, so it is little wonder why scholars have struggled addressing these questions in a historical sense when so much of the concept and experience of children and childhood was defined and recorded by adults.

In order to address these questions, the first half of this chapter explores concepts of children and childhood and how one might define what it is to be a child in early modern England and New England. The latter half of this chapter then traces the rise and trajectory of children in demonological writings and witchcraft trials in Continental Europe. Understanding the role children played in Continental European trials provides a helpful comparison from which to inform and juxtapose how children behaved in English and New English trials. To best understand this, it is imperative to first explore questions of: what is a child, children and childhood.

Of course, every adult was once a child and has their own formative memories relating to their childhood. Due to a lack of written records by children, their voices are rarely recorded. Historians are left with diaries,

DOI: 10.4324/9781003685319-2

letters or other sources from an adult perspective reminiscing or reflecting on what it was to be a child but not from the child itself. Conversely, the witch-hunting phenomena has afforded the historian with a plethora of sources that come from children. Children did not record these sources themselves, and they are doubtlessly distorted, even perhaps manipulated by the adults that compiled the documents, but through these sources, historians can gain a glimpse of the child's voice. Thus, it is imperative to this study to locate the early modern child and their voice amongst centuries of silence.

There are many ways to define a child. Biologically speaking, historian Erica Burman claimed that Charles Darwin's 'Biographical Sketch of an Infant' was the first study that defined and described the features of a child as being separate from an adult.[2] Scientifically speaking then, a child could be defined as being in a physiological and developmental stage between infancy and adulthood, a period of life when the body and mind are in a constant state of liminality: ever-changing and ever-growing until it reached adulthood. This definition situates the child as conforming to the boundaries of age, as we perhaps understand it in modern terms. However, this definition is problematic and comes with a multitude of caveats. Firstly, it is ahistorical to assume that all cultures at all times defined a child by age. Even many Western cultures – that have defined a legal consenting adult as an eighteen-year-old – may be flawed, as recent studies have shown that one might be considered a child as late as twenty-four years of age.[3] To relegate the definition of a child to a series of life stages and developmental milestones is to harken back to nineteenth-century and particularly Victorian attitudes that saw children as an 'unstable perception', 'lacking affective maturity' and those who are 'vulnerable or helpless'.[4] In this way, children were considered to be akin to women and the mentally impaired, an inherent weakness in society open to influence and corruption with one scholar even describing them as 'pollution'.[5]

Furthermore, it may be inaccurate to assume that people in early modern England and New England thought age was as important as we do in our current society. As stated in the introduction, a total of 16% of the English and New English children examined in this study are of an unknown age, as it was not thought significant by the recorder to make a note of it (or the children themselves did not know how old they were). Birth records, particularly amongst the poor or socially marginalised in society, were not well kept. Hence, many parents simply did not know the age of their children. For example, it is frequently recorded that a child was described as being 'around fifteen or sixteen' as either the recorder was not aware, or the parents of the child were unclear of the accurate age of their child.[6] Another example comes from a 'census' from 1599 in Ealing, which revealed that Annis Lawrence, herself aged sixty-seven, had three children: a four year old, a one year old and a nine month old; whether Annis was confused about her own age or the age of her children is unclear, but this shows that numerical age was clearly still a language that not all understood.[7] One's age was certainly becoming more important – not more so than social status or gender – but it could still be useful in helping to ascertain how someone would be treated, what authority they could enjoy and what behaviour/decorum they were expected to show in public.[8] Therefore, relying on numerical age alone to define the early modern child is a problematic way to understand this important historical group.

The concept of an early modern child is not a transhistorical or transcultural consistent being that can be understood solely in terms of biology or brain development. Instead, the idea of being a child is a social construction, constituting sets of different meanings in liminal spaces, transiting between the divides of total innocence or uninhibited sinfulness, purely derivative or truly original, freely sexual or without any sexuality at all.[9] The early modern child, then, is an anomalous body, an 'abhuman', not an infant or an adult. In this way, it exists outside the barriers of age. This definition also helps explain why Edward Fairfax referred to his twenty-one-year-old daughter as a child just as he did his eight-year-old daughter. To Fairfax, his eldest daughter was still considered a child because she was unmarried and lived at home. More importantly, she displayed the classic, almost formulaic behaviour of a demoniac, which had almost become completely dominated and monopolised by children.[10]

It is important to remember that children, like all those living in early modern society, were nurtured and shaped by the dominant social norms at the time, and the early modern world was a spiritual one. In this way, the concept of a 'cultural phenomenon' is a much more helpful way to understand early modern English and New English children, as opposed to one that relies solely on numerical age. Rather than necessarily representing age as life stages, the concept of being a child represented a nexus of positivity but also one of fear; the early modern child is not mature, not socialised, and not wholly accepted by society. Therefore, the concept of being a child is less defined by those who are actually in it and more by the adults who impose their ideals upon them.[11] It is within these constraints that the historian must try to locate and attempt to differentiate between the 'imagined' and 'real' voices of early modern children.

Locating the Early Modern Child: A Brief Historiographical Glance

It is only recently that scholars have paid any serious attention to the recent changes and revisions in child and childhood studies, which have decided to put the child 'back' into the history of the early modern world.[12] One of the earliest works on the history of early modern childhood was Philippe Ariès' *Centuries of Childhood*. Ariès' work has become like an unmoveable foundation for most historians of early modern childhood or family studies. Ariès' study, written in the 1960s, posited that during the Middle Ages, there was no concept of childhood as we know it today. That is, childhood innocence and the idea that childhood was a special part of life (that adults would want to nurture and protect) is only a recent phenomenon that emerged at the end of the eighteenth century.[13] The Ariès thesis claimed that parental love towards children developed only when children's life expectancies increased. He argued that parents did not love or treasure their children as we do today due to high mortality rates and therefore would not grieve for them in ways that we would recognise as 'normal' in more recent historical times. In the seventeenth century, Ariès claimed that people were gradually realising that children were different to adults and enjoyed coddling them, but children were also seen as innocent and morally weak, which was championed by moralists and philosophers at the time. As this chapter will demonstrate further on, this idea was promoted by some witch-hunters and demonologists who also saw children as prime targets for Satan due to their inherent moral weakness.

Ariès' arguments proceeded to shape the historiography of the 1970s and 1980s. Lawrence Stone's work went even further than Ariès and claimed that not only did parents not love their children, but they also let them die due to 'indifference' and neglect: 'the neglect was caused in part by the high mortality rate, since there was small reward from lavishing time and care on such ephemeral objects as small babies'.[14] Stone's thesis has been summed up as being 'dramatic and dogmatic' with 'not one shred of sound logic and convincing evidence to support it'.[15] Yet, it has also been labelled an 'important book' in the shaping of ideas about early modern childhood.[16] Indeed, other scholars proposed similar theories around the same time as Stone. Keith Thomas, for example, argued that children were not valued in the same ways as they are now. Child labour was rampant, and pauper children as young as five were often 'swept off the street' and put out to masters.[17] Not only was this idea borne out of the notion that longer apprenticeships were beneficial from a practical and economic point of view, but it also came from an attitude that sought to give priority to the older generation; access to trades should be made difficult, and the next generation should be kept waiting as long as possible.[18] In Thomas' view, children were not so much valued as in loved and cherished; rather, they were valued in terms of how they could be useful to society. Hence, adults sought to prolong their period of 'legal and social infancy' for as long as possible for their own benefit.[19]

Since Ariès, other historians have attempted to bring a different and more nuanced approach to the history of childhood. Linda A. Pollock, using mainly diaries as her primary sources, argued against the Ariès thesis, stating that while children may not have necessarily been thought of in the same terms as today, they were recognised as being different from adults.[20] Using similar primary source material, Ralph A. Houlbrooke described how parental love in this period was 'the closest of human bonds'.[21] Houlbrooke demonstrated that although the evidence has its shortcomings, the period of adolescence actually provides historians with the richest number of sources. To give just one example, four years after the devastating Salem witchcraft trials, the diary of Samuel Sewall, one of the former judges, was full of expressions of what one might describe as sincere love and grief for his still-born son:

> found my wife as well as usually; but I was grievously stung to find a sweet desirable Son dead, who had none of my help to succour him and save his Life. The Lord pardon all my Sin, and Wandering and Neglect, and sanctify to me this singular Affliction. These tears I wept over my abortive Son.[22]

It is significant to note that while Houlbrooke uses the term 'adolescent', he stated that historically speaking, people of this age bracket (from the onset of puberty to mid-late twenties) were 'perhaps more commonly described in terms appropriate to children'.[23]

Hugh Cunningham's work is the most recent in this area of study which has been referred to as 'middle-class ideology'.[24] Cunningham's aim was to trace the development of twentieth-century ideals of childhood belief. Cunningham claimed that children are only real children if their life experience revolved around a particular set of ideals about childhood, which Cunningham identified as: innocence, school, fun, games, friends, nature and sweets.[25] In this way, Cunningham made a somewhat obvious but important distinction between the 'child' and 'childhood'. In fact, it was not until historians who were interested in the early modern family (which incorporated a particular awareness of the 'child') that the two terms were separated: one (child) now referred to a physical state while the other (childhood) referred to a changing set of ideals and life experiences.

Another contribution by Cunningham was the observation that much of the historiographical debate surrounding the history of children and childhood focussed on whether parents loved their children. Whether or not children loved their parents was apparently a non-issue. Cunningham's notion that scholars have not asked whether the love between children and their parents was reciprocated further demonstrates how research on children, even in studies which were outwardly dedicated to them, focuses on attitudes towards adults and not children.

Cunningham further argued that historians would 'not recognise love if we saw it' and that because it is not an inanimate object, the question of finding love in historical documents is 'impossible to answer'.[26] It might be easier to write with more confidence, stated Cunningham, about the history of childhood than the history of children. However, this does not mean that the idea of 'love' cannot be explored and fruitful insight gained.[27] Studying the abundance of sources available through the prism of early modern witch-hunting, the historian can understand more about the early modern child and ask deeper questions that extend beyond parental love. Furthermore, contrary to Cunningham's assertation that it is impossible to find emotions like love in the primary sources, emotions such as love, anger and frustration can be discerned within sources when historical actors are given autonomy.[28] An analysis of the role of children in early modern witch-hunting tells us much about the child itself: its needs, desires, fears and its delicate and tenuous place in a society. In a deeply religious society, infused with religious sacraments and ceremonies, children straddled the transitional space between infancy and adulthood, representing both a threat and a promise to their community; they could be righteous God-fearing adults or, if not moulded correctly, Devil-worshipping sinners.[29]

In-Between God and the Devil: The Family, Discipline and Education in Early Modern England and New England

To best understand the role of children in early modern English and New English witch-hunting, it is first necessary to briefly outline what family life consisted of. Understanding concepts of discipline and education is essential in establishing context as well as informing children's roles in witch-hunting.[30] The early modern English and New English 'family' usually comprised of what we now call the nuclear family, that is, a couple with their immediate dependent children. It is unlikely that most households were multi-generational as men and women typically married well into their twenties, so, statistically speaking, their parents were most likely deceased by the time they produced children.[31] Up to one-third of families in England had servants living with them at any given time, meaning that domestic servants were not just perquisites of wealth and position.[32] In fact, servants and apprentices were an integral feature of everyday family life in England.[33]

At this stage, it is important to clarify that the term 'family' did not necessarily denote feelings of affection and close bonds, as one would associate with the word today. It was simply a term used to define those who shared a household together for any extended period of time. Of course, family members may have experienced love and feelings of kinship, but in early modern England and New England, particularly in homes with servants and apprentices, there was very little separation between the domestic and economic head of the family. Apprentices were often thought of as extra sons and daughters in the sense that they could be expected to be fed, clothed and educated, but in return they were obliged to obedience, forbidden to marry and were often unpaid and dependent on their master until the age of twenty-one or in some cases much later.[34]

Children who were not yet old enough to be apprentices or whose family could not economically afford to be without them performed tasks and labour around the home appropriate to their gender and age. Young women prepared meals, churned butter and tended to livestock. Young men tilled, ploughed and did any other hard manual labour. Younger children could be tasked with scaring crows off crops, catching vermin or collecting firewood.[35] Most of the children in this study were either apprentices – if they were teenagers – or lived in some kind of family structure, whether that be their own nuclear family home or under someone else's care. Most probably assisted with daily chores or were being prepared for domestic/married life if they were part of the gentry/upper class.

To understand discipline and control in the family structure, one must first understand the influence of Humanism on Catholicism and Protestantism. Of particular value is the Dutch Humanist Desiderius Erasmus, who, in the 1520s, wrote a series of books and pamphlets on the education of children and how to properly raise them into upstanding adults.[36] Of course, historians should be wary of sources such as these, as it should not be assumed that these advice manuals were put into practice widely. They were of course only used by the literate and those who could afford to own books in the first place. Nonetheless, historian Hugh Cunningham asserts that Erasmus' teachings were 'not confined to Florence or Italy'.[37] Secondly, it was a new departure from medieval advice books, a new child-rearing formula that was created from both classical as well as Christian culture.[38]

Erasmus emphasised the need for early education, otherwise he – and it was always a son Erasmus was referring to – would '...most certainly turn out to be an unproductive brute unless at once and without delay he is subjected to a process of intensive instruction'.[39] It is important to note that Erasmus was an illegitimate son of a priest and spent most of his childhood in schools or in the residences of a pious lay brotherhood; he had little experience with a traditional nuclear family.[40] Erasmus, like many other Humanist writers, compared the child to wax, to be moulded, while it is still soft; if not, human's evil inclinations would set in 'unless you mould and shape the mind of your child, you will be the father of a monster, not of a human being'.[41] While Erasmus' main influence was classical, his work still impacted both Protestantism and Catholicism. While both – particularly Protestants – drew their authority on child-rearing from the Bible, their conclusions about the nature of children and how to raise them did not differ much from Erasmus' teachings, resulting in similar assumptions and ideals.[42] What is important to remember is that Protestantism represented what Christopher Hill coined as the 'spiritualisation of the household', that is, that the family represented a microcosm of the church and state. Hence, the rearing of children was taken as a serious and personal endeavour.[43]

Protestant households believed faith was personal, without the need for an intermediary like the Pope or a priest. Therefore, it was left to the family (usually the father) to discipline and instruct the child in the ways of God. The perfect Protestant child can be summed up by Nuremberg reformer Veit Dietrich when he stated: 'there is nothing more precious, friendly, lovable thing on earth than a pious, disciplined, obedient, and teachable child'.[44] For Protestant families, the Bible gave some indication on how to obtain such results in a child, as can be found in Proverbs 22:15: 'Foolishness is bound in the heart of the child; but the rod of correction shall drive it far from him'.[45] Hard discipline like this occurred, but it should not be assumed that parents routinely flogged their children. An example of Protestant discipline that demonstrates the challenges of administering such reprimanding can be found in the writings of the life of Thomas Cawton, Minister of London and then of Rotterdam:

> he took a great deal of pains to instruct and catechise ... to bring them in the nurture and admonition of the Lord ... [when he had to punish them] he was so moved with compassion, his fatherly bowels did so yearn over them, that the tears would trickle apace from his eyes when he was correcting them: nothing ever wrought upon me like this sight, which did plainly convince his Children of his unwillingness to chastise, but that he was forced to it; his tears did sink so deep into their hearts...[46]

Of course, it would be a mistake to assume that there was a single defined Protestant approach to child rearing. For example, Philip Greven's work on Puritan New England identified three 'modes' with regard to the rearing of children that stretches from the seventeenth to the mid-nineteenth century. First there were the evangelicals or the 'self-suppressed', whose ideas about the body and self were connected to themes of pollution and monstrosity.[47] The idea that the 'will' of the child had to be broken appears to align with Humanist and Protestant ideas. Next were the moderates or the 'self-controlled', where the will had to be 'bended' and children needed to have the 'seeds of virtue' planted in them to ensure their path to salvation. Lastly, the genteel or the 'self-asserted', where children were 'much indulged' and nourished in order for them to thrive and grow into acceptable adults.[48] Between 1640 and 1660, Puritans wrote twice as many books as any other group providing directions for raising children.[49] It is no surprise then that historians have stated that the Puritan movement has its 'roots in the family' and that 'we cannot even begin to understand it if we leave the family out of the account'.[50]

Focussing on the spiritual health of the family – particularly children – was an essential part of every Puritan's life in colonial Massachusetts. In a 1679 tract, Increase Mather echoed aforementioned sentiments about the dangers of childhood claiming 'youth is commonly the unclean part of a man's age'.[51] In this, Mather insinuated that cleaning the sin of youth and walking 'according to the way of God', not only reflected upon the child, but also on the family and the community as whole.[52] Therefore, the 'spiritualisation of the household' was thought to permeate not only through the individual but also through society. In times of witch-hunt outbreaks, when the spiritual vitality of the individual and community was shaken to its foundations, the ensuing chaos surrounding the state of the individual's and the collective community's soul often resulted in devastating consequences. In fact, it will be shown in subsequent chapters how the perceived apostasy of the third generation of the Salem village community seemed to be a large contributing factor to the outbreak of the witchcraft trials. Overall, a sense of discipline and early education was key to Anglicans and Puritans if their child was to be cleansed of original sin and not be allowed to grow wildly and succumb to the vices of humankind.[53] Only through Biblical teachings and complete submission to the idea of God's freely granted grace could one expect to be accepted into society as a model adult. Catholic families had similar ideas and beliefs which also began with Humanistic teachings. Humanist ideas arguably influenced Catholics more deeply, for it was in Catholic Italy that they had their origins.

In 1558 when Elizabeth I ascended to the throne, she not only re-established Protestantism as the official religion but also instilled a series of laws outlawing Catholicism in England. Despite this, Catholic communities still managed to exist and thrived in many parts of England, particularly Lancashire. As they remained a religious minority, there are comparatively fewer sources reflecting England's Catholic past.[54] This, combined with an assumption within the relevant historiography that English Catholic children were not important, has left the experience of Catholic children in England a largely neglected area of study. Nevertheless, the work that has been done in this area has provided fascinating insights into this forgotten area of England's history of childhood.[55]

During the Council of Trent, the early modern Catholic Church reaffirmed its position that children were essentially on the same continuum as adults. As a result, children were to be baptised for the remission of original sin in infancy and thereafter would be considered full Christians. As they grew older, they would receive other sacraments of initiation: Eucharist, Confirmation and Penance. At the same time, childhood was also considered to be a time of formation when they required education and religious instruction. Unlike Protestants, Catholics believed that children were largely incapable of sin until they reached the 'age of reason' which was seven-years old.[56] Hence, the period between infancy and seven was one of unique innocence, but it was tentative. Catholics, like Humanists, recognised the child's inclination to sin, so religious training and education was essential so the child would be moulded correctly. Yet, Catholic hagiography and iconography frequently depicted children as holy and innocent, reflecting a curious inversion of the 'normal' framework of adults teaching children, as it is the child that was often depicted as virtuous.[57]

Historians such as Hugh Cunningham argued that what separated Catholicism and Counter-Reformation Catholicism from Protestantism is the significance of schools as centres for rearing children: 'schools became a centre of power and authority often rivalling and threatening to displace the family'.[58] Schools were also important to Protestants, but they were seen as a way to work alongside the family, rather than outside it. This was more the case in Catholic Europe than in England where Catholicism was illegal and no Catholic schools existed, at least officially. Arthur Beales' *Education under Penalty* was the first study to look at Catholic schools in England and found that eighty existed in the Elizabethan era and then seventy-three between 1603 and 1642.[59] Most were located in prisons (where an abundance of Catholic clergy were incarcerated), in gentry houses where priests could hide or even in towns where the law enforcements either chose not to notice them or were Catholics themselves.[60] It is likely then, as Catholic schools were not always available, that family devotion played a key role in the experience of Catholic children in early modern England. Familial piety has often been downplayed as a feature of Catholicism as it has been argued that, as priests were the intermediary between God and humans, the responsibility of religious instruction was passed on to the church, rather than the family. Yet, this does not mean that the family played no role in rearing children or that it was left entirely to the church, especially in England where there was no public Catholic church to attend and worship was legally restricted to the home.

Overall, understanding the meaning of 'children' and 'childhood' in early modern England and New England is essential in an analysis of their roles in witchcraft trials. Although historians have spent decades debating different aspects of early modern families, the concept of being a child was understood to be a formative time in someone's life. In a deeply religious society, childhood was fraught with spiritual danger and laced with temptations that one would have to combat if one was to be accepted into society.[61] Childhood, then, was liminal, both physically and spiritually. In this way, it appears unsurprising that children were seen as supernatural agents. Sometimes chosen by God to be mouthpieces of angels and prophets, children could be venerated and seen as uniquely innocent and holy, certainly in the Catholic faith.[62] Yet, children were just as likely to be viewed as diabolical lightning rods, in need of strict religious instruction and discipline; their simple, soft minds and souls were the perfect target for the snares of Satan.[63] Both Protestants and Catholics implemented techniques to ensure their children would be moulded correctly and emerge into society as acceptable adults. However, just as God ordained strength out of the mouths of babes and sucklings, so too did he create children of wrath.[64]

Children and Witch-Hunting in Continental Europe

It is imperative to dedicate some discussion to the role of children in witchcraft discourse and trials in Continental Europe, as the events in early modern England and New England neither occurred in a vacuum nor arose *ex nihilo*. The extent to which England and New England were influenced by the Continent is a contentious matter, but a comparison is useful in understanding the complex and multifaceted role children played in early modern witch-hunting. It also places this topic in a broader context, which helps clarify issues surrounding previous historiographical patterns of seeing English and New English witch-hunting as 'unique' in its witch-hunting endeavours.[65] The first section focusses on what Continental demonologists said about children and then explores the dominant role children played in Germany, Sweden and the Basque region in Spain. The second section then compares this to English demonological perspectives to inform our understanding of children in England and New England.

Demonological Interpretations on the Role of Children in Witch-Hunting

The *Malleus Maleficarum,* or The Hammer of Witches, is arguably the most notorious demonological treatise of the late medieval/early modern period.[66] First published in 1486, the *Malleus* appeared only a generation after the introduction of the moveable type printing press in Western Europe. While its notoriety is undeniable, its influence and authority has been overstated, particularly for England and New England. For example, Montague Summers, a twentieth-century Catholic priest who believed in the dangers of witchcraft and was the early translator of the *Malleus*, wrote on its alleged prestige: 'there are few demonologists and writers upon witchcraft who do not refer to its pages as an ultimate authority. It was continually quoted and appealed to in the witch trials of Germany, France, Italy and England…'.[67] More current research has demonstrated that there is little evidence to support that the *Malleus* had the widespread and dominant authority that Summers purported.[68] While the *Malleus* may not be directly influential in England or New England, by the sixteenth century, it had (directly or indirectly) shaped the thinking of many Continental demonologists.[69] Thus, the *Malleus* had already shaped the discussion of witches and children in other works, long before witch-hunting in England had begun. Moreover, it was one of the earliest treatises written on the nature of witchcraft and witch-hunting and was republished thirteen times before 1520, so its inclusion of children and their role in witchcraft is worth highlighting for establishing context and precedent.

According to Henricus Institoris and Jacobus Sprenger (the authors of the *Malleus*) children were awarded very little agency in witchcraft-related activities and were typically seen as the victims of malevolent midwives and to a lesser extent, their mothers.[70] In fact, children were hardly discussed, but this should be seen as unsurprising as the over-arching purpose of the *Malleus* was to demonstrate the reality of witches against the scepticism of secular and ecclesiastical critics. Further, the *Malleus* was aimed at delineating the practices of witches and how to counteract their magic, as well as outlining procedural methods of how to eradicate them through their conviction and execution.[71] It is worth noting that midwives were the author's main target of hostility, as they possessed 'the most impressive occult arsenal' and became 'Institoris' and Sprenger's archetype, standing for all others'.[72] Therefore, because midwives dealt exclusively within the realm of childbirth and child-rearing, the authors of the *Malleus* seemed more concerned with the protection of children than perhaps historians have previously thought, demonstrating that although the children in the *Malleus* had little to no agency, they were nonetheless deemed remarkably important.

The first explicit reference to children in the *Malleus* appears in question two of part one, where the authors discussed the impressionability of children with relation to the evil eye. The authors mentioned that men and women are able to afflict children with the evil eye due to their 'great tenderness'.[73] Through introducing children in this way, the *Malleus* set the scene for children to be viewed by the reader as innocent victims of the witches' malice, which has broader implications for their conclusion that witches were evil and deserving of extermination. From this, the fullest inclusion of children comes in the discussion on what harm midwife witches were thought to cause. According to the *Malleus*, women were more susceptible to becoming witches than men. It is unsurprising, then, that large portions of the text are dedicated to discussions surrounding how women – in spheres where women had influence such as procreation, childbearing and child rearing – were subverting Christendom by conducting sorcery in these areas. Hence, midwives, in the words of the *Malleus*, 'surpass all others in evil'.[74]

Midwives are first discussed in any depth in part one, question eleven, where the authors outline how – outside of impeding conception and causing miscarriages – midwives will eat babies or offer them to demons. The authors then provide an example from Bormio (a German town in modern-day Italy) where forty-one midwives were burnt for allegedly killing and eating babies. According to the authors of the *Malleus*, the message is clear: 'in these practices midwife sorceresses cause greater losses than anyone...no one harms the Catholic Faith more than do midwives'.[75] Explicitly tying the significance of children to the harm and destruction caused by witches was an important step in witch-hunting theory. This idea transcended historical and geographic bounds and became a prominent idea, including hundreds of years later in England and New England.

Midwives are further discussed in part two, chapter thirteen, in terms of killing babies and offering them to demons through dedicating them by a curse which is described at great length by the authors.[76] It is not until later in this section where the notion of 'tainted children' is raised, and this powerful idea became deeply engrained in Continental witch-hunting ideology. The *Malleus* claimed that after a child has unwittingly been offered to demons by its mother 'it was only with the greatest difficulty that they could be freed in adulthood… '.[77] On the next page, however, the *Malleus* claimed that these 'tainted' children are 'disposed to commit acts of sorcery until the ends of their lives'.[78] The authors use mothers and daughters as an example of this and discuss how the entire progeny becomes tainted as the demon is always in need of a successor. The most significant part of this discussion is how the authors of the *Malleus* link this theory of 'tainted children' to ideas of agency and, through this, come up with their own theory to explain how there could be child witches:

> how could it have happened that immature girls of eight or ten years, as very often been found to be the case, stirred up storms or hail if the mother had not dedicated the baby to the Devil with a curse…For by themselves children could not, as a result of a renunciation of the Faith, achieve such effects in the ways that grown-up sorceresses are able to do from the beginning, since they probably have no awareness of any Article of the Faith.[79]

In this way, the authors of the *Malleus* argued that children became witches not of own desire but through the misdeeds of their mothers. They do not and indeed cannot become witches because they do not yet have comprehension of the 'Articles of Faith'.[80] Thus, they are incapable of making a pact with Satan. The idea that children are not complicit in witch-hunting in this way has broader implications regarding agency, as well as their accountability and responsibility in witchcraft. Certainly, the little influence the *Malleus* appeared to have in England and New England can be seen in this theory, where questions of children's agency and accountability became prominent discussion points amongst the hundreds of witchcraft trials that involved children in these regions. Many people saw children as reliable witnesses who used their supernatural insight to accuse and denounce witches. However, there were sceptics who did not believe children were reliable witnesses, while others believed children could themselves be guilty of witchcraft. Pondering the culpability of children is necessary, as the *Malleus* was an influential text in many areas on the Continent where large numbers of child witches were executed. Therefore, understanding the harm witches were thought to do, as well as how children fit into the witch-hunting narrative, is essential in placing them accurately into the wider witchcraft phenomenon.

In part three, question fifteen, the *Malleus* made a brief but intriguing reference to the 'sorcery of silence'. The *Malleus* stated that in the town of Hagenau (modern-day France), a sorceress described how to 'bring about the following variety of the sorcery of silence'.[81] A newborn, unbaptized, firstborn, male baby would be killed and roasted in an oven with other objects 'which is not a good idea to mention' until they were all reduced to ashes.[82] If any sorceress or criminal carried this with them they would never confess their crimes. The *Malleus* concluded: 'if one hundred thousand children were used, they could never achieve such silence as a result of natural tendency. Rather… the Devil makes use of these practices to damn their souls and offend God's majesty'.[83] The authors of the *Malleus* stated that using the ashes of unbaptized, newborn, firstborn, male babies was a charm that prevented the confession of witches.[84] It is striking that the authors of the *Malleus* chose to tie the 'sorcery of silence' to children. This further highlights the extent to which children were becoming entangled in the evolving witch-hunting narrative.

Although the authors of the *Malleus* seemed unfamiliar with what would become conventional details about the Sabbat and the baby-eating debauchery that was described as occurring there, they were nonetheless able to paint a picture of witchcraft that involved children as victims. Children were midwife murder victims, tainted progeny from their mothers or essential ingredients in sorcery and magic. Children were central then, to the witch-hunting lore the *Malleus* authors promoted. Infanticide and the ritual murder and abuse of children, even by the time of the *Malleus'* creation, was a 'powerful and evocative symbol in the hands of witch-theorists, a symbol of the witch's identity with the devil, her spiritual depravity, and her responsibility for a particularly awful form of concrete social harm'.[85] Moreover, because infanticide had long been associated with demonised enemies of Christendom, accusations of child murder served to reinforce the intellectual, conceptional and theological links between heresy and witchcraft. This further strengthened the idea of the witch as 'the other'. Thus, the significance of children to the witch-hunting narrative is deep-rooted and integral not just to the *Malleus Maleficarum* but to its very existence as a phenomenon.

While other demonologists reinforced the sentiments about children found in the *Malleus*, new details reflected children's shifting role in Continental witchcraft trials. Jean Bodin, a French jurist, wrote *On the Demon-Mania of Witches* in 1580. Bodin supported much of the *Malleus'* conclusions on children, but he added further details that the *Malleus* was silent on. Bodin, like the *Malleus*, refers to children who have 'no knowledge of witchcraft' and similarly only refers to child witches as 'tainted children': 'if the mother is a witch, so also is the daughter'.[86] In this way, Bodin seemingly removes direct agency from the children and applies it to their mothers who dedicated them to Satan at birth. Unlike the *Malleus*, Bodin does not mention midwife witches, but instead attributes the evil witches do to children to all witches: 'for there is nothing more normal for witches than to murder children'.[87] Bodin moved away from the midwife witch as the main source of harm to children and identified all witches as a threat to children, thereby extending the need for their protection.

The new detail Bodin made in his book that the *Malleus* did not discuss was the torture of children. While the *Malleus* recognised that there could be child witches from when mothers dedicated their babies to Satan, it did not offer any recommendations on how to deal with these child witches. There is only one story in the *Malleus* where the authors allude to consequences for child witches. In part two, chapter thirteen, the *Malleus* described a story from Swabia where a father stood in a field with his eight-year-old daughter, who said she could make it rain, cause hail and storms. When the father asked how she could do this, she replied her mother taught her. After witnessing his daughter bring hail over their crops, he brought her and her mother before the judge. According to the authors of the *Malleus*, the mother was burnt and the little girl was described as being 'baptised anew and dedicated to God and after that she could no longer produce those effects'.[88] Hence, the authors of the *Malleus* appeared to extend a very lenient hand to child witches, offering only renewed baptism for offenders. This is in direct contradiction to what historians know happened in many jurisdictions on the Continent where children as young as seven were burnt for association with witchcraft.[89]

It appeared as if the role of children in demonological treatises was beginning to coincide with their changing role in witchcraft trials. When the *Malleus* was published in 1486, children were not routinely executed on the Continent. By the time Bodin wrote *On the Demon-Mania of Witches* in 1580, the role of children in trials was becoming more pervasive. In parts of Germany, the number of children executed for witchcraft had likely reached into the hundreds.[90] Perhaps this demonstrates how the *Malleus's* influence, in this respect, tapered off and other demonologists, like Bodin, became more authoritative. Bodin was one of the first demonologists to recommend introducing children, particularly small children or young girls to the 'torment with terror', while others 'be submitted to it' (that is, torture) if they should not confess.[91] Why the 'solution' to the problem of child witches changed from re-baptism to torture and then eventually to execution is doubtlessly complicated and multifaceted. It is unclear whether re-baptism was ever the conventional method to deal with child witches, or maybe there was no standard solution until child witches became more prevalent in the mid- to late 1500s. Yet, Bodin was not the only demonologist who found the growing role of children in witchcraft a challenging and perturbing development.

Only nine years after Bodin, Peter Binsfeld, a bishop and theologian from Trier, was the first to seriously consider a 'minimum age' for children's participation in witch trials.[92] Using his own experience in the Trier trials, Binsfeld fundamentally affirmed the use of torture for children. However, the nature of torture would be different to that used on adults, such as being frightened with torture or being hit with a rod or leather strap.[93] Binsfeld noted that the exceptional nature of the crime of witchcraft transgressed the usual procedural norms which excluded children from participating in such legal spheres. Children could therefore be tortured and their testimony be used as evidence against adults. According to Wolfgang Behringer, this modification on the concept of circumstantial evidence was decisive in setting the course for the new role of children in witchcraft trials: they could now actively intervene in the proceedings and, under certain circumstances, even trigger trials or persecutions.[94] Therefore, the role of children in Continental demonologies was developing from silent victims to the child who could wield some degree of power and agency, albeit with a degree of pain and suffering involved. Children were becoming more prominent in Continental witchcraft trials and the work demonologists created around this time reflected the predominance of children in the trials as they struggled to combat, justify and deal with this developing issue.

The Continental demonologist who addressed this issue the most in-depth appeared to be Henri Boguet in his *Examen of Witches*, which can be traced to around 1590. Boguet was a Burgundian jurist who wrote much of the *Examen* from his own personal experience, as well as building on the work done by Bodin and Binsfeld. Hence, some of Boguet's ideas, such as believing that witchcraft was hereditary, were not new. Boguet affirmed this, explaining: 'I am in this respect but imitating the example of most who have written before me'.[95] Boguet did contribute many new or noteworthy ideas in relation to child witches and child witnesses with direct reference to his experience as a judge. This significant development further brought children out of the sphere of victimhood and gave them more responsibility, accountability and agency in witchcraft discourse. The likelihood of this change occurring on a court-base level is almost certain given the growing involvement of children in witchcraft trials. The fact that Boguet's popular treatise laid out descriptions and possible solutions to the problem of child witches and child witnesses helped usher in a renewed reflection on their role in the witchcraft trials.[96]

Boguet begins his *Examen* with an analysis of the case of Loyse Maillat, an eight-year-old girl who was said to be possessed with five devils through the malevolence of a woman called Françoise Secretain. After detailing the basic narrative of the case and explaining Françoise's motivations for bewitching Loyse, Boguet outlined his justification for using the evidence of an eight-year-old girl. He stated that while children are considered 'unstable' and 'light-headed', Boguet maintained that Loyse's depositions were 'so very precise and never varied'.[97] This appears to imply that although in age she was only a child, in court she acted like an adult, and thus her testimony should be treated as if from one. Boguet further stated that because witchcraft is an abominable, secret crime: 'it [does] not call for such positive proof as would be required in the case of any other crime'.[98] The exceptional nature of the crime meant that the normal conventions of the law were circumvented, meaning the belief in gullibility and susceptibility of children was suspended and replaced with ideas of their innocence and apparent inability to lie. This is evident in Boguet's writing when he further justifies using Loyse's testimony by stating that 'numberless' witches have been discovered and brought to their just punishment by means of a child.[99] This, Boguet explained, is part of the secret judgement and glory of God.[100] However, in the next sentence, Boguet mentioned that 'several other children' were 'instruments' being judged guilty of witchcraft which Boguet lamented is 'no less strange than pitiable'.[101] The fact that Boguet highlighted both children's inherent innocence, as well as their culpability in witch-hunting, is a dichotomy most judges, demonologists and ordinary peoples would come to recognise as the witch-hunts progressed.

Two other interesting case studies Boguet mentioned in his *Examen* surround a fourteen-year-old girl called Christofle and a twelve-year-old boy called Pierre.[102] Boguet included their case studies as two examples highlighting how and why they were treated leniently (most likely as a guide for other judges who might have to deal with young offenders). Boguet stated that, in addition to their young age, neither Pierre nor Christofle had been to the Sabbat in two years and therefore distinguished between their cases by their level of participation in witchcraft. Boguet stated that Pierre had never been dedicated to the Devil and did not commit any act of witchcraft. Christofle, on the other hand, admitted that she had been given to the Devil and that she had killed a cow by rubbing some kind of ointment on its behind. In the end, Pierre's next of kin was ordered to have him catechised and instructed in the proper Catholic faith. Christofle was banished from Saint Oyan and was commanded to be present at the execution of four other witches 'so that she might be afraid to continue in the service of Satan and that the gravity of the punishment which she saw them suffer might be the occasion of her changing her life'.[103] Boguet concluded this segment stating that a stricter judge would have surely condemned her to death, emphasising that her tender age was no excuse: 'for in cases of serious and atrocious crime little count is taken of the criminal's age... '.[104] Boguet further supported this assertion: 'And consequently it has been known for children of not more than fifteen years to be punished with death in accordance with the law, which is strict in this matter'.[105] Boguet then stated that the witch's punishment should be mitigated if the offender had not reached the age of puberty, further defending the sentence passed down on Christofle.[106] Yet, the most interesting reason for Christofle's sentence surrounded malice and revenge. Boguet stated that because of her prompt and simple answers, there was no malice in her which, as Boguet noted, was a crucial element in the guilt of a witch. Finally, Boguet concluded: 'for my part I shall always maintain that... they should be put to death...they never change their manner of living'.[107]

The case studies of Pierre and Christofle are significant in giving a detailed outline of (supposedly) real examples of how to deal with child witches that other judges could use to assist in their sentences. There was little discussion of their inherent innocence, and while Boguet took their 'tender age' into consideration, he concluded it was 'no excuse' for such an abominable crime as witchcraft.[108] The extent to which Boguet's ideas regarding child witches affected England and New England is debatable, but as the first Continental demonologist to give a detailed overview on this matter, it likely affected people's thinking and writing on this complex subject.

At the end of his book Boguet listed seventy articles which provided concise advice for judges handling witchcraft cases. In Article LVI, Boguet stated that judges should permit the evidence of children under the age of puberty as witches are known to take young children to the Sabbat and 'seeing that the crime is hidden and secret...there is no one who can better witness to it than those who have been to the Sabbat'.[109] In Article LXIII, Boguet stated that Bodin believed that children under the age of puberty who are guilty of witchcraft should be sentenced to the lash.[110] He then noted that Binsfeld stated that the death sentence should not be passed on a child of less than sixteen years of age. Boguet had the harshest opinion stating that children in general – regardless of whether they had reached puberty – should be sentenced to death if one can prove they acted out of malice.[111] The importance of motivation and intention has far-reaching implications, particularly when the witch-hunts developed further and cases of fraud or 'counterfeiting' became rife on the Continent, England and New England. Indeed, malice would be one of the core features of the role of children in the English and New English witchcraft trials, but proving it, as Boguet implied, was more difficult than it seemed.

Lastly, Boguet mentioned that sons and daughters should be treated equally in the eyes of the law. This creates an interesting, almost ahistorical gender equality in a phenomenon that historians generally assume to be largely female dominated. Through examining the *Malleus Maleficarum* and the works of Bodin, Binsfeld and Boguet, it becomes increasingly obvious how the role of children developed and changed from voiceless victims to persons of increased agency. Demonologists, particularly Binsfeld and Boguet, struggled with what to do with children in witchcraft in spheres outside of victimhood. Hence, there was never a unified procedure in dealing with child witnesses or child witches. Instead, in areas where children were heavily involved in witch-hunting, the response of the authorities varied greatly, sometimes with devastating results.

Demonologies in Practice: German, Swedish and the Basque Witchcraft Trials

The three geographic locations that saw the heaviest involvement of children in witchcraft trials on the Continent were Germany, the Basque region in Spain and Sweden. Wolfgang Behringer noted that, chronologically speaking, it was not until the large Trier trials of 1585 when children began to feature not just in cases of demonic possession but in cases of witchcraft. This aligns with the demonological works of Binsfeld and Boguet, who were writing in the late 1580s, as more children became embroiled in witchcraft proceedings not just as victims but as witnesses and witches. The reason why child witch trials began to change in the 1580s remains unknown. One theory posited that increased parental control triggered children's desire for rebellion and revenge.[112] Another theory suggested that the Reformation led to an amplified belief in children's capacity for sin, thereby increasing their accountability.[113] A distinct lack of evidence means these theories remain conjecture, and a monocausal answer may not be possible.

The historiography on the German trials is extensive and will not be covered in any exhaustive detail. Yet, it worth noting how the role of children developed and shaped many witchcraft trials in a place which has been described as 'the classic land of witchcraft'.[114] Wolfgang Behringer was one of the first scholars to pay any serious attention to the role of children in German witchcraft trials in his 1989 study. Behringer stated that after the large Trier trials of 1585, children were crystallising their role in witchcraft trials in three main ways: either through outbreaks of witchcraft accusations in orphanages or boarding schools, denouncing people during Catholic exorcisms, while they were in the throes of demonic possession or as self-confessors who voluntarily admitted to being witches.[115] The developing role of children in German witchcraft trials seemed unstoppable. Though witchcraft trials gradually declined after their peak in 1630, child witch trials remained relatively constant.[116] In fact, statistically speaking, from 1630 onwards a significant portion of persecuted victims were now children rather than old women.[117] Understanding how this developed in some brief case studies may help to inform our understanding of the role of children in witch-hunting more broadly.

Under the reign of the prince-bishop Phillip Adolf von Ehrenburg, the Franconian territory of Würzburg became notorious for its extensive persecution of witches, especially child witches between 1623 and 1631.[118] Group dynamics were key in these trials and over-zealous witch-hunters were ruthless in their persecutions of school-aged children ranging from eight to thirteen.[119] The trial of thirteen-year-old Hans Philipp Schuh provides a useful example of the thorough techniques used to extract confessions from accused children. Schuh, the son of a choirmaster, initially denied any charge of witchcraft when he was examined in October 1628. He maintained his innocence after he was subjected to judicial torture in the form of forty-six stripes of the lash. After receiving a further seventy-seven stripes he made a full confession. Schuh stated that he was introduced to witchcraft by a schoolmate who persuaded him to renounce God. He also confessed that he had had intercourse with a young girl whose private parts were 'soft and warm'.[120] Schuh also implicated other classmates, provoking more arrests. On 9 November 1628 he was executed for his crimes.[121] Although this appears to be far removed from anything historians know occurred in England and New England, there are parallels that challenge former ideas of England's 'exceptionalism', which will be explored in depth further on.[122] What is important to note is that the authorities were not afraid to wield whatever weapon they had at their disposal to address the problem of child witches. It is also significant that the stories the children created were demonological ideas or imaginative fantasies they had probably heard from their parents, church or from leading questions asked from the interrogators.

While the total number of child witches might never be known – since many of Würzburg's primary sources have been lost – historians can gain some insight from a letter written from Würzburg's chancellor in August 1629:

> In conclusion of this lamentable matter, there are some 300 children of three or four years who have had intercourse with demons. I have seen children of seven executed, brave scholars of ten, twelve, fourteen and fifteen years. I can write no more about this misery.[123]

Even allowing for the likelihood that a horrified chancellor may have exaggerated these figures, it is clear that child witchcraft trials in Würzburg were extensive. Indeed, not only did the role of children extend and develop in Germany over this period, but they also seemed to have the longest lasting impact. This can be seen well into the end of the seventeenth century with the infamous 'Zaubererjackl' trials in Salzburg where over 70% of the estimated 140 victims were under the age of twenty-two.[124] Lyndal Roper's studies on the outbreaks of child witchcraft cases in the city of Augsburg in 1723 also demonstrated the longevity of this issue, even when trials had declined or basically disappeared almost everywhere else.[125] As a result, children's proportional importance increased dramatically, and as Behringer noted in his study, they were essential figures right until the very end of the witch-hunting phenomena:

> Whether it was the last witch execution in Bavaria in 1756, in Germany in 1775 or in Europe in 1782: every one of these trials began with the accusations made by an underaged child. At the end of the age of European

witch persecutions, the witch problem had increasingly become a problem of dealing with witch children.[126]

For a multitude of different reasons, the role of children changed from voiceless victims to active participants in the witchcraft trials from 1580s onwards. Rather than simply being cursed as witches from doomed mothers, accusations could now go either way. Through demonic fits, children found agency and power in denouncing others as witches as the lines between demonic 'possession' and 'obsession' began to blur. Voluntary self-confessions posed a moral panic throughout towns, as parents and authorities struggled with the idea that dozens of children freely admitted to having renounced their baptism and were having sex with Satan. Demonological treatises emerged to help instruct the authorities on how to deal with such problems, but the balance of power appeared to be shifting. Unlike Germany, where there were many over-zealous witch-hunters eager to root-out witchcraft, in the Basque region in Spain, Alonso de Salazar Frias, sometimes referred to as the 'witches advocate', helped avoid catastrophic conditions in his perusal of justice.[127]

Between 1609 and 1614 Inquisitors at Logrono in northern Spain were dealing with what historian Gustav Henningsen claimed as the greatest witch trial in history, comprising of almost 7000 cases.[128] After the auto da fé in 1610, eleven out of thirty-one witches were burned to death, but a temporary halt in proceedings was called as the Inquisitors believed the witch cult spanned a much wider area than first anticipated.[129] Hence, an Edict of Grace was declared, during which time anyone who voluntarily confessed themselves to be a witch and named accomplices escaped punishment. Alonso de Salazar Frias travelled the Basque lands, taking the Edict of Grace to the witches. The denunciations that rolled in were staggering: after almost a year, Salazar had come back with 1,802 confessions with 1,384 of those coming from children between the ages of seven and fourteen years old.[130] For the Inquisitors in Logrono, the 5000 newly accused persons from the Edict of Grace and the influx of self-confessed child witches created a moral dilemma not yet seen in the Spanish region. Its significance cannot be overstated; the gravity of persecutions would not be seen again, and it took the Inquisitors eighteen months to process the 11,000 pages of reports Salazar compiled during his travels around the Basque regions. But Salazar had not simply compiled the reports; he sought to *understand* them. He wanted to know the origins and nature of the accusations, and unlike his two senior colleagues, he was unwilling to move ahead with prosecuting the thousands of accused individuals, citing a lack of empirical evidence. This enraged his two senior colleagues who were more swayed by demonological treatises than Salazar whose background was firmly rooted in Canon Law. His colleagues claimed that Salazar was 'blinded by the Devil' and remained unshakably convinced by the witches' confessions.[131]

The fact that most of the self-confessed were children only heightened the intensity of the situation which made Salazar all the more determined to understand the origins of the panic as rationally as he could.[132] He discovered the three main components that occurred in all the Basque regions: indoctrination, stereotyped dreams and forced confessions.[133] Rather than fuelling local animosities and allowing witchcraft accusations to spiral out of control, Salazar implemented a policy of 'silence and discretion' whereby witchcraft trials in the area slowly began to decline, and by 1613 they had almost completely disappeared.[134] Hence, on 29 August, after intense debate and discussion between Salazar and his two colleagues, the Inquisitorial council ruled that all pending trials at Logrono should be dismissed.[135] At the same time, new instructions were being issued (based on a draft prepared by Salazar himself) that made the rules for accepting evidence in witchcraft trials so rigorous that it basically brought witch-hunting in Spain to a halt long before this happened for the rest of Europe.

The 'witches advocate' prevented cataclysmic conditions involving thousands of children, who might have been burned for their stories of night flying and Sabbat participations had they been arrested elsewhere. This is significant not just for number of children involved, but also because of how it was handled by Salazar. His discretion stands in stark comparison to the prince-bishop in Würzburg or even to Matthew Hopkins in England. The Swedish witchcraft trials were also unique as they involved the accusations of thousands of children, but also because they were specifically referred to by the Puritans in New England who were shaken by the news of diabolical disturbances in another Godly commonwealth.[136]

The Great Northern Witch Trial in Sweden (1668–1678) rivals the Basque outbreak in its intensity; both in its spread geographically and by the fact that it began and was spurred on by thousands of children aged mostly between five and fifteen years old.[137] The trials began in northern Dalarna where children began telling stories about being taken to Blåkulla (the mythical site of the witches' Sabbat). Similar to the first recorded witchcraft trial in England, the themes, peculiarities and characteristics about witches' familiars were already well established by the time stories of nocturnal transvections to Blåkulla were inquired into by the local court. In all, eighteen death sentences were passed, four of which were for minors below the age of fifteen. However, the Court of Appeal in Stockholm confirmed only seven of the adult's death sentences who were subsequently beheaded and then burned.[138]

By May 1669, the trials had spread to Mora where parents urged the government for more 'energetic measures' to protect their children.[139] Afraid the people would take the law into their own hands – thereby questioning royal and governmental authority – the government in Stockholm established a commission to investigate witchcraft accusations in the north of Sweden. In 1670, reports of at least 300 suspected witches and thousands of possessed children poured into the governments and the Court of Appeal. Other than panicked parents, the problem of reliable witnesses threatened the credibility of the trials. Older Swedish case law stated that witnesses had to be at least fifteen years old to testify. Suddenly, the court found itself with thousands of minors who told terrifying tales of being taken to Blåkulla with seemingly no way to get around the law to permit their evidence in court. To solve this problem, children under the legal age were counted as half or a tenth of a full witness. For example, a five-year-old child may have been considered as one-tenth of a witness while a fourteen-year-old as at least half; by adding the fractions, the court soon arrived at the minimum two competent adult witnesses.[140]

The agency and influence of these children should not be underestimated. In fact, most accusations were made by a small and rather busy group of the same children, while the others seemed to simply follow their lead. For example, in one parish, 20% of the child witnesses who were the most active were responsible for about half of all the charges made.[141] While most children in English and New English witchcraft cases acted alone, similar group dynamics existed where small groups of children became ‘leaders’ and others simply followed suit.[142]

It was not until the witch trials reached Stockholm in 1676 where they finally ended. For the first time since the trials begun, the leading politicians and judges saw the proceedings up close, and suspicion slowly overcame the court. Several death sentences were passed, but suddenly, the children began to confess that their Blåkulla stories were purely fictious, and the accused witches were innocent. Trials ended abruptly, and the most recently condemned women were set free. In an unprecedented move, the most active child witnesses were prosecuted and received the ultimate punishment: four of them, including a thirteen-year-old boy, were sentenced to death and were executed for providing false witnesses against innocent persons.[143] This did not signal the end of witchcraft trials in Sweden, and in the 1720s, tales of Blåkulla and kidnapped children surfaced once again in Värmland. In the lower courts, minors were again admitted as witnesses, torture was illegally resorted to, and several women were sentenced to death. All verdicts were reversed by the Court of Appeal, and once again, the most active child persecutors were punished.

To return to the Great Northern Witch Trial of the 1660s/1670s, where over 250 people were executed by the end of the panic, children played an extensive role. These children, sometimes, but not always acting on their own initiative, denounced adults for a multitude of different reasons: to get attention, to get goods or clothes, to practise extortion, to experience some kind of an adventure or excitement, to exercise power over life and death, to be popular amongst other children, to rid society of mean and hated adults, coercion or peer pressure or to settle old scores. Bengt Ankarloo’s work showed that some children, usually poor orphans, accepted food and drink from people in return for not defaming them.[144] Others travelled as professional witch-finders and could 'see' who travelled to Blåkulla and were paid for their services out of the parish coffers.[145] The motivations for doing such activities have no historical boundaries. The very same motivational pursuits can be seen in the witchcraft trials in England and New England by children of similar ages. Greed, power, manipulation, fear, and the desire to be seen and heard are not fixed by geographic boundaries but cultural and religious understandings, particularly by a societally marginalised group like children. What is additionally significant in the Great Northern Witch Trial in Sweden is that the beliefs and stories told about the travels to, and occurrences at Blåkulla, were children's creations since there are no other traditions in Swedish folklore where children play such a central role.[146]

Through analysing demonological discourses, as well as assessing children's involvement in Continental witchcraft trials, one can gain a better understanding and a deeper appreciation for the complex and multifaceted role children played in the European witch-hunts. It is now imperative to juxtapose the role of children on the Continent with relation to England and New England. There is inherent value in ascertaining the differences between the Continental, English and New English witchcraft cases, but there is evidence that demonstrates many similarities between the five geographic locations.

A Sceptical Tradition? The English Perspective

Unlike the Continent, which had no shortage of demonological treatises spouting revelations about what witches were thought to do and how to deal with them, England had comparatively few such sources. The sources England did publish did not contain the same level of baby boiling and night-flying debauchery that was championed by works such as the *Malleus Maleficarum*. In fact, the first treatise to appear on witchcraft in 1584 was a sceptical work written by a well-educated Kentish gentleman called Reginald Scot.[147] Out of all of the English demonologists, Scot appears to have the most to say regarding children, lamenting their use as witnesses in witchcraft trials.[148] To further emphasise his point that 'witchcraft and enchantment is the cloak of ignorance' Scot relayed multiple stories of English children who were later found out to be frauds or 'counterfeits' when they acted bewitched and accused old, poor women of vexing them.[149] Scot recalled the infamous stories of Mildred Norrington, Rachel Pindar and Agnes Briggs and a lesser-known account of the daughter of one M. L. Stuppenie to demonstrate how the entire witchcraft phenomenon is based on 'lies and folly'.[150] It is noteworthy that the first demonological work in England was sceptical and Scot, through masterfully blending concepts from the Continent with stories that happened in England at the time, helped demonstrate the fluidity of ideas between England and Europe. Scot cited Continental practices in his work and used this to condemn English witchcraft cases that involved children. Thus, it might appear that England's witch-hunting narrative is not as 'exceptional' as once thought.

Of course, Scot was just the first to mention the role of children in English demonological treatises. In 1587, George Gifford (a Puritan preacher) also commented on how children accused their own mothers, finding it 'vile and monstrous'.[151] Gifford noted how only later, when the children came to 'years of discretion', did they confess that 'they were enticed to accuse'.[152] Like Scot, Gifford also used children as examples that showed the need for discretion in witchcraft trials, which may give insight into how both men might have reflected on the overall use of children's involvement in witchcraft procedures.

The prominent English author Richard Bovet's *Pandemonium* or *The Devil's Cloyster* relayed the story of four children of Mr Meredith of Bristol whose ages ranged from eight to fourteen years old. Unlike Scot and Gifford, Bovet truly believed in the existence of witchcraft. Bovet relayed the story of the Meredith children to affirm the existence of bewitchment and possession in direct opposition to the findings of the physician who attended to the children and concluded that they were suffering from a physical illness.[153] The Puritan preacher, Richard Baxter, also relayed stories of English children who were embroiled in witchcraft cases. He referred to a nine-year-old girl who passed urine stones. As a result, the old woman she accused of bewitching her was executed. He also told the reader of a 'youth' called Nathan Crab who consulted a white witch when he thought he was possessed.[154] These stories, according to Baxter, were added to bolster his polemical purpose of reinforcing belief in the existence of witches.

In the latter half of the seventeenth century, those who accepted the reality of demonic possession and witchcraft tended to be English dissenters (the heirs of the seventeenth-century New England Puritans).[155] It is perhaps unsurprising, then, that Baxter also included the account of the 1681 possession of the Boston-born Goodwin children in his work in order to justify his stance on the reality of spirits, as well as strengthen connections with his New English compatriots who also found themselves facing preternatural dilemmas.[156] It is interesting that both sceptics (like Scot and Gifford), as well as English demonologists who affirmed the existence of witchcraft (like Bovet and Baxter), highlighted the role of children in witchcraft trials. These sources perhaps demonstrate the complex nature of children in witchcraft discourse and trials. Those who supported witchcraft accusations affirmed the idea of children as supernatural agents. Conversely, those who questioned the reality of witchcraft also conceded that children had the ability to influence the invisible world.

Outside of demonological treatises, the three English laws written about witchcraft (1541, 1562 and 1604) only included children as victims and gave no clarity about child witches or witnesses.[157] Not even King James' infamous *Daemonologie* said anything about the status of children; there was no English equivalent of Bodin or Boguet attempting to give advice or direction on how to deal with such a complicated issue. Hence, the English legal system, though very different to the Continental one, was left in the dark as to what to do when children became entangled in witchcraft proceedings. Children were pervasive in English witchcraft trials, and perhaps the lack of clarity surrounding their legal or even cultural status is partly to blame for their prevalence. New England, implementing the same legal status as England and having similar cultural and social ties, saw a similar preponderance of children in witchcraft trials; the leaders of their society also struggled with how to effectively manage this issue.

Through analysing the changing role of children in Continental Europe, we gain a better understanding of how they transitioned from the silent victims in the *Malleus* to child witches and witnesses by the time of the Trier trials in the 1580s. The direct impact this had on England and New England cannot be known, but it is doubtful it would have been nil. In fact, Jean Bodin's work directly influenced the presiding judge at the St Osyth trials in 1582, and in New England, Cotton Mather explicitly referred to the Swedish trials in his treatise on the Salem witch trials in 1692.[158] Though the legal system and witch-hunting lore varied, at least some residents of both England and New England were aware of what was happening on the Continent. Finally, it is striking that there were witchcraft trials in England and New England – that all involved children – that included 'Continental elements' such as night flying, demonic Sabbats as well as baby boiling and eating. The significance of this in the fabric of England's and New England's overall witch-hunting tapestry should not be understated, the fact that historians have appeared to overlook this has only added to the misrepresented stereotype of England's and New England's so-called 'unique' witch-hunting narrative.

The lack of explicit direction or instruction from English judges or theologians on how to deal with children in witchcraft proceedings is an interesting divergence from demonological trends on the Continent. Gaining some understanding of Continental beliefs and practices helps to inform our knowledge and insight into the role of children in England and New England, as there are more similarities than historians have perhaps given credence to. For example, the role of children evolved from silent victims to more independent witnesses and even to being accused of witches themselves, just like in England and New England. Coercion and manipulation enticed children to accuse scores of people and sometimes swallowed up entire families. There are, of course, nuances in this argument as the differences do not allow for direct comparisons; even the quantity of people accused is different, as England and New England never saw the kind of large-scale hunts like those on the Continent. However, the development of the role of children in witchcraft trials nonetheless progressed; the emotions, reactions and the devastation that followed as a consequence of their changing role endured.

Notes

1 William Shakespeare, *As You Like It: A Shakescleare Translation*, Matt Cosby, ed. 2014, LitCharts LLC, act 2, scene 7, lines 142–169, www.litcharts.com/shakescleare/shakespeare-translations/as-you-like-it/act-2-scene-7.
2 Erica Burman, *Deconstructing Developmental Psychology* (London and New York: Routledge, 1994), p. 10.
3 Susan M. Sawyer, Peter S. Azzopardi, Dakshitha Wickremarathne and George C. Patton, 'The age of adolescence', *Viewpoint* 2 (No. 3, 2018), p. 223.
4 Margarita Georgieva, *The Gothic Child* (New York: Palgrave Macmillan, 2013), p. 2.
5 Mary Douglas, *Purity and Danger: An Analysis of Concepts of Pollution and Taboo* (London and New York: Routledge, 2003), p. 67.
6 C. L'Estrange Ewen, *Witchcraft and Demonism: A Concise Account Derived from Sworn Depositions and Confessions Obtained in the Courts of England and Wales* (London: Heath Cranton Limited, 1933), p. 374.
7 K. J. Allison, 'An Elizabethan Village "Census"', *Bulletin of the Institute of Historical Research* 93 (1963), p. 102.
8 Keith Thomas, 'Age and Authority in Early Modern England', *Proceedings of the British Academy* 65 (1976), p. 205.
9 Karin Lesnik-Oberstein, 'Childhood and Textuality: Culture, History, Literature' in *Children in Culture: Approaches to Childhood*, ed. Karin Lesnik-Oberstein (New York: Palgrave Macmillan, 1998), p. 2.
10 Edward Fairfax, *A Discourse of Witchcraft as It Was Acted in the Family of Mr Edward Fairfax…*, communicated by R. M. Milnes, 1621, in *Miscellanies of the Philobiblon Society*, vol. 5 (London: printed by Charles Whittingham, 1858–1859), p. 32, passim.
11 Simon Bacon and Leo Ruickbie, 'Introduction' in *The Cultural Construction of Monstrous Children: Essays on Anomalous Children from 1595 to the Present Day*, eds. Simon Bacon and Leo Ruickbie (London and New York: Anthem Press, 2020), p. 4.
12 Anna French, 'Locating the early modern child' in *Early Modern Childhood: An Introduction*, ed. Anna French (Oxford and New York: Routledge, 2020), p. 7
13 Philippe Ariès, *Centuries of Childhood: A Social History of Family Life*, Robert Baldick, trans. (New York: Alfred A. Knopf, 1962), p. 15, passim.
14 Lawrence Stone, *The Family, Sex and Marriage in England 1500-1800* (London: Weidenfeld and Nicolson, 1977), p. 81.
15 Linda A. Pollock, *Forgotten children: parent-child relations from 1500 to 1900* (Cambridge and New York: Cambridge University Press, 1983), p. 59.

16 Alan Macfarlane, 'Reviewed work(s): The Family, Sex and Marriage in England 1500-1800 by Lawrence Stone', *History and Theory* 18 (No. 1, 1979), p. 103.
17 Keith Thomas, 'Age and Authority in Early Modern England', *Proceedings of the British Academy* 65 (1976), p. 215.
18 Keith Thomas, 'Age and Authority in Early Modern England', *Proceedings of the British Academy* 65 (1976).
19 Keith Thomas, 'Age and Authority in Early Modern England', *Proceedings of the British Academy* 65 (1976), p. 214.
20 Linda A. Pollock, *Forgotten children: parent-child relations from 1500 to 1900* (Cambridge and New York: Cambridge University Press, 1983), p. 1.
21 Ralph A. Houlbrooke, *The English Family 1450-1750* (London and New York: Longman, 1984), p. 134.
22 Samuel Sewall, 'Diary of Samuel Sewall 1674-1729. Vol I. 1674-1700', diary entry, 18 May 1696 in *Collections of the Massachusetts Historical Society*, vol. 5, fifth series (Boston: published by the society, 1877), p. 426.
23 Ralph A. Houlbrooke, *The English Family 1450-1750* (London and New York: Longman, 1984), p. 166.
24 Anna French, 'Locating the early modern child' in *Early Modern Childhood: An Introduction*, ed. Anna French (Oxford and New York: Routledge, 2020), p. 9.
25 Hugh Cunningham, *Children and Childhood in Western Society Since 1500*, 2nd edn. (Harlow: Pearson, 2005), p. 1.
26 Hugh Cunningham, *Children and Childhood in Western Society Since 1500*, 2nd edn. (Harlow: Pearson, 2005), p. 2.
27 Hugh Cunningham, *Children and Childhood in Western Society Since 1500*, 2nd edn. (Harlow: Pearson, 2005), pp. 2–3.
28 Charlotte-Rose Millar, *Witchcraft, the Devil, and Emotions in Early Modern England* (London and New York: Routledge, 2017), p. 82, passim.
29 On 'fear' and its significance in early modern European society see Penny Roberts and William G. Naphy, 'Introduction' in *Fear in Early Modern Society*, eds. William G. Naphy and Penny Roberts (Manchester and New York: Manchester University Press, 1997), pp. 1–9, and Jean Delumeau, *Sin and Fear: The Emergence of a Western Guilt Culture 13th to 18th Centuries*, trans. Eric Nicholson (New York: St. Martin's Press, 1990), esp. pp. 1–6; with particular reference to fear and witchcraft see Ronald Hutton, *The Witch: A History of Fear, from Ancient Times to the Present* (New Haven: Yale University Press, 2017), p. 151; Aaron John Henry Larsen, 'Darkest Forests and Highest Mountains: The Witches' Sabbath and Landscapes of Fear in Early Modern Demonologies' *European Review of History* 31 (No. 1, 2024), pp.157–174, and Peter Dinzelbacher, *Angst im Mittelalter: Teufels-, Todes-und Gotteserfahrung: Mentalitätsgeschichte und Iknonographie* (Paderborn: Ferdinand Schoeningh, 1996). Dinzelbacher argues that ordinary people might be advocates or instruments of the Devil, and his book presents a vivid portrait of the medieval mentality and culture of fear.
30 It is important to note that the scholarship on the New England child is not as rich and diverse as England. Despite this, much of the social and cultural structures of England were carried over to the new world and much of what is said for England can be easily replicated for New England. Where differences arise, particularly when it comes to themes encompassing 'Puritanism', this will be noted.

31 Charlotte-Rose Millar, *Witchcraft, the Devil, and Emotions in Early Modern England* (London and New York: Routledge, 2017), p. 83.
32 Peter Laslett, *The World We Have Lost: Further Explored*, 3rd edn. (New York: Routledge, 1983), p. 13.
33 Ilana Krausman Ben-Amos, *Adolescence and Youth in Early Modern England* (New Haven: Yale University, 1994), p. 69.
34 Peter Laslett, *The World We Have Lost: Further Explored*, 3rd edn. (New York: Routledge, 1983), p. 3.
35 Hugh Cunningham, *Children and Childhood in Western Society Since 1500*, 2nd edn. (Harlow: Pearson, 2005), p. 84.
36 P. Gavitt, *Charity and Children in Renaissance Florence: The Ospedale degli Innocenti, 1450-1536* (Ann Arbor: University of Michigan Press, 1990), p. 273.
37 Hugh Cunningham, *Children and Childhood in Western Society Since 1500*, 2nd edn. (Harlow: Pearson, 2005), p. 43.
38 Hugh Cunningham, *Children and Childhood in Western Society Since 1500*, 2nd edn. (Harlow: Pearson, 2005), p. 42.
39 Desiderius Erasmus, 'A Declamation on the Subject of Early Liberal Education for Children De pureis statim ac liberaliter instituendis declamation', in *Literary and Educational Writings, 3 and 4: Volume 3: De conscribendis epistolis/Formula/De civilitate. Volume 4: De pureis instituendis/De recta pronuntiatione, [The Collected Works of Erasmus, volumes 25-26]*, trans. and annot. by Beert C. Verstraete, ed. J. K. Sowards (Toronto: University of Toronto Press, 1985), p. 301.
40 Cornelis Augustijn, *Erasmus: His Life, Works, and Influence*, trans. J.C. Grayson (Toronto: University of Toronto Press, 1991), pp. 22–23.
41 Desiderius Erasmus, 'A Declamation on the Subject of Early Liberal Education for Children De pureis statim ac liberaliter instituendis declamation', in *Literary and Educational Writings, 3 and 4: Volume 3: De conscribendis epistolis/Formula/De civilitate. Volume 4: De pureis instituendis/De recta pronuntiatione, [The Collected Works of Erasmus, volumes 25-26]*, trans. and annot. by Beert C. Verstraete, ed. J. K. Sowards (Toronto: University of Toronto Press, 1985), p. 305.
42 Margo Todd, *Christian Humanism and the Puritan Social Order* (Cambridge: Cambridge University Press, 1987), p. 97.
43 See Christopher Hill, *Society and Puritanism in Pre-revolutionary England* (London: Secker and Warburg, 1964), pp. 443–481.
44 Steven Ozment, 'Raising a Loving Child in Late Medieval and Early Modern Europe (1400-1700)' in *The Best Love of the Child: Being Loved and Being Taught to Love as the First Human Right*, ed. Timothy P. Jackson (Grand Rapids: William B. Eerdmans Publishing Company, 2011), p. 93.
45 Proverbs 22:15, The Bible, King James Version.
46 John Morgan, *Godly Learning: Puritan Attitudes towards Reason, Learning and Education, 1560-1640* (Cambridge: Cambridge University Press, 1986), pp. 169–170.
47 Philip Greven, *The Protestant Temperament: Patterns of Child-Rearing, Religious Experience, and the Self in Early America* (New York: Alfred A. Knopf, 1977), pp. 12–14.
48 Philip Greven, *The Protestant Temperament: Patterns of Child-Rearing, Religious Experience, and the Self in Early America* (New York: Alfred A. Knopf, 1977), pp. 65 and 74.

49 Lawrence Stone, *The Family, Sex and Marriage in England 1500-1800* (London: Weidenfeld and Nicolson, 1977), p. 175.
50 L. K. Shücking, *The Puritan Family*, trans. B. Battershaw (New York: Routledge, 1970), p. 56.
51 Increase Mather, *A Call from Heaven to the Present and Succeeding Generations...* (Boston: Printed by John [?], 1679), p. 111.
52 Increase Mather, *A Call from Heaven to the Present and Succeeding Generations...* (Boston: Printed by John [?], 1679)
53 Due to the long chronological scope of this book, it is important to acknowledge how ideas around childhood changed for Anglicans and Puritans. For example, children were not seen as inherently innocent by staunch Reformed Protestants, who did not view any post-lapsarian person as intrinsically innocent. See Nancy Jiwon Cho, 'Extending Moral and Religious Verse for Children from Puritan Adults' Warnings to Romantic Children's Insights: Ann and Jane Taylor's Pedagogic Achievements in *Hymns for Infant Minds* (1810)' *Feminist Studies in English Literature* 23 (No. 1, 2015), pp. 14–15.
54 For a thorough discussion on England's Catholic past, see Eamon Duffy, *The Stripping of the Altars: Traditional Religion in England 1400-1580*, 2nd edn. (New Haven and London: Yale University Press, 2005).
55 See for example Lucy Underwood, *Childhood, Youth, and Religious Dissent in Post-Reformation England* (New York: Palgrave Macmillan, 2014).
56 Lucy Underwood, 'Catholics' in *Early Modern Childhood: An Introduction*, p. 141.
57 See the frequent depictions of Madonna and Christ child. The earliest depiction dates back to the 6th century: 'The Virgin and Child Enthroned between St Theodore and St George', painted icon, Constantinople, sixth or seventh century, *Mount Sinai*, Monastery of Saint Catherine. See John Beckwith, *Early Christian and Byzantine Art* (New Haven and London: Yale University Press, 1970), pp. 92–94. For information on child martyrs, child saints and their surrounding 'cults' in medieval and early modern Europe, see Patricia Healy Wasyliw, *Martyrdom, Murder, and Magic: Child Saints and their Cults in Medieval Europe* (New York: Peter Lang, 2008).
58 Hugh Cunningham, *Children and Childhood in Western Society Since 1500*, 2nd edn. (Harlow: Pearson, 2005), p. 57.
59 A. C. F. Beales, *Education under Penalty: English Catholic Education from the Reformation to the Fall of James II* (London: Athlone Press, 1963), pp. 83, 205 and 215.
60 Lucy Underwood, 'Catholics' in *Early Modern Childhood: An Introduction*, p. 151.
61 Anna French, *Children of Wrath: Possession, Prophecy and the Young in Early Modern England* (Oxford and New York: Routledge, 2016), p. 13.
62 Anna French, *Children of Wrath: Possession, Prophecy and the Young in Early Modern England* (Oxford and New York: Routledge, 2016), p. 14.
63 Anna French, *Children of Wrath: Possession, Prophecy and the Young in Early Modern England* (Oxford and New York: Routledge, 2016).
64 Psalm 8:2 and Ephesians 2:3, The Bible, King James Version; Hieronymus Magomastix, 'The Strange Witch at Greenwich...' (London: Printed by Thomas Harper, 1650), p. 4.

65 See for example James Sharpe, *Instruments of Darkness: Witchcraft in Early Modern England* (Philadelphia: University of Pennsylvania Press, 1997), p. 77, and G.R. Quaife, *Godly Zeal and Furious Rage: The Witch in Early Modern Europe* (London and New York: Routledge, 1987), pp. 59–60.
66 Christopher S. Mackay, *The Hammer of Witches: A Complete Translation of the Malleus Maleficarum* (Cambridge: Cambridge University Press, 2009), p. 1.
67 Montague Summers, *Malleus Maleficarum: Translated with an Introduction, Bibliography and Notes* (London: John Rodker, 1928), pp. xxxviii–xxxix.
68 Brian Levack, *The Witch Hunt in Early Modern Europe*, 4th edn. (London and New York: Routledge, 2016), p. 51.
69 Brian Levack, *The Witch Hunt in Early Modern Europe*, 4th edn. (London and New York: Routledge, 2016).
70 There is debate surrounding how much authorship should be attributed to Jacobus Sprenger. Mackay, *The Hammer of Witches*, p. 2.
71 Christopher S. Mackay, *The Hammer of Witches: A Complete Translation of the Malleus Maleficarum* (Cambridge: Cambridge University Press, 2009), p. 7.
72 Hans Peter Broedel, *The Malleus Maleficarum and the Construction of Witchcraft: Theology and Popular Belief* (Manchester and New York: Manchester University Press, 2003), p. 30.
73 Christopher S. Mackay, *The Hammer of Witches: A Complete Translation of the Malleus Maleficarum* (Cambridge: Cambridge University Press, 2009), p. 115.
74 Christopher S. Mackay, *The Hammer of Witches: A Complete Translation of the Malleus Maleficarum* (Cambridge: Cambridge University Press, 2009), p. 161.
75 Christopher S. Mackay, *The Hammer of Witches: A Complete Translation of the Malleus Maleficarum* (Cambridge: Cambridge University Press, 2009), pp. 211–212. It is interesting to note how the authors appear to use the terms 'babies' and 'children' interchangeably. This is also apparent in the Latin version of the text.
76 Christopher S. Mackay, *The Hammer of Witches: A Complete Translation of the Malleus Maleficarum* (Cambridge: Cambridge University Press, 2009), pp. 366–374.
77 Christopher S. Mackay, *The Hammer of Witches: A Complete Translation of the Malleus Maleficarum* (Cambridge: Cambridge University Press, 2009), p. 372.
78 Christopher S. Mackay, *The Hammer of Witches: A Complete Translation of the Malleus Maleficarum* (Cambridge: Cambridge University Press, 2009), p. 373.
79 Christopher S. Mackay, *The Hammer of Witches: A Complete Translation of the Malleus Maleficarum* (Cambridge: Cambridge University Press, 2009), p. 374.
80 The authors of the *Malleus* do not specify what exactly they mean by this.
81 Christopher S. Mackay, *The Hammer of Witches: A Complete Translation of the Malleus Maleficarum* (Cambridge: Cambridge University Press, 2009), p. 552.
82 Christopher S. Mackay, *The Hammer of Witches: A Complete Translation of the Malleus Maleficarum* (Cambridge: Cambridge University Press, 2009).
83 Christopher S. Mackay, *The Hammer of Witches: A Complete Translation of the Malleus Maleficarum* (Cambridge: Cambridge University Press, 2009), pp. 552–553. Francesco Maria Guazzo, 130 years after the *Malleus*, also promoted that the fat of boiled babies was used as an ointment to make witches fly. Francesco Maria Guazzo, *Compendium Maleficarum*, trans. E. A. Ashwin, ed. Montague Summers (New Jersey: University Books, 1974), p. 34.

84 Christopher S. Mackay, *The Hammer of Witches: A Complete Translation of the Malleus Maleficarum* (Cambridge: Cambridge University Press, 2009), p. 552.
85 Hans Peter Broedel, *The Malleus Maleficarum and the Construction of Witchcraft: Theology and Popular Belief* (Manchester and New York: Manchester University Press, 2003), p. 129.
86 Jean Bodin, *On the Demon-Mania of Witches*, trans. Randy A. Scott (Toronto: Centre for Reformation and Renaissance Studies, 2001), p. 199.
87 Jean Bodin, *On the Demon-Mania of Witches*, trans. Randy A. Scott (Toronto: Centre for Reformation and Renaissance Studies, 2001), p. 182.
88 Christopher S. Mackay, *The Hammer of Witches: A Complete Translation of the Malleus Maleficarum* (Cambridge: Cambridge University Press, 2009), pp. 374–375.
89 Robert S. Walinski-Kiehl, 'The Devil's Children: Child Witch-Trials in Early Modern Germany', *Continuity and Change* 11 (No. 2, 1996), p. 176.
90 Henry Charles Lea, *Materials Toward a History of Witchcraft*, vol. 3, arranged and ed. Arthur C. Howland, introduction, George Lincoln Burr (add city: University of Pennsylvania Press, 1939), pp. 1075, 1132, 1187 and 1282.
91 Walinski-Kiehl, 'The Devil's Children: Child Witch-Trials in Early Modern Germany', p. 201.
92 Binsfeld identified a child as being under the age of fourteen. Wolfgang Behringer, 'KINDERHEXENPROZESSE: Zur Rolle von Kindern in der Geschichte der Hexenverfolgung' *Zeitschrift für Historische Forschung* 16 (No. 1, 1989), pp. 34–35.
93 Wolfgang Behringer, 'KINDERHEXENPROZESSE: Zur Rolle von Kindern in der Geschichte der Hexenverfolgung' *Zeitschrift für Historische Forschung* 16 (No. 1, 1989).
94 Wolfgang Behringer, 'KINDERHEXENPROZESSE: Zur Rolle von Kindern in der Geschichte der Hexenverfolgung' *Zeitschrift für Historische Forschung* 16 (No. 1, 1989), p. 35.
95 Henri Boguet, *An Examen of Witches*, ed. Montague Summers (New York: Dover Publications, 2009), p. xx.
96 Gary K. Waite, *Heresy, Magic and Witchcraft in Early Modern Europe* (Basingstoke: Palgrave Macmillan Publishers, 2003), pp. 165–168. The popularity of Boguet's work is reflected by the fact that it went through at least eight editions in ten years.
97 Henri Boguet, *An Examen of Witches*, ed. Montague Summers (New York: Dover Publications, 2009), p. 6.
98 Henri Boguet, *An Examen of Witches*, ed. Montague Summers (New York: Dover Publications, 2009), p. 7.
99 Henri Boguet, *An Examen of Witches*, ed. Montague Summers (New York: Dover Publications, 2009).
100 Henri Boguet, *An Examen of Witches*, ed. Montague Summers (New York: Dover Publications, 2009).
101 Henri Boguet, *An Examen of Witches*, ed. Montague Summers (New York: Dover Publications, 2009), p. 8.
102 Henri Boguet, *An Examen of Witches*, ed. Montague Summers (New York: Dover Publications, 2009), pp. 167–171.

103 Henri Boguet, *An Examen of Witches*, ed. Montague Summers (New York: Dover Publications, 2009), p. 168.
104 Henri Boguet, *An Examen of Witches*, ed. Montague Summers (New York: Dover Publications, 2009), p. 169.
105 Henri Boguet, *An Examen of Witches*, ed. Montague Summers (New York: Dover Publications, 2009).
106 Boguet does not specify what the age of puberty is.
107 Henri Boguet, *An Examen of Witches*, ed. Montague Summers (New York: Dover Publications, 2009), p. 171.
108 Henri Boguet, *An Examen of Witches*, ed. Montague Summers (New York: Dover Publications, 2009), p. 169.
109 Henri Boguet, *An Examen of Witches*, ed. Montague Summers (New York: Dover Publications, 2009), p. 230. This is the first reference I have found in any demonological work that refers to child witnesses.
110 Henri Boguet, *An Examen of Witches*, ed. Montague Summers (New York: Dover Publications, 2009), p. 233.
111 Henri Boguet, *An Examen of Witches*, ed. Montague Summers (New York: Dover Publications, 2009), p. 234.
112 G.R. Quaife, *Godly Zeal and Furious Rage: The Witch in Early Modern Europe* (London and New York: Routledge, 1987), p. 189.
113 Behringer, 'KINDERHEXENPROZESSE…', p. 47.
114 Rossell Hope Robbins, *The Encyclopedia of Witchcraft and Demonology* (London: Girard and Stewart, 1959), p. 215.
115 Wolfgang Behringer, 'KINDERHEXENPROZESSE: Zur Rolle von Kindern in der Geschichte der Hexenverfolgung' *Zeitschrift für Historische Forschung* 16 (No. 1, 1989), pp. 36–37.
116 Wolfgang Behringer, 'KINDERHEXENPROZESSE: Zur Rolle von Kindern in der Geschichte der Hexenverfolgung' *Zeitschrift für Historische Forschung* 16 (No. 1, 1989), p. 39.
117 Wolfgang Behringer, 'KINDERHEXENPROZESSE: Zur Rolle von Kindern in der Geschichte der Hexenverfolgung' *Zeitschrift für Historische Forschung* 16 (No. 1, 1989), p. 37
118 Walinski-Kiehl, 'The Devil's Children: Child Witch-Trials in Early Modern Germany', p. 176.
119 Walinski-Kiehl, 'The Devil's Children: Child Witch-Trials in Early Modern Germany', p. 175.
120 Walinski-Kiehl, 'The Devil's Children: Child Witch-Trials in Early Modern Germany'.
121 Walinski-Kiehl, 'The Devil's Children: Child Witch-Trials in Early Modern Germany', p. 176
122 One of the elements from Schuh's case that transcends geographic or chronological boundaries relates to the corporal punishment of children. While children in England and New England were not routinely (if at all) executed for participating in witchcraft, other punishments did exist. Indeed, corporal punishment (in the form of discipline and household violence) was commonplace throughout England and New England during the early modern era. See Susan

Dwyer Amussen, 'Punishment, Discipline, and Power: The Social Meanings of Violence in Early Modern England', *Journal of British Studies* 34 (No. 1, 1995), esp. p. 18, and Joan E. Durrant, 'Corporal Punishment: From Ancient History to Global Progress' in *Handbook of Interpersonal Violence Across the Lifespan*, eds. R. Geffner, J.W. White, L.K. Hamberger, A. Rosenbaum, V. Vaughan-Eden and I.V. Veith (Berlin: Springer Nature, 2022), esp. pp. 347–348.

123 Robert S. Walinski-Kiehl, 'The Devil's Children: Child Witch-Trials in Early Modern Germany', *Continuity and Change* 11 (No. 2, 1996), p. 176.

124 There is a wide array of scholarship on the Zaubererjackl trials. See for example Thomas Robisheaux, 'The German Witch Trials' in *The Oxford Handbook of Witchcraft in Early Modern Europe and Colonial America*, ed. Brian P. Levack (Oxford: Oxford University Press, 2014), p. 185.

125 Lyndal Roper, ' "Evil Imaginings and Fantasies" ': Child-Witches and the End of the Witch Craze', *Past & Present* (No. 167 2000), pp. 107–139.

126 Binsfeld identified a child as being under the age of fourteen. Wolfgang Behringer, 'KINDERHEXENPROZESSE: Zur Rolle von Kindern in der Geschichte der Hexenverfolgung' *Zeitschrift für Historische Forschung* 16 (No. 1, 1989), p. 41.

127 Gustav Henningsen, *The Witches' Advocate: Basque Witchcraft and the Spanish Inquisition (1609-1614)* (Reno: University of Nevada Press, 1980), passim.

128 Gustav Henningsen, 'The Greatest Witch-Trial of All: Navarre, 1609-1614' *History Today* 30 (No. 11, 1980), p. 36.

129 Gustav Henningsen, 'The Greatest Witch-Trial of All: Navarre, 1609-1614' *History Today* 30 (No. 11, 1980).

130 Gustav Henningsen, 'The Greatest Witch-Trial of All: Navarre, 1609-1614' *History Today* 30 (No. 11, 1980).

131 Gustav Henningsen, 'The Greatest Witch-Trial of All: Navarre, 1609-1614' *History Today* 30 (No. 11, 1980), p. 37.

132 Lu Ann Homza, *Village Infernos and Witches' Advocates: Witch-Hunting in Navarre, 1608-1614* (University Park: The Pennsylvania State University Press, 2022), p. 120.

133 Gustav Henningsen, *The Witches' Advocate: Basque Witchcraft and the Spanish Inquisition (1609-1614)* (Reno: University of Nevada Press, 1980), passim, p. 39.

134 Gustav Henningsen, *The Witches' Advocate: Basque Witchcraft and the Spanish Inquisition (1609-1614)* (Reno: University of Nevada Press, 1980), passim.

135 Gustav Henningsen, *The Witches' Advocate: Basque Witchcraft and the Spanish Inquisition (1609-1614)* (Reno: University of Nevada Press, 1980), passim.

136 Cotton Mather, *Wonders of the Invisible World: Being an account of the Tryals of Several Witches Lately Executed in New England* (London: John Russell Smith, 1862), pp. 167–172.

137 Jari Eilola, 'Interpreting Children's Blåkulla Stories in Sweden (1675)' in *Demonology and Witch-Hunting in Early Modern Europe*, eds. Julian Goodare, Rita Voltmer and Liv Helene Willumsen (Oxford and New York: Routledge, 2020), p. 327.

138 Bengt Ankarloo, 'Sweden: The Mass Burnings' in *Early Modern European Witchcraft: Centres and Peripheries*, eds. Bengt Ankarloo and Gustav Henningsen (New York: Oxford University Press, 1993), p. 295.

139 Bengt Ankarloo, 'Sweden: The Mass Burnings' in *Early Modern European Witchcraft: Centres and Peripheries*, eds. Bengt Ankarloo and Gustav Henningsen (New York: Oxford University Press, 1993), p. 295.
140 Bengt Ankarloo, 'Sweden: The Mass Burnings' in *Early Modern European Witchcraft: Centres and Peripheries*, eds. Bengt Ankarloo and Gustav Henningsen (New York: Oxford University Press, 1993), p. 303.
141 Bengt Ankarloo, 'Sweden: The Mass Burnings' in *Early Modern European Witchcraft: Centres and Peripheries*, eds. Bengt Ankarloo and Gustav Henningsen (New York: Oxford University Press, 1993).
142 76% of the twenty-nine cases in England used in this study involved only one child. In New England, 55% of the eleven cases used in this study involved only one child.
143 Bengt Ankarloo, 'Sweden: The Mass Burnings' in *Early Modern European Witchcraft: Centres and Peripheries*, eds. Bengt Ankarloo and Gustav Henningsen (New York: Oxford University Press, 1993), p. 300.
144 Bengt Ankarloo, 'Sweden: The Mass Burnings' in *Early Modern European Witchcraft: Centres and Peripheries*, eds. Bengt Ankarloo and Gustav Henningsen (New York: Oxford University Press, 1993), p. 302.
145 Bengt Ankarloo, 'Sweden: The Mass Burnings' in *Early Modern European Witchcraft: Centres and Peripheries*, eds. Bengt Ankarloo and Gustav Henningsen (New York: Oxford University Press, 1993).
146 Per-Anders Östling, 'Witchcraft Trials in 17th Century Sweden and the Great Northern Swedish Witch Craze of 1668–1678', *Studia Neophilologica* 84 (No. 1, 2012), p. 102.
147 Scot was later known for his work as a horticulturalist. Sydney Anglo, *The Damned Art: Essays in the Literature of Witchcraft* (London: Routledge and Kegan Paul, 1977), p. 107.
148 Reginald Scot, *The Discoverie of Witchcraft*, 1691 edn. (London: publisher unknown), pp. 18–19.
149 Reginald Scot, *The Discoverie of Witchcraft*, 1691 edn. (London: publisher unknown), p. 8.
150 Reginald Scot, *The Discoverie of Witchcraft*, 1691 edn. (London: publisher unknown), pp. 127, 132 and 259, respectively.
151 George Gifford, *A Discourse on the Subtil Practise of Devils by Witches...* (London: Imprinted for Toby Cooke, 1587), sig. Hv.
152 George Gifford, *A Discourse on the Subtil Practise of Devils by Witches...* (London: Imprinted for Toby Cooke, 1587), sig. Hv.
153 Richard Bovet, *Pandemonium or The Devils Cloyster...* (London: Printed for Thomas Malthus, 1684), pp. 168–170.
154 Richard Baxter, *The Certainty of the Worlds of Spirits* (London: Printed for T. Parkhurst, 1691), pp. 44–45 and pp. 47–52.
155 Brian P. Levack, *The Devil Within: Possession and Exorcism in the Christian West* (New Haven and London: Yale University Press, 2013), p. 73.
156 Baxter, *The Certainty of the Worlds of Spirits*, p. 2, refers to using both English and New English sources in his work including Joseph Glanvil, Henry More as well as Cotton and Increase Mather. The brief reference to the Goodwin case appears on p. 80.

157 Brian Levack, *The Witch Hunt in Early Modern Europe*, 4th edn. (London and New York: Routledge, 2016), p. 83.

158 W. W., *A True and Just Recorde of the Information, Examination and Confession of All the Witches…*, sig. A3r–A3v and Mather, *Wonders of the Invisible World*, pp. 167–172.

2

PRE-1589, THE CHILDREN WHO SET THE SCENE

Under normal circumstances, children in early modern England held little power or influence, especially in adult-dominated spheres. However, as liminal beings in a deeply religious society, children were understood to have some level of connection with the supernatural world. It is through this association that they would become involved in witchcraft trials. In a community where they were supposed to be seen and not heard, their role in supernatural affairs was first seen as minor, since they were thought not to be capable of being truly responsible for their actions; this will be seen in the brief case study of Elizabeth Crofts (1554). Ten years later, Anne Mylner demonstrated her connection with the invisible world, giving insight into the signs and symptoms of bewitchment and possession which would come to be mimicked for decades. In 1566, Agnes Brown set the precedent as the first minor whose evidence was permitted in a witchcraft trial. Brown's ability to enumerate demonological features at twelve years old showed that not only would children's beliefs and ideas about witchcraft be heard by a magisterial court, but they were also trusted and believed. Joan Waterhouse, also in this trial, demonstrated that children could also be accused of being witches.

While other children like Agnes Briggs, Rachel Pindar and Mildred Norrington were later exposed as frauds, their stories add valuable information to the evolution of the multifaceted role of children in witchcraft trials. Like Mylner, these cases would be mimicked and built on. In the years before the turn of the sixteenth century, Thomas Lever created a new role for children in witchcraft trials when he was imprisoned as a conjuror's assistant. Children like Waterhouse and Lever reflected the dual nature of their role as agents of the invisible world as they often walked a fine line between accusing and being accused themselves. Finally, the second Chelmsford trial (1579),

DOI: 10.4324/9781003685319-3

the St Osyth trial (1582) and the third Chelmsford trial (1589) demonstrate the deadly consequences of what could happen when children influenced witchcraft trials without restraint because they facilitated the judge's need for confessions and guilty verdicts. In the years prior to 1589, children's involvement in witchcraft trials grew from relatively minor to almost indispensable; they became accused as witches and learnt how to influence a system that legally should have never allowed them to participate in it. These children had set the scene with devastating consequences.

'The Spirit in The Wall': Elizabeth Crofts

In 1554, while the Catholic Queen Mary was on the throne, an obscure London maid aged about eighteen became involved in a highly politicised religious scandal. Elizabeth Crofts was either persuaded, paid or even came up with the idea to conceal herself behind the false exterior wall of a house on Aldersgate Street, which was a part of London with a large Protestant population. Behind the wall, Elizabeth uttered anti-Catholic propaganda, which many listeners took to be the words of an invisible angel or spirit. Hence, she was dubbed the 'Spirit in the Wall' or the 'Bird in the Wall', as she also used a special whistle one of her conspirators called Drake gave her.[1] Elizabeth spoke against Queen Mary, King Philip and the Catholic Church, apparently drawing an audience of 17,000 people by the second morning.[2] It was several days before her imposture was discovered, the wall was pulled down and Elizabeth was arrested. Either on 6 or 15 July (the accounts vary) Elizabeth appeared at Paul's Cross to confess and atone for her sins.[3] Initially, in the presence of the Archdeacon of Middlesex, Elizabeth stated that she had done it because 'the Lord's word caused her so to do'.[4] Then, the source stated that 'the poor wench...afterwards' made an 'open confession'.[5] Whether this implied that Elizabeth was coerced into admitting her imposture, we will never know, but it is interesting that initially, she insinuated it was her own religious beliefs that inspired her actions. Elizabeth's confession appears *pro forma* as she stated:

> this present day have I ... have brought me to offend God and the Queen's majesty in this my late practice, and to be a gazing stock to the whole world to my great shame. And therefore, beware good people, beware of the heretics, for as they have undone me in counterfeiting time to attempt this wicked enterprise, so they will undo you all, unless you take heed by times of their naughty opinions.[6]

The purpose of Elizabeth's confession was not simply to admonish her but also serves as a warning to other heretics who might also be harbouring 'dangerous' thoughts. Thus, one can see that Elizabeth's punishment – being briefly imprisoned – served as a warning. Her other conspirators were handed more serious punishments, and it could be argued that Elizabeth was never held fully responsible for her actions. Elizabeth may have just been a pawn in a much larger game or was simply in the wrong place at the wrong time, yet she certainly made an effective weapon for both sides during the tumultuous years of the Reformation. What is significant about the 'Spirit in the Wall' account is that this young girl was clearly very successful in attracting attention, which was no doubt the purpose of the performance. The performance itself was obviously a group effort, but even if Elizabeth was not involved in the planning, it was clearly more convincing to involve a child in the execution of the ploy. Croft's story helps reveal that children played a key role, not only in stories of preternatural occurrences, but also in anti-Catholic propaganda; the fact that, in this case, the invisible world was made up behind a wall made little supposed difference to the people who believed down on Aldersgate Street.

While, at this point, Elizabeth Crofts' actions did not culminate in any accusations of witchcraft per se, it would not be long before these spiritual visitations took a more sinister turn. Indeed, English demonic possession cases involving children occurred only ten years later in 1564. From there, the role of children in English witchcraft trials flourished even before the notorious Throckmorton case of 1589. While the witch-hunts already raged in Europe, English children began to assert themselves firmly as preternatural agents. Establishing themselves as demoniacs, accusers, counterfeits and accused witches, children played a multitude of complex and diverse roles. This, in turn, set the precedent for children's involvement in witchcraft trials for decades. Although their roles evolved and developed, patterns and themes persisted throughout decades of social and cultural upheaval. One of the most important pamphlets appeared in 1564, outlining the signs and symptoms that came to be associated with demonic possession and/or bewitchment. While they were likely influenced by Biblical and Continental ideas about what possession or bewitchment 'looked like', it is significant to note that a child represented one of the first recorded English demonic possession cases. To be possessed was a role that would be almost dominated by children by the end of the sixteenth century; it all began with an eighteen-year-old girl called Anne Mylner.

'No, no, no more for God's sake': Anne Mylner

Mylner's story comes from a short pamphlet written mostly by eyewitnesses, including Sir William Cawley Knight, Richard Hurleston Esquire and John Fisher. These men recorded the account 'for that the thing is so rare and notable that it should not be kept from...posterity'.[7] It is important to acknowledge the various 'voices' that make up pamphlet accounts and their agenda in creating them. The purpose of recording Mylner's account was clearly to affirm a belief in the supernatural and disparage Catholic beliefs.

Mylner's 'most monstrous and horrible kind of torment and disease' began on 17 October 1564 when she was sent to bring her father's cows in from the fields.[8] Returning home, she was 'suddenly taken with great fear' as she thought she saw 'a white thing compassing her about'.[9] From the next morning Mylner felt herself 'grieved and very sore in all the parts of her body'.[10] For the first five days of her sickness, Mylner did not take any sustenance whatsoever and only slept three hours a night. The foregoing of any sustenance was more common in divine prophecy cases, but there was a belief that people who were possessed with bad spirits were prevented from eating by the Devil who inhabited their bodies.[11] Another example of this arose in the New English demonic possession case of Mercy Short when Cotton Mather stated that one of the 'miseries' of her case was 'extreme fasting for many days together'.[12] Mylner's sickness drew a lot of attention in the city of Chester where John Pierce, one of the Canons of Chester Cathedral, made a special prayer to her at the end of his sermon, praying for her deliverance.[13] As Protestants, devout prayer was all that could be done to relieve Mylner's torments.

At the end of January the following year, John Lane, a fellow of Christ's College, was asked whether Mylner was perhaps 'possessed with spirits as in times past' and he confirmed that she was, and in fact, argued that it could be 'nothing else'.[14] On 16 February, around 2 pm, Lane was brought to the Cawley household where Mylner was staying. Mylner was described as lying on the bed with her eyes half open, half shut, her mouth mostly open with her tongue 'doubling between', her face mostly red and her head heavy.[15] But her two symptoms that were more closely aligned with demonic possession were described in detail:

> her belly began to move, swelling up and down, sometimes beneath her chest…in such vehemency that a man would have thought she would have burst. Then suddenly she lift[ed] herself up in her bed, bending backwards in such order, that almost her head and feet met, falling down sometimes on the one side…but rising again so suddenly that the beholders could not imagine how it might be possible so quickly she could without aid of hand, cast herself (her belly upward) into the form of a hoop.[16]

According to Brian Levack, the swelling of the throat, belly or tongue was 'rarely cited as evidence of a true possession'.[17] Yet is frequently cited by English children as apparent proof of their possession or bewitchment. Mylner was the first but instances of 'swelling' would also arise in the cases of: Alexander Nyndge (1573), Katherine Wright (1586), Agnes Briggs and Rachel Pindar (1574), the Throckmorton children (1589), William Sommers

(1597), Mary Cooper (1597), the Starkie Seven (1597), Mary Glover (1602) and Abraham Swift (1683).[18] These cases all had varying levels of success in terms of proving their bewitchment or possession. While some, like Briggs and Pindar, were shown to be frauds, the Throckmorton and afflicted Starkie household were effective in getting their accused tormentors executed.

When Lane saw Mylner in the position described above, he asked if no one had been able to hold her down. Those around her stated that when they had tried, they had almost been cast into the fire. Lane then asked if he 'could hold this doleful woman down' and pulled her feet down, sat on her legs and held her hands down.[19] After two hours, Lane was visibly sweating with the struggling Mylner and called for vinegar to use on the demoniac. Those around them argued that using vinegar on demoniacs had been 'oftentimes attempted but to no purpose'.[20] Nonetheless, Lane put the vinegar into his mouth and blew it into Mylner's nostrils whereupon she cried out for the Virgin Mary: 'a Lady, Lady'.[21] Lane admonished her for resorting to Catholic piety and willed her to cry out for God and specifically the blood of Christ instead. Lane called for more vinegar, upon which Mylner cried 'no, no, no more for God's sake'.[22] Lane then called for food and clothes to be brought and then commanded Mylner to walk. Those around him affirmed that she could not walk as it had been seventeen weeks since she had moved whereupon Lane stated: 'the same God which gave her speech could give her strength also to go'.[23] Mylner ate and was able to walk after which Lane told her to occupy herself in prayer and stay steadfast in her faith with Christ. The next day, Lane preached at Saint Mary's and Mylner attended alongside John Chrogmatron Esquire and The Queen's High Justice in Chester, who had become personally interested in the case. Mylner was in 'perfect health and liking' and according to the account remained so.[24]

Mylner's case is often overlooked by scholars interested in witchcraft cases involving children as she is not usually considered a child at age eighteen. As the previous chapter demonstrated, numerical age is only one factor that should be considered when assessing whether an early modern English person is a child. Considering Mylner was in her teens, unmarried and still living with her father, it is not unreasonable to conclude that she would have been thought of as a child by her contemporaries. Indeed, throughout the pamphlet, Mylner is referred to as a 'maid' which was frequently used as a synonym for a child in cases that involve young, unmarried girls. While it is true that her case did not involve any explicit witchcraft accusations, Mylner's case is an important starting point as the signs and symptoms she displayed as a demoniac were seen in later demonic possession and bewitchment cases. Furthermore, while many of the behaviours and actions between Lane and Mylner were celebrated, they would be seen in different light only two decades later during the intense ecclesiastical upheaval in the Darrell Controversy.[25]

The men who captured Mylner's story were not peasants but men of high social status. It would be extremely difficult – if not impossible – to demonstrate how widely Mylner's account was circulated and known (especially among the poorer class), but the fact that it attracted the attention of the Queen's High Justice shows that it had become quite infamous. Mylner's story included many of the behaviours that were associated with symptoms of possession, and these would be mimicked and built on by children for subsequent decades. Even if they were not directly referencing Mylner's case, this does not mean that children did not hear about it via rumour or gossip, which is how most news spread in this period. Mylner's demonic possession case, being one of the first of its kind in the country, likely garnered at least some attention.[26] The alternative options to children learning from Mylner's case are simply that it was all coincidental; that early modern English children experienced very similar fits and contortions throughout a relatively small chronological and geographic timeframe, or there really was an epidemic of demons infecting English children during the early modern period. The evidence at the historian's disposal gives credence to the idea that children were learning, copying and building on the behaviour from earlier cases for a variety of different reasons and motivations, some of which are obtainable, while others remain speculative. Hence, it is fair to propose that Mylner's influence on the role of children in witch-hunting may be more significant than previously thought. Mylner's story then provides insight into the themes and connections that prevail over the following decades. This provides clues as to how children may have learned to act possessed or bewitched, as well as how adults learnt to perceive or manipulate them; it would only take two more years for the first documented witchcraft case in England to appear, this time in Essex. The accuser was a twelve-year-old girl called Agnes Brown. Unlike Anne Mylner, Agnes Brown did not contort her body and therefore did not 'act' possessed. Brown introduced a new tactic into the role of accuser; she used nothing but her words.

A Deadly Precedent: Agnes Brown and Joan Waterhouse

The anonymously written pamphlet *The Examination and Confession of certain Witches at Chelmsford in the County of Essex* is famously known as the first witchcraft pamphlet to be published in England in 1566. Most of the assertions in the pamphlet can be corroborated with the trial records and indictments. Marion Gibson agrees, stating that the first main section appeared to comprise of almost unaltered examination documents.[27] What makes this pamphlet particularly unique is that it is composed of two sections, which gives the impression that it may have originally been conceived to be printed as two separate works. Gibson noted that this is the only pamphlet to be printed in such instalments.[28] Only the second section mentions

Agnes Brown, which Gibson believed to be a mixture of trial documents and journalistic exaggerations, a feature of all witchcraft sources to some extent. The third and final section (which was likely meant as an addition to the second instalment) dealt with the sentence of death and execution of one of the witches.[29] Understanding how the pamphlet was 'intended' to be published is important to acknowledge, as the collation and organising of the documents may have distorted the narrative.

The fact that this pamphlet may have initially been written as two separate instalments is not the only element that makes it unique. One of the most fascinating aspects about this pamphlet is that its witch-hunting concepts and beliefs appear fully formed and come seemingly out of nowhere only four years after Queen Elizabeth's new witchcraft law passed in 1562. Certainly, the establishment of a new law does not necessarily mean that ideas about witchcraft were not circulating among the populace before this; but it is somewhat surprising that fully fledged ideas about the witch's mark, the pact between the witch and the Devil as well as the witch's familiar – an element unique to England, New England and the Basque region of Spain – were exposed in this pamphlet without any explanation to their origins.[30] What is more significant is how these elements were (allegedly) clearly articulated by twelve-year-old Agnes Brown. One wonders how a likely illiterate twelve-year-old girl from Essex became so well versed in demonological matters. The last important detail about this case surrounds Brown's ability to combine demonological ideas in her accusations against another child, an eighteen-year-old girl called Joan Waterhouse. Joan's role in this case should not be understated as she was the first child not only to confess to familiarity with the Devil, but she also gave evidence against her mother, Agnes Waterhouse. Both Agnes Brown and Joan Waterhouse set a precedent for roles which other English children built on for years after this trial. While scholars have usually focussed on the adults, the pattern these children set in motion was significant, setting a deadly precedent for decades to come.

According to Joan Waterhouse's indictment, Agnes Brown had suffered from Joan's witchcraft, being 'decrepit in her right leg and in her right arm'.[31] Her physical condition was only mentioned in the indictment and not in the oral evidence Brown gave in court. This means that the pamphleteer either thought it was not interesting enough to include in the document or perhaps Brown did not think to mention it and thought she needed only her words to accuse Joan. Agnes Brown was called in to give testimony against Joan, and she was first asked how old she was.[32] In later cases, the question of numerical age would come up less frequently in the examinations of children, indicating that perhaps it became less important or was simply neglected.

After Brown stated that she thought she was about twelve years old, the attorney asked her what she had to say, and Brown relayed her evidence: She stated that she was churning butter and then something came to her 'a thing like a black dog with a face like an ape and a short tail and a silver whistle... about his neck and a pair of horns on his head and in his mouth [the] key of the milk house door'.[33] Brown's description of the witch's familiar seemed noteworthy at the time considering that a drawn depiction of the demonic familiar known as 'Sathan' – showing him exactly as Brown described him – was found within the pamphlet itself.[34] The fact that Sathan is depicted how Brown described him, in contrast to how the accused witches Elizabeth Francis and Agnes Waterhouse described him earlier in the document (as a cat and even a toad), might reflect the pamphleteer's inclination to believe the child's insight rather than the accused witches.[35] This further elevated the position of children as authorities in matters pertaining to the supernatural world. How a twelve-year-old girl came up with such a vivid description of a demonic creature is fascinating and perhaps sheds light into the early modern child's imagination.

Instead of defending herself by disputing Brown's evidence, Joan simply stated that Brown lied only in the description of Sathan, who did not have a face like an ape, 'for this that came to me was like a dog'.[36] Joan's defence was more sophisticated than it first appears. The belief that witchcraft was hereditary – especially between mothers and daughters – had been firmly established in demonological discourse.[37] Furthermore, the hereditary aspect of witchcraft had been mentioned even before Joan and Agnes Waterhouse reached the bar by another accused witch in this trial called Elizabeth Francis. Francis stated that when she was twelve she learnt 'this art of witchcraft...from her grandmother'.[38] By the time Joan was in court, her mother had already confessed to being a witch.[39] Hence, the pressure on Joan to confess as her daughter would have been almost insurmountable. Perhaps in a sophisticated manner of self-protection, thinking that denying she was a witch might offer little safeguard, Joan tried to protect herself by stating that she was supposed to learn this art from her mother 'this last winter' but did not end up doing so, the reason not being given.[40] Joan frequently tried to mitigate how much involvement she had in her mother's witchcraft, possibly trying to secure the juries' mercy by minimising her guilt. Although Joan initially tried to mitigate her familiarity with Satan, under cross-examination, she admitted that after she begged for food from Agnes Brown (leaving dissatisfied) she went to her mother's familiar Sathan and told him to 'make such a girl afraid' for not fulfilling her request for alms.[41] Agnes Brown was then called in to give her side of the story. The fact that these two children are called in (one not even old enough to legally supply evidence in court) to settle a capital case serves as an explosive precedent for the history of the role of children in English witch-hunting.[42]

Though Joan indeed seemed guilty for consorting with familiars and sending them to frighten Agnes Brown, she was acquitted of all charges.[43] While the jury may have pitied her on account of her young age, it is important to recognise the agency Joan enacted throughout her trial, which possibly helped save her life. While Joan Waterhouse escaped punishment, children in later trials were imprisoned after being accused of witchcraft.[44] Conversely, some children used very similar tactics to try to protect themselves as they too were accused alongside relatives.[45]

The first Chelmsford witchcraft trials (1566) set the precedent for a number of roles that English and New English children played in witchcraft trials in the coming decades. Agnes Brown's bout as an accuser not only demonstrated that children under the legal age of fourteen could now be used as witnesses in witchcraft trials, but it also solidified the idea that children could be useful in the pursuit of witch-hunting.[46] Willing or coerced, Brown showed that children had information the judges and jury were willing to hear. Whether she was able to secure the jury's mercy through her own means or through their freely applied pity, Joan's agency and sophistication in minimising her involvement in her mother's witchcraft may have significantly altered her fate. The most important aspect of this case is that for the first time, space had been made for children to give evidence, testify and confess to adults who were willing to hear, accept and believe them. In this way, the 1566 Chelmsford trials were more influential than has been previously thought by historians who have overlooked the children in this case. For it was Agnes Brown and Joan Waterhouse who ushered in a deadly precedent that allowed children under the legal age to act as accusers in court and also saw other children become accused themselves.

'Marvellous Delusions': Rachel Pindar and Agnes Briggs

In London in 1574, rather than being believed and accepted, Rachel Pindar and Agnes Briggs were discovered as frauds or 'counterfeit' demoniacs, but this did not make them irrelevant. In fact, instances of fraud were seen throughout English and New English trials that involved children. In some rare cases, a discovery of fraud did not even inhibit the child's ability to help secure a guilty verdict from the jury.[47] However, some children were eventually punished when exposed as frauds, making 'counterfeits' a complex and fascinating part of the role of children in witchcraft trials, and it seemed to all start with Rachel Pindar and Agnes Briggs.

On Sunday 25 August 1574, twenty-year-old Agnes Briggs and eleven-year-old Rachel Pinder publicly admitted that they had faked being possessed by the Devil and repented before the congregation gathered at Paul's Cross in London.[48] About a month earlier, on 16 July, Pindar had been dispossessed by two – probably dissenting – ministers: William Turner and William Long.[49] According to Agnes Briggs' confession, the saga began when Briggs, Pinder and Pinder's mother were gathered at John Foxe's house, the latter being the author of *Acts and Monuments,* more commonly known as *Foxe's Book of Martyrs*. It is interesting to note that the diagnosis of bewitchment and possession (as both feature in the case of Pinder) come from Pinder's mother, which likely reflects a level of manipulation and coercion on the part of Mistress Pinder, for reasons unknown. Perhaps she took her daughter to John Foxe so he would endorse her belief that her daughter was indeed 'possessed with a devil', thinking that the young girl might serve as a new form of martyr, persecuted by Satan alongside Foxe's other Protestant martyrs who were persecuted by the State.[50]

Sometime after this came the dispossession of Pinder which was a highly evocative display, full of Biblical imagery and remnants of Catholic exorcist rituals. For example, both William Long and William Turner conversed directly with the demon inside Pinder, first asking it: '...you Satan in the blood of Jesus Christ, speak and tell me why you came here?'[51] The demon eventually replied that 'Old Joan' sent the demon into the girl, blurring the lines between possession and bewitchment.[52] In line with another Catholic exorcist rite, the ministers asked the demon what its name was, and the demon replied multiple times: 'Legion'.[53] A long discourse then proceeded between the men and Legion whereby the demon asked for various things such as an apple, bread, thread and blood from them. The men refused and commanded the demon to depart.[54]

Soon afterwards, 'Old Joan' was identified as Joan Thornton. In a demonstration of anti-Catholic sentiment, when Legion was asked how Joan commanded him to appear, he responded: 'she said the Pater Noster three times, and then I did come'.[55] At the end of the document, Pinder was finally dispossessed but not before she displayed classic symptoms of possession that went beyond what Anne Mylner had performed. Not only did her throat swell, but she could speak in a loud voice without her lips moving and later, as her confession indicated, she was able to vomit mysterious objects such as hair, a feather and black silk thread.[56] While her mother may have manipulated or coerced Pinder into acting possessed, it is still impressive how an eleven-year-old was able to put on such a display which seemed to be very earnestly believed by at least six adult witnesses. Furthermore, it is not unfeasible to suggest that Pinder had taught herself to act possessed after hearing about Mylner's story or the story of Alexander Nyndge, a young boy who was also demonically possessed a year earlier in Suffolk.[57] It seemed that demonic possession was in the air and for whatever reason, whether that be a chance for attention or some other form of mental instability, Agnes Briggs was next.[58]

Agnes Briggs was the twenty-year-old daughter of William Briggs, a cloth worker in London.[59] According to Briggs' confession, she first became possessed after meeting Rachel Pinder and her mother at Foxe's house. When she was asked why she was there in the first place, Briggs replied that she was 'much troubled in mind' possibly alluding to some kind of mental or emotional instability.[60] When Briggs heard how the young Pinder acted possessed, she confessed she was 'determined to practise the like'.[61] The motivating factors for why she decided to mimic Pinder are unclear; nonetheless, when Briggs got home that night, she 'on purpose...fell into a trance'.[62] Her confession described how she vomited 'a little piece of lace which she had pulled out her sleeve...and a tenterhook' which, she said, she 'took out of a corner of a window in the chamber...and had put the same in her mouth'.[63] Briggs also vomited other items such as crooked pins, nails and hair which she had pulled from her own head. She was also able to 'disfigure herself with divers strange countenances' and was able to speak in 'strange voices', just like Rachel Pinder.[64] Historians have no account of any attempted dispossession of Briggs so it is assumed that her fits ceased when she admitted her fraud at Paul's Cross.

While it may seem that Briggs' attempt at acting demonically possessed was nothing but a failed side show act, it is still historically significant. At twenty years old, she conducted such a display she claims 'nobody was privy to... but herself'.[65] Furthermore, the details of how she got the mysterious objects into her mouth likely provided other children with information on how to get away with it themselves, albeit more successfully than Briggs.[66] It may be impossible to determine just how widely stories like these were known, but the circulation of these accounts and the influence of gossip should not be underestimated. Just as Briggs became possessed through seeing Pinder at Foxe's house, other children became possessed and bewitched through hearing accounts from neighbours, parents and other people in the town. Indeed, one of the most significant aspects surrounding the role of children in English and New English witch-hunting is persistent and recurring themes that arose over different geographical and chronological timeframes. It may be too tenuous to suggest they were all learning from each other in any kind of explicit, conspiracy-like manner, but there is evidence to suggest that children mimicked one another after learning about preceding trials, usually through word of mouth. For example, vomiting foreign objects – while not an entirely new phenomena in demonic possession cases – occurred substantially more often after the case involving Rachel Pinder and Agnes Briggs, despite them both being discovered as frauds. Rather than focussing on what was happening (the fraud they enacted) it is perhaps more important to focus on why it was happening. Certainly, one could postulate whether both girls suffered from allotriophagy (pathological swallowing) to explain the desire to swallow hair, nails and pins, but this theory alone does not take into consideration the profound affect demonic possession/bewitchment had on the person, family and the community that believed in Satan's malice. As Brian Levack explained: 'all such psychiatric diagnoses are ahistorical. They suffer from the assumption that pathological or abnormal behaviour in all societies and at all periods of time can be attributed to the same psychopathological syndromes of complexes'.[67] This does not mean that such theories are useless, but understanding the actions of the girls in terms of a cultural performance sheds greater insight, rather than simply pathologising them.

Outside of trying to view possession and bewitchment cases through a purely medical lens, we are left with two other options to help explain how and why these stories were spreading, as well as why children mimicked each other. The first was that it was simply a coincidence. Yet, this view appears far too simplistic, as it does not effectively explain how hundreds of children across the entirety of England over a vast chronological timeframe all came up with similar ideas, patterns and behaviours. It also ignores the evidence available where children admitted to having learnt their possession/bewitchment act from another child's case.[68] The only other option to consider was that there really was an epidemic of demonic possession and witchcraft occurring in early modern England. Without substantial evidence to prove the existence of an army of Satanic demons bent on subverting Christendom, the most logical answer appears to be that oral communication allowed these children to learn from one another and use their influence to manipulate witchcraft trials. Certainly, adults took advantage of this for their own gain and children were sometimes used as pawns, while others became targets for accusations. Yet, this only makes children's role in the witchcraft trials more complex and multifaceted. Rather than being one-dimensional or unimportant to the witchcraft trials, children were often integral to their flourishing and functioning.

The significance of Rachel Pinder's and Agnes Briggs' actions was how they built on what Anne Mylner had done as a demoniac, as well as what Agnes Brown had done as an accuser. It is doubtful they did this consciously, but this evolution of roles was significant in the history of English witchcraft trials and the role that children played in them. Of course, it is important to remember the religious agenda in this and all cases, as they do not occur in a vacuum. The dispossession of Rachel Pinder was clearly meant to demonstrate that the dissenting ministers – and not just the Catholic church – had the power to exorcise demons. The capacity in which children became involved in witchcraft trials was growing. For historians, the motivating factors for their involvement are puzzling: why would children want to become involved in such proceedings? Current scholarship has provided no shortage of postulations, such as a need for attention or rebelling against an oppressive religious system.[69] However, a closer examination of the primary evidence reveals more nuanced and complex needs and wants from society's silent majority. Mildred Norrington is one of the first cases that gives historians a clearer view of why children manipulated their role as agents of the invisible world.

'A Ventrilioqua': Mildred Norrington

Mildred's case is captured in Reginald Scot's *A Discoverie of Witchcraft* where Scot stated that he was close to where Mildred was 'practising', only six miles away in Westwell, Kent.[70] Scot's purpose in writing his book was to debunk belief in witchcraft and the trials as a whole.[71] Moreover, Peter Elmer stated that in his relaying of Mildred's story in particular, Scot was attempting to 'tar the Kentish puritans with the brush of excessive zeal and superstition through their promotion of witchcraft and related ideas'.[72] Hence, Mildred's story was brought up by others attempting to either disprove the reality of witchcraft (such as Francis Hutchinson in 1718) or to disprove the reality of dispossession (like Samuel Harsnett in 1599).[73] Yet, it is the individual agency that Mildred displayed that is the most important aspect of her case, one that has not been given due credit.

Mildred Norrington was the illegitimate daughter of Alice Norrington from Westwell, Kent. At the time of her affliction, Mildred was a servant to a man called William Spooner of the same village. On 13 October 1574, Mildred suddenly fell into a fit: 'roaring, crying, striving and gnashing of teeth...so strong in the maid that four men could scarce hold her down'.[74] This continued for the space of about two hours before the men around Mildred entreated the demon inside her to speak. When he did speak, he spoke 'very strangely' in a voice that did not sound like Mildred's own.[75] Between the roaring and screaming the demon told the men they would kill Mildred, and the men asked who sent him: 'Old Alice', he replied. When they asked which Alice, the demon clarified, 'in Westwell street'.[76] Historian Wallace Notestein confirmed that this Alice was in fact Mildred's mother, Alice Norrington.[77] The demon stated that he was kept behind Alice's house 'in two bottles'.[78] When asked what Alice wanted the demon to do, the demon responded that Alice wanted him to 'kill her maid'.[79] When asked why, the demon claimed 'because she did not love her'.[80] The men then told the demon to depart, which he did. Afterwards the men noted: 'Satan's voice did differ much from the maid's voice and all that he spoke was in his own name'.[81] The account that Scot included was signed by eight adult witnesses, including the two vicars who dispossessed young Mildred. Scot continued his retelling of Mildred's account by rhetorically asking: 'how could mother Alice escape condemnation and hanging being arraigned upon this evidence...'.[82] He then stated that Mildred was brought in front of Thomas Wotton and George Darrell, two men he described as being 'discreet [in the] handling of the matter' and from there the two men got Mildred to confess her fraud.[83] Scot stated that Mildred 'received consign punishment' but did not clarify what this was.[84]

Unsurprisingly, given how politically and religiously useful Mildred's case was at the time for sceptics such as Scot, Francis Hutchinson and Samuel

Harsnett, too much has been made out of the fact that Mildred was discovered as a fraud. Conversely, Mildred Norrington's case reveals important evidence about motivation for why children actively participated in witchcraft trials. Using ventriloquy to convey her message, Mildred told the adults around her that she believed her mother did not love her, using a language they would understand: bewitchment. Obviously, Mildred was discovered as a fraud before any formal proceedings against Alice Norrington could be processed. It is not unlikely that Mildred's goal was to have her mother imprisoned, possibly even executed, given that she accused her mother of intending to enact fatal *maleficia*; this was perhaps revenge for a loveless relationship, possibly related to the fact that she was her illegitimate daughter. Nonetheless, Mildred's acumen to use ventriloquy – and ability to convince eight adults of its veracity – to expose her mother's alleged mistreatment of her demonstrates how possession/bewitchment was becoming a powerful weapon, one that children were learning how to use. Children may have been taken advantage of, but this does not exclude them from understanding how they could use bewitchment to gain adult attention. For example, where Agnes Brown failed in her attempt to secure a conviction against Joan Waterhouse in the first set of Chelmsford trials in 1566, in the second Chelmsford trials of 1579, the young child of Ellen Smith further extended children's influence in witchcraft trials.

'Away with the witch!': More Essex Trials, 1579

Only thirteen years after the first Chelmsford trials, the second of three Chelmsford witchcraft trials shook the terrified inhabitants of this Essex community. It is not difficult to imagine that any kind of misfortune must have been interpreted as *maleficia,* as memories of the 1566 trial lingered. In fact, Elizabeth Francis, who had been accused in 1566 and 1572, found herself accused again, this time for bewitching Mrs. Poolc.[85] Although it is known as the second Chelmsford trial (in a singular form) the four accused women were all unconnected to one another both in terms of alleged crimes committed and by relation. In a deviation from the first set of trials where one can see a degree of leniency against the accused – on the basis that Joan Waterhouse was acquitted – all but one woman in these trials were executed. Mother Noakes escaped the noose because neither manslaughter nor murder could be proven against her due to her indictment being incorrectly filled; someone had not recorded the owner's names of the beasts she supposedly killed using *maleficia*.[86] Of the four women, Ellen Smith's case is the most relevant with regard to the developing role of children in English witchcraft trials.

In a similar way to Joan Waterhouse, Ellen Smith must have felt a sense of pressure and fear when she entered the court room knowing she was the daughter of an executed witch. Five years earlier, in 1574, Alice Chaundeler (Ellen's mother) was executed for witchcraft, an event responsible for the first of four separate charges against Smith.[87] In 1579, the first charge Smith was indicted for involved her refusing to pay money back to her father-in-law that he thought she owed him. After an altercation, Smith became enraged and threatened John Chaundeler stating 'that it had been better for him he had never fallen out with her', after which he reportedly 'wasted away' and died.[88] Interestingly, this accusation of death by *maleficia* against an adult was not the main piece of evidence Smith was convicted on. Rather, the charges Smith was inevitably sentenced to death over rested on the accusations of a four-year-old girl and the confessions of her own son.

The second charge Ellen Smith was indicted for was relayed to the court by Smith's illegitimate thirteen-year-old son who had gone to John Estwood's house to beg for alms.[89] After being 'chid away' by Estwood, the boy returned home and told his mother what had happened, whereupon Estwood was 'taken with very great pain in his body'.[90] That night, Estwood apparently saw a rat run up the chimney and fall down in the form of a toad. Putting the toad into the fire, it turned the fire blue and almost put it out. At the burning of the toad, 'Ellen Smith was in great pain' and came to Estwood's house 'and asked to see how [they] did' before leaving.[91] The fact that Smith's young, illegitimate child was able to describe such vivid demonological elements of a witch's demonic familiar, or the idea that burning them could summon the witch, is remarkable. His agency should not be understated, and while we cannot know if he was coerced, there must have been some excitement, even for a brief moment, of being the most important person in the room amid the solemnities and terror of an Assize court. His role was important, accepted and, most significantly, believed. Yet, the evidence from children in Ellen Smith's case had only just begun.

The main charge against Ellen Smith was that she had bewitched to death a four-year-old girl called Susan Webbe. Ellen Smith's daughter and Susan Webbe came 'to blows' during which Ellen Smith struck Susan across the face, whereupon Susan languished for two days and then died crying, 'away with the witch!'[92] It is on this indictment alone that Ellen Smith was found guilty and executed.[93] The fact that Susan, a four-year-old girl on her deathbed, was able to influence a witchcraft trial of an adult with these four words is astonishing. Why this evidence was considered to be more important than the evidence of *maleficia* Smith had supposedly done to two adult men is even more interesting and perhaps sheds light on the sanctity of children: the need to protect, believe or avenge them.

Just in case Susan's words were not enough to convict Smith, her son was brought back into the courtroom to see if he would further testify against her. It cannot be known whether the boy was encouraged or simply enjoyed his time in the spotlight, but Ellen Smith's young son appeared willing to give further evidence against his mother, sealing her fate. He told the court that his mother kept three spirits: 'Great Dick was enclosed in a wicker bottle, the second named Little Dick was put into a leather bottle and the third termed Willet she kept in a wool pack'.[94] This is reminiscent of Mildred Norrington's accusation that her mother kept her familiars in two bottles. This may simply be a coincidence; however, when one analyses the fact that these accounts took place only a year apart, geographically close to one another and by two illegitimate children accusing their mothers, it appears to suggest evidence of learnt behaviour. After the young boy spoke of his mother keeping spirits, her house was commanded to be searched. Smith's son may have felt validated after being believed by a group of adults; however, the pamphleteer noted that while the bottles and packs of wool were found 'the spirits were vanished away'.[95] Nonetheless, combined with bewitching to death Susan Webbe, the jury considered this enough evidence to convict Ellen Smith, and she was executed on 2 April 1579.

In the short span of only fifteen years, the role of children in witchcraft trials had grown markedly in terms of agency and influence. A four-year-old girl, Susan Webbe, had succeeded where Agnes Brown had failed in successfully convincing a jury of a guilty verdict against an adult, no less. Joan Waterhouse escaped punishment, and her tactics of guilt minimisation – by lessening her involvement in her mother's witchcraft – was harnessed by children in later trials. Rachel Pinder and Agnes Briggs significantly developed Anne Mylner's demonic possession behaviour and intertwined it with bewitchment, adding the swallowing of objects to the repertoire of symptoms. Unlike Mildred Norrington, whose condemnation of her mother ended in realisations of her own imposture, the confessions of Ellen Smith's illegitimate son assisted in his mother's eventual execution. While some children may not have realised they were developing witchcraft theory or increasing their role in witchcraft trials, adults certainly took advantage of their testimony. Still, children remained essential in witch-hunting lore and procedure. As adults manipulated children in matters pertaining to witchcraft cases, they revealed that children had some level of influence or value in them. Certainly, it must have become increasingly obvious, especially after the second Chelmsford trials, that the influence children exhibited over matters of life and death was terrifying. Yet, in the same year, a thirteen-year-old boy called Thomas Lever found himself accused of being a conjuror's assistant. Lever's case sheds further light on how children's liminality was also reflected in their status as agents of the invisible world; they could be both accusers – seeing into the invisible world – and accused – looking out from it.

The Conjuror's Assistant: Thomas Lever

Although Thomas Lever's case holds an intriguing amount of detail, Lever is rarely mentioned in secondary sources. The reasons for this are unclear, but perhaps it is because Lever does not fit the stereotype of other children in English witchcraft trials and is therefore left out of the discussion altogether. However, this renders a distorted view of children's involvement in witchcraft trials. Lever's case is unique, as he appears to be one of only two children who were imprisoned for dabbling in the dark arts.[96] His case then sets a precedent which disrupts the pattern of other accusatory children and demonstrates a different, less explored aspect of English children in such cases.

On 28 November 1579, William Randall of Ipswich was arraigned in Essex for conjuring for the purposes of finding hidden treasure.[97] With him were four other men who were also arraigned for helping him. Additionally, there was a thirteen-year-old boy called Thomas Lever, 'who was said to be his [Randall's] assistant and helped in all matters of conjuration'.[98] It was said that Randall could 'bewitch and summon spirits and call the Devil to his tune'.[99] His assistant, the 'boy Thomas Lever mixed his potions and was familiar with all his workings'.[100] Whether Lever was simply a loyal apprentice and did what he was told or was actually keenly interested in the dark arts, historians can only speculate, but the fact that he actively participated in Randall's witchcraft indicated that he had some level of significance in the latter's treasure-finding enterprise.

The trial eventuated in guilty verdicts for Randall and the four other men. Randall was executed, but the four others were reprieved. There did not seem to be any formal charges pressed against Lever, yet he remained in prison.[101] Unsurprisingly confused by the matter of proceedings, Lever's mother, Katherine Lever, wrote a petition to the Privy Council in London, stating that since her son had done no witchery himself – based on the fact there were no formal charges against him – he should be set free.[102] The Council then sent a letter to Lord Brian Darcy and Sir Thomas Lucas, the Justices of the Assize in Essex, stating: 'their Lordships not remembering any particular cause why the child should be either committed or remain so long time as he hath done [in prison] do require them...to give order for his setting at liberty'.[103] However, the letter was clear: 'but if they find good cause why he should be detained, then to advise their Lordships thereof, to the end that his mother may be satisfied with a reasonable answer'.[104] Katherine Lever was clearly unsatisfied, and while little else is known of her, one has to admire her efforts to free her son. She persisted in writing to the Privy Council who, more urgently, wrote to the Essex Justices. The Council required the Justices 'at the next Assize within that county' to either formulate a charge for Lever, otherwise he is 'to be set at liberty'.[105] Unfortunately, after this, Thomas Lever disappears from the record and his fate remains unknown.

Thomas Lever's role as a conjuror's assistant who spent over a year in prison despite no formal charges adds new depth and insight into the role of children in English witchcraft cases. Lever's case demonstrated a shift in attitude as the authorities were clearly moving away from former practices of leniency shown in the case of Joan Waterhouse. While Lever was not arraigned on any formal charges, the fact the thirteen-year-old was put in prison for over a year for merely assisting in his master's witchcraft showed a change in any relative mercy the court had shown in years prior. As the influence and agency of children in witchcraft trials grew, so too did their accountability.

Children's accusations and condemnations of adults were increasingly believed and accepted, which, in turn, appeared to have the unintended consequence of raising suspicions about their own culpability. Lever's case served as a warning that children, as influential and important as they could be in matters pertaining to witchcraft, had to be careful not to fall into the invisible world themselves. Whether consciously or unconsciously, the lesson was learned, and over subsequent decades children did not make the same mistakes as Lever. In fact, the next two cases brought children back to the forefront of the courtroom as accusers against their parents and other relatives. Patterns and themes from earlier cases linger throughout the infamous St Osyth and third set of Chelmsford trials. What makes these unrelated trials unique is the evidence of adult manipulation on the part of the judges, which allowed the power of the accusatory children in these trials to proliferate almost without restraint.

'Can ye not keep your imps from my children?': The Witches of St Osyth

At over one hundred pages long, the pamphlet attached to the St Osyth witchcraft trial of 1582 is the longest witchcraft pamphlet to that date.[106] It was most likely written by the Justice of the Peace that presided over the trials, Brian Darcy, who took the examinations of the witches involved. The source captured Darcy's intent to shine as a successful witch-hunter as the details of the case were carefully kept; the pamphlet included all the pre-trial processes against the witches, including the information from witnesses and victims. The pamphlet also has what Marion Gibson described as a 'wonderfully obsessive, almost loving' fold-out table of statistics attached to the back of the pamphlet.[107] In the table, each witch is numbered with her crimes and spirits listed in an attempt to 'control, classify and thus capture definitely the spattering of stories and accusatory suggestions laid out in the main text'.[108] However, the pamphlet is marred with flaws and errors which can make it challenging to understand. For example, there is little detail on the conclusion of the trials on 29 March 1582; most of the sentences were merely gestured to at the end of the pamphlet. Furthermore, the table omits some sources while providing verbose detail on others, rendering a 'multiform' account which is essentially 'confused and ungraspable', rather than 'coherent and solid' which one feels was Darcy's original purpose in writing the source.[109] Despite this, the three most noteworthy elements focus on the explicit ties to Continental demonological practices, the involvement of children and their manipulation by Darcy, as well as Darcy's apparent distortion of the dates in the pamphlet. These elements reveal an intriguing insight into the emotional turmoil of those involved in this trial, which Gibson described in a more recent microhistorical survey of the trials as: 'a mix of fear, grief, anger and worry, occasionally wonder and thrill'.[110] These emotions are explicit in the depositions provided by the children captured in these trials whose accusations against their own family members are a striking feature of this trial.

The preface of *A true and just Record* is taken directly from Jean Bodin's *On the Demon-mania of Witches*, which likely reflects Darcy's admiration for the French jurist's methods. Bodin wrote:

> Now if ever there was a way to appease the anger of God, to obtain His blessing, to dismay some by the punishment of others, to preserve some of the infection of others, to reduce the number of the wicked...and to punish the most despicable wickedness's that the human mind can imagine, it is to chastise witches with the utmost rigour. However, the word 'rigour' is a misnomer, since there is no penalty cruel enough to punish the evils of witches...[111]

Darcy paraphrased Bodin's words but perfectly captured the sentiment in his pamphlet, only adding wise-women to the 'evils of witches' which was more fitting to the English setting.[112] What is important is that Bodin's 'rigour' in witch-hunting is echoed throughout the pamphlet. For example, in his interrogation of Elizabeth Bennet, Darcy threatened to have her 'burnt and hanged'.[113] In England, burning was reserved only for witches who had committed petty treason using *maleficia*, so Darcy's threat of burning Bennet can be seen more to reflect his commendation of Continental procedure more than anything else.[114] It mattered not that Bodin had said practically nothing about child witnesses, as the precedent had been well and truly established in England by this point that the evidence of minors was permissible in court. Children featured prominently in this heavily documented case, and it appeared that – rather than the children being manipulated and bullied – it was the accused adults that were compelled to accept the children's testimony, many of whom were their own sons and daughters.

Due to the 'mosaic mass of stories' encapsulated in this source, the following discussion focuses on five of the main children involved in the proceedings: Thomas Rabbet, the eight-year-old illegitimate son of Ursley Kempe; Febey Hunt, the eight-year-old stepdaughter of Ales Hunt; Henry and John Sellys, the nine- and six-year-old children of Henry and Cysley Sellys; as well as Annis Dowsing, the seven-year-old illegitimate daughter of Annis Herd.[115] One of the most remarkable aspects of this case was not only the creative stories these children told about their parents, but also the ways in which the parents were pressured into responding to the accusations their children made about them.

Brian Darcy may have attempted to circumvent any allegations of unfairness or manipulation on his part as Justice of the Peace by changing the dates of the examinations and depositions of the children and parents. These changes made it appear that the children were simply affirming the adult's testimony. In reality, it seemed that the adults were being forced to accede to the children's allegations; they had told about their parents *first*. Two conclusions can be drawn from this: firstly, that children were being deliberately used as willing or coerced (evidence would appear to give credence to the former) instruments to extract confessions from witches to gain guilty verdicts. Secondly, Darcy's attempt to alter the order of proceedings in his pamphlet minimised the level of control and influence the children had during the trial, which offers some insight into how he wanted to be perceived by a larger audience. Darcy indisputably wanted a successful career, and while children's participation had precedent in witchcraft trials, obscuring their participation no doubt affirmed and validated his witch-hunting methods, making him seem like a more palatable judge in the face of sceptics; regardless, Reginald Scot later vented his disgust at the handling of the trial in his *Discoverie*.[116]

Although the children's information about their parents always appears first in the pamphlet, the dates attached to the depositions and examinations always make it appear as if the child was affirming the adult's response and not the other way around. However, a close reading of the evidence contained in these depositions and examinations casts serious doubt on the dates Darcy ascribed in his pamphlet. The first example came from Thomas Rabbet, the eight-year-old illegitimate son of Ursley Kempe, who featured prominently throughout the trials. Thomas told the court that his mother had:

> four several spirits, the one called Tyffin, the other Tettey, the third Pigine and the fourth Jacke and being asked of what colours they were, saith that Tettey is like a little grey cat, Tyffin is like a white lamb, Pygine is black like a toad and Jacke is black like a cat. And he saith he hath seen his mother at times to give them beer to drink and of a white loaf or cake to eat and saith that in the night time the said spirits will come to this mother and suck blood of her upon her arms and other places of the body.[117]

Thomas' deposition against his mother demonstrated an impressive knowledge of the lore on familiars, as well as being able to clearly articulate exactly what the judges wanted to hear about his mother's affiliation with them. Thomas' information appeared first in the pamphlet and was dated as 25 February. His mother, Ursley Kempe's examination appeared later in the pamphlet but was dated 20 February; Kempe's information appears to be the origin of Thomas' story about his mother's familiars. Hence, it is unclear, in this instance, whether Thomas simply affirmed his mother's story about her familiars or whether Kempe confirmed her son's story; certainly, the dates would appear to support the former. Yet, later evidence from children created obvious loopholes in Darcy's dating system.

Febey Hunt, also aged eight, was the stepdaughter of Ales Hunt, and she claimed that her stepmother had 'two little things like horses, the one white, the other black, the which she kept in a low earthen pot with wool…she hath seen her mother to feed them with milk out of a black trening dish'.[118] Firstly, it is notable that the keeping of spirits in a pot full of wool was a feature mentioned by Ellen Smith's thirteen-year-old son, also from Essex only three years previously. It is not impossible that Febey was copying the same demonic elements from trials she had heard about previously in order to build a believable story of witchcraft using local lore. After this information, the constable took the little girl to her house where 'she showed them the place where [the pots] stood and the board that covered them and this examinate chose out the dish, out of which they were fed, from amongst many other dishes'.[119] The emphasis on Febey's ability to discern exactly which dish her stepmother used to feed her spirits was an attempt to add weight to her credibility as a witness; at only eight years old, Febey seemed completely willing to not only give oral evidence against her mother, but also provide them with physical 'proof' too.

Perhaps some clues as to the motivation behind this surfaced when she confessed 'that her mother had charged her not to tell anything, what she had seen, and if she did those things would take her'.[120] Whether her mother intended for this to be a playful game or was some kind of nasty threat, historians cannot know. Notwithstanding, Febey was clearly afraid and willing went against her stepmother's orders, accusing her openly as a witch. This act of defiance, from a child whose place in society at eight years old was to be obedient and loyal to one's parents, demonstrates how their visionary abilities enabled them to have influence, control and power in ways that were usually far out of reach. Whether Febey was used as an instrument against her stepmother by the judges does not take away from the fact that she provided them with the necessary evidence they needed to denounce her. These children, of course, needed the magistrates on their side in order for their accusations to lead to convictions, but it was becoming increasingly obvious the magistrates were relying on the children too.

The fact that the judges relied on the evidence of children was explicit in the examination of Ales Hunt when she was confronted with the aforementioned spirit-feeding dish her stepdaughter provided to the court. Hunt was first asked whether she had a falling out with the Haywards of Frowick (which was another accusation made by Febey). When the judges were unsuccessful in getting Hunt to admit to this or to owning any spirits, the judges pressed further with more leading questions, using details from Febey's story. They asked if Hunt '...never did feed her spirits with milk out of a little trening dish'.[121] When Hunt replied that she did not, she was confronted with the physical dish Febey identified from their house. Hunt stood firm and denied that it was her dish, claiming that she did not have a dish like that in her house. The court, clearly unsatisfied with her answers, simply committed Hunt to prison. Upon hearing this, Hunt desired to speak alone with Darcy. Whether it was the confrontation with the dish or the commitment to prison, Ales Hunt snapped: 'she then falling upon her knees with weeping tears confessed and said that she [had] two spirits, like unto little colts, the one black and the other white...'.[122] Being confronted with the dish Febey identified and Hunt's admission about the keeping of spirits – that looked just like Febey described them – is made further interesting when one examines the dates placed for these two pieces of evidence.

Unlike Thomas Rabbet and his mother, where the truth of whose story came first is unclear, the series of events for Ales Hunt's case is obvious. Clearly, Febey gave her information about the dish and the nature of her stepmother's familiars before Hunt was examined about them. However, the dates given in the documents stated that Febey's deposition was given on 25 March, while her mother's examination and confession were given the day before, on 24 March. This, of course, is illogical given the sequence of events describing the nature of the evidence in both the deposition and the examination. This demonstrates how Darcy may have deliberately misdated the documents in an attempt to show that the children merely affirmed their parent's admonitions. Nonetheless, the evidence reveals that Ales Hunt was pressured into accepting her eight-year-old stepdaughter's story about black and white horse-like familiars, and this, combined with being committed to prison, seemed to force her to confess.

Febey's information against her stepmother provided the most dramatic example in this trial of children's evidence being used to influence an adult, but it was not the last. The Sellys brothers, Henry and John, aged nine and six respectively, both told the court about the demonic activities of their parents, highlighting the domestic disturbances they lived with. Henry told the court that something 'like his sister...but that it was all black' grabbed his little brother John's left leg and little toe around midnight one night'.[123] Frightened, the young boy called out to his father asking for his help, whereupon Henry stated that his father said to his mother, 'why thou whore cannot you keep your imps from my children? Whereat she presently called it away from her son'.[124] The next day, Henry told his mother he was so afraid of the thing that grabbed John in the middle of the night 'he sweat... that he could scarce get his shirt from his back: his mother answering thou lyest thou lyest whoresonne'.[125] Not only does this provide a clear picture of children's fears (real or imagined), but it also gives historians an insight into what appeared to be quite a disruptive if not abusive home, where cursing and swearing were the norm.[126] What this may indicate about the children and their decision to testify against their parents remains speculative, but it is possible they were more willing to testify due to possible feelings of harboured resentment and fear.

John's testimony differs little from his elder brothers', only in that his father called his mother a 'stinking whore' when his father asked her why she could not keep her imps away from his children.[127] John, only six, was asked the curious question of whether his parents 'bade him that he should say nothing' as a possible way to assess his mother's and father's guilt.[128] John replied that his 'mother said unto him that he should go before a gentleman and willed him to take heed and tell no tales nor lies'.[129] This is perhaps one of the only references to what a child was told by their parent before going to court to testify in a witchcraft case. Whether at this point John's mother knew her son was going to testify against her is unclear; this, conceivably, might have altered her directions to him.

In John's deposition, he told the court more details about the demonic familiars and placed more blame on both his parents, saying his mother and father fed them. When he was asked what their names were, he said that his father called the black one John and 'mocked him because his name was so'.[130] Whether this was some kind of playful game or mean joke to scare the child is unclear, but it appears John did not appreciate his father's demonic pet being named after him. The last note on John's testimony was that there was a scar on his leg where it was said the spirit took him. The nail on his little toe was also described as being 'unperfect'.[131] Like Febey, John had physical 'proof' to show the court not only of his parent's malevolence and dealings with the invisible world but also of their failure as parents to protect him from it.

Henry Sellys' deposition is strangely not dated, but it is likely it was given the same day as his brother John's which was dated 3 March. As is with all the children's testimony in this pamphlet, the examination of the parents – this time Henry and Cysley Sellys – is dated 1 March, two days before the information given by their children. This appears illogical given the nature of the questions they are asked to respond to. The pamphlet reports that two days *before* the information was given by their children, Henry Sellys was asked whether his children did cry out to him in the middle of the night, as well as whether he did call his wife a 'stinking whore'. He denies both claims, but the pamphlet simply noted that he was condemned anyway (in fact, both Henry and Cysley were acquitted but died in prison).[132] During her examination, Cysley was also asked whether her child 'cried out in the night to his father', but she also denied this. Again, one wonders how Henry and Cysley Sellys were asked such specific questions if they were examined two days before their children? As with the other examples given, the only logical explanation is that Darcy misdated the records.

The young Henry and John Sellys' stories must have strengthened Darcy's presumption of guilt as he appointed three local women to search Cysley for the witches' mark. According to one of the appointed women, Cysley had 'many spots very suspicious...that they be much like the sucked spots, that she [the searcher] hath seen upon the body of Ursley Kempe...'.[133] Unable to break the adult Sellys down and extract a confession, substantiating the children's information with the physical 'proof' of the witch's mark must have seemed to Darcy more than enough evidence to convict Cysley Sellys. The fact that the elder Henry Sellys was committed to prison on the children's evidence alone demonstrated that the examination of the witches' mark was simply an addition to Cysley's proof of guilt and not the linchpin that sealed her fate.[134]

The last influential child in this case was seven-year-old Annis Dowsing, the illegitimate daughter of Annis Herd. Dowsing was first asked whether her mother had any 'little things' or 'little imps'.[135] Dowsing responded that her mother had 'avices or blackbirds' in one box and things like 'cows... as big as rats' in another box.[136] She said that her mother had given her two of these creatures, which were named Crowe and Donne. Dowsing goes into detail about what Herd fed them, and when she was asked if they ever sucked from her mother, she used her own body as a tool of demonstration to show exactly which familiars sucked from which body parts.[137] Dowsing also seemed to implicate her brother in this, who is not mentioned further in the pamphlet, by saying that he also fed the birds and let them suck from him. This is likely why the judges asked her this last question: 'and being asked how one spot upon the back of her hands came...like the other, she saith the same was burnt'.[138] Children who saw into the supernatural world were often caught in a tenuous position; it is evidence like this that demonstrates that accusing children had to be careful not to implicate themselves.

Again, the dates for the information and examination between child and adult are suspicious and give credence to the idea that Darcy manipulated the way in which the reader interpreted the trial. The pamphlet stated that Dowsing's information was given on 18 March and that her mother, Annis Herd, was examined the day before on 17 March. Again, this does not make logical sense given the questions and evidence Herd was forced to respond to. In Herd's examination, she was asked whether she had, 'any imps, avices or blackbirds or any kine [cows] called Crowe or Donne...' which she denied any knowledge of. How would the court have known to ask Herd such specific questions had her daughter not given them the information before the examination? The pamphlet stated that Herd was committed to prison but was in the end acquitted. The fact that this method of pressuring adults with information brought forth from their own children shows that Darcy thought it was useful and yielded results. This trial marks an important moment in the history of the role of children in English witchcraft trials, as forcing of adults to confront children's accusations about them highlights the influence and control children could have over witchcraft trials when the magistrates were willing to let it develop freely.

'Commended them greatly for telling the truth': The 1589 Chelmsford Trials

Not only were the accusations of children allowed to thrive in the third set of Chelmsford witchcraft trials in 1589, but also they were actively encouraged and commended by the highly esteemed judges: Robert Clarke, Baron of the Exchequer, and John Puckering, the Queen's Sergeant.[139] The surviving trial records indicated that one man and nine women were brought into court accused of witchcraft. However, the pamphlet attached to this case only included the confessions and executions of three witches: Joan Prentice, Joan Cunny or Cony and Joan Upney. This not only highlights the need to substantiate pamphlet evidence with trial documents (where available), but it also alludes to the pamphlet writers' possible motivations for only including three women in his work. Perhaps the three confessions he included created the best story for his audience, as the judges were seen to have done the Lord's work by sending the most wicked of the witches to their deaths, rather than including four of the accused who were found not guilty.

The most relevant parts of this trial focus on the Cony or Cunny family. The trial documents noted their name as 'Cony', but the pamphleteer recorded them as 'Cunny'. It is unclear whether this was simply a spelling deviation, but Marion Gibson noted that Cunny, a slur for vagina, might have been used on purpose as an added joke or way to further degrade the family.[140] The author of the pamphlet made it clear that he believed the Cony family were 'living very lewdly', describing the daughters as being, 'no better than naughty packs'.[141] The pamphleteer also noted that the daughters had 'two bastard sons' who were described as 'chief witnesses' and 'gave in great evidence against their grandmother and mothers'.[142] It is for this reason that the Cony family makes a useful case study to examine the role of children in witchcraft trials at the end of the sixteenth century.

The pamphlet did not provide the names of the boys and stated only that the eldest one was around ten or twelve years old. The details of the evidence the boys gave against their mothers and grandmother are relatively brief compared to the St Osyth trial, but this does not make it any less valuable. The elder boy stated that his mother first went to Harry Finches' house 'to demand some drink' but when she did not receive any, it is said that Finches' wife became 'grievously taken in her head' for a week before she died.[143] After giving this information, Joan Cony confessed, stating that she had sent her spirit to torment Finches' wife. In a similar way to the St Osyth trial, it seemed that Joan Cony was pressured into responding to the information her child accused her of. Perhaps emboldened by this, the boy's next accusation was even more detailed and elaborate.

The boy described how his grandmother asked him to gather some wood which he did, but then another boy stole it from him, so he came home without any. When the boy told his grandmother he had lost the wood, she replied 'she would have wood enough' and told the boy to go to Sir Edward Huddlestone's ground and to take Jack the spirit with him.[144] The boy claimed that no one could see the spirit but himself and when Huddlestone and the boy came to a mighty oak tree, the boy watched as Jack 'went about it' and 'presently the tree blew up at the roots and no wind at all stirring at this time', something which Huddlestone also confirmed was true.[145] The fact that the boy told the court that he could see and use Jack the familiar just as well as his grandmother demonstrates his dual role as a preternatural agent, one who could look into the invisible world as well as out of it. That the judge did not reprimand him for his participation in the occult is even more remarkable but may show how invaluable the boy had made himself to the proceedings; he was more useful as an accuser than an accused. Indeed, the pamphlet noted that at the end of the proceedings, the judge:

> very wisely with a great foresight called in the two bastard children … and commended them greatly for telling the truth of that which he should ask them, concerning their grandma and their mothers, which they did, and having said what they could, together with the depositions of sundry other witnesses, they having confessed sufficient matter to prove the indictments.[146]

This statement alone indicates the level of power and influence these young, illegitimate children had over the life and death of their mother and grandmother. Joan Cony, Avis Cony and Margaret Cony were all found guilty. Joan was hanged; Avis was reprieved for a year after it was found she was pregnant but was hanged in 1590 after the birth. Margaret was imprisoned for a year and served four rounds in the pillory as her bewitchment of a man did not result in death.[147] The Cony children not only stepped up in societal and cultural defiance against their mother and grandmother, they were also actively encouraged and praised for doing so. It was the deadly consequence of what could happen when the influence of children and unbridled magisterial support joined together in the pursuit of witch-hunting.

Of course, this was not always the case. Children were not always supported by the court in their denunciations of witches. Some, like Agnes Briggs and Rachel Pinder, were discovered as frauds, and hence, their accusations never made it to court. Other children, like Thomas Lever, broke away from the stereotype of being an accuser through being imprisoned as a conjuror's assistant. Other children still, like Elizabeth Crofts and Anne Mylner, established further precedents by involving themselves in matters pertaining to the supernatural. These early contributions from Crofts and Mylner are often overlooked, yet it is still important to recognise just how much the role of children in witchcraft grew and developed in the late sixteenth century.

From 1564 to 1589, children established themselves in witchcraft trials as important accusers who influenced the nature of witchcraft trials and demonically possessed individuals capable of captivating adult audiences, as well as those like Joan Waterhouse and Thomas Lever, who found themselves denounced. The evidence demonstrates that children were learning and mimicking behaviour from earlier trials, pushing boundaries and asserting themselves in adult spheres through their liminality; they gave insight and information that was otherwise unobtainable. In the second set of Chelmsford trials, the St Osyth trials and third Chelmsford trials, one can observe that once the court discovered how useful children could be, their influence grew and restrictions or other safeguards protecting the accused were lifted. In these trials, it is clear how the magistrates placed the information and authority of children above that of adults, almost forcing them to confront – and hopefully confess – to whatever the children accused them of. The consequences of this method, in most cases, were devastating and showed what could happen when magistrates allowed children's accusations to dominate the courtroom almost without restraint.

In the years after 1589, children exerted themselves in witchcraft trials more so than ever, culminating in the infamous John Darrell Controversy. The consequence of this controversy and the role children played in it should not be underestimated: the controversy ended two Puritan preachers' careers, established a Canon on dispossession that was not reversed in the Anglican Church until 1969 and seemed to permanently tarnish the validity of children's role as demoniacs.[148] Outside of this, other children followed in the footsteps of the precedents set by the children in this chapter, making themselves indispensable in witchcraft trials. Conversely, other children, trying similar tactics, were not believed. However, their stories of fraud provide just as much valuable information about motivation and cultural perceptions surrounding the growing place of children in witchcraft trials.

Notes

1 Gilbert Burnet, *The History of The Reformation of The Church of England*, vol. 2, part 2, book 2 (New York: D. Appleton & Company, 1843), p. 425.
2 Daniel Hahn, 'Elizabeth Crofts', *Oxford Dictionary of National Biography*, ed. David Cannadine (2004), https://doi.org/10.1093/ref:odnb/6725, unpaginated.
3 Daniel Hahn, 'Elizabeth Crofts', *Oxford Dictionary of National Biography*, ed. David Cannadine (2004), https://doi.org/10.1093/ref:odnb/6725. Paul's Cross was a preaching cross and an open-air pulpit in St Paul's Churchyard near the grounds of Old St Paul's Cathedral in London.
4 Miles Huggarde, *The Displaying of the Protestants...* (London: Robert Caly, 1556), sig. 120v.
5 Miles Huggarde, *The Displaying of the Protestants...* (London: Robert Caly, 1556).
6 Miles Huggarde, *The Displaying of the Protestants...* (London: Robert Caly, 1556), sig. 120v–120r.
7 John Fisher, William Cawley and Richard Hurleston, *The Copy of a Letter Describing the Wonderful Work of God in Delivering a Maiden with the City of Chester...* (London: Imprinted by John Awdely, 1564), im. 3r.
8 John Fisher, William Cawley and Richard Hurleston, *The Copy of a Letter Describing the Wonderful Work of God in Delivering a Maiden with the City of Chester...* (London: Imprinted by John Awdely, 1564), im. 4v.
9 John Fisher, William Cawley and Richard Hurleston, *The Copy of a Letter Describing the Wonderful Work of God in Delivering a Maiden with the City of Chester...* (London: Imprinted by John Awdely, 1564).
10 John Fisher, William Cawley and Richard Hurleston, *The Copy of a Letter Describing the Wonderful Work of God in Delivering a Maiden with the City of Chester...* (London: Imprinted by John Awdely, 1564).
11 Brian P. Levack, *The Devil Within: Possession and Exorcism in the Christian West* (New Haven and London: Yale University Press, 2013), pp. 10–11.
12 Cotton Mather, 'A Brand Pluck'd out of the Burning', 1693, in *Narratives of the Witchcraft Cases 1648-1706*, ed. George Lincoln Burr (New York: Charles Scribner's Sons, 1914), p. 265.
13 John Fisher, William Cawley and Richard Hurleston, *The Copy of a Letter Describing the Wonderful Work of God in Delivering a Maiden with the City of Chester...* (London: Imprinted by John Awdely, 1564), im. 4r.
14 John Fisher, William Cawley and Richard Hurleston, *The Copy of a Letter Describing the Wonderful Work of God in Delivering a Maiden with the City of Chester...* (London: Imprinted by John Awdely, 1564), im. 5v.
15 John Fisher, William Cawley and Richard Hurleston, *The Copy of a Letter Describing the Wonderful Work of God in Delivering a Maiden with the City of Chester...* (London: Imprinted by John Awdely, 1564), im. 6v–6r.
16 John Fisher, William Cawley and Richard Hurleston, *The Copy of a Letter Describing the Wonderful Work of God in Delivering a Maiden with the City of Chester...* (London: Imprinted by John Awdely, 1564), im. 6r.
17 Brian P. Levack, *The Devil Within: Possession and Exorcism in the Christian West* (New Haven and London: Yale University Press, 2013), p. 9.
18 See Edward Nyndge [?], *A Book Declaring the Fearful Vexation of one Alexander Nyndge...* (London: imprinted by Thomas Collwell, 1573); Edward Nyndge,

A True and Fearful Vexation of One Alexander Nyndge… (London: imprinted for W. B., 1615). The latter version embellishes some of the details found in the earlier pamphlet; Samuel Harsnett, *A Discovery of the Fraudulent Practices of John Darrell…*(London: Imprinted by John Wolfe, 1599); Anon., *The Disclosing of a Late Counterfeited Possession by the Devil in Two Maidens within the City of London…* (London: printed by Richard Watkins, 1574); Anon., *The Most Strange and Admirable Discoverie of Three Witches of Warboys…* (London: printed by the Widow Orwin for Thomas Man and John Winnington, 1593); Anon., *A Brief Narration of the Possession, Dispossession and Repossession of William Sommers…*, Amsterdam: S.N, 1598); Samuel Harsnett, *A Discovery of the Fraudulent Practices of John Darrell…* (London: Imprinted by John Wolfe, 1599); John Darrell, *A Detection of That Sinnful, Shamful, Lying and Ridiculous Discours of Samuel Harshnet…* (London: Imprinted by the English secret press, 1600); Edward Jorden, *A Briefe Discourse of a Disease Called the Suffocation of the Mother* (London: publisher unknown,1603); John Swan, *A True and Briefe Report of Mary Glovers Vexation, and of Her Deliverance by Fastings and Prayer* (London: publisher unknown, 1603); J. Horsfall Turner, ed. *Rev. Oliver Heywood, 1630-1702: His Autobiography, Diaries, Anecdote and Event Books Illustrating the General and Family History of Yorkshire and Lancashire*, vol. 4 (Bingley: printed for the editor, 1885), pp. 53–54.

19 John Fisher, William Cawley and Richard Hurleston, *The Copy of a Letter Describing the Wonderful Work of God in Delivering a Maiden with the City of Chester…* (London: Imprinted by John Awdely, 1564), im. 7v.

20 John Fisher, William Cawley and Richard Hurleston, *The Copy of a Letter Describing the Wonderful Work of God in Delivering a Maiden with the City of Chester…* (London: Imprinted by John Awdely, 1564), im. 8v.

21 John Fisher, William Cawley and Richard Hurleston, *The Copy of a Letter Describing the Wonderful Work of God in Delivering a Maiden with the City of Chester…* (London: Imprinted by John Awdely, 1564), im. 8r.

22 John Fisher, William Cawley and Richard Hurleston, *The Copy of a Letter Describing the Wonderful Work of God in Delivering a Maiden with the City of Chester…* (London: Imprinted by John Awdely, 1564).

23 John Fisher, William Cawley and Richard Hurleston, *The Copy of a Letter Describing the Wonderful Work of God in Delivering a Maiden with the City of Chester…* (London: Imprinted by John Awdely, 1564), im. 9v.

24 John Fisher, William Cawley and Richard Hurleston, *The Copy of a Letter Describing the Wonderful Work of God in Delivering a Maiden with the City of Chester…* (London: Imprinted by John Awdely, 1564), im 10v.

25 John Darrell and the surrounding controversy are discussed in more depth in Chapter 3.

26 According to historian Margaret Spufford, cheap, religious publications (which include but are not limited to accounts such as Mylner's) found a 'ready market' in early modern England. However, Spufford affirms that by 'no means' can historians know the extent to which these books 'demonstrate changes in emphasis and thought'. Margaret Spufford, *Small Books and Pleasant Histories: Popular Fiction and its Readership in Seventeenth-Century England* (London: Methuen & Co., 1981), pp. 197 and 213.

27 Marion Gibson, *Early Modern Witches: Witchcraft Cases in Contemporary Writing* (London and New York: Routledge, 2000), p. 10.
28 Marion Gibson, *Early Modern Witches: Witchcraft Cases in Contemporary Writing* (London and New York: Routledge, 2000), p. 11.
29 Marion Gibson, *Early Modern Witches: Witchcraft Cases in Contemporary Writing* (London and New York: Routledge, 2000).
30 The witch's familiar is a phenomenon unique to England, New England and the Basque region in Spain. Its origins and why it did not appear regularly in Continental European witchcraft trials remain obscure.
31 C. L'Estrange Ewen, *Witch Hunting and Witch Trials: The Indictments for Witchcraft from the Records of 1373 Assizes Held for the Home Court AD 1559-1736* (London: Kegan Paul, 1929), p. 120.
32 Anon., *The Examination and Confession of Certain Witches at Chelmsford in the County of Essex...* (London: printed by William Powell, 1566), im. 16r.
33 Anon., *The Examination and Confession of Certain Witches at Chelmsford in the County of Essex...* (London: printed by William Powell, 1566), im. 17v.
34 See im. 16r for the depiction of 'Sathan'.
35 Both Elizabeth Francis and Agnes Waterhouse were eventually found guilty.
36 Anon., *The Examination and Confession of Certain Witches at Chelmsford in the County of Essex...* (London: printed by William Powell, 1566), im. 19r.
37 See previous chapter.
38 Anon., *The Examination and Confession of Certain Witches at Chelmsford in the County of Essex...* (London: printed by William Powell, 1566), im. 6r.
39 Anon., *The Examination and Confession of Certain Witches at Chelmsford in the County of Essex...* (London: printed by William Powell, 1566), im. 9r.
40 Anon., *The Examination and Confession of Certain Witches at Chelmsford in the County of Essex...* (London: printed by William Powell, 1566), im 11r.
41 Anon., *The Examination and Confession of Certain Witches at Chelmsford in the County of Essex...* (London: printed by William Powell, 1566), im. 12r.
42 Ronald Seth, *Children Against Witches* (London: Robert Hale, 1969), p. 35.
43 C. L'Estrange Ewen, *Witch Hunting and Witch Trials: The Indictments for Witchcraft from the Records of 1373 Assizes Held for the Home Court AD 1559-1736* (London: Kegan Paul, 1929), p. 120.
44 See for example the cases of Thomas Lever (explored later in this chapter) and Mary Clarke (discussed briefly in the conclusion).
45 For example, this can be seen in the Pendle trials of 1612 and later in New England in the Salem trials of 1692, discussed in Chapters 4 and 6, respectively.
46 According to Geoffrey Gilbert, who wrote *The Law of Evidence*: 'idiots, madmen and children under the age of common knowledge' were excluded from testifying. Gilbert clarifies that children 'under the age of fourteen are not regularly admitted as witnesses' but noted 'the reason and sense of their evidence is to appear from the questions propounded to them and their answers to them'. Sir Geoffrey Gilbert, *The Law of Evidence* (London: printed by Henry Lintot, 1756), pp. 146–147; for a thorough discussion of the legal status of children, see Orna Alyagon Darr, *Marks of an Absolute Witch: Evidentiary Dilemmas in Early Modern England* (Oxford and New York: Routledge, 2016), pp. 199–204.
47 See the 1662 Bury St Edmunds trial explored in Chapter 4.

48 Anon., *The disclosing of a late counterfeited possession by the devil in two maidens within the city of London…* (London: printed by Richard Watkins, 1574), im. 3v.
49 Philip C. Almond, *Demonic Possession and Exorcism in Early Modern England: Contemporary Texts and their Cultural Contexts* (Cambridge: Cambridge University Press, 2004), p. 59.
50 Anon., *The Disclosing of a Late Counterfeited Possession by the Devil in Two Maidens within the City of London…* (London: printed by Richard Watkins, 1574), im. 8v.
51 Anon., *The Disclosing of a Late Counterfeited Possession by the Devil in Two Maidens within the City of London…* (London: printed by Richard Watkins, 1574), im. 4v.
52 Anon., *The Disclosing of a Late Counterfeited Possession by the Devil in Two Maidens within the City of London…* (London: printed by Richard Watkins, 1574), im. 4r.
53 Anon., *The Disclosing of a Late Counterfeited Possession by the Devil in Two Maidens within the City of London…* (London: printed by Richard Watkins, 1574), im. 5v; this is clearly a reference to Mark 5:9 where Jesus spoke to the Gadarene demoniac: 'And he [Jesus] asked him, What is thy name? And he answered, saying, My name is Legion: for we are many'. Mark 5:9, The Bible, King James Version.
54 Anon., *The Disclosing of a Late Counterfeited Possession by the Devil in Two Maidens within the City of London…* (London: printed by Richard Watkins, 1574), im. 5v–6r.
55 Anon., *The Disclosing of a Late Counterfeited Possession by the Devil in Two Maidens within the City of London…* (London: printed by Richard Watkins, 1574), im. 7v.
56 Anon., *The Disclosing of a Late Counterfeited Possession by the Devil in Two Maidens within the City of London…* (London: printed by Richard Watkins, 1574), im. 9r.
57 See Edward Nyndge [?], *A Book Declaring the Fearful Vexation of One Alexander Nyndge…* (London: imprinted by Thomas Collwell, 1573), and Edward Nyndge, *A True and Fearful Vexation of One Alexander Nyndge…* (London: imprinted for W. B., 1615). The latter version embellishes some of the details found in the earlier pamphlet.
58 Gary K. Waite, *Heresy, Magic and Witchcraft in Early Modern Europe* (Basingstoke: Palgrave Macmillan Publishers, 2003), p.140, stated that the frequency of demonic possession often paralleled the escalation of religious polemics and conflict, which may be one contributing factor to the seemingly 'catching' nature of possession seen in the case of Pinder and Briggs.
59 Anon., *The Disclosing of a Late Counterfeited Possession by the Devil in Two Maidens within the City of London…* (London: printed by Richard Watkins, 1574), im. 8v.
60 Anon., *The Disclosing of a Late Counterfeited Possession by the Devil in Two Maidens within the City of London…* (London: printed by Richard Watkins, 1574).
61 Anon., *The Disclosing of a Late Counterfeited Possession by the Devil in Two Maidens within the City of London…* (London: printed by Richard Watkins, 1574), im. 8v–8r.

62 Anon., *The Disclosing of a Late Counterfeited Possession by the Devil in Two Maidens within the City of London...* (London: printed by Richard Watkins, 1574), im. 8r.
63 Anon., *The Disclosing of a Late Counterfeited Possession by the Devil in Two Maidens within the City of London...* (London: printed by Richard Watkins, 1574).
64 Anon., *The Disclosing of a Late Counterfeited Possession by the Devil in Two Maidens within the City of London...* (London: printed by Richard Watkins, 1574), im. 9v.
65 Anon., *The Disclosing of a Late Counterfeited Possession by the Devil in Two Maidens within the City of London...* (London: printed by Richard Watkins, 1574).
66 Anon., *The Disclosing of a Late Counterfeited Possession by the Devil in Two Maidens within the City of London...* (London: printed by Richard Watkins, 1574). im. 9r.
67 Brian P. Levack, *The Devil Within: Possession and Exorcism in the Christian West* (New Haven and London: Yale University Press, 2013), pp. 28–29.
68 Other than Agnes Briggs (who confessed to acting bewitched after seeing Rachel Pinder) there are examples of children admitting that they learnt how to act bewitched/possessed from other cases. For example, William Sommers claimed he had watched Thomas Darling in his fits to learn how to act bewitched. Sommers also purportedly claimed to have read the Throckmorton account as an inspiration for his fits. Even if Sommers did not watch Darling or read the Throckmorton case, the fact that he had knowledge of what to say/who to mention demonstrates how such accounts may have circulated. See Samuel Harsnett, *A Discovery of the Fraudulent Practices of John Darrell...*(London: Imprinted by John Wolfe, 1599), esp. p. 85 and p. 97.
69 See for example Samuel Eliot Morison, *The Intellectual Life of Colonial New England* (New York: New York University Press, 1956), p. 259, and G.R. Quaife, *Godly Zeal and Furious Rage: The Witch in Early Modern Europe* (London and New York: Routledge, 1987), p. 189.
70 Reginald Scot, *The Discoverie of Witchcraft*, 1691 edn. (London: publisher unknown), p. 127.
71 Scot was also responding to Dutch/German physician Johan Wier's explanation of such behaviour in Germany, as well as to his own neighbourhood. See Hans de Waardt, 'Inflating the Prestige of Demons: Johan Wier's Role-Playing' *Church History and Religion* 101 (2021), pp. 234–262.
72 Peter Elmer, *Witchcraft, Witch-Hunting and Politics in Early Modern England* (Oxford: Oxford University Press, 2016), p. 21.
73 See Francis Hutchinson, *An Historical Essay Concerning Witchcraft: With Observations Upon Matters of Fact...* (London, printed for R. Knaplock, 1718), pp. 189–192, and Samuel Harsnett, *A Discovery of the Fraudulent Practices of John Darrell...* (London: Imprinted by John Wolfe, 1599), p. 16.
74 Reginald Scot, *The Discoverie of Witchcraft*, 1691 edn. (London: publisher unknown), p. 127.
75 Reginald Scot, *The Discoverie of Witchcraft*, 1691 edn. (London: publisher unknown), p. 129.
76 Reginald Scot, *The Discoverie of Witchcraft*, 1691 edn. (London: publisher unknown), p. 128.

77 Wallace Notestein, *A History of Witchcraft in England from 1558-1718* (Washington D.C.: The American Historical Association, 1911), p. 59.
78 Reginald Scot, *The Discoverie of Witchcraft*, 1691 edn. (London: publisher unknown), p. 128.
79 Reginald Scot, *The Discoverie of Witchcraft*, 1691 edn. (London: publisher unknown).
80 Reginald Scot, *The Discoverie of Witchcraft*, 1691 edn. (London: publisher unknown).
81 Reginald Scot, *The Discoverie of Witchcraft*, 1691 edn. (London: publisher unknown), p. 129.
82 Reginald Scot, *The Discoverie of Witchcraft*, 1691 edn. (London: publisher unknown), p. 130.
83 Reginald Scot, *The Discoverie of Witchcraft*, 1691 edn. (London: publisher unknown)p. 131.
84 Reginald Scot, *The Discoverie of Witchcraft*, 1691 edn. (London: publisher unknown).
85 Marion Gibson, *Early Modern Witches: Witchcraft Cases in Contemporary Writing* (London and New York: Routledge, 2000), p. 41.
86 C. L'Estrange Ewen, *Witchcraft and Demonism: A Concise Account Derived from Sworn Depositions and Confessions Obtained in the Courts of England and Wales* (London: Heath Cranton Limited, 1933), p. 152.
87 C. L'Estrange Ewen, *Witchcraft and Demonism: A Concise Account Derived from Sworn Depositions and Confessions Obtained in the Courts of England and Wales* (London: Heath Cranton Limited, 1933), p. 150
88 C. L'Estrange Ewen, *Witchcraft and Demonism: A Concise Account Derived from Sworn Depositions and Confessions Obtained in the Courts of England and Wales* (London: Heath Cranton Limited, 1933).
89 Anon., *A Detection of Damnable Driftes, Practized by Three Witches Arraigned at Chelmisforde in Essex, at the Laste Assises There holden, Whiche Were Executed in April, 1579* (London: Imprinted for Edward White, 1579), im. 6r. The name of Ellen Smith's son is not given.
90 Anon., *A Detection of Damnable Driftes, Practized by Three Witches Arraigned at Chelmisforde in Essex, at the Laste Assises There holden, Whiche Were Executed in April, 1579* (London: Imprinted for Edward White, 1579).
91 Anon., *A Detection of Damnable Driftes, Practized by Three Witches Arraigned at Chelmisforde in Essex, at the Laste Assises There holden, Whiche Were Executed in April, 1579* (London: Imprinted for Edward White, 1579).
92 Anon., *A Detection of Damnable Driftes, Practized by Three Witches Arraigned at Chelmisforde in Essex, at the Laste Assises There holden, Whiche Were Executed in April, 1579* (London: Imprinted for Edward White, 1579), im. 7v.
93 C. L'Estrange Ewen, *Witch Hunting and Witch Trials: The Indictments for Witchcraft from the Records of 1373 Assizes Held for the Home Court AD 1559-1736* (London: Kegan Paul, 1929), p. 137.
94 Anon., *A Detection of Damnable Driftes, Practized by Three Witches Arraigned at Chelmisforde in Essex, at the Laste Assises There Holden, Whiche Were Executed in April*, im. 7v.
95 Anon., *A Detection of Damnable Driftes, Practized by Three Witches Arraigned at Chelmisforde in Essex, at the Laste Assises There Holden, Whiche Were Executed in April*, im. 7v.

96 The other child is Mary Clarke whose case is explored briefly in the conclusion.
97 Raphael Holinshed, 'The Chronicles of England, Scotland and Ireland', 1684 edn., in *The Witchcraft Papers: Contemporary Records of the Witchcraft Hysteria in Essex 1560-1700*, ed. Peter Haining (London: Robert Hale and Company, 1974), p. 44.
98 Raphael Holinshed, 'The Chronicles of England, Scotland and Ireland', 1684 edn., in *The Witchcraft Papers: Contemporary Records of the Witchcraft Hysteria in Essex 1560-1700*, ed. Peter Haining (London: Robert Hale and Company, 1974).
99 Raphael Holinshed, 'The Chronicles of England, Scotland and Ireland', 1684 edn., in *The Witchcraft Papers: Contemporary Records of the Witchcraft Hysteria in Essex 1560-1700*, ed. Peter Haining (London: Robert Hale and Company, 1974).
100 Raphael Holinshed, 'The Chronicles of England, Scotland and Ireland', 1684 edn., in *The Witchcraft Papers: Contemporary Records of the Witchcraft Hysteria in Essex 1560-1700*, ed. Peter Haining (London: Robert Hale and Company, 1974).
101 Raphael Holinshed, 'The Chronicles of England, Scotland and Ireland', 1684 edn., in *The Witchcraft Papers: Contemporary Records of the Witchcraft Hysteria in Essex 1560-1700*, ed. Peter Haining (London: Robert Hale and Company, 1974), p. 85.
102 *Acts of the Privy Council of England, vol. 11, 1578-1580*, ed. John Roche Dasent (London: Her Majesty's Stationery Office, 1896), pp. 370–371.
103 *Acts of the Privy Council of England, vol. 11, 1578-1580*, ed. John Roche Dasent (London: Her Majesty's Stationery Office, 1896), p. 370.
104 *Acts of the Privy Council of England, vol. 11, 1578-1580*, ed. John Roche Dasent (London: Her Majesty's Stationery Office, 1896), pp. 370–371.
105 *Acts of the Privy Council of England, vol. 12, 1580-1581*, ed. John Roche Dasent (London: Her Majesty's Stationery Office, 1896), p. 102.
106 Marion Gibson, *Early Modern Witches: Witchcraft Cases in Contemporary Writing* (London and New York: Routledge, 2000), p. 72.
107 Marion Gibson, *Early Modern Witches: Witchcraft Cases in Contemporary Writing* (London and New York: Routledge, 2000), p. 73.
108 Marion Gibson, *Early Modern Witches: Witchcraft Cases in Contemporary Writing* (London and New York: Routledge, 2000).
109 Marion Gibson, *Early Modern Witches: Witchcraft Cases in Contemporary Writing* (London and New York: Routledge, 2000).
110 Marion Gibson, *The Witches of St Osyth: Persecution, Betrayal and Murder in Elizabethan England* (Cambridge and New York: Cambridge University Press, 2022), p. 278.
111 Jean Bodin, *On the Demon-Mania of Witches*, trans. Randy A. Scott (Toronto: Centre for Reformation and Renaissance Studies, 1995), p. 204.
112 W. W., *A True and Just Recorde of the information, Examination and Confession of All the Witches...* (London: Imprinted by Thomas Dawson, 1582), sig. A3r–A3v.
113 W. W., *A True and Just Recorde of the information, Examination and Confession of All the Witches...* (London: Imprinted by Thomas Dawson, 1582), sig. B6v.
114 W. W., *A True and Just Recorde of the information, Examination and Confession of All the Witches...* (London: Imprinted by Thomas Dawson, 1582).

115 Marion Gibson, *Early Modern Witches: Witchcraft Cases in Contemporary Writing* (London and New York: Routledge, 2000), p. 73.
116 Reginald Scot, *The Discoverie of Witchcraft*, 1691 edn. (London: publisher unknown), pp. 17, 50, 543, 544–545.
117 W. W., *A True and Just Recorde of the information, Examination and Confession of All the Witches...* (London: Imprinted by Thomas Dawson, 1582), sig. A4v.
118 W. W., *A True and Just Recorde of the information, Examination and Confession of All the Witches...* (London: Imprinted by Thomas Dawson, 1582), sig. A6v–A6r. Trening means wooden.
119 W. W., *A True and Just Recorde of the information, Examination and Confession of All the Witches...* (London: Imprinted by Thomas Dawson, 1582), sig. A6r.
120 W. W., *A True and Just Recorde of the information, Examination and Confession of All the Witches...* (London: Imprinted by Thomas Dawson, 1582).
121 W. W., *A True and Just Recorde of the information, Examination and Confession of All the Witches...* (London: Imprinted by Thomas Dawson, 1582), sig. C4v.
122 W. W., *A True and Just Recorde of the information, Examination and Confession of All the Witches...* (London: Imprinted by Thomas Dawson, 1582).
123 W. W., *A True and Just Recorde of the information, Examination and Confession of All the Witches...* (London: Imprinted by Thomas Dawson, 1582), sig. Dr.
124 W. W., *A True and Just Recorde of the information, Examination and Confession of All the Witches...* (London: Imprinted by Thomas Dawson, 1582).
125 W. W., *A True and Just Recorde of the information, Examination and Confession of All the Witches...* (London: Imprinted by Thomas Dawson, 1582), sig. D1v.
126 For a thorough discussion on how family violence occurred in early modern English families see Susan Dwyer Amussen, '"Being stirred to much unquietness": Violence and Domestic Violence in Early Modern England', *Journal of Women's Histry* 6 (No. 2, 1994), pp. 70–89.
127 W. W., *A True and Just Recorde of the information, Examination and Confession of All the Witches...* (London: Imprinted by Thomas Dawson, 1582), sig. D2r.
128 W. W., *A True and Just Recorde of the information, Examination and Confession of All the Witches...* (London: Imprinted by Thomas Dawson, 1582), sig. D2r–D3v.
129 W. W., *A True and Just Recorde of the information, Examination and Confession of All the Witches...* (London: Imprinted by Thomas Dawson, 1582), sig. D2r–D3v.
130 W. W., *A True and Just Recorde of the information, Examination and Confession of All the Witches...* (London: Imprinted by Thomas Dawson, 1582), sig. D3v.
131 W. W., *A True and Just Recorde of the information, Examination and Confession of All the Witches...* (London: Imprinted by Thomas Dawson, 1582).
132 J.S. Cockburn, *Introduction to Calendar of Assize Records. Home Circuit Indictments. Elizabeth I and James I* (London: Her Majesties Stationary Register, 1985), p. 146.
133 W. W., *A True and Just Recorde of the information, Examination and Confession of All the Witches...*, sig. D4r.
134 W. W., *A True and Just Recorde of the information, Examination and Confession of All the Witches...*, sig. D4v.
135 W. W., *A True and Just Recorde of the information, Examination and Confession of All the Witches...*, sig. F4v.

136 W. W., *A True and Just Recorde of the information, Examination and Confession of All the Witches....* Note the term 'avices' is no longer in the Oxford English Dictionary.
137 W. W., *A True and Just Recorde of the information, Examination and Confession of All the Witches...*, sig. F5v the signature reads as G5 here.
138 W. W., *A True and Just Recorde of the information, Examination and Confession of All the Witches....*
139 Barbara Rosen, *Witchcraft in England 1558-1618* (Amherst: University of Massachusetts Press, 1991), p. 182.
140 Marion Gibson, *Early Modern Witches: Witchcraft Cases in Contemporary Writing* (London and New York: Routledge, 2000), p. 129.
141 Anon., *The Apprehension and Confession of Three Notorious Witches Arraigned and by Justice Condemned and Executed in Chelmsford in the County of Essex, the 5th day of July, last past. 1589. With the Manner of Their Devilish Practices and Keeping of Their Spirits Whose Forms Are Herein Truly Proportioned* (London: imprinted for Edward Allde, 1589), sig. A4r
142 Anon., *The Apprehension and Confession of Three Notorious Witches Arraigned and by Justice Condemned and Executed in Chelmsford in the County of Essex, the 5th day of July, last past. 1589. With the Manner of Their Devilish Practices and Keeping of Their Spirits Whose Forms Are Herein Truly Proportioned* (London: imprinted for Edward Allde, 1589).
143 Anon., *The Apprehension and Confession of Three Notorious Witches Arraigned and by Justice Condemned and Executed in Chelmsford in the County of Essex, the 5th day of July, last past. 1589. With the Manner of Their Devilish Practices and Keeping of Their Spirits Whose Forms Are Herein Truly Proportioned* (London: imprinted for Edward Allde, 1589).
144 Anon., *The Apprehension and Confession of Three Notorious Witches Arraigned and by Justice Condemned and Executed in Chelmsford in the County of Essex, the 5th day of July, last past. 1589. With the Manner of Their Devilish Practices and Keeping of Their Spirits Whose Forms Are Herein Truly Proportioned* (London: imprinted for Edward Allde, 1589), sig. A5v
145 Anon., *The Apprehension and Confession of Three Notorious Witches Arraigned and by Justice Condemned and Executed in Chelmsford in the County of Essex, the 5th day of July, last past. 1589. With the Manner of Their Devilish Practices and Keeping of Their Spirits Whose Forms Are Herein Truly Proportioned* (London: imprinted for Edward Allde, 1589).
146 Anon., *The Apprehension and Confession of Three Notorious Witches Arraigned and by Justice Condemned and Executed in Chelmsford in the County of Essex, the 5th day of July, last past. 1589. With the Manner of Their Devilish Practices and Keeping of Their Spirits Whose Forms Are Herein Truly Proportioned* (London: imprinted for Edward Allde, 1589), sig. B3r.
147 C. L'Estrange Ewen, *Witchcraft and Demonism: A Concise Account Derived from Sworn Depositions and Confessions Obtained in the Courts of England and Wales* (London: Heath Cranton Limited, 1933), p. 166.
148 Francis Young, *A History of Anglican Exorcism Deliverance and Demonology in Church Ritual* (New York, Bloomsbury Publishing, 2018), p. iii.

3

1589–1604, THE CHILDREN THAT SHOOK THE ADULT WORLD

Before 1589, witchcraft cases involving children generally only circled amongst local villages that mostly involved peasants or people from the lower-middle social stratum. One of the most significant developments in the role of children in the fifteen-year-period between 1589 and 1604 is the dramatic increase in children's participation in witchcraft cases that concerned the upper-middle estates. As a result of including more influential people and becoming embroiled in bigger, theological debates, these children shaped and influenced not just small, village squabbles but their entire world. The news surrounding these cases spread quicker and wider than ever before. For example, the Throckmorton case (or the Witches of Warboys) became one of the most well-known witchcraft trials in English history. The five bewitched Throckmorton girls added an impressive arsenal of signs, symptoms and behaviours to the role of children in witchcraft trials which was learnt and imitated by other children for decades.

When children became the centre of accusations and debate during the infamous John Darrell Controversy – which centred around the efficacy of exorcism and the threat Puritan exorcists made to the Church of England – those in higher authority realised the potential power children held as mediators of the unseen. For example, the bewitchment stories of Thomas Darling and Mary Glover, while incorporating demonological elements, also seemed divinely inspired, reflecting the religious-political turmoil at the time.[1] Their cases directly influenced the establishment of Canon 74 of the Church of England which forbade exorcisms without a special license from the bishop; the fact that children were essential in effecting ecclesiastical change is a remarkable display of agency and influence, with insight to shape not only ecclesiastical but public opinion in the wake of religious

DOI: 10.4324/9781003685319-4

upheaval. Darrell's condemnation as a fraud, as well as other notable cases of counterfeit demoniacs in this period, such as Anne Gunter, both increased people's interest in demonic possession and bewitchment but also made them more suspicious of it. As a result, the burden of proof for witchcraft trials increased and demoniacs were put under more pressure to justify their fits and appear more credible. The Throckmorton girls showed what could happen when children's agency and power was encouraged and unrestrained. Yet, as a consequence of the Darrell Controversy and fraudulent demoniacs like Gunter, adults more frequently questioned the credibility of children and their involvement remained tenuous. To best understand how this development occurred, it is necessary to undertake an in-depth examination of one of the most influential witchcraft trials in English history, the so-called story of the Witches of Warboys.

'Oh that I had her!': The Throckmorton Children or the Case of the Witches of Warboys

The 1589 Witches of Warboys trial has become a *cause célebrè* not just amongst English witch-hunting narratives but amongst early modern European witch-hunting as a whole. Unlike the cases in the preceding chapters, which nearly all involved illegitimate children and poor families, the accusing family in this instance was neither poor nor were the children illegitimate. The Throckmortons were relatively affluent and had close ties to prominent families like the Cromwells and the Pickerings who also feature in this case. In fact, it could be argued that part of the reason why the Witches of Warboys trial is so infamous is it is the first case where the accusing family was of the upper-middle estate, meaning the children might have been considered slightly more important than the poor, illegitimate children who came before them. As such, the Witches of Warboys case had a deep and lasting impression on the witchcraft trials that followed. It may have also created an impetus to the passing of the 1604 Witchcraft Act due to the involvement of Henry and Oliver Pickering who were part of the political elites that made laws.[2] The Witches of Warboys case was so influential; the agency and authority exerted by children in the years previously were pushed to new extremes and new precedents were set. In the decades following the trial, the Warboys case frequently arose as a reference point of inspiration for children who wished to imitate the Throckmorton girls; their influence can even be seen in the chaotic Salem trials of 1692. The ways in which the Throckmorton girls brought the actions and influence of children in the lower classes to the gentry, successfully using it in their witchcraft accusations, are a remarkable display of control that ended in the total eradication of the entire Samuels family. By showing their supernatural insight to the higher social estates, the Throckmorton children were able to create much larger ripples in a society where the wealthy and well-connected had the means to make the biggest waves.

The details of the Warboys case are taken from the lengthy and anonymously written pamphlet titled, *The Most Strange and Admirable Discoverie of the Three Witches of Warboys*, which seemed to be hastily printed after the conclusion of the proceedings in early 1593.[3] The body of the text itself appears to give clues as to the authorship of the work; it seems that Robert Throckmorton, the father of the afflicted children, contributed to, edited and published the pamphlet with the help of the copious notes that were kept of the children's behaviour during their three-and-a-half-year bewitchment. There is also evidence within the pamphlet of authorial contributions by Gilbert and Henry Pickering – the former of which took care of Elizabeth Throckmorton for a period of time – as well as the Throckmortons' physician Dr Dorrington and the presiding judge, Edward Fenner.[4] The urgency of publishing the pamphlet indicated that it was intended to be seen as a full explanation and validation of the trial against the Samuels family by the Throckmortons: that the children really were bewitched by them and that the Samuels were responsible for the death of Lady Cromwell. Hence, the Throckmortons were justified in using the full force of the law against the family that, in their eyes, tormented their children for over three years. However, though the text attempted to present the Samuels family as victimisers, we can only read them as victims.[5] The fact that they were the direct victims of the *children's* malice is obvious and makes it terrifyingly apparent to those involved in this trial what children were capable of.

The Witches of Warboys case focussed on the five daughters of the Throckmorton family, located in Warboys, Huntingdonshire. The affliction began with Jane, described as being ten or eleven but it soon spread to her other sisters: Joan around fifteen, Elizabeth, thirteen, Mary, twelve, and Grace, nine. The youngest child, Robert, around six, showed no symptoms and is briefly mentioned only once in the pamphlet. Seven other maidservants in the household also became bewitched but are similarly barely mentioned in the pamphlet. This is significant and possibly reflected the author's belief that the children were considered more important than the servants. Hence, any other strange behaviour in the household that was not from the children was thought not worth mentioning. Barbara Rosen postulated that the omission of the maidservants from the pamphlet is made further interesting by the fact that she believes the servants possibly provided the children with most of their 'supernatural' information.[6] Clearly not all of the information came from the servants, as Alice Samuels' denunciation as a witch came first from the children, demonstrating that many of the cues came from the Throckmorton children themselves.

The account of the Witches of Warboys began around 10 November 1589 when Jane Throckmorton 'fell unto a strange kind of sickness and distemperance of body'.[7] Although it seemed as if Jane displayed the classic symptoms of bewitchment, these were not the first suggestions made by the Throckmorton family who assumed Jane was physically unwell. For example, the account stated that Jane's belly would 'begin to swell and heave up…so as none was able to bend her or keep her down' combined with her shaking all over she was thought to be as if '[she] had been infected with the running palsy'.[8] However, Jane soon articulated to the adults around her that it was not a physical illness that was the origin of her sickness but a supernatural disturbance. Not only that, but Jane knew who was responsible for her bewitchment and was not afraid to call this to the attention of those around her, setting in motion the eventual demise of the Samuels family.

Jane suffered with this affliction for two or three days when Alice Samuels, a neighbour of the Throckmortons, came to visit Jane who was sitting near the fireplace with her mother and grandmother. When Jane saw Mother Samuels come into the room, her fits grew worse and she exclaimed:

> Grandmother, look where the old witch sitteth (pointing to Mother Samuels) did you ever see (said the child) one more like a witch than she is? Take off her black thrummed cap, for I cannot abide to look on her.[9]

The directness in which the ten/eleven-year-old Jane spoke to her elders was a remarkable display of boldness. By accusing Alice Samuels as a witch to her face, simply by looking at her, Jane attempted to change the narrative of her illness, not as one of physical sickness but something with malevolent origins. What is more important is that the accusation was not immediately supported or accepted by the adults around Jane, which likely meant that accusing Alice Samuels as a witch – for whatever reason – came from no one else but Jane herself. In fact, after the outburst from Jane against Alice, Jane's mother quickly became 'very angry with her child and rebuked her for saying so…thinking that it might proceed of some lightness in the child's brain… .'[10] Clearly, Jane's mother did not appreciate the brashness of her daughter and was not willing, at this stage, to accept bewitchment as the cause of her malady.

Jane's condition did not improve, so her parents sent her urine to Cambridge Doctor Barrow who thought she might be 'troubled with worms', which was a common diagnosis for children who were otherwise thought to be demonically possessed.[11] Jane continued to worsen and her parents eventually sent for the doctor three times with no resolution. After the third time the doctor asked, 'whether there was no sorcery or witchcraft suspected in the child, the answer was made, no'.[12] Still unwilling to accept witchcraft as a possibility, the Throckmortons called in a different physician for a second opinion but this doctor's advice was not taken into consideration as he also diagnosed worms which had already been ruled out as a possibility.[13] Finally, Robert Throckmorton decided he would not spend any more money on doctors for he concluded that because 'he had some experience of the malice of some witches', he accepted that there might be some kind of malevolent influence in the child.[14] Jane's ability then, from the outset of her symptoms, to control the narrative, attempting to assert her affliction as bewitchment from Alice Samuels, rather than any physical sickness, is a significant display of autonomy and control from a child whose family were clearly unwilling to initially accept a supernatural diagnosis. However demonically inspired Jane's symptoms might have been in origin, it appeared they were contagious, for it was not long before two more sisters (most likely Mary and Elizabeth) also fell into similar fits and cried out against Alice Samuels as their tormentor.

About a month later, two more sisters (described as being 'two or three years' older than Jane) 'fell into the same like extremities' but this time Alice Samuels did not even have to be present in the room to be denounced as a witch; the girls simply cried out: 'take her away, look where she standeth here before us in a black thrummed cap...It is she, said them, that hath bewitched us and she will kill us if you do not take her away'.[15] This is one of the first mentions of seeing someone's 'spectre' in the history of English witch-hunting, a phenomenon that became a formidable weapon which was used frequently by children after the Warboys trial.[16] Children ran, screamed and acted as if they were being tortured by someone's apparition when the real person may have been standing in the corner of the room in chains. It was certainly a difficult accusation to deny for those who believed in reality of spectral evidence. It also strengthened the position of children as preternatural agents; the spectres were something only they could see as they had the power and control to decide whose spectre appeared when and where, and they decided what it would do and to whom. Particularly when spectral evidence became more important in cases, adults – including the judges – found themselves relying principally on children for their information about who was guilty of doing what, when and where.[17] This became true with the Throckmorton children. However, the motivation for why they denounced Alice Samuels was a question that plagued their parents as the pamphlet makes clear: '...yet devising what cause it should be wrought upon them or their children, they could not imagine; for they were but newly come to the town to inhabit'.[18] The fact that the Throckmorton parents paused to question why Alice Samuels might want to bewitch their children is intriguing. Unfortunately, this moment of critical thinking was not enough to stop the proceedings. The children were bent on bewitchment, and it soon spread to the Throckmorton's eldest daughter, Joan, and the youngest daughter, Grace, who also cried out against Mother Samuels.

The pamphlet stated that because Joan was the eldest and thereby having more 'strength…and striving more with the spirit than the rest' she was more 'grievously tormented'.[19] Whether it was a deliberate decision on Joan's part to struggle more than the rest of her sisters cannot be known but the pamphlet certainly gives the impression that it became some kind of game or competition between the sisters to see who could be the most afflicted. The possible motivation behind this is unknown, but it certainly had an effect on the adults around them who desperately sought to keep the five young girls under control: 'the more they laboured to help them and to keep them down, the more violently they were handled…'.[20] The way in which the girls became senseless in their fits and came out not remembering anything they said or did diffused accountability and minimised any possible repercussions or consequences, like when Jane was reprimand by her mother when she first accused Alice Samuels as a witch. However, the children made sure to let the adults know they still maintained some level of control with their connection to the invisible world. For example, in one of her fits, Joan stated:

> the spirit as it should seem would sound in her ears … that there should be twelve of them which should be bewitched in that house in one sort or other, and named them all unto her, being all women kind, and servants in the house, herself and her sisters being five of the number…[21]

Within a short space of time, all of this came true and twelve girls/women were bewitched just as Joan predicted. This display of clairvoyance from Joan signified to the adults around her that supernatural knowledge belonged to her and her sisters; the maid servants, as discussed earlier, apparently mattered little.

The only mention the maidservants received is that when they fell into their fits, they cried out against Alice Samuels saying, 'take her away Mistress, for God's sake, take her away and burn her, for she will kill us all if you let her alone…'.[22] The mention of burning is curious and either reflects an ignorance of English witchcraft execution procedure or perhaps the maid servants had some Continental knowledge of witchcraft process and thought Alice deserved to be burnt, rather than hanged. Nevertheless, we are told the servants were sent away and from then, most became well and were no longer afflicted.

In early February the following year, Gilbert Pickering, who later became involved in another witchcraft trial in his home county of Northamptonshire, visited the Throckmorton children as he was the children's uncle.[23] About half an hour after Pickering's arrival he found out that some people had gone to convince Mother Samuels to visit the children. Pickering assumed, because they took so long in getting her, they had failed in persuading her. The author of the pamphlet noted this as suspicious given Mother Samuels had formerly stated she would 'venture her life in water up to the chin and lease some part of her best blood to do them any good'.[24] These admissions from Alice Samuels (if she ever made them at all) were references to the swimming test and another folkloric English witchcraft belief which claimed that extracting blood from the accused witch would un-bewitch the afflicted.[25] The mention of swimming witches in the Warboys case might have inspired Pickering to put it into practice in 1612. Nonetheless, the pamphlet makes clear that whatever Alice Samuels had said regarding her willingness to prove her innocence, now, it seemed 'her mind was clean altered'.[26] Her reason being that now more than one child cried out against her 'she feared the common practice of scratching would be used on her'.[27] The purposes of this process were to extract blood for the reasons aforementioned.[28] Pickering assured her that himself and the Throckmorton parents did not 'intend' to use this on her as they had consulted 'good divines of the unlawfulness thereof'.[29] The significance of the fact that scratching Alice Samuels at the behest of the young girls occurred despite this only adds to the influence and power the Throckmorton sisters exhibited in the face of waning parental control.

Pickering eventually convinced Alice Samuels to visit the Throckmorton children. When she entered the house, the reaction was instant:

> the said three children fell down upon the ground strangely tormented so that if they had been let lie still on the ground they would have leaped and sprung like a quick pickerel newly taken out of the water, their bellies heaving up their head and their heels touching the ground as though they had been tumblers; and would have drawn their heads and their heels together backwards, throwing out their arms with great groans most strangely to be heard, to the great grief of the beholders.[30]

Although it cannot be known for certain, it is likely this behaviour was learnt from earlier cases or trials, as they were very similar to the signs and symptoms of Anne Mylner, Agnes Briggs and Rachel Pinder.[31] Coincidence is possible but using a medium – bewitchment and possession – that had specific behaviours required a performance that followed a particular cultural script, one that had already been established by other children years earlier. The Throckmorton children's ability to perform this cultural script in addition to adding new elements to it (while still retaining their credibility throughout) is just one component that makes their case a turning point in the history of the role of children in English witchcraft trials.

After the initial outburst from the children, Jane was taken out of the room where she was put on a bed where Master Whittle 'lying in a manner with his whole body and weight over her...' struggled to hold the nine-year old down.[32] When Pickering entered the room, Jane started screaming: 'Oh that I had her!' and though Pickering knew scratching was 'merely unlawful', he succumbed to the pressure Jane placed on him and fetched Alice Samuels. Though he first tested Jane by placing different hands in front of her to see if she could discern the difference, when he eventually thrust an unwilling Alice Samuels' hand at her: 'the child scratched her with such vehemency that her nails [broke] into spills with the force and earnest desire that she had to revenge'.[33] The violence enacted upon Alice Samuels by the young Jane is challenging to dissect in terms of motivation; even if she did suspect Alice to be a witch, committing such an act against an elder certainly took a degree of audacity most children dared not express. Manipulating the adults to go against the advice they had received from the aforementioned 'good divines' regarding scratching also reflected the level of power Jane wielded in her role as an afflicted person.

Another demonstration of manipulation on the part of the Throckmorton children against the adults around them was their revulsion to prayer. Exhibiting disgust at fundamental Christian rituals was a traditional symptom of possession and bewitchment. In Catholic countries, showing fear or repulsion at sacred objects had a long history in exorcism rites. As Protestantism was a religion of the book, Protestant demoniacs mostly indicated their rejection of religious culture by demonstrating their inability to read the Bible or even listen to it being read.[34] The Throckmorton children were a prominent example of this. After Alice Samuels was forcibly taken to the house and was scratched by Jane, Doctor Dorrington suggested that the company engages in prayer. As soon as Dorrington began to pray, the children became 'wonderfully tormented, as though they should have been torn in pieces'.[35] When Dorrington stopped praying, the children stopped shrieking. When he started to pray again, they too resumed screaming. Using their position as afflicted individuals to remove themselves from having to engage in prayer was a clever way of subverting their expected duties without punishment. In a similar way, Barbara Rosen observes: 'the children's fits seemed to be based on two contradictory desires: the desire to *get* attention and the desire to avoid *paying* attention'.[36] While this was only the first instance of the children being unable to participate in prayer, their outright repulsion of prayer, the Bible or parental edification in general worsened over time. Whether this was because the children were learning how far they could push the boundaries of their rebellious behaviour or there was some real pathological element of trauma is unclear; the answer is likely a complicated mixture of both. It is possible they were using their fits to be able to control and manipulate what they engaged with, when and how. Conversely, it is likely that over the course of their three-and-a-half years of these episodes, the children became convinced of their own bewitchment. Regardless, it is clear that their parents were compelled to devote all their time and effort into caring for their children but frequently found themselves unable to control or discipline the girls who were so often 'deaf' to them.

Not only is it evident that the children manipulated the adults through the revulsion of prayer, but their 'deafness' in their fits and not remembering anything when they came out of them provided an excellent veil in case anyone dare question the validity of their symptoms. For example, when Pickering took Elizabeth back to his home in Titchmarsh Grove, he observed:

> above all things she delighteth in play: she will pick out some one body to play with her at cards, and but one only not hearing, seeing or speaking to any other, but being awake she remember nothing that she heard or spoke, affirming that she was not sick but only slept.[37]

Elizabeth's ability to persuade a household of adults that she played cards asleep as part of Mother Samuels' bewitchment of her surely speaks volumes to her astuteness as a thirteen-year old.

Furthermore, we should not assume that all the adults in this narrative were gullible or vacuous, some might have been, but Elizabeth consistently demonstrated agency and determination in her role as an accuser. At supper, Elizabeth screeched and raged during grace and other prayers, yet those around her persisted in prayer and found that John 1:1 in particular vexed the Devil: 'In the beginning was the Word, and the Word was with God, and the Word was God.'[38] Rather than stop, there was a conviction that it was wrong to do anything that the Devil wanted, leading the parents and friends of the bewitched children not to avoid but persist in actions which brought on the fits. In modern psychology, similar techniques are still used. When treating obsessive fears, patients are sometimes confronted repeatedly with the fear until they crack and become receptive to new suggestions.[39] In the case of the Throckmorton children, this tactic might have either encouraged their fits, convinced them further of the 'reality' of their bewitchment or a combination of both.

It seemed as if not all prayer was repulsive to Elizabeth, as Pickering recorded: 'on the 26th of February she read and sung Psalms, being well all the day until the evening'.[40] Whether this was because singing Psalms was considered more 'fun' than any other type of prayer is unknown, but it is a tantalising insight into the mind of a child and their attitudes towards prayer. The lack of comment on this by any adult watching her is curious, yet it only adds to Elizabeth's credibility as an afflicted person; she was never accused of being a counterfeit. In fact, having fun seemed to be a large part of the bewitchment of the Throckmorton children. While this may seem contradictory to the Devil's plans, in the minds of the Godly parents and friends watching the children be 'merry' and 'full of exceeding laughter' was nothing short of sinful; as the author of the pamphlet makes clear: 'if they had been awake they would have been ashamed thereof'.[41] To our modern minds, it seems as if these children merely wanted to be children, with the freedom to laugh and play cards with those around them as Elizabeth frequently did. However, their opportunities, as children growing up in a religiously strict gentry family, were limited. The repressive nature of these households may have been overstated by the scholarship but there is some truth to it; being bewitched did allow these children to behave like children.[42]

Gilbert Pickering was meticulous in his recording of Elizabeth's time with him which was around seven months from February to August.[43] One perplexing element of Pickering's notes indicated that the 'spirit' inside Elizabeth was thought to be Catholic. Pickering seemed to particularly enjoy testing the spirit and on 11 March he asked it a series of questions: 'love you the word of God? Whereat she was sore troubled and vexed. But love your witchcraft? It seemed content.... but love you Papistry? It was quiet. Love you prayer? It raged. Love your Mass? It was still.'[44] The purpose of this was clearly anti-Catholic propaganda which became another prominent feature amongst some demonically possessed/bewitched children. It also demonstrated that Elizabeth knew how to respond appropriately to the kinds of questions and tests Pickering often put to her, further solidifying her credibility in the eyes of the adults around her. Pickering 'tested' the spirit in Elizabeth by feeding her milk with a quill, bringing her inside and outside, taking her on horseback near her home in Warboys to see if she could discern where she was and checking up on the statements she made about her sisters. Elizabeth's ability to stay one step ahead of those investigating her is a testament to her intuitiveness.[45] As Rosen astutely remarks: 'Elizabeth is always one jump ahead, changing the rules as fast as they discover them.'[46]

Amongst all this, Alice Samuels is not forgotten. Elizabeth complained that Alice Samuels tried to force a mouse down her throat on 31 August. She also claimed that she saw the spectre of Alice Samuels in a white sheet with a black child sitting on her shoulder.[47] Both instances seemed to cause genuine terror to all those involved.[48] While a combination of deliberate fraud and being slowly convinced of the 'reality' of her bewitchment cannot be ruled out as explanations for Elizabeth's actions, it was clear she successfully manipulated and influenced the Pickering household. Finally, Elizabeth was reunited with her sisters at Warboys. About a month afterwards, the situation for the Samuels family worsened with the arrival of Lady Cromwell.[49]

Lady Cromwell came to visit the Throckmorton children after she heard about their fits. The pamphlet stated that she was so moved she could not 'abstain from tears' and demanded that Alice Samuels be sent for.[50] When Alice Samuels arrived at the house the children were worse than ever and Lady Cromwell took Alice aside and they exchanged 'hard speeches'.[51] When Alice Samuels complained that she had never given Master or Mistress Throckmorton any reason to accuse her, Lady Cromwell clarified: 'that neither M. Throckmorton or his wife accused her, but the children themselves in their fits did…'.[52] This demonstrates that even without overt parental support of their witchcraft accusation, the children were still dominating and influencing the adults around them, attempting to bend them to their whim. Overhearing this, Joan claimed there was something that 'squealed very loud in her ears and marvelled that nobody could hear it, wishing the old woman to listen to it'.[53] Joan's challenge to Alice Samuels is important, as it was only the first of many torments the children put to Alice directly, subverting the usual societal order of respecting one's elders.

After Lady Cromwell found that she could get nowhere with Alice Samuels, she took off Alice's kercher and clipped off some of her hair and hair lace, giving them to Mistress Throckmorton to burn. Recognising this as a folkloric method to un-bewitch the afflicted, Mother Samuels uttered these unfortunately phrased words to Lady Cromwell: 'madame why do you use me thus? I never did you any harm *as yet*'.[54] After this altercation, Lady Cromwell had nightmares involving Alice Samuels, fell sick and died a year and a quarter after meeting her. The aforementioned 'as yet' words from Mother Samuels were 'never out of her mind'.[55] Now that Alice Samuels appeared responsible for the death of someone – no less the wife of a knight – the children took this as an opportunity to capitalise on the death of Lady Cromwell, adding it to their repertoire of torments against the Samuels family.

Around Christmas 1591, Henry Pickering and some others confronted Alice Samuels near her house and desired to ask her some questions. The most significant of these concerned what she believed about the children's fits:

> The greatest part of her speech was railing words against Master Throckmorton and his children, saying that he did misuse her in suffering his children so to play the wantons in accusing of her and bringing her name into question; often repeating that the children's fits was nothing but wantonness in them and, if they were her children, she would not suffer them so to escape without punishment one after the other.[56]

It is unsurprising that Alice Samuels thought such sentiments about the children who accused her as a witch but it is interesting that no one else seemed to question the veracity of the children's fits. In fact, after Alice Samuels refused to answer any more questions and returned home, Henry Pickering responded to Alice's statement thus:
…yet there was no way to prevent the judgements of God but by her confession and repentance; which if she did not in time, he hoped one day to see her burned at a stake, and he himself would bring fire and wood, and the children should blow the coals.[57] Again, the mention of burning seems to be raised not because Pickering was ignorant of English procedure, but because he felt it was a more fitting death for Alice Samuels. Meanwhile,

at the Throckmorton house, Joan (who seemed to be having a moment of clairvoyance) recited every word that passed between her uncle and Alice Samuels as it was happening. With relation to her uncle's statement she stiffly declared: 'for I myself, said she, would blow the coals'.[58] Too much should not be made out of Joan's statement but it is important to note that this was the first statement by a child in English witch-hunting that gives any direct indication that they knew explicitly that what they were doing could lead to a death sentence for the accused.

Sometime in 1592, the children became bolder and more frequently accused Alice Samuels to her face claiming: 'they shall not be well ... except [if] they continue in her house, or she be brought to continue with them'.[59] This is a curious statement as later witchcraft trials demonstrated the opposite effect that their bewitchment or possession symptoms did not usually ease until the witch was out of the presence of the afflicted. Yet, for whatever reason, the children demanded that Alice Samuels be near them at all times. This was done probably in an attempt to control her and torment her continuously with basically no discipline or restriction from the other adults involved. Master Throckmorton stalled for weeks 'still thinking that the spirits might lie' and that he would not have to resort to having Mother Samuels live with them or vice versa. However, it seemed his children were more persistent than him and he eventually gave in to their demands.[60] He spoke to Alice Samuels' husband, John Samuels, and offered him ten pounds and the best servant in Huntingdonshire if he allowed his wife to come live with him. Or, if he would not allow his wife to go, whether he would let the children live with him and Master Throckmorton would pay for their 'necessities'.[61] John Samuels simply stated that he would starve the children if they stayed with him. Eventually, it was agreed that Alice Samuels would stay with the Throckmortons. Before she went, it is claimed that John beat Alice Samuels with a cudgel in the presence of Master Throckmorton and others for telling them something she apparently should not have. Mother Samuels was then placed on house arrest in the Throckmorton home by Master Throckmorton despite the assertion that she was treated as a 'welcome guest'.[62] For the next ten days, seeing as the children finally got what they wanted, they had no fits for the first time in years. Whether it was pre-planned or something that simply evolved with her being there, the children further denounced Alice Samuels in almost every way possible, making her claim of innocence increasingly difficult to deny.

While Alice Samuels remained with the children they taunted and mocked her stating,

> Look you here Mother Samuels, do you not see this thing that sits here by us? She would answer no, not she. Why they would say again, I marvelled that you do not see it, look how it leaps, skips and plays up and down....[63]

In this way, the children demonstrated to the adults that Alice Samuels had spectral sight too; she was simply not admitting it. It was a clever way to denounce someone as a witch and an almost impossible accusation to deny. Once the children claimed that Alice Samuels had spectral sight, how could she prove that she did not? The children also imparted their clairvoyance onto Mother Samuels and told her 'twenty times' to her face that she will 'confess this matter' on 6 January; the pamphlet confidently read: 'that whatsoever the spirits foretold, proved most true.'[64] In other words, the children would force a confession out of Mother Samuels, one way or another. The confidence in which the children persisted in their harassment of Alice Samuels is nothing short of remarkable. Their tactics of manipulation and control soon broke Alice and embroiled her husband and their daughter in the denunciations.

It was probably not a coincidence that 6 January – the day the children marked as Alice's confession day – was the Quarter Sessions day at Huntingdon which was presided over by Justices of the Peace.[65] The children wanted Alice Samuels' confession in a courtroom, in the hope that she would finally, after two years, be indicted as a witch. However, the children's efforts to force Alice to confess did not work, as she stated she would not 'confess [to] which she never did know of, nor consented unto'. [66] The children then used a different tactic, stating that: 'they would not wish her to accuse herself for anything… yet they said that they enforced no more upon her than what the spirits…told them'[67]. If Mother Samuels would not take them seriously as children, she had no choice but to face their accusations from the invisible world.

In their fits, the children took turns chastising Mother Samuels on nearly every aspect of her life, so much so, that the pamphlet recorded: 'that if a man had heard it he would not have thought himself better edified at ten sermons'.[68] The children talked about the joys of heaven – which Alice Samuels would lose – and the torments of hell she would endure if she should be found guilty without confessing. The children 'rehearsed likewise unto her naughty manner of living, her usual cursing and banning of all that displeased her, and especially of their parents…her negligent coming to church and slackness in God's service'. Amazingly, Alice Samuels confessed to all these things and stated 'she would now begin to amend'.[69] For the Throckmorton sisters, however, this was not enough. They continued to rebuke her for 'her lewd bringing up of her daughter, in suffering her to be her dame both in controlling of her and beating of her … and she herself had also confessed.'[70] Lastly, to demonstrate their power and control over Alice Samuels, they reminded her of an earlier time when Alice said that their fits were merely due to some 'wantonness' in them. They asked her now whether 'she was still in that same mind or not? She answered no'.[71] Such bold behaviour from children towards adults was highly unlikely to be tolerated in any other sphere except where children were thought to hold certain levels of authority and could persuade adults of afflictions only they could 'prove'. This was a role that clearly the Throckmorton girls masterfully learnt; one which gained them sympathy and cast villainy unto the Samuels family.

Sometime around Christmas 1592, after mounting pressure from the children (which was backed primarily by Master Throckmorton) Alice Samuels confessed. This occurred at the Throckmorton house where Alice was still forcibly confined. Master Throckmorton heard the children calling out once again for Alice to confess, whereupon he reminded her:

> ...you hear what the children say, which is that if you confess this fact, they should be presently well; and they say that you must confess it before it be long and you know that they have not used to tell lies in their fits.[72]

Finally, it seemed as if Alice had had enough for she fell to her knees, and wept: 'I have been the cause of all this trouble to your children...I have forsaken my maker and given my soul to the Devil.'[73] However, a day later, when Alice Samuels returned to her own home, she retracted the confession. When Master Throckmorton went to her house and confronted her about this, their recorded conversation offers an intriguing insight into the motivation behind false confessions. When Alice Samuels was asked by Master Throckmorton why she confessed if it was not true, she answered '...for joy. For joy, said she, smiling to herself ... and why for joy? Because, said she, I did see your children so presently well after your good prayers and mine'.[74] This declaration by Alice Samuels may also reflect her genuine desire to end the torments of the children, whether she believed she was responsible for them or not. It seemed to be a sincere attempt at ending their afflictions, regardless of the effect it would have on her own life. Furthermore, months of house arrest at the Throckmortons, compounded by the incessant harassment from the young girls, no doubt emotionally and mentally affected Alice Samuels; it may be possible that she had simply given in and said anything to end her anguish. This appears to be confirmed not long after when the constables arrested Alice and her daughter Agnes Samuels. Before they were taken away, Alice hastened to confess again to Master Throckmorton stating:

> I would have never denied it but for my husband and my daughter, who said that I was a fool in confessing [and it would] have been better for me to have died in the same estate I was in than to confess myself a witch; for now everybody will call me old witch while I live.[75]

John Samuels, hearing Alice had confessed again, called her a 'foul term' and told her he would have beaten her had people not been standing in his way.[76] Alice's succumbing to her role as a witch only added further strength to the power of the children's tactics. They had successfully turned Alice Samuels into the witch they had made her out to be for almost three years. For Alice's part, her motivation for why she provided a false confession, retracted it, then confessed again is important insight into the motivation and emotions of witches, a detail rarely seen in early modern trials.[77]

The next few pages of the pamphlet cover the confession of Alice Samuels taken on 26–29 December 1592 when she finally provided details about the owning of spirits the children so frequently accused her of.[78] On 9 January, Master Throckmorton went to great lengths to bail the young Agnes Samuels out of prison for the purposes of having her live at his house 'to see if it might please God whether any such evidences of guiltiness would appear against her as had before appeared in the children against her mother.'[79] As with earlier cases, the children proved to be almost indispensable weapons in provoking guilt in the accused; if Agnes would not confess and prison would not render her more likely to admit her guilt, surely the Throckmorton children could manipulate her into confessing as they had successfully done with her mother. When Agnes Samuels first arrived at the house, the children did not have fits for two or three days. However, it was not long before they were 'grievously afflicted' as before.[80] The children accused 'the daughter as...they did the mother' and told those around them that Alice had sent her spirits to Agnes to bewitch them all over again adding 'she will deal worse with them than ever her mother did'.[81] The Throckmorton sisters were nothing short of tenacious in their persecution of the Samuels family and it seemed as if they would not stop until Agnes suffered akin to her mother.

The eldest sister, Joan, was particularly loquacious about the spirits that talked to her, at one point being described as talking 'very familiarly' with them, though she was never accused of being on the 'wrong' side of the invisible world.[82] Joan used her position to rebuke those around her for not being strict enough with Agnes Samuels. After asking where Agnes was, Joan stated: 'that she [Agnes] had too much liberty and that she must be more straightly looked in to'.[83] Joan's reprimand of the adults for not watching Agnes more closely could only be tolerated in an environment where Joan's authority was seen as more influential than the adults who would usually be the ones reprimanding her. Joan exercised her authority over Agnes who at this point was brought into the room where Joan charged her to her face: 'you have spun a fair thread, your devils...will be no longer at your commandment, it will be no better with us, said she, until you and your mother be both hanged'.[84] The confidence with which the Throckmorton girls denounced the Samuels family to their faces is a remarkable display of power but one they were careful to align with their role as accusers. This is shown when almost immediately after she charged Agnes to her face, Joan came out of her fit and claimed she had been asleep and knew nothing of what she had said.[85] Situating herself carefully within her role, Joan could almost do or say anything she pleased without taking responsibility for her actions just in case they did not have a favourable outcome. These competing desires – to want to be seen and heard without wanting accountability of one's actions – is a curious feature of the Throckmorton case but is also a recurring theme in many witchcraft trials that involved children; it was a way to get attention, in whichever way they wanted, without facing the consequences that came with it.

After Agnes had stayed with the Throckmortons for a while, the girls developed a new technique that tested Agnes' guilt, proving to be effective 100% of the time. When the children were in their fits they forced Agnes to say the following words: 'I charge thee thou devil as I love thee and have authority over thee and am a witch and guilty of this matter that thou suffer this child to be well at this present.'[86] Once Agnes spoke these words, the children immediately wiped their eyes and came out of their fit. While the incantation may have not been overly complicated, it was certainly a clever tool of manipulation, one that arose later in the trial as evidence of guilt against the accused Samuels family. Joan, who always added more detail to any discussion about her fits, added the following words to the formula Agnes had to say: 'As I am a witch, and consenting to the death of Lady Cromwell, so I charge thee to depart and to let her come forth of her fit, you should presently be well.'[87] The pamphlet records the 'open' discussions Joan had with the spirits, which included whether Joan should scratch Agnes, foreshadowing her fits she would have on the Assizes day and stating that she should have no more after then. If she did have more fits after the Assize, Joan noted with obvious animosity: 'then woe be to Agnes Samuels, for then…I will make her pay for it.'[88]

On 1 March, Mary Throckmorton, who had not had any fits since January, suddenly fell 'into a marvellous great quaking and trembling'.[89] Mary, now around fourteen, had no trouble announcing her intentions to those around her: 'this is the day wherein I must scratch the young witch. I am heartily glad for it… .'[90] Unlike Joan, who seemed unable to bring herself to scratch Agnes, Mary declared her intent with joy as the terrified Agnes Samuels was brought into the girl's chamber. Upon seeing Agnes, Mary called out to her 'art thou come thou young witch, who hast done all this mischief?' The pamphlet noted that even Agnes stood 'amazed at those words' as she was not used to hearing 'any such hard speeches from the child'.[91] It is worth noting that Mary was not reprimanded for these comments and Agnes persisted in going through with the scratching. No sooner had Agnes come within reaching distance did the child, '[fall] on scratching of her so eagerly and so fiercely as that it was a wonder to all that saw it'.[92] Mary's admonishing of Agnes continued: 'I will scratch you, you young witch, and pay you home for this punishing of me and my sisters!'[93] For her part, Agnes bowed her head and 'cried very pitifully' while Mary (now on her knees) scratched violently at her face. It seemed as if Agnes could not or would not move her head away as Mary furiously scolded her: 'I know you cry, but the spirit told me that I should not hear you because I should not pity you…you cannot get away from me.'[94] The viciousness with which Mary scratched Agnes' face was brutal, as the pamphlet noted that she took skin off to 'the breadth of a shilling'.[95]

This act of uncontrollable cruelty against Agnes Samuels is challenging to understand; perhaps Mary's belief in her own bewitchment really did convince her to enact such violence against Agnes in an attempt to ease her and her sisters' suffering. Whatever the cause, it seems Mary's actions – while it seemed to provoke genuine excitement – also caused her genuine distress. After it was done, Mary claimed that she would not have done it except the spirit in her 'forced me thereunto'.[96] For the rest of the night, Mary refused to believe she had done it; the pamphlet recorded that she was altogether 'ignorant of any such thing', yet when she was shown what she had done to Agnes' face, she '[broke] into tears and was marvellously sorry to see it'.[97] After this, it was noted that Mary had no more fits. However, not wanting to remove herself entirely from her role as an accuser, Mary claimed that it was because the spirit told her she was well because she had scratched Agnes Samuels. Wanting the spirit to come to them and will them to scratch Agnes so they too would have no more fits, her sisters carried on with their persecution of the Samuels family.[98]

Nine days later, on 9 March, Elizabeth and Grace were the next sisters to exhibit rage against Agnes. Agnes was forced to hold both girls in their fits until Elizabeth turned in a 'marvellous anger to her, now I can see the young witch which I could never do before since she came to the house…'.[99] Those with them at supper were stunned at the girl's comments:

> …the company that sat at supper thought there was some extraordinary matter in working that the child should call the young maid witch for it was never heard by anybody that ever she gave either her or her mother any evil word before either in her fit or out of her fit.[100]

The observation by the pamphlet that these admonitions were contrary to the usual nature of the child acts as further validation of their bewitchment; rather than a perception that the child was disobedient or rude like the lewd and uncontrollable daughter they tried to make Agnes Samuels out to be. Within moments of Elizabeth's outburst, she fell to her knees, grabbing one of Agnes' hands and scratched it, which was 'most fiercely to see' saying:

> oh thou young witch … young witch, fie upon thee, fie upon thee, who ever heard of a young witch before and thus she cried with such vehemence of speech and eagerness of scratching as both her breath and strength had failed her.[101]

Like Mary, Elizabeth demonstrated unbridled anger against Agnes which culminated in a vicious scratching incident. However, unlike Mary, this did not 'cure' Elizabeth, though she too seemed to feel genuine remorse for her actions afterwards. Yet, this remorse did not seem to last long. Afterwards, Elizabeth stood up and gave a long speech willing Agnes to confess to her witchcraft and warned her of the torments of hell. Although only a child herself, Elizabeth scolded Agnes, belittling her: 'but thou art a wicked child… thy mother is a witch, thy father is a witch and thou art a witch, but of all the three thou art the worst, thou wicked child, thou art a wicked child…'.[102] The fact that Elizabeth referred to Agnes as a child is interesting as Agnes' age is never mentioned; she is referred to as a 'maid' or 'Nan' but later in the trial it is suggested that she is old enough to plead pregnancy (therefore being old enough to have sexual intercourse) but if she was perceived as a child by those around her, this makes her role as a witch even more significant.

The next few pages of the pamphlet go into detail about Joan and her 'open' discussion with her spirits about whether she will or will not scratch Agnes Samuels. This culminated in both Joan and Elizabeth scratching Agnes, finding it 'marvellously joyful' when the blood came from Agnes' face and hands 'very abundantly'.[103] It is significant to note that Joan and Elizabeth's last scratching of Agnes contained no remorse afterwards, only joy. The last comment to make about the Throckmorton sisters before their final appearance at the Assize pertains to Jane, who started it all three-and-a-half years earlier. The pamphlet noted that Jane, rather than Joan, was the 'most extremely dealt with all' and recorded her frequent attempts at self-harm and suicide.[104] Jane allegedly tried to 'cast herself into the fire and the water and to deprive herself of life by cutting her throat with her own knife'.[105] Significantly, the young Jane only ever made attempts on her life when people were watching her. Nonetheless, having thoughts or attempts at self-harm or suicide (whether genuine or not) is a recurring theme amongst children involved in witchcraft trials. Whether this relates to their emotional/mental well-being or was simply another tactic to gain attention cannot be known for certain, but it does provide more insight into their multifaceted role. Jane was also the last person to scratch Agnes, scratching her with such fierceness and rage 'as if she would have pulled the flesh of her hand from the bones'.[106] Like Elizabeth and Joan, there was no remorse afterwards, only exhaustion from the effort exerted in her act of cruelty against Agnes.

As if Agnes had not suffered enough, she was admonished by Doctor Dorrington:

> saying that God would surely not suffer her to be thus cried out upon by these wicked spirits and afflicted in this sort by these innocent children contrary to their wills if she was not consenting or at the least concealing

> and of some knowledge of these wicked practice which her mother had confessed.[107]

Dorrington's words aptly sum up the impression of the Throckmorton girls and their role throughout the trials: they saw the wicked spirits and charged the Samuels family as guilty; since the children had fully persuaded those around them of their innocence, there was only one answer as to who was responsible for the bewitchment and torment of the girls. The fate of Alice, Agnes and John Samuels seemed inevitable, but the girls continued their fits, eventually manipulating the Samuels family into condemning themselves with terrifying tenacity.

On 4 April, the day of the Assize, Joan was taken to Huntingdon where she fell into fits in front of the judge. The pamphlet claimed that 'five hundred men' came and visited her at various times throughout the day.[108] Joan continued to have fits until Agnes was forced to repeat the aforementioned 'formula' until she had well and truly implicated herself in front of the judges.[109] Through making the Samuels family say the formula, the Throckmorton sisters made the Samuels family act as the witches and the exorcisers; those who had the power to cause harm and those who had the power to command the spirits to depart. In the courtroom, it also resulted in the generation of indictments against all three members of the Samuels family: for bewitching to death Lady Cromwell and for bewitching the five daughters of Master Throckmorton.

On the same day that Joan was being used to convict Agnes Samuels, Jane was being used against John. While Jane stood in court, in a fit unable to speak, John Samuels was brought to the bar but refused to say the 'formula' that would unbewitch Jane whereupon the judge stated: 'if he would not speak the words of the charm, the court would hold him guilty of the crimes whereof he was accused'.[110] That the court was willing to find him guilty whether he said the 'formula' or not is testament to the effectiveness of the bewitchment Jane and her sisters exhibited for three-and-a-half years. The court clearly believed that the Throckmorton sisters were bewitched and that the Samuels family was responsible for it; the fact that they were insistent in getting John Samuels to speak the 'formula' perhaps provided an element of satisfaction both to the girls and to the court. John Samuels, realising his fate was sealed either way, spoke the formula and Jane came out of her fit. Jane successfully made her point and it was her final act of malice against the Samuels family; it did not take the jury long to deliver the verdict of *billa vera* against all of the accused.[111]

The rest of the pamphlet dealt with the passing of the death sentences and the execution of the Samuels family. While these details are important, the Throckmorton children disappear almost entirely from the narrative until, at the end, we are told that they had no more fits after the executions.[112]

The Witches of Warboys trial is an incredible account demonstrating how five young girls from a gentry family used their agency and tactics of manipulation to eradicate an entire family. Of course, they needed to have their parents and the law on their side to ignite judicial proceedings, but the fact that witchcraft was not suspected until the girls persisted with their fits demonstrated the level of influence they exhibited over the adults around them. Indeed, the Throckmorton sisters were able to demonstrate unprecedent levels of authority and got away with not participating in prayer as well as indulging in other rebellious behaviour. Yet, their harassment and torment of Alice and Agnes Samuels would not have been tolerated in any other circumstances other than one where they were given power.

Through using their spectral sight, the Throckmorton girls surpassed their lowly social status as children and became much more influential, having access to information the adults around them were not privy to. Being able to see into the invisible world and divulge the wicked secrets of the Samuels family to the invested adults, the Throckmorton sisters became the linchpin of evidence needed to find the Samuels guilty. This explains why Joan and Jane were taken to the Assize in Huntingdon; the testimony of the adults was not as powerful as the physical writhings of the young girls, who only became aware of their senses after the accused was forced to say the special 'formula'. It should not be forgotten that the 'formula' was apparently devised by the children, a technique that proved effective each time it was used until the end of the Samuels' lives.[113]

In the end, the Throckmorton sisters were successful in their denunciation and eradication of the Samuels family. They triumphed in getting Alice Samuels to confess and were also able to implicate Agnes and John even though they died obstinate in their professions of innocence. Hence, the Warboys case represented a major development in the history of children in English witchcraft trials. Not only did their role evolve substantially by adding new elements and themes, but their case was highly publicised and became incredibly influential. In fact, Sir Henry Cromwell (husband of the deceased Lady Cromwell) as lord of the manor, received the forfeit of goods and chattels of the executed Samuels. He used the money to fund an annual sermon at Huntingdon, to be delivered by a fellow of Queen's College, Cambridge, who was to preach against the wicked sin of witchcraft; this tradition continued until 1812.[114] Although the sermon was eventually used to denounce a belief in witchcraft, for many years the sermon served as an annual reminder, for those in Huntingdon and around, of what detestable sins the Samuels had committed against the Throckmorton girls. The behaviour of the girls – which arguably became the most well-known case of bewitchment since the beginning of England's witchcraft trials – inspired the behaviour of children in later trials for decades.[115] While the Throckmorton children's actions eliminated an entire family, possibly influenced the passing of the 1604 Witchcraft Act as well as initiated an annual sermon, the children involved in the John Darrell Controversy facilitated the establishment of a new Church Canon and assisted in the imprisonment of two Puritan ministers. Using their status as supernatural agents, children exerted their influence like never before, shaking the religious foundations of the adult world.

'A marvellous bug to scare the Devil': The John Darrell Controversy

The tumultuous events surrounding the short-lived career of the so-called Puritan Exorcist, John Darrell has attracted a multitude of opinions from scholars seeking to understand what became known as the 'Darrell Controversy'.[116] Marion Gibson stated that since his trial at the High Commission in 1599, 'Darrell's memory has gathered a thick dusting of abuse for the past four hundred years'.[117] John Darrell was accused of teaching 'four to counterfeit', as well as performing fake exorcisms. The four fraudulent demoniacs were Katherine Wright (1586), Thomas Darling (1596) as well as Mary Cooper and William Sommers (1597). Darrell alongside his Puritan colleague George More were both implicated and stood on the same charges. After months of inquiries and languishing in gaol, both men were eventually found guilty and were defrocked. After the Controversy, both men disappear into relative obscurity. During the events, however, Darrell himself felt wrongly judged and accused, listing some of the epithets he had been labelled: '...a cozener, a juggler, an exorcist, a counterfeit, a devil-flinger, a devil-driver, a seducer [and] a deceiver...'.[118] To his enemies, Darrell was seen as a threat to the unity of the Church of England; at worse, he was seen as an imposter and a liar. At best, Darrell was seen as a fool and was used as comedic inspiration, which can be seen in Shakespeare's *Twelfth Night*, when Malvolio and Feste the clown conduct a mock exorcism.[119] Clearly a stand-in for the disgraced Darrell, Malvolio is described as: 'the devil a puritan that he is ... an affectioned ass, that cons state without book, and utters it by great swaths...'.[120]

The ripples of the Controversy were felt so strongly that King James VI and I, shortly after his coronation in 1603, became aware of the affair, as it would have been his business to know of all pertinent religious and political matters affecting the realm. This is evident in the sarcastic remark King James made in his treatise on the possible virtues of tobacco smoke: 'and if it could by the smoke thereof chase out devils...it would serve for a precious relic both for the superstitious priests and the insolent Puritans, to cast out devils withall'.[121] More recently, historians have described Darrell as 'the singularly unlovable Puritan exorcist', highlighting the contempt he has gained over the centuries.[122] However, some historians have attempted to be more understanding and at times, more sympathetic to Darrell.[123] Current scholarship on the Darrell Controversy has sought to analyse it in terms of the literary, political and theological aspects. Yet, what recent scholars have failed to do in earnest is analyse the role of the children in this saga.[124] Whole monographs have been written about the Darrell Controversy, as there survives approximately ten lengthy primary sources split between the pro-Darrell and pro-Harsnett sides that give various details about this event.[125] This discussion focusses chiefly on elements that surround the agency of the children encapsulated in this drama. Of course, their stories need to be placed in a broader context but exhaustive narratives of their cases – including the back-and-forth slandering that occurred principally between Harsnett and Darrell – are best analysed in other works that have chosen not to focus on the children involved in this drama.

Much has been commented concerning the character of Darrell and the theological significance of his procedures in performing dispossessions of children between 1586 and 1597. However, the influence of the children that spurred the proceedings against Darrell has not been given their due credit.[126] Their involvement in the Darrell Controversy was of course part of a much larger, adult discussion about the efficacy of exorcism and the supremacy of the Church of England. Yet, without their accusations against Darrell, the High Commission inquiry against him might have come to naught. Moreover, their individual accounts of bewitchment, their motivations and agency are often overlooked, as historians have given precedence to this larger theological-political picture. Anna French aptly summarises this sentiment: '...the authority and power Darrell and Harsnett fought for, and the religio-political power their historians have sought to recreate, did not simply or truly belong to the exorcist or bishop: they belonged, most accurately and extraordinarily, to the child'.[127]

'A young damsel': Katherine Wright

Katherine Wright was seventeen-years old when she first began to have fits in Derbyshire, 1586.[128] According to her confession in one of Samuel Harsnett's anti-Darrell tracts, Wright went out one morning to fetch water from a well and upon imagining that she saw a 'child without feet' she grew 'greatly afraid' and began faking her fits.[129] Harsnett explained that Wright suffered from swelling in her body which caused 'some stopping of humours', claiming this was 'not unknown to divers women'.[130] Of course, in John Darrell's account of Wright's possession, he says that her 'supposed feats were either impossibilities...or the effects of an unclean spirit and not counterfeitings'.[131] Darrell then supplied a list of indications, such as supernatural knowledge and strength, demonstrating that Wright did not faking her fits. According to Harsnett's account, which gives the fullest details on Wright's case, Darrell accused a woman called Margaret Roper as the one who bewitched

Wright.[132] He claimed that she had sent her demonic familiar Middlecub into Wright (though he stated that she eventually had nine devils inside her).[133] It is also alleged that Wright scratched Roper, an accusation that Darrell denied, pleading ignorance, as he was not in the room at the time.[134]

Harsnett's account outlined Wright's confession where she allegedly confessed to being a counterfeit and detailed all of Darrell's misdealings with her. One of the more serious accusations being that he, a young man at the time, had 'lay on Katherine Wright's belly' during one of her fits.[135] The strong insinuation being that this was a sexual act and therefore immoral. Men laying on top of younger girls in the middle of their fits arose in the case of Anne Mylner and the Throckmortons, yet, it is only in the Darrell Controversy where Harsnett raises it as a moral dilemma; this was clearly a tool to tarnish the reputation of a man they were so keenly trying to discredit. In this, children, again, act as the most valuable weapon. Darrell initially stated that he was merely trying to hold Wright down but then tried to protect himself further by stating that 'he lay not upon her belly but on her side'.[136] Hence, Wright's agency and voice within the Controversy is utterly distorted by the two men in this drama. In Harsnett's account, she is a confessing counterfeit, willingly denouncing and detailing all that Darrell had done to her to prove the case against him. In Darrell's account, Wright 'sorrowfully confessed her perjury and was most miserable ... through trouble in mind because of the same'.[137] Darrell further claimed that Wright only confessed because Harsnett threatened 'to burn her feet' if she did not confess to counterfeiting.[138] It is often challenging to find the voice of the child in the back-and-forth slandering pamphlet writings that proliferated between the Darrell and Harsnett parties, yet, there is evidence that reveals more about these children and their role in the witchcraft drama than might appear at first blush.

One of the most important elements of Wright's case is her revelation of motivation for why she began to have fits. This admission comes from her confession in Harsnett's account, which, of course, was an attempt to show Darrell and all of the children he dealt with as frauds. However, not even Darrell himself denied the claim Wright made. Wright stated that her step-father, John Mekin, beat and abused her regularly. It is unclear whether she or Harsnett believed that this, 'want of sleep' caused her 'to be idle-headed' but the abuse clearly affected her mental and physical well-being.[139] Nevertheless, Wright found that when she began having fits, Mekin now 'made much of her', so she continued in performing the fits until she was thirty-years old.[140]

In two of his pamphlets, Darrell did not deny that Mekin abused his step-daughter but stated that this did not mean Wright counterfeited her fits. His argument revolved around the fact that faking fits for thirteen years, in the 'prime of her [life]...depriving herself of many if not all the comforts of this life [such as] marriage...' did not seem worth it considering she did not, 'reap profit by her counterfeiting…'.[141] Darrell summarised his argument by affirming that he no doubt believed Mekin beat Wright, however: 'who of understanding will believe either him [Harsnett] or her seeing there were more easy and honest ways to have avoided the "hard usage of her father in law" then this of [pretending] to be possessed with the devil?…'.[142] Clearly, the truth and hence the power, of this situation rested with Wright who found more affection from Mekin once she started having fits. The idea that children simulated fits in order to evoke empathetic responses from those around them is not a new idea but Wright's admission of it further strengthens the complexities of their role. Exhibiting symptoms of demonic possession or bewitchment were used to garner kindness from adults around them; it was a coping mechanism using a language that adults understood, believed and clearly, as Mekin did, empathised with. Although Darrell allegedly dispossessed her twice, Wright became repossessed a third time and the sources stated that she remained so.[143]

While it may seem that Wright had very little agency in this affair – especially if Darrell's accusations of threats of torture are to be believed – in fact, her ability to use bewitchment as a way to cease the violence she suffered at the hands of her step-father was a sophisticated way of coping with abuse. Furthermore, whether she was coerced or not does not change the reality that Harsnett clearly relied on her testimony to proceed with the case against Darrell. While Harsnett did not believe she had dealt with spirits, he believed that her role allowed her to discern that Darrell had not dispossessed her and therefore had not glimpsed the invisible world either.

After the mostly unsuccessful dispossession of Katherine Wright, it was another ten years before Darrell attempted another dispossession, this time, on a thirteen-year-old boy called Thomas Darling. Darrell's unsuccessful career as an exorcist was thwarted by the Anglican authorities who had the resources and the means to supress his endeavours. However, the children Darrell dealt with continued to act and inspire demonic possession and bewitchment cases despite outright hostility; their connection to the supernatural surpassed attempts by Anglican authorities to gatekeep dispossession. Therefore, the keys of the invisible world surreptitiously remained in the hands of children. This is clearly displayed in the case of one of Darrell's star pupils, Thomas Darling.

The 'Boy of Burton': Thomas Darling

The story of the bewitchment-cum-possession of Thomas Darling has become one of the most well-known accounts in the early modern English context.[144] Brendan Walsh, an expert on this case, stated that every notable source surrounding the Darrell Controversy addressed the dispossession of Darling in some capacity.[145] This is likely due to the extensive detail and insight it gives into the lore on spirits, witchcraft, demonic possession as well as divine possession. Yet, most modern historiography on Darling usually discusses him strictly with reference to the Darrell Controversy and gives little credence to the agency he displayed in the fits he performed.

Darling demonstrated an impressive level of religious knowledge which was doubtlessly fuelled by the Puritanism he grew up around. His Puritan background was also reflected in his aspirations to be a preacher when he grew up. The fact that he was allegedly tortured, beaten and starved into accusing Darrell, only to retract his confession and stand by his belief that he was in fact possessed, further demonstrates Darling's struggle to control his own narrative, a powerful thing to fight for at thirteen-years old. After his entanglement in the Controversy, Darling's religious allegiance and sense of justice clearly did not waiver, because, in 1602, a nineteen-year-old Thomas Darling was publicly whipped and had his ears cut off for committing libel against the Vice Chancellor of Oxford on account of his apparently ungodly conduct.[146] However, the focus of this discussion surrounds the 1597 incident.

The saga began on 27 February 1597 when Robert Toone, Darling's uncle, took the young boy out to hunt hare in the woods outside Burton-upon-Trent, Staffordshire.[147] At one point, Darling became separated from his uncle and came across a woman whom he later described as the stereotypical caricature of a witch: 'I met a little old woman; she had a grey gown with a black fringe about the cape. A broad thrummed hat and three warts on her face.'[148] The reference to the thrummed hat is notable as it parallels the first thing Jane Throckmorton mentioned about Alice Samuels when she first accused her of being a witch. Historians know that Darling read the Witches of Warboys account and thinking that a broad thrummed cap was a notable part of the first accusation against Alice Samuels, perhaps Darling mentioned it in his account to make his story more believable.[149] Upon walking past the old woman, Darling passed wind, which the woman took offence at, cursing him: 'gyp with a mischief and fart with a bell, I will go to heaven and thou shalt go to hell'.[150] Darling then recognised her as Alice Gooderidge, the daughter of Elizabeth Wright who had a reputation as a cunning woman.[151] Immediately after this interaction, Darling came home and felt 'very sick, vomiting and casting up what he had eaten at dinner'.[152] The most curious thing, however, is that Darling did not mention his meeting with Alice Gooderidge in the woods for another week, despite the deterioration of his physical health. One would think that the incident Darling described – the imagery of Gooderidge and her highly specific rhyming curse – would have been the first thing he mentioned when he came home feeling unwell, thinking himself a victim of her witchcraft. Clearly then, Darling and his family did not initially suspect bewitchment as the cause of his misfortunes and a doctor was sent for. The doctor analysed Darling's urine and postulated that he may be infected with worms but was otherwise unable to come up with a diagnosis, though he doubted the boy was bewitched.[153] The accusation against Gooderidge was therefore relayed with retrospection after other options were postulated for the cause of Darling's illness.

Before Darling admitted to his meeting with Gooderidge, his fits seemed to be a unique mixture of both demonic and divine possessions. It is almost as if Darling himself did not know how he wanted to interpret or perform his supernatural malady. Hence, it was not until he heard his aunt and Jesse Bee (a family friend and likely the author of the relevant pamphlet) discussing whether Darling was bewitched did Darling relay the story about Gooderidge, presumably to give his bewitchment story some traction.[154] As Darling's story progressed, it became evident that Darling never seemed to make up his mind on whether he was bewitched or divinely possessed. Perhaps Darling decided that while he was bewitched, his aspiration to be a preacher made him want to appear like Job – who he referenced frequently in his torments – so Darling's fits were not so much like those of the Throckmorton girls (rebellious and rude) but a spiritual battle between good and evil erupting inside him, fighting for his soul, truly, an agent of the invisible world.[155]

Before Darling's relaying of meeting Gooderidge in the woods, both divine and demonic possession elements were described by Darling: in his fits pointed and said: 'look where green angels stand in the window' and not long after he would complain that a green cat troubled him.[156] Darling's discursive sophistication to understand, manage – or perhaps more accurately manipulate – these two spiritual phenomena at age thirteen is impressive and adds further complexities to the role of children in witchcraft trials. Using the blurred lines of bewitchment and demonic possession as a battleground for the child's soul became a powerful display of religious expression. Divine prophecy cases involving children did occur in England, notably that of William Withers in 1580 and Sarah White in 1647.[157] But Darling's unique blend of divine and demonic possession – which also involved accusations of witchcraft – created a new and complex element to children's role in witchcraft trials. Not only did Darling discern bad spirits and name witches, he also purported himself to be a mouthpiece of God.

In the week before Alice Gooderidge was accused by Darling, the pamphlet stated that Darling spent the time between his fits exuding 'the fruits of his education which was religious and godly.'[158] Darling seemed to take 'great pleasure' in conferring with other 'good Christians' especially about his readiness to die and meet Christ: 'he extended thus far that, if God had been pleased, he might have lived to be a preacher…'.[159] Unlike the Throckmorton girls, who could not stand to have the Bible read to them in their fits, Darling asked his friends to read scripture to him even though it tormented him; these all ended in vomiting, whereby Darling praised the Lord, perhaps as a way of cleansing his soul.[160] It was during these moments that Bee and Darling's aunt discussed whether the boy was bewitched and

Darling, possibly seizing the opportunity, relayed the story of Gooderidge, who was then sent for. When Gooderidge entered the room, Darling fell into 'a marvellous sore fit' and those around the boy asked him whether he should scratch her 'which he did upon the face and the back of the hands so that the blood came out apace'.[161] Rather than being afraid, Gooderidge stroked the back of her hands upon the boy saying 'take blood enough child God help thee', to which Darling rebuked her stating 'pray for thyself, thy prayer can do me no good'.[162] Darling's narrative now seemed to follow the pattern of typical witchcraft accusations and since the Throckmorton case, scratching appeared much more frequently in trials as a folkloric way to cure the bewitched. Darling, however, continued to discuss the spiritual battle that apparently raged within him.

After the scratching incident and more inquiries against Gooderidge, Darling conversed with Satan and outlined his temptations:

> does thou say thou art my god, and that I am thy son? Avoid Satan, there is no God save the Lord of hosts ... and would thou have me worship a molten calf? I will worship nothing but the Lord God and him only will I serve ... wilt thou give me three towns if I will worship thee? Avoid Satan, it is written, I shall worship the Lord God only. And does thou say that if I will not worship thee, thou wilt torment me three times more, if thou torment me three hundred times, yet thou [cannot] touch my soul.[163]

This display of godly knowledge – likely inspired by the temptation of Jesus in Matthew: 4 – from the young Darling touched those around him as the bystanders were 'moved ... to commiseration and pity for the child so distressed estate'.[164] Consequently, the pressure against Gooderidge and Elizabeth Wright mounted and both women were searched for witches' marks, whereby there were found suspicious 'teats' and 'warts' on both women.[165] Darling's loud battles with Satan, rather than attacking the witches directly like the Throckmorton girls, added a new and indirect way of mounting pressure and guilt onto the accused, one that played on the religious turmoil at the time. On more than one occasion, Bee turned to Darling and asked if he wanted to 'provoke him [Satan] to battle?' whereupon Darling always answered 'yes, very willingly'.[166] Interpreting Darling's afflictions as a battleground of good and evil, whereupon Darling eventually triumphed, helped demonstrate that his religious affiliation – which was undeniably Puritan – was the strongest faith, able to defeat the Devil in the fight over the boy's soul.[167] Darling's complex addition to the role of children in witch-hunting was hence inextricably caught up in the religio-political agenda at the time, but he clearly had his own individual motivations for performing his bewitchment-cum-possession. His aspirations to be a preacher very likely motivated his desire to want to be seen as the site for such a holy battle; winning the spiritual war was an internal and external battle, one that thirteen-year-old Darling wanted to be a part of and actively involved himself in.

Darrell finally entered the story by arriving at the household on 26 May and assured everyone that Darling was indeed 'possessed by an unclean spirit'.[168] Curiously, Darrell provided everyone with directions on how to prepare for the dispossession of Darling but did not stay for it, noting that he did not need the 'vainglory'.[169] Significantly, Darrell stated that he did not see his presence necessary 'by reasons of the child's strong faith'.[170] Hence, in a unique turn of events, Darling took the lead in his own dispossession. He named the devils inside him and charged them to depart while also asking God to forgive Gooderidge for bewitching him.[171] Darling even took to exhorting the adults in the room, requesting that one 'man of bad life' who had entered the parlour be removed, which the company around him did.[172] The capacity with which Darling controlled himself during this performance, as well as the adults in the room, is an incredible display of authority. Then, like the demonic possession cases in the Bible: 'A voice was heard to say "my son arise up and walk, the evil spirit is gone from thee, arise and walk"' and Darling walked with no difficulty and fell flat upon the ground 'giving God thanks for his wonderful deliverance and that in such excellent manner as was to be admired in a child.'[173]

The pamphlet noted that Darling became briefly repossessed (which was common in demonic possession cases) before finally dispossessing himself again whereupon, 'he and all the company joining with him humbled themselves before the Lord God'.[174] The pamphlet quickly concluded that Alice Gooderidge died in prison: 'had she lived, she should have been executed'. This last note is unlikely as under Elizabeth I's Witchcraft Act, Gooderidge likely would have been placed in prison for a year and then in the pillory as she was a first offender.[175] Admonitions such as these remind the historian to interrogate claims made by sources.

Thomas Darling's story is often overshadowed by his involvement in the Darrell Controversy. Recent historiography has not paid enough attention to the level of influence Darling enacted in entwining his own religious aspirations with existing features of demonic possession and bewitchment. In this way, Darling created a new and complex role, fashioning himself truly to be an agent of the invisible world in discoursing with Satan, angels and effectively single-handedly imprisoning Alice Gooderidge. Of course, Darling's personal motivations and aspirations are intricately tied to the religio-political debates at the time, especially surrounding Puritanism and non-conformism – which was essentially the focus of the Darrell Controversy – but this does not remove his personal agency. In fact, the significance of Darling's actions proved long-lasting and far-reaching, for Mary Glover used similar tactics in her bewitchment case years later in 1602 as another poignant demonstration of faith-based tribulations. Furthermore, Richard Bancroft and Samuel Harsnett, the same men who spearheaded the attack against Darrell, also involved themselves in Glover's case in another attempt to thwart Puritan hegemony.[176] Far from being seen and not heard, children became the centre of highly charged religious and political debates.

'I will tell you it is not natural': Mary Glover

Mary Glover's case survives in three sources, the most in-depth of which is Stephen Bradwell's *Mary Glover's Late Woeful Case*... .[177] Bradwell's source dealt mainly with the bewitchment aspect of Mary's case, whereas John Swan's pamphlet explored Glover's dispossession after Elizabeth Jackson's imprisonment as the alleged witch. Glover is described as a fourteen-year-old girl who, on 30 April 1602, ran into 'old chairwoman' Elizabeth Jackson while on an errand.[178] Jackson found reason to quarrel with Glover and rebuked her for allegedly making fun of her daughter's clothes: '...it had been better that you had never meddled with my daughter's apparel... my daughter shall have clothes when thou art dead and rotten'.[179] Glover went home where one of the servants of her household noted that Glover's 'countenance and colour' were 'much altered'.[180] A few days later, while Glover was at her father's shop eating posset, Jackson came in again, wishing to speak with Glover's mother. When she was told she was not in, 'the old woman, having fiercely beheld her [Glover] snappishly replied that she must speak with her [and] departed'.[181] Suddenly, Glover's throat became 'locked up' that she could not eat one more mouthful.[182] From the outset, it seemed that Glover's afflictions followed one of the typical patterns of a bewitchment case: Elizabeth Jackson cursed her for mocking her daughter's clothes and suddenly Glover suffered physical torments whenever Jackson was near her. While Glover went through extreme trials to 'test' the validity of her fits, she too, like Thomas Darling, fashioned herself to be divinely inspired, as she continued to have fits even after Jackson was imprisoned.

After Glover's fits worsened, Mr Crooke, a recorder of London, sent a warrant out for both Jackson and Glover to appear before him on 18 October. Crooke exhorted Glover 'not to be a false accuser of anybody' and likewise told Jackson to 'acknowledge her fault'.[183] To test the validity of Glover's fits, Crooke chose a woman who looked like Elizabeth Jackson and made them switch most of their clothes whereupon he made Glover walk by her and touch her. When he saw no change in her behaviour he reported, 'I am glad to see this Mary; I hope thou shalt touch her freely many times hereafter and never be afraid.' But as soon as Glover saw Elizabeth Jackson, who was disguised as the other women, 'the maids countenance altered'.[184] The test of distinguishing the witch by her clothes is significant and reoccurred most notably in the Salem witchcraft trials. However, Crooke had only just begun testing Glover. When Glover threw herself on a bed, Mr Crooke got a candle and a needle and after heating the needle up, placed it against Glover's cheek and then near her eye to see if she felt anything and apparently, she did not.[185] Then he lit some rolled up paper on fire and put it into her right hand until the fire was consumed. He did this twice more 'so as her hand ... was effectually burned in several places'.[186] One can only speculate how and why Glover did not feel any pain or sensation during these torturous experiences, for when the experiment was repeated on Jackson, she 'cried upon him [Crooke] not to burn her'.[187] Although Crooke became convinced that Glover did not counterfeit, public opinion towards demoniacs had wavered since the scandalous Darrell Controversy. As a result, Glover was publicly slandered during Jackson's trial. Glover's status as supernatural agent was tested, yet her integrity and determination to demonstrate that she was bewitched is a testament to the agency she so desperately tried to exert in the face of outright hostility.

Glover was brought into Jackson's trial on 1 December 1602 and like the Throckmorton girls, it was thought that her physical fits in the courtroom were the most effective proof to determine Jackson's guilt. Unlike the Throckmorton girls, Glover was called a counterfeit by those on the bench and though the judge Lord Anderson told her to proceed in her evidence, she was continuously interrupted by those around her crying out against her: 'bring the fire, and hot irons for this counterfeit come we will mark her on the cheek for a counterfeit...'.[188] Despite the threats and accusations of counterfeiting, eight out of twelve pieces of evidence used against Jackson focussed solely on Glover's fits and words against her.[189] Even the eminent doctor Edward Jorden, who first coined the term *Passio Hysterica* to try to prove that Glover's fits were natural and not supernatural, could not convince the judge or jury that Glover was not bewitched.[190] The jury returned a guilty verdict and Elizabeth Jackson was sentenced to a year's imprisonment and four rounds in the pillory. Although psychiatric historian Michael MacDonald stated that Jackson was 'quickly released from prison' and 'certainly escaped' punishment, this is not verified by primary source documents.[191]

It seems quite extraordinary then, that despite the hostility Glover faced from the public, as well as a strong attack from Jorden and Bancroft (who actively mobilised Jackson's defence), she was still convincing enough to persuade the judge and jury of her bewitchment. Unlike earlier trials where the burden of proof seemed easier to gain, what Jackson's case had essentially done was make it harder to resolve individual cases decisively in favour of the supernatural. Though Glover's condemnation of Jackson seemed hard won, Glover wanted to further illustrate her role and thus her torments did not end when Jackson's sentence was passed down. Glover, like Darling, was engaged in a much larger religio-political game, and through showing herself to be a vessel of demonic and divine conflict, Glover demonstrated to Bancroft, Jorden and the other sceptics that she was well and truly an agent of the invisible world.

Mary Glover's dispossession began on 14 December where 'ten or twelve ministers' met to undertake prayer and fasting to relieve Glover's torments.[192] Two days later, however, a total of twenty-four people gathered to dispossess Glover. Like Darling, Glover read the Bible and when she struggled 'being pane and wane coloured' she wept and 'prayed to God to be merciful unto her and to help her'.[193] Glover also demonstrated an impressive display of religious knowledge and spoke four separate prayers, the first of which covered three pages of the pamphlet.[194] Glover's control of the room throughout her spiritual torment is also a remarkable display of agency; when it seemed that she was going to stop talking and be interrupted, another person apparently said: 'leave her alone, you shall see she will do it herself, she will produce her own deliverance'.[195] When the moment of deliverance came, Glover uttered the words: 'he is come, he is come ... the comforter is come, O Lord thou hast delivered me'.[196] These words are particularly important as they were thought to be the exact words Mary's grandfather, Robert Glover, spoke when he was burned alive as a martyr in Oxford in 1555.[197] The religious significance of this would not have been lost on those around Glover, nor would it have been lost on those who read the account of Glover's dispossession. Like Darling's dispossession and divinely inspired words, Glover's account was clearly entrenched in the religious and political turmoil at the time, which is further evidenced in the concluding comments of the pamphlet. Swan commented on Samuel Harsnett's 'dangerous points', stating that in his last book 'he broached a concept as if there were no witches at all'.[198] Swan then listed many notable examples of 'the strange works of God' mentioning many infamous cases of bewitchment and possession – all of which involved children – as a way to further validate Glover's case.[199]

Glover's eventual dispossession – though it was clearly used as a political weapon against those who attacked non-conformism – does not discredit the agency she exhibited in an increasingly hostile environment. The Darrell Controversy ignited the public and ecclesiastical interest in demonic possession but his condemnation as a fraud brought demoniacs under increasing suspicion of counterfeiting. Although Glover secured a guilty verdict against Jackson, Anglican heavyweights like Bancroft and Harsnett eventually came out victorious against Puritans and other non-conformists with regard to the efficacy of exorcism, thereby securing the supremacy of the Church of England. This is evidenced by the establishment of Canon 74 which came into effect in 1604. This prohibited all exorcisms – including those that utilised Biblically sanctioned methods of fasting and prayer – without a license from the bishop.[200] While it may seem as though Puritan demoniacs such as Thomas Darling and Mary Glover lost the battle, it did not mean they stopped fighting in the spiritual war; just because the burden of proof in witchcraft cases increased and demoniacs were now more suspected as counterfeits, this did not mean that children stopped actively engaging in witchcraft trials. In fact, in the same year that Canon 74 was established, the bishop of Chester, Richard Vaughan, granted a license authorising certain nominated preachers (all well-known Puritans) to conduct a service of fasting and prayer over an eleven-year-old boy called Thomas Harrison.[201] This is the first license historians know to have passed seal; it further demonstrates that children still had the capacity, agency and influence to act as mediators of the supernatural world in a society that made their admission in witchcraft trials increasingly difficult.[202] To further complicate matters, a high-profile case caught the attention of King James, who personally intervened in a bewitchment case that was brought to one of the highest courts in England.

The intricate details of Anne Gunter's case have been thoroughly explored in sources elsewhere but what is important to note here is how her case added to the growing attitude of scepticism towards child demoniacs. Gunter was about twenty when she started to experience fits in 1604.[203] Gunter's case is significant, since she was examined in the Star Chamber by the King's Privy Councillors on charges of counterfeiting.[204] Gunter threw herself on the mercy of the court and told the Councillors that her father pressured her into acting bewitched. She also admitted to having knowledge of the Throckmorton account from which she learnt how to imitate their fits.[205] The fact that her case, which began as a village squabble between her father and three local women, ended up in Westminster and attracted the attention of the newly crowned King, is an astonishing development in the role of children in witch-hunting. It shows how firmly bewitchment and possession were established in local society but it also showed how credibility and the burden of proof became more difficult to attain.

It is also important to note that one of the last of Darrell's demoniacs, William Sommers, also impacted the integrity of demoniacs in this period.[206] Fraudulent demoniacs such as Gunter and Sommers tested the authenticity and integrity that other demoniacs like Darling and Glover had fought for. These children well and truly brought their role out of the shadows and into the spotlight through their involvement in important ecclesiastical and political matters, which had now caught the attention of the King.

In the short period between 1589 and 1604, the Throckmorton girls almost single-handedly brought about the destruction of the entire Samuels family by introducing torments of bewitchment to the gentry, making it a larger and louder problem than ever before. The Darrell Controversy and cases like Anne Gunter's heightened society's interest in bewitchment and demonic cases, making people more aware of the role children played within witchcraft trials. Children demonstrated that they could be powerful and dangerous forces of social, political and religious change when encouraged by invested adults or left uncontrolled. While the Darrell Controversy centred on the threat of non-conformism to the unity of the Church of England, it also demonstrated that children held more power over matters pertaining to the spiritual world than those in higher authority might have preferred to admit. Thus, the prohibition of exorcism not only sought to weaken the power of zealous Puritan preachers like Darrell but also lessened the power of demoniacs and sought to reign control of the spiritual world back into the Church of England and out of the hands of children.

Though the Church of England seemed to emerge victorious in the exorcism affair, the fact that a license to cast demons out of young Thomas Harrison was granted shows that the validity of child demoniacs did not completely vanish. However, as Anne Gunter's case showed, it was coming increasingly under suspicion. In the next few decades, this evolution culminated in cases whereby some children displayed almost unrestrained power and influence, where other children struggled to secure credibility. As a consequence of the Darrell Controversy and the children who became entrapped in it, children now found their status increasingly harder to justify; some maintained their position with devastating results, while others faced the consequences of being found out as frauds. The lessons learned by these children were swiftly learnt by others in the following decades, though the adults had learnt too.

Notes

1 For a useful discussion about the effects of politics and religion on witchcraft outbreaks see Peter Elmer, *Witchcraft, Witch-Hunting and Politics in Early Modern England* (Oxford: Oxford University Press, 2016).
2 George Lyman Kittredge, *Witchcraft in Old and New England* (New York: Russell & Russell, 1929), p. 305.
3 Anon., *The Most Strange and Admirable Discoverie of Three Witches of Warboys…* (London: printed by the Widow Orwin for Thomas Man and John Winnington, 1593).
4 Philip C. Almond, *Demonic Possession and Exorcism in Early Modern England: Contemporary Texts and Their Cultural Contexts* (Cambridge: Cambridge University Press, 2004), pp. 72–73
5 Philip C. Almond, *Demonic Possession and Exorcism in Early Modern England: Contemporary Texts and Their Cultural Contexts* (Cambridge: Cambridge University Press, 2004), p. 74.
6 Barbara Rosen, *Witchcraft in England 1558-1618* (Amherst: University of Massachusetts Press, 1991), p. 241.
7 Anon., *The Most Strange and Admirable Discoverie of Three Witches of Warboys…* (London: printed by the Widow Orwin for Thomas Man and John Winnington, 1593), sig. A3.
8 Anon., *The Most Strange and Admirable Discoverie of Three Witches of Warboys…* (London: printed by the Widow Orwin for Thomas Man and John Winnington, 1593).

9 Anon., *The Most Strange and Admirable Discoverie of Three Witches of Warboys...* (London: printed by the Widow Orwin for Thomas Man and John Winnington, 1593); Herbert Norris, *Tudor Costume and Fashion* (New York: Dover Publications, 1997), p. 854, stated that these thrummed caps were most commonly worn by English seamen; Cheryl A. Fury, 'The Elizabethan Maritime Community', in *The Social History of English Seamen, 1485-1649*, ed. Cheryl A. Fury (Woodbridge: The Boydell Press, 2012), p. 120, stated that sailors certainly had a reputation of 'binge drinking and free spending' and that even the most illustrious of seamen often lived 'on the edges of the law' and therefore it is possible that Alice's wearing of such a hat was interpreted by the young Jane as a sign of Alice's wantonness, which may have contributed to Jane's conviction she was a witch. The fact that Herbert Norris, *Tudor Costume and Fashion* (New York: Dover Publications, 1997), p. 854, stated that these hats were most commonly blue and brown is further interesting, in that Alice Samuel's hat was black, which Jane may have also associated with malevolence.

10 Anon., *The Most Strange and Admirable Discoverie of Three Witches of Warboys...* (London: printed by the Widow Orwin for Thomas Man and John Winnington, 1593), sig. A3–A3v.

11 Anon., *The Most Strange and Admirable Discoverie of Three Witches of Warboys...* (London: printed by the Widow Orwin for Thomas Man and John Winnington, 1593), sig., A3v; On worms being a common diagnosis in cases of bewitchment and demonic possession see James Sharpe, *Instruments of Darkness: Witchcraft in Early Modern England* (Philadelphia: University of Pennsylvania Press, 1997), p. 197.

12 Anon., *The Most Strange and Admirable Discoverie of Three Witches of Warboys...* (London: printed by the Widow Orwin for Thomas Man and John Winnington, 1593), sig. A3v.

13 Anon., *The Most Strange and Admirable Discoverie of Three Witches of Warboys...* (London: printed by the Widow Orwin for Thomas Man and John Winnington, 1593), sig. A3r.

14 Anon., *The Most Strange and Admirable Discoverie of Three Witches of Warboys...* (London: printed by the Widow Orwin for Thomas Man and John Winnington, 1593).

15 Anon., *The Most Strange and Admirable Discoverie of Three Witches of Warboys...* (London: printed by the Widow Orwin for Thomas Man and John Winnington, 1593).

16 The legal status of spectral evidence was affirmed in 1690 by Michael Dalton in his popular book *The Country Justice*. In it, he stated: 'their apparition to the sick party in his fits is one of the felonies by statute'. Michael Dalton, *The Country Justice: Containing the Practice of the Justices of the Peace out of their Sessions...* (London: printed by William Rawlins and Samuel Roycroft), p. 384. With relation to New England, historian Thomas Hutchinson wrote:

> the court justified themselves from books of law, and the authorities of Keble, Dalton and other lawyers, then of the first character, who lay down rules of conviction as absurd and dangerous, as any which were practised in New England.
>
> (Thomas Hutchinson, *The History of the Province of Massachusetts-Bay* 2nd edn., vol. 2 (Boston: Thomas & John Fleet, 1768), p. 27).

17 The use of spectral evidence came to be a highly important but also contentious topic of debate in English witchcraft trials; it was most famously used – and abused – in the Salem witchcraft trials in 1692 which are discussed in Chapter 6.
18 Anon., *The Most Strange and Admirable Discoverie of Three Witches of Warboys*... (London: printed by the Widow Orwin for Thomas Man and John Winnington, 1593).
19 Anon., *The Most Strange and Admirable Discoverie of Three Witches of Warboys*... (London: printed by the Widow Orwin for Thomas Man and John Winnington, 1593), sig. A4v.
20 Anon., *The Most Strange and Admirable Discoverie of Three Witches of Warboys*... (London: printed by the Widow Orwin for Thomas Man and John Winnington, 1593).
21 Anon., *The Most Strange and Admirable Discoverie of Three Witches of Warboys*... (London: printed by the Widow Orwin for Thomas Man and John Winnington, 1593).
22 Anon., *The Most Strange and Admirable Discoverie of Three Witches of Warboys*... (London: printed by the Widow Orwin for Thomas Man and John Winnington, 1593).
23 Anon., *The Most Strange and Admirable Discoverie of Three Witches of Warboys*... (London: printed by the Widow Orwin for Thomas Man and John Winnington, 1593), sig. B.; For Pickering's involvement in another witchcraft trial in Northamptonshire, see Anon., *The Witches of Northamptonshire*... (London: printed by Thomas Purfoot, 1612); There is another manuscript that adds more information to this pamphlet which can be found at BL, Sloane MS 972, fol. 7. There does not seem to be any evidence suggesting that the executed witch Agnes Brown in this case was the same child Agnes Brown from the 1566 Essex trials though this remains a possibility.
24 Anon., *The Most Strange and Admirable Discoverie of Three Witches of Warboys*... (London: printed by the Widow Orwin for Thomas Man and John Winnington, 1593), sig. B.
25 Again, it is worth noting Gilbert Pickering's involvement in both cases. While James Sharpe claimed that the 1612 Northamptonshire case was the first English witchcraft trial to swim witches, it was actually the Warboys case that first mentioned the practice. James Sharpe, *Instruments of Darkness: Witchcraft in Early Modern England* (Philadelphia: University of Pennsylvania Press, 1997), pp. 99 and 218.
26 Anon., *The Most Strange and Admirable Discoverie of Three Witches of Warboys*... (London: printed by the Widow Orwin for Thomas Man and John Winnington, 1593), sig. B.
27 Anon., *The Most Strange and Admirable Discoverie of Three Witches of Warboys*... (London: printed by the Widow Orwin for Thomas Man and John Winnington, 1593).
28 Scratching the witch has origins in the thirteenth century and persisted until the nineteenth century as a way of relieving the bewitched victim's afflictions. The rationale for this supernatural counter-magic was not articulated and it seemed as if no one knew exactly how it worked. See Orna Alyagon Darr, *Marks of an Absolute Witch: Evidentiary Dilemmas in Early Modern England* (Oxford and New York: Routledge, 2016), p. 173.

29 Anon., *The Most Strange and Admirable Discoverie of Three Witches of Warboys...* (London: printed by the Widow Orwin for Thomas Man and John Winnington, 1593), sig B.
30 Anon., *The Most Strange and Admirable Discoverie of Three Witches of Warboys...* (London: printed by the Widow Orwin for Thomas Man and John Winnington, 1593), sig. B1v.
31 See Chapter 2.
32 Anon., *The Most Strange and Admirable Discoverie of Three Witches of Warboys...* (London: printed by the Widow Orwin for Thomas Man and John Winnington, 1593), sig. B1v–B2r.
33 Anon., *The Most Strange and Admirable Discoverie of Three Witches of Warboys...* (London: printed by the Widow Orwin for Thomas Man and John Winnington, 1593), sig. B2r.
34 Brian P. Levack, *The Devil Within: Possession and Exorcism in the Christian West* (New Haven and London: Yale University Press, 2013), p. 14.
35 Anon., *The Most Strange and Admirable Discoverie of Three Witches of Warboys...* (London: printed by the Widow Orwin for Thomas Man and John Winnington, 1593), sig. B4r.
36 Barbara Rosen, *Witchcraft in England 1558-1618* (Amherst: University of Massachusetts Press, 1991), p. 251. Emphasis in the original.
37 Anon., *The Most Strange and Admirable Discoverie of Three Witches of Warboys...* (London: printed by the Widow Orwin for Thomas Man and John Winnington, 1593), sig. B5v.
38 John 1:1, The Bible, King James Version; D. P. Walker, *Unclean Spirits: Possession and exorcism in France and England in the late sixteenth and early seventeenth centuries* (Philadelphia: University of Pennsylvania Press, 1981), p. 103, stated that becoming tormented at the beginning of the Gospel of John has 'ancient and persistent tradition' in cases of possession but stated that the cause of which remains unknown.
39 Barbara Rosen, *Witchcraft in England 1558-1618* (Amherst: University of Massachusetts Press, 1991), p. 250.
40 Anon., *The Most Strange and Admirable Discoverie of Three Witches of Warboys...* (London: printed by the Widow Orwin for Thomas Man and John Winnington, 1593), sig. B7v.
41 Anon., *The Most Strange and Admirable Discoverie of Three Witches of Warboys...* (London: printed by the Widow Orwin for Thomas Man and John Winnington, 1593), sig. Cr.
42 Keith Thomas, "Children in Early Modern England" in *Children and Their books: A Celebration of the Work of Iona and Peter Opie*, eds., Gillian Avery and Julia Briggs (Oxford: Clarendon Press, 1989), see esp. pp. 46–47, 51–55, and 62–63. The connection between children's witchcraft accusations and children's play is explored in Lyndal Roper, *The Witch in the Western Imagination* (Charlottesville and London: University of Virginia Press, 2012), see esp. pp. 133–134.
43 Pickering noted Elizabeth's fits and other strange behaviour over a substantial number of pages (Anon., *The Most Strange and Admirable Discoverie of Three Witches of Warboys...* (London: printed by the Widow Orwin for Thomas Man and John Winnington, 1593), sig. B4v–D3v).

44 Anon., *The Most Strange and Admirable Discoverie of Three Witches of Warboys...* (London: printed by the Widow Orwin for Thomas Man and John Winnington, 1593), sig. C2r.
45 Anon., *The Most Strange and Admirable Discoverie of Three Witches of Warboys...* (London: printed by the Widow Orwin for Thomas Man and John Winnington, 1593), sig., B4v–D3v.
46 Barbara Rosen, *Witchcraft in England 1558-1618* (Amherst: University of Massachusetts Press, 1991), p. 252.
47 Anon., *The Most Strange and Admirable Discoverie of Three Witches of Warboys...* (London: printed by the Widow Orwin for Thomas Man and John Winnington, 1593), sig. C5r.
48 Anon., *The Most Strange and Admirable Discoverie of Three Witches of Warboys...* (London: printed by the Widow Orwin for Thomas Man and John Winnington, 1593), sig. Cr.
49 Anon., *The Most Strange and Admirable Discoverie of Three Witches of Warboys...* (London: printed by the Widow Orwin for Thomas Man and John Winnington, 1593), sig. D4v.
50 Anon., *The Most Strange and Admirable Discoverie of Three Witches of Warboys...* (London: printed by the Widow Orwin for Thomas Man and John Winnington, 1593).
51 Anon., *The Most Strange and Admirable Discoverie of Three Witches of Warboys...* (London: printed by the Widow Orwin for Thomas Man and John Winnington, 1593), sig. D5r.
52 Anon., *The Most Strange and Admirable Discoverie of Three Witches of Warboys...* (London: printed by the Widow Orwin for Thomas Man and John Winnington, 1593).
53 Anon., *The Most Strange and Admirable Discoverie of Three Witches of Warboys...* (London: printed by the Widow Orwin for Thomas Man and John Winnington, 1593).
54 Anon., *The Most Strange and Admirable Discoverie of Three Witches of Warboys...* (London: printed by the Widow Orwin for Thomas Man and John Winnington, 1593), emphasis added.
55 Anon., *The Most Strange and Admirable Discoverie of Three Witches of Warboys...* (London: printed by the Widow Orwin for Thomas Man and John Winnington, 1593), sig. D6v.
56 Anon., *The Most Strange and Admirable Discoverie of Three Witches of Warboys...* (London: printed by the Widow Orwin for Thomas Man and John Winnington, 1593), sig. Er.
57 Anon., *The Most Strange and Admirable Discoverie of Three Witches of Warboys...* (London: printed by the Widow Orwin for Thomas Man and John Winnington, 1593).
58 Anon., *The Most Strange and Admirable Discoverie of Three Witches of Warboys...* (London: printed by the Widow Orwin for Thomas Man and John Winnington, 1593), sig. E1v.
59 Anon., *The Most Strange and Admirable Discoverie of Three Witches of Warboys...* (London: printed by the Widow Orwin for Thomas Man and John Winnington, 1593), sig. E6v.

60 Anon., *The Most Strange and Admirable Discoverie of Three Witches of Warboys...* (London: printed by the Widow Orwin for Thomas Man and John Winnington, 1593).
61 Anon., *The Most Strange and Admirable Discoverie of Three Witches of Warboys...* (London: printed by the Widow Orwin for Thomas Man and John Winnington, 1593), sig. Fr.
62 Anon., *The Most Strange and Admirable Discoverie of Three Witches of Warboys...* (London: printed by the Widow Orwin for Thomas Man and John Winnington, 1593).
63 Anon., *The Most Strange and Admirable Discoverie of Three Witches of Warboys...* (London: printed by the Widow Orwin for Thomas Man and John Winnington, 1593), sig. F1v.
64 Anon., *The Most Strange and Admirable Discoverie of Three Witches of Warboys...* (London: printed by the Widow Orwin for Thomas Man and John Winnington, 1593), F4v.
65 Anon., *The Most Strange and Admirable Discoverie of Three Witches of Warboys...* (London: printed by the Widow Orwin for Thomas Man and John Winnington, 1593); Barbara Rosen, *Witchcraft in England 1558-1618* (Amherst: University of Massachusetts Press, 1991), p. 268. This is later recorded in the pamphlet as 9 January.
66 Anon., *The Most Strange and Admirable Discoverie of Three Witches of Warboys...* (London: printed by the Widow Orwin for Thomas Man and John Winnington, 1593), sig. F5r.
67 Anon., *The Most Strange and Admirable Discoverie of Three Witches of Warboys...* (London: printed by the Widow Orwin for Thomas Man and John Winnington, 1593).
68 Anon., *The Most Strange and Admirable Discoverie of Three Witches of Warboys...* (London: printed by the Widow Orwin for Thomas Man and John Winnington, 1593).
69 Anon., *The Most Strange and Admirable Discoverie of Three Witches of Warboys...* (London: printed by the Widow Orwin for Thomas Man and John Winnington, 1593).
70 Anon., *The Most Strange and Admirable Discoverie of Three Witches of Warboys...* (London: printed by the Widow Orwin for Thomas Man and John Winnington, 1593).
71 Anon., *The Most Strange and Admirable Discoverie of Three Witches of Warboys...* (London: printed by the Widow Orwin for Thomas Man and John Winnington, 1593).
72 Anon., *The Most Strange and Admirable Discoverie of Three Witches of Warboys...* (London: printed by the Widow Orwin for Thomas Man and John Winnington, 1593), sig. G2v.
73 Anon., *The Most Strange and Admirable Discoverie of Three Witches of Warboys...* (London: printed by the Widow Orwin for Thomas Man and John Winnington, 1593), sig. G3r.
74 Anon., *The Most Strange and Admirable Discoverie of Three Witches of Warboys...* (London: printed by the Widow Orwin for Thomas Man and John Winnington, 1593), sig. G5r.

75 Anon., *The Most Strange and Admirable Discoverie of Three Witches of Warboys...* (London: printed by the Widow Orwin for Thomas Man and John Winnington, 1593), sig. G6v.
76 Anon., *The Most Strange and Admirable Discoverie of Three Witches of Warboys...* (London: printed by the Widow Orwin for Thomas Man and John Winnington, 1593), sig. Hr.
77 For a useful discussion about emotions and early modern English witches see Charlotte-Rose Millar, *Witchcraft, the Devil, and Emotions in Early Modern England* (London and New York: Routledge, 2017).
78 Anon., *The Most Strange and Admirable Discoverie of Three Witches of Warboys...* (London: printed by the Widow Orwin for Thomas Man and John Winnington, 1593), sig. H1v–H2v.
79 Anon., *The Most Strange and Admirable Discoverie of Three Witches of Warboys...* (London: printed by the Widow Orwin for Thomas Man and John Winnington, 1593), sig. H2v.
80 Anon., *The Most Strange and Admirable Discoverie of Three Witches of Warboys...* (London: printed by the Widow Orwin for Thomas Man and John Winnington, 1593), sig. H4v.
81 Anon., *The Most Strange and Admirable Discoverie of Three Witches of Warboys...* (London: printed by the Widow Orwin for Thomas Man and John Winnington, 1593).
82 Anon., *The Most Strange and Admirable Discoverie of Three Witches of Warboys...* (London: printed by the Widow Orwin for Thomas Man and John Winnington, 1593), sig. H5r.
83 Anon., *The Most Strange and Admirable Discoverie of Three Witches of Warboys...* (London: printed by the Widow Orwin for Thomas Man and John Winnington, 1593), sig. H6v
84 Anon., *The Most Strange and Admirable Discoverie of Three Witches of Warboys...* (London: printed by the Widow Orwin for Thomas Man and John Winnington, 1593), sig. Ir.
85 Anon., *The Most Strange and Admirable Discoverie of Three Witches of Warboys...* (London: printed by the Widow Orwin for Thomas Man and John Winnington, 1593).
86 Anon., *The Most Strange and Admirable Discoverie of Three Witches of Warboys...* (London: printed by the Widow Orwin for Thomas Man and John Winnington, 1593), sig. I2r.
87 Anon., *The Most Strange and Admirable Discoverie of Three Witches of Warboys...* (London: printed by the Widow Orwin for Thomas Man and John Winnington, 1593), sig. J6v.
88 Anon., *The Most Strange and Admirable Discoverie of Three Witches of Warboys...* (London: printed by the Widow Orwin for Thomas Man and John Winnington, 1593).
89 Anon., *The Most Strange and Admirable Discoverie of Three Witches of Warboys...* (London: printed by the Widow Orwin for Thomas Man and John Winnington, 1593).
90 Anon., *The Most Strange and Admirable Discoverie of Three Witches of Warboys...* (London: printed by the Widow Orwin for Thomas Man and John Winnington, 1593), sig. K2r.

91 Anon., *The Most Strange and Admirable Discoverie of Three Witches of Warboys...* (London: printed by the Widow Orwin for Thomas Man and John Winnington, 1593).

92 Anon., *The Most Strange and Admirable Discoverie of Three Witches of Warboys...* (London: printed by the Widow Orwin for Thomas Man and John Winnington, 1593).

93 Anon., *The Most Strange and Admirable Discoverie of Three Witches of Warboys...* (London: printed by the Widow Orwin for Thomas Man and John Winnington, 1593).

94 Anon., *The Most Strange and Admirable Discoverie of Three Witches of Warboys...* (London: printed by the Widow Orwin for Thomas Man and John Winnington, 1593), sig. K2v.

95 Anon., *The Most Strange and Admirable Discoverie of Three Witches of Warboys...* (London: printed by the Widow Orwin for Thomas Man and John Winnington, 1593).

96 Anon., *The Most Strange and Admirable Discoverie of Three Witches of Warboys...* (London: printed by the Widow Orwin for Thomas Man and John Winnington, 1593).

97 Anon., *The Most Strange and Admirable Discoverie of Three Witches of Warboys...* (London: printed by the Widow Orwin for Thomas Man and John Winnington, 1593).

98 Anon., *The Most Strange and Admirable Discoverie of Three Witches of Warboys...* (London: printed by the Widow Orwin for Thomas Man and John Winnington, 1593).

99 Anon., *The Most Strange and Admirable Discoverie of Three Witches of Warboys...* (London: printed by the Widow Orwin for Thomas Man and John Winnington, 1593), sig. K5r.

100 Anon., *The Most Strange and Admirable Discoverie of Three Witches of Warboys...* (London: printed by the Widow Orwin for Thomas Man and John Winnington, 1593).

101 Anon., *The Most Strange and Admirable Discoverie of Three Witches of Warboys...* (London: printed by the Widow Orwin for Thomas Man and John Winnington, 1593), sig. K6v.

102 Anon., *The Most Strange and Admirable Discoverie of Three Witches of Warboys...* (London: printed by the Widow Orwin for Thomas Man and John Winnington, 1593), sig. Lr–L1v.

103 Anon., *The Most Strange and Admirable Discoverie of Three Witches of Warboys...* (London: printed by the Widow Orwin for Thomas Man and John Winnington, 1593), sig. M4v–M5r.

104 Anon., *The Most Strange and Admirable Discoverie of Three Witches of Warboys...* (London: printed by the Widow Orwin for Thomas Man and John Winnington, 1593), sig. M6v.

105 Anon., *The Most Strange and Admirable Discoverie of Three Witches of Warboys...* (London: printed by the Widow Orwin for Thomas Man and John Winnington, 1593).

106 Anon., *The Most Strange and Admirable Discoverie of Three Witches of Warboys...* (London: printed by the Widow Orwin for Thomas Man and John Winnington, 1593), sig. N1v.

107 Anon., *The Most Strange and Admirable Discoverie of Three Witches of Warboys...* (London: printed by the Widow Orwin for Thomas Man and John Winnington, 1593), sig. N2r.
108 Anon., *The Most Strange and Admirable Discoverie of Three Witches of Warboys...* (London: printed by the Widow Orwin for Thomas Man and John Winnington, 1593), N3r–N4v.
109 Anon., *The Most Strange and Admirable Discoverie of Three Witches of Warboys...* (London: printed by the Widow Orwin for Thomas Man and John Winnington, 1593), N5r.
110 Anon., *The Most Strange and Admirable Discoverie of Three Witches of Warboys...* (London: printed by the Widow Orwin for Thomas Man and John Winnington, 1593), O1v.
111 Anon., *The Most Strange and Admirable Discoverie of Three Witches of Warboys...* (London: printed by the Widow Orwin for Thomas Man and John Winnington, 1593). Billa vera meaning true bill.
112 Anon., *The Most Strange and Admirable Discoverie of Three Witches of Warboys...* (London: printed by the Widow Orwin for Thomas Man and John Winnington, 1593), sig. O1v–O5r.
113 A similar scenario – where children devised a formula and made adults speak it over them to un-bewitch them – can be seen in the cases of John Smith and Elizabeth Mallory, discussed in Chapter 4.
114 Barbara Rosen, *Witchcraft in England 1558-1618* (Amherst: University of Massachusetts Press, 1991), p. 297.
115 Philip C. Almond, *Demonic Possession and Exorcism in Early Modern England: Contemporary Texts and their Cultural Contexts* (Cambridge: Cambridge University Press, 2004), p. 71.
116 Brian P. Levack, *The Devil Within: Possession and Exorcism in the Christian West* (New Haven and London: Yale University Press, 2013), p. 94.
117 Marion Gibson, *Possession, Puritanism and Print: Darrell, Harsnett, Shakespeare and the Elizabethan Exorcism Controversy* (London and New York: Routledge, 2006), p. 27.
118 John Darrell, *A Detection of that sinnful, shamful, lying and ridiculous discours of Samuel Harshnet...* (London: Imprinted by the English secret press, 1600), sig. Ar.
119 William Shakespeare, *Twelfth Night* (London: Cassell & Company, 1889), act two, scene three, lines 145–152.
120 William Shakespeare, *Twelfth Night* (London: Cassell & Company, 1889), lines. 145–148.
121 King James VI and I, *A Counterblaste to Tobacco* (London: R. Barker, 1604), sig. C3r.
122 Barbara Rosen, *Witchcraft in England 1558-1618* (Amherst: University of Massachusetts Press, 1991), p. 235.
123 See especially D. P. Walker, *Unclean Spirits: Possession and Exorcism in France and England in the Late Sixteenth and Early Seventeenth Centuries* (Philadelphia, University of Pennsylvania Press, 1981), p. 62.
124 See Brendan Walsh, *The English Exorcist: John Darrell and the Shaping of Early Modern English Protestant Demonology* (New York and London: Routledge, 2021); Marion Gibson, *Possession, Puritanism and Print: Darrell, Harsnett,*

Shakespeare and the Elizabethan Exorcism Controversy (London and New York: Routledge, 2006).

125 For a detailed overview of the primary sources attached to the Darrell Controversy see Brendan Walsh, *The English Exorcist: John Darrell and the Shaping of Early Modern English Protestant Demonology* (New York and London: Routledge, 2021), pp. 15–17.

126 Not included in this discussion are the five bewitched children in the Starkie household as they were not invited to give evidence against Darrell and for reasons of scope were considered less influential than the other children in the Darrell Controversy.

127 Anna French, *Children of Wrath: Possession, Prophecy and the Young in Early Modern England* (Oxford and New York: Routledge, 2016), p. 86.

128 Samuel Harsnett, *A Discovery of the Fraudulent Practices of John Darrell...* (London: Imprinted by John Wolfe, 1599), p. 1.

129 Samuel Harsnett, *A Discovery of the Fraudulent Practices of John Darrell...* (London: Imprinted by John Wolfe, 1599), p. 297. The page is incorrectly recorded as 279 in the pamphlet.

130 Samuel Harsnett, *A Discovery of the Fraudulent Practices of John Darrell...* (London: Imprinted by John Wolfe, 1599), p. 298.

131 Anon., *The Triall of Maist. Dorrell, or A collection of defences against allegations not yet suffered to receive convenient answer. Tending to clear him from the imputation of teaching Sommers and others to counterfeit possession of devils. That the mist of pretended counterfeiting being dispelled, the glory of Christ his royal power in casting out devils (at the prayer and fasting of his people) may evidently appear* (Middelburg: Imprinted for R, Schilders, 1599), p. 17.

132 Samuel Harsnett, *A Discovery of the Fraudulent Practices of John Darrell...* (London: Imprinted by John Wolfe, 1599), p. 310. Harsnett does contain what appears to be transcriptions of Darrell's responses to questions he might have been asked at the High Commission Inquiry.

133 Samuel Harsnett, *A Discovery of the Fraudulent Practices of John Darrell...* (London: Imprinted by John Wolfe, 1599).

134 Samuel Harsnett, *A Discovery of the Fraudulent Practices of John Darrell...* (London: Imprinted by John Wolfe, 1599), p. 311.

135 Anon., *The Triall of Maist. Dorrell, or A collection of defences against allegations not yet suffered to receive convenient answer. Tending to clear him from the imputation of teaching Sommers and others to counterfeit possession of devils. That the mist of pretended counterfeiting being dispelled, the glory of Christ his royal power in casting out devils (at the prayer and fasting of his people) may evidently appear* (Middelburg: Imprinted for R, Schilders, 1599), p. 18.

136 Anon., *The Triall of Maist. Dorrell, or A collection of defences against allegations not yet suffered to receive convenient answer. Tending to clear him from the imputation of teaching Sommers and others to counterfeit possession of devils. That the mist of pretended counterfeiting being dispelled, the glory of Christ his royal power in casting out devils (at the prayer and fasting of his people) may evidently appear* (Middelburg: Imprinted for R, Schilders, 1599), p. 20–21.

137 Anon., *The Triall of Maist. Dorrell, or A collection of defences against allegations not yet suffered to receive convenient answer. Tending to clear him from the imputation of teaching Sommers and others to counterfeit possession of devils.*

That the mist of pretended counterfeiting being dispelled, the glory of Christ his royal power in casting out devils (at the prayer and fasting of his people) may evidently appear (Middelburg: Imprinted for R, Schilders, 1599), p. 20.

138 Anon., *The Triall of Maist. Dorrell, or A collection of defences against allegations not yet suffered to receive convenient answer. Tending to clear him from the imputation of teaching Sommers and others to counterfeit possession of devils. That the mist of pretended counterfeiting being dispelled, the glory of Christ his royal power in casting out devils (at the prayer and fasting of his people) may evidently appear* (Middelburg: Imprinted for R, Schilders, 1599), p. 18.

139 Samuel Harsnett, *A Discovery of the Fraudulent Practices of John Darrell...* (London: Imprinted by John Wolfe, 1599), p. 297.

140 Anon., *The Triall of Maist. Dorrell, or A collection of defences against allegations not yet suffered to receive convenient answer. Tending to clear him from the imputation of teaching Sommers and others to counterfeit possession of devils. That the mist of pretended counterfeiting being dispelled, the glory of Christ his royal power in casting out devils (at the prayer and fasting of his people) may evidently appear* (Middelburg: Imprinted for R, Schilders, 1599), p. 18.

141 Anon., *The Triall of Maist. Dorrell, or A collection of defences against allegations not yet suffered to receive convenient answer. Tending to clear him from the imputation of teaching Sommers and others to counterfeit possession of devils. That the mist of pretended counterfeiting being dispelled, the glory of Christ his royal power in casting out devils (at the prayer and fasting of his people) may evidently appear* (Middelburg: Imprinted for R, Schilders, 1599).

142 John Darrell, *A Detection of That Sinnful, Shamful, Lying and Ridiculous Discours of Samuel Harshnet...* (London: Imprinted by the English Secret Press, 1600), p. 186.

143 Anon., *The Triall of Maist. Dorrell, or A collection of defences against allegations not yet suffered to receive convenient answer. Tending to clear him from the imputation of teaching Sommers and others to counterfeit possession of devils. That the mist of pretended counterfeiting being dispelled, the glory of Christ his royal power in casting out devils (at the prayer and fasting of his people) may evidently appear* (Middelburg: Imprinted for R, Schilders, 1599), p. 18.

144 Brendan Walsh, *The English Exorcist: John Darrell and the Shaping of Early Modern English Protestant Demonology* (New York and London: Routledge, 2021), p. 61.

145 Brendan Walsh, *The English Exorcist: John Darrell and the Shaping of Early Modern English Protestant Demonology* (New York and London: Routledge, 2021).

146 John Chamberlain, *Letters Written by John Chamberlain During the Reign of Queen Elizabeth*, ed., Sarah Williams (Westminster: J. B. Nichols and Sons, 1861), p. 179.

147 I. D., *The Most Wonderful and True Storie of a Certaine Witch Named Alse Gooderige...* (London: printed for I.O., 1597), p. 1.

148 I. D., *The Most Wonderful and True Storie of a Certaine Witch Named Alse Gooderige...* (London: printed for I.O., 1597), p. 4.

149 Brendan Walsh, *The English Exorcist: John Darrell and the Shaping of Early Modern English Protestant Demonology* (New York and London: Routledge, 2021), p. 78.

150 I. D., *The Most Wonderful and True Storie of a Certaine Witch Named Alse Gooderige...* (London: printed for I.O., 1597), p. 4
151 I. D., *The Most Wonderful and True Storie of a Certaine Witch Named Alse Gooderige...* (London: printed for I.O., 1597).
152 I. D., *The Most Wonderful and True Storie of a Certaine Witch Named Alse Gooderige...* (London: printed for I.O., 1597), p. 2.
153 I. D., *The Most Wonderful and True Storie of a Certaine Witch Named Alse Gooderige...* (London: printed for I.O., 1597), p. 2
154 I. D., *The Most Wonderful and True Storie of a Certaine Witch Named Alse Gooderige...* (London: printed for I.O., 1597), p. 4.
155 I. D., *The Most Wonderful and True Storie of a Certaine Witch Named Alse Gooderige...* (London: printed for I.O., 1597), p. 1 and pp. 29–30.
156 I. D., *The Most Wonderful and True Storie of a Certaine Witch Named Alse Gooderige...* (London: printed for I.O., 1597), p. 1.
157 See John Philips, *The Wonderfull Worke of God Shewed upon a Chylde whose name is William Withers...* (London: printed by Robert Waldergrave, 1581) and Henry Jessey, *The Exceeding Riches of Grace Advanced by the Spirit of Grace, in an empty nothing creature, viz. Mris. Sarah Wight...* (London: Printed by Matthew Simmons, 1648).
158 I. D., *The Most Wonderful and True Storie of a Certaine Witch Named Alse Gooderige...* (London: printed for I.O., 1597), p. 2.
159 I. D., *The Most Wonderful and True Storie of a Certaine Witch Named Alse Gooderige...* (London: printed for I.O., 1597).
160 I. D., *The Most Wonderful and True Storie of a Certaine Witch Named Alse Gooderige...* (London: printed for I.O., 1597), p. 3.
161 I. D., *The Most Wonderful and True Storie of a Certaine Witch Named Alse Gooderige...* (London: printed for I.O., 1597), p. 5.
162 I. D., *The Most Wonderful and True Storie of a Certaine Witch Named Alse Gooderige...* (London: printed for I.O., 1597), p. 6.
163 I. D., *The Most Wonderful and True Storie of a Certaine Witch Named Alse Gooderige...* (London: printed for I.O., 1597), p. 10.
164 I. D., *The Most Wonderful and True Storie of a Certaine Witch Named Alse Gooderige...* (London: printed for I.O., 1597), p. 12.
165 I. D., *The Most Wonderful and True Storie of a Certaine Witch Named Alse Gooderige...* (London: printed for I.O., 1597), p. 13.
166 I. D., *The Most Wonderful and True Storie of a Certaine Witch Named Alse Gooderige...* (London: printed for I.O., 1597), p. 17 and pp. 18–19.
167 Brian P. Levack, *The Devil Within: Possession and Exorcism in the Christian West* (New Haven and London: Yale University Press, 2013), p. 70.
168 I. D., *The Most Wonderful and True Storie of a Certaine Witch Named Alse Gooderige...* (London: printed for I.O., 1597), p. 33.
169 I. D., *The Most Wonderful and True Storie of a Certaine Witch Named Alse Gooderige...* (London: printed for I.O., 1597).
170 I. D., *The Most Wonderful and True Storie of a Certaine Witch Named Alse Gooderige...* (London: printed for I.O., 1597), p. 34.
171 I. D., *The Most Wonderful and True Storie of a Certaine Witch Named Alse Gooderige...* (London: printed for I.O., 1597), pp. 34–35.

172 I. D., *The Most Wonderful and True Storie of a Certaine Witch Named Alse Gooderige…* (London: printed for I.O., 1597), p. 36.
173 I. D., *The Most Wonderful and True Storie of a Certaine Witch Named Alse Gooderige…* (London: printed for I.O., 1597), p. 38.
174 I. D., *The Most Wonderful and True Storie of a Certaine Witch Named Alse Gooderige…* (London: printed for I.O., 1597), p. 43.
175 This is the 1563: *Act against Conjurations, Enchantments and Witchcrafts*, 5 Eliz. 1. c. 16. In *Witchcraft and the Act of 1604*, John Newton and Jo Bath, eds. (Leiden and Boston: Brill, 2008).
176 James Sharpe, *Witchcraft in Early Modern England* (London: Pearson Education, 2001), p. 29.
177 Stephen Bradwell, *Mary Glovers Late Woeful Case, Together with Her Joyful Deliverance* (London: publisher unknown, 1603) in *Witchcraft and Hysteria in Elizabethan London: Edward Jorden and the Mary Glover Case*, ed. Michael MacDonald (London and New York: Routledge, 1991); Edward Jorden, *A Briefe Discourse of a Disease Called the Suffocation of the Mother* (London: publisher unknown, 1603); John Swan, *A True and Briefe Report of Mary Glovers Vexation, and of Her Deliverance by Fastings and Prayer* (London: publisher unknown, 1603).
178 Stephen Bradwell, *Mary Glovers Late Woeful Case, Together with Her Joyful Deliverance* (London: publisher unknown, 1603), p. 3. A chairwoman or charwoman denotes someone who worked in the domestic sphere, often as a cleaner.
179 Stephen Bradwell, *Mary Glovers Late Woeful Case, Together with Her Joyful Deliverance* (London: publisher unknown, 1603).
180 Stephen Bradwell, *Mary Glovers Late Woeful Case, Together with Her Joyful Deliverance* (London: publisher unknown, 1603).
181 Stephen Bradwell, *Mary Glovers Late Woeful Case, Together with Her Joyful Deliverance* (London: publisher unknown, 1603), pp. 3–4. Posset was a drink made of hot milk curdled with ale, wine or other alcohol, typically flavoured with spices.
182 Stephen Bradwell, *Mary Glovers Late Woeful Case, Together with Her Joyful Deliverance* (London: publisher unknown, 1603), p. 4.
183 Stephen Bradwell, *Mary Glovers Late Woeful Case, Together with Her Joyful Deliverance* (London: publisher unknown, 1603), p. 19.
184 Stephen Bradwell, *Mary Glovers Late Woeful Case, Together with Her Joyful Deliverance* (London: publisher unknown, 1603), pp. 20–21.
185 Stephen Bradwell, *Mary Glovers Late Woeful Case, Together with Her Joyful Deliverance* (London: publisher unknown, 1603), p. 21.
186 Stephen Bradwell, *Mary Glovers Late Woeful Case, Together with Her Joyful Deliverance* (London: publisher unknown, 1603).
187 Stephen Bradwell, *Mary Glovers Late Woeful Case, Together with Her Joyful Deliverance* (London: publisher unknown, 1603).
188 Stephen Bradwell, *Mary Glovers Late Woeful Case, Together with Her Joyful Deliverance* (London: publisher unknown, 1603), p. 23.
189 C. L' Estrange Ewen, *Witchcraft and Demonism: A Concise Account Derived from Sworn Depositions and Confessions Obtained in the Courts of England and Wales* (London: Heath Cranton Limited, 1933), pp. 197–198

190 Stephen Bradwell, *Mary Glovers Late Woeful Case, Together with Her Joyful Deliverance* (London: publisher unknown, 1603), p. 27.
191 C. L' Estrange Ewen, *Witchcraft and Demonism: A Concise Account Derived from Sworn Depositions and Confessions Obtained in the Courts of England and Wales* (London: Heath Cranton Limited, 1933), pp. 196–199
192 John Swan, *A True and Briefe Report of Mary Glovers Vexation, and of Her Deliverance by Fastings and Prayer* (London: publisher unknown, 1603), p. 4.
193 John Swan, *A True and Briefe Report of Mary Glovers Vexation, and of Her Deliverance by Fastings and Prayer* (London: publisher unknown, 1603), p. 13.
194 John Swan, *A True and Briefe Report of Mary Glovers Vexation, and of Her Deliverance by Fastings and Prayer* (London: publisher unknown, 1603), p. 25.
195 John Swan, *A True and Briefe Report of Mary Glovers Vexation, and of Her Deliverance by Fastings and Prayer* (London: publisher unknown, 1603), p. 23.
196 John Swan, *A True and Briefe Report of Mary Glovers Vexation, and of Her Deliverance by Fastings and Prayer* (London: publisher unknown, 1603), p. 47.
197 Anna French, *Children of Wrath: Possession, Prophecy and the Young in Early Modern England* (Oxford and New York: Routledge, 2016), p. 89; See John Foxe, *Acts and Monuments*, 1583 edn., pp. 1526, 1733, 1738 and 2095. See www.dhi.ac.uk/foxe/index.php. Accessed 23 February 2024.
198 John Swan, *A True and Briefe Report of Mary Glovers Vexation, and of Her Deliverance by Fastings and Prayer* (London: publisher unknown, 1603), p. 68.
199 John Swan, *A True and Briefe Report of Mary Glovers Vexation, and of Her Deliverance by Fastings and Prayer* (London: publisher unknown, 1603), p. 70.
200 Anna French, *Children of Wrath: Possession, Prophecy and the Young in Early Modern England* (Oxford and New York: Routledge, 2016), p. 84.
201 See William Hinde, *A Faithful Remonstrance of the Holy Life and Happy Death of John Bruen…* (London: Printed by R.B, 1641), pp. 148–154.
202 Francis Hutchinson, *An Historical Essay Concerning Witchcraft* (London: Printed for R. Knaplock, 1718), p. 210.
203 James Sharpe, *The Bewitching of Anne Gunter: A Horrible and True Story of Deception, Witchcraft, Murder, and the King of England* (New York: Routledge, 2001), p. 5.
204 James Sharpe, *Instruments of Darkness: Witchcraft in Early Modern England* (Philadelphia: University of Pennsylvania Press, 1997), p. 191
205 James Sharpe, *Instruments of Darkness: Witchcraft in Early Modern England* (Philadelphia: University of Pennsylvania Press, 1997), p. 192.
206 There are no fewer than fifteen primary sources that mention William Sommers. For the most detailed account see Anon., *A Brief Narration of the Possession, Dispossession and Repossession of William Sommers…* (Amsterdam: S.N, 1598).

4

1612–1662, THE CHILDREN WHO CALLED THE SHOTS AND THE CHILDREN NO ONE BELIEVED

By the turn of the seventeenth century, children became involved in highly publicised witchcraft trials and fraudulent demoniac cases. These cases were sometimes linked with influential social, political and religious matters that affected not just village-level squabbles but English society as a whole. As supernatural agents, children's authority and influence were demonstrated through cases like the Throckmorton's but clerical and magisterial scepticism was roused by counterfeit demoniacs like Anne Gunter and those associated with the disgraced Puritan exorcist John Darrell. The effect this had on the role of children in English witchcraft trials throughout the 1600s was an imperfect dichotomy which saw some children believed, while others lost credibility and support. These cases reveal what could happen when scepticism arrived too late for those wrongly accused of witchcraft. However, intriguing observations about chronological developments can be seen through analysing some of the most important witchcraft trials during this period.

Firstly, children like Jennet Device were believed and championed in the first set of Pendle witchcraft trials of 1612, yet, at the same time, Grace Sowerbutts' accusations were rejected due to her religious affiliations. Secondly, John Smith had a mixed role of being believed by the local magistrates in Leicestershire while also being found to be an imposter by King James I. Thirdly, a string of counterfeits that were discovered in the 1620s – including William Perry and Katherine Malpas – led to further growth in clerical and judicial scepticism. However, in 1634, the second set of Lancashire witchcraft trials saw Edmund Robinson (similar to John Smith) being believed by the magistrates but then forced to confess his fraud to the King. The Civil War disrupted English society in every capacity, but children

DOI: 10.4324/9781003685319-5

still acted as mediators between the visible and invisible worlds. After the Restoration, children continued to play an integral role in witchcraft trials. This can be seen in Elizabeth Mallory's case and the Bury St Edmund's trial in 1662, which demonstrate the return to an acceptance of children's testimony and the sanctity of their evidence in witchcraft trials. Though the early seventeenth century saw a lapse in the belief in children's testimony and accusations, by the end of the 1600s, children once again regained their position as essential weapons in the fight against witches. These are the children who called the shots and the children no one believed.

'Wonderful Work of God': Jennet Device and the 1612 Pendle Witchcraft Trials

Along with the Witches of Warboys case, the Pendle witchcraft trials of 1612 is perhaps one of the most well-known English witchcraft trials in history.[1] The 1612 Pendle trial that occurred in Lancashire is unique for a number of reasons. Firstly, the nineteen persons tried at the Lancaster Assizes in August of 1612 constituted the largest number of witches to be tried at one Assize in England up until that time; ten witches were executed which, numerically speaking, is significant amongst the estimated 500 executions for witchcraft that occurred in England between the first witchcraft act in 1542 and the repeal of all witchcraft statutes in 1736.[2] Secondly, Lancashire – particularly the Pendle area – had a reputation for being a wild, magical place (with a large population of Catholic recusants) so it seems unsurprising that Thomas Potts, who wrote the lengthy treatise on the trials, called the area 'fit' for a witch's 'profession'.[3] The Pendle trial is also unique because it appeared to encapsulate a rift between two families led by the matriarchs Elizabeth Southerns (Old Demdike) and Anne Whittle (Old Chattox), who more than likely did (or believe they did) participate in magic or act as cunning folk for nearby villages. This was seen in the fascinating detail given in their evidence against one another. For this discussion, the most important element of the Pendle trials revolves around the evidence given by nine-year-old Jennet Device against her mother, brother and sister which culminated in their eventual executions.

The narrative of the Pendle witches is fairly well-known and is covered in-depth in other academic works. However, a basic overview is useful in order to understand young Jennet Device's essential role in it. On 18 March 1612, Alizon Device (Old Demdike's grand-daughter) met John Law, a pedlar, on a highway near Colne field. According to one version of the story in Potts' account, Alizon asked John for some pins. John Law claimed that Alizon begged him for pins but after he refused, she became 'very angry' with him.[4] After he had gone only a short distant past her, he fell down and became 'lame in great extremity'.[5] Alizon claimed that she offered to buy pins from the pedlar. While she did not admit to becoming angry with him, she did confess to having met a black dog who appeared to her and 'sucked' from her. The spirit then asked Alizon what she would have him do to the pedlar? The creature offered a suggestion: 'I can lame him', upon which Alizon replied, 'lame him'.[6] It was in this moment that John Law fell down. There was a third description of the event from Abraham Law, John Law's son. According to Abraham's evidence, he received a letter from his father which claimed that Alizon asked to buy pins from John Law but she had no money. Notwithstanding, John apparently gave her some pins but both men still blamed Alizon for causing John's lameness through witchcraft.[7]

While it is important to question the veracity of Potts' narrative in choosing to champion one account – where Alizon took revenge on John Law for not supplying her with pins – it is just as important not to spiral into the tyranny of taxonomy. Attempting to decipher what was definitely 'true' and 'factual' from what was not is a worthwhile pursuit, but it should not be used anachronistically to discredit what was 'real' to those living in early modern England.[8] Potts relayed all three stories in his account and made no attempt to resolve the inconsistencies between them, nor did he note the contradictions. In this way, it is perhaps an honest relaying of information between three separate people who all saw one event very differently. As a man of his time, writing in the aftermath of the trials, Potts focussed on how Alizon, 'this odious witch', revenged herself upon John Law through her witchcraft.[9] It was, after all, the story that was most likely to secure a conviction. It was also the story that brought Roger Nowell, a Justice of the Peace, to the Pendle area to examine Alizon; it was not long before Nowell believed an entire witchcraft conspiracy had been discovered in Pendle.

Nowell examined a number of people between 3 March and 2 April and, to his surprise, found that Old Demdike, Old Chattox and Alizon Device were ready to confess to their familiarity with Satan. They also openly accused the opposing family of *maleficia*. Anne Redfearne (Old Chattox's daughter) did not confess but Old Demdike said she saw her making clay figures.[10] Consequently, all four women were committed to Lancaster prison. A few days after their imprisonment, James Device stole a sheep from a neighbour for a meeting held at Malkin Tower (Elizabeth Device's house) for the next night (which was Good Friday). In Potts' account, the meeting at Malkin Tower was not just a simple gathering of friends and family to enjoy a meal, but it was an assembly 'of all the most dangerous, wicked and damnable witches in the county far and near'.[11] According to Potts, the meeting at Malkin Tower was akin to European Continental Sabbats; Potts claimed that the witches plotted to procure the release of the entrapped inmates, blow up Lancaster Castle and murder Thomas Covell and Thomas Lister.[12] Upon receiving information about the meeting from suspicious neighbours, Nowell conducted examinations of Elizabeth, James and Jennet Device. The details of what transpired (or what Potts thought transpired) at the Malkin Tower meeting, as well as who attended the gathering, came from none other than nine-year-old Jennet Device. What is especially striking about the Malkin Tower meeting, and the 1612 Pendle trials generally, is the weight and significance placed upon the testimony of young Jennet Device.

At this stage, it is important to note that historians such as Ronald Seth have miscalculated the ages of some of the accused in the 1612 Pendle trials. Jennet Device is the only young person whose age is specified (for reasons unknown) but it is significant that historians know her age at all. Knowing Jennet Device was only nine when she played such a central role in one of the biggest witchcraft trials in English history adds immense value to the corpus of information on the role of children in witch-hunting. The fact that other historians have incorrectly asserted the ages of other people in this trial requires clarification so that further misrepresentations of the past can be avoided. For example, Seth stated that Anne Redfearne was eleven-years old. Seth appeared to have gotten this information from Rossell Hope Robbins' work who claimed she was the daughter of Elizabeth Device.[13] Both statements are inconsistent with the available evidence. According to the primary source documents, Redfearne was the daughter of Anne Whittle (Old Chattox) and it is unlikely she was eleven at the time of her execution because she was accused of a murder which she supposedly committed eighteen years prior to the trial.[14] Anne was also old enough to be married to a man called Thomas Redfearne, making the claim of her being eleven even more dubious.[15] Seth also claimed that Alizon Device was eleven-years old and though there is no evidence to prove the contrary – as her age is not specified in the trial documents – if Alizon was eleven, she would have been by far the youngest executed witch in English witch-hunting history, a significant event that would have surely been noted by at least one primary source account during or post-trial.[16] The question of age in the Pendle witchcraft trials has been distorted by some scholars but if we are to rely on Potts and believe that Jennet Device was nine-years old, her influential role in the 1612 Pendle witchcraft trials is made even more disturbing.

Jennet Device's first appearance in Potts' narrative came in the arraignment and trial of her mother, Elizabeth Device. With echoes reminiscent of the *Malleus Maleficarum* on how witches offer up their children to the Devil, Potts described Elizabeth Device as a 'barbarous and inhumane monster … so far from sensible understanding of thy own misery as to bring thy own natural children into mischief and bondage…'.[17] Potts went on to describe how Elizabeth made her children – Alizon and James Device – witches and 'provided [them] with spirits'.[18] Remarkably, Potts never suspected that Jennet, the youngest of Elizabeth's children, was also made a witch by her mother, though Jennet's own testimony would hint as much; she proved more useful as an accuser rather than an accused. When Jennet was called in and 'commanded' to stand up to give evidence against her mother, Potts stated that Elizabeth began, 'outrageously cursing [and] cried out against the child in such a fearful manner...'.[19] Jennet, with 'weeping tears' cried out to the judge and told him that she was 'not able to speak in the presence of her mother'.[20] While Elizabeth's reaction might be fairly attributed to the knowledge that her daughter was about to give evidence against her, it is also possible that her outburst signified a darker reality; that she might have been a harsh or even an abusive mother towards Jennet. Like other children who may have had abusive parents – such as the Sellys brothers in the St Osyth trial – Jennet appeared more than willing to testify against her own mother.[21]

When no means could stop Elizabeth's 'cursing and threating of the child', the judge commanded her to be taken away, whereupon Jennet was set 'upon the table' so that she could be witnessed by the whole court and give her evidence without interruption.[22] With her mother out of the room, Jennet told the court in no uncertain terms that her mother was a witch and that she had seen her spirit come to her 'in the likeness of a brown dog which she called Ball'.[23] Jennet then proceeded to tell the court how long her mother had been a witch, what exactly her mother had asked Ball to do and to whom.[24] The details Jennet outlined to the court from atop a table at only nine-years old was an incredible display of influence and control. Although Ronald Seth claimed that Jennet had been 'coached' (though he does not speculate by whom), Jennet signified to the court that she had access to the invisible world and used that knowledge to successfully condemn her mother.[25] Yet, Jennet's role as an accuser had only just begun and proved to be an invaluable witness against other accused witches.

In Jennet's second examination, she relayed to the court details of the Malkin Tower gathering. Jennet stated that they had gathered to give a name to her sister Alizon's spirit and that there were about twenty people present, supplying the names of six of them. Though Jennet admitted that she did not know the names of the rest of them, she assured the court that her mother and brother were both there.[26] Then, Jennet confessed that her mother taught her two 'prayers': one to cure the bewitched and the other 'to get drink'.[27] Amazingly, it did not seem that either the court or Potts thought that Jennet herself was a witch despite this admission. It seemed, in this case, that the child's role was too important to be circumvented by an accusation of witchcraft. Far from being suspected as a witch by the court, Potts appeared to almost venerate her in his writing. For example, before Jennet's examination against her brother James Device, Potts noted:

> but do observe the wonderful work of God to raise up a young infant, the very sister of the prisoner, Jennet Device, to discover, justify and prove these things against him [James] at the time of his Arraignment and Trial....[28]

Jennet was not only encouraged to give evidence against members of her family – like the unnamed boys in the 1589 Chelmsford trials – she was commended highly for doing so.

Similar to her evidence against her mother, Jennet readily confirmed that her brother James was a witch and had been one for three years.[29] She told the court that James had a spirit in the shape of a black dog called Dandy and outlined with great 'modesty, government and understanding' what James commanded Dandy to do.[30] It is clear to the reader that Potts – like Henri Boguet when he wrote about Loyse Maillat – attempted to portray Jennet as a rational and logical accuser in an effort to dissuade any sceptic from attacking the court's decision to use a child as the linchpin in a capital trial.[31]

Although Jennet was not suspected as a witch, to test the validity of her claims (and perhaps, more accurately, ensure sceptics could be quelled), Jennet was put through a series of tests regarding who was at the gathering at Malkin Tower. In the examination of Alice Nutter – a wealthy woman whose denunciation alone was questionable amongst the court and townspeople alike – Jennet was asked whether she would know the faces of those at the meeting at Malkin Tower if she saw them. Jennet replied that she would.[32] Jennet was then taken out of the room and Thomas Covell commanded: 'to set all his prisoners by themselves and betwixt every witch another prisoner and some other strange women amongst them, so as no man could judge the one from the other'.[33] Jennet was then brought back into the room and took Alice Nutter by the hand, accused her of being at the Malkin Tower gathering and even told her who she sat next to and what conversation they had.[34] Potts attributed great significance to this, stating that it was 'the very act of God to discover her'.[35] Alice Nutter, though she did not confess, was executed on the denunciation of Jennet Device's words alone. In fact, this experiment was deemed so important, it was repeated three more times against Katherine Hewitt, Jane Bulcock and John Bulcock; the outcome was exactly the same as it was with Alice Nutter, proving to be effective 100% of the time.[36] These three – though they pleaded not guilty – were found guilty and executed based largely on the accusation of young Jennet Device.

While the Malkin Tower gathering was probably a real event that Jennet Device attended, her ability to either distort or take advantage of the meeting as a gathering of witches is a remarkable display of ingenuity for a nine-year old. The motivation behind why Jennet accused so many remains elusive; without direct evidence demonstrating that she was coached, historians must look for other alternatives. She was certainly encouraged, but it appeared as if it was Jennet's own discursive sophistication that made her act out against her potentially neglectful family, triggering her accusations against her mother and brother. Jennet's reasons for accusing Katherine Hewitt as well as Jane and John Bulcock might have been less complicated in nature; perhaps she was simply telling the court who was at the Malkin Tower feast, or perhaps she enjoyed her status as the most important person in the room and was clever enough to know what the court wanted to hear.

Whatever the motivating factors were, it is clear that nine-year-old Jennet Device was able to use her role as a preternatural actor to assert dominance in one of the biggest witchcraft trials in English history, which ultimately, ended in the destruction of her entire family. Jennet's ability to feed relevant information to the court about the activities of witches – without implicating herself – is a pronounced display of astuteness shown within the role of children in English witchcraft trials. Of the nine executed witches, six of them were sent to the gallows based almost solely on the evidence given by Jennet Device. Others gave evidence against the six condemned witches but it was Jennet's evidence and her 'experiment' which showed to the court who was at the Malkin Tower meeting. This was the piece of evidence that sealed the fate of each of the six executed witches. At the same time Jennet Device exerted her agency and gave essential information in the Pendle trial, a fourteen-year-old girl named Grace Sowerbutts was slandered as an 'impudent wench' by Thomas Potts for bringing accusations of witchcraft against three women in neighbouring Salmesbury.[37]

'This Impudent Wench': Grace Sowerbutts and the Salmesbury Witches

Inserted almost in the middle of Pott's *Discovery of Witches*, the account of the Salmesbury witches of 1612 remains an obscure part of England's witch-hunting narrative; despite it being rich in details that challenge what is considered the 'norm' of English witch-hunting lore. According to Potts' account, Grace Sowerbutts accused Jennet Bierley (her grandmother), Ellen Bierley (her aunt), Old Doewife (though she featured little in Grace's actual accusations) and Jane Southworth of being witches. These women were accused of dragging Grace 'violently [by]...the hair of the head and laid her on the top of a hay-mowe'.[38] Grace claimed that she saw Jennet Bierley change from her own shape into the likeness of a dog and attempted to persuade Grace to drown herself; a mortal sin.[39] So far, Grace's accusations against the three women align with those told by children in preceding trials. However, Grace's next accusations took a much more sinister turn.

Under oath, Grace claimed that Jennet and Ellen Bierley took her to Thomas Walshman's house.[40] Grace claimed that Jennet took the man's baby out of his bed, whereupon Jennet thrust a nail into the navel of the infant, putting a 'pen' into the hole and then, 'did suck there a good space' before putting the child back into the bed.[41] Grace clarified that the child did not cry when it was hurt but she did 'think that the said child did thenceforth languish and not long after it died'.[42] These extraordinary claims appear to come straight from Continental demonological treatises but Grace had not finished detailing a narrative that to the English justices must have provoked credulity, or perhaps sheer terror. Grace claimed that after the infant died, Jennet and Ellen Bierley exhumed the corpse, brought it home and boiled it. They then ate some of it and melted the fat off the bones, allegedly telling Grace that they would anoint themselves: 'thereby they might sometimes change themselves into other shapes'.[43] Though Grace seemed perceptive enough to detail these horrors to the court, she had played a passive role throughout the baby killing debauchery she described thus far. However, the next time she was sworn in to give evidence, Grace (for reasons unknown) freely implicated herself.

If the simple Malkin Tower gathering was thought to be the first English Sabbat, it would have deeply disturbed the English public had Grace's account of her Sabbat been believed and disseminated. Grace told the court that six months before her appearance as a witness, herself, Ellen and Jennet Bierley and Jane Southworth all went to a place called Redbank. Grace stated that every Thursday and Sunday night, there were four 'black things, going upright, and yet not like men in the face' that carried the four women across the river where the eight of them ate meat and danced.[44] After dancing, each of the 'black things' did 'pull down the said three women and did abuse their bodies'.[45] Potts adds: 'as this exanimate thinks, for she says, that the black thing that was with her, did abuse her body'.[46] Astonishingly, though she openly admitted to having sexual intercourse with a demonic entity, Grace was not accused of being a witch herself. Grace's intimate supernatural knowledge was enriched with graphic details that the English court had doubtlessly only heard about from Continental trials, so why did Grace's convictions lack credibility? As a supernatural actor, Grace's accusations were initially accepted on face value as she was the key witness in this case, giving valuable information that could not be discerned by anyone else. However, evidence soon came to light that broke apart Grace's narrative.

The essential piece of information discrediting Grace's confession in the Salmesbury witch trial was the discovery by the authorities that she was coached by a Jesuit priest. Therefore, the reason that Grace's testimony against the three women was not believed seemed to have nothing to do with the fact she was a child; it was because she was influenced by Popish superstition. The persecution of Catholics had deep roots in Elizabeth I's reign, particularly with the establishment of the Act Against Jesuits and Seminarists that banned Catholic priests from entering the country; those within England had forty days to leave or risk persecution.[47] By the time of King James, Protestantism had almost completely erased any remnants of England's Catholic past. Yet, there were still places in England – particularly Lancashire – where Catholic recusants survived and practiced in secret. In his relaying of the account, Potts first undermined the evidence Grace gave, pointing out flaws in her story, which, significantly, he did not do with Jennet Device's, highlighting the influence of his personal religious convictions.[48] Both were children, both gave fascinating tales of witchcraft, but one was not believed because of Catholic influences that helped inspire Grace's stories; this anti-Catholic sentiment ironically had the positive side effect of saving the lives of three accused women.[49] However, it was not just Potts whose religious convictions motivated his actions in this account. When the judge pressured the accused and asked them why Grace accused her own grandmother, aunt and Jane Southworth, they replied that the Jesuit priest 'Thompson' (later identified in the account as Christopher Southworth) had 'instructed and taught her this accusation against them, because they were once obstinate Papists, and now came to church'.[50] Clearly, the Jesuit priest recognised Grace as a believable vessel whereby witchcraft accusations would be heard. He then persuaded her to accuse the three women of witchcraft for abandoning the Catholic faith. The extent of Grace's reliance on Southworth was realised; had her influence from a Catholic priest not been discovered by the Salmesbury authorities; the history surrounding the story of Grace Sowerbutts and the Salmesbury witches might have been very different.

The reasons why Grace Sowerbutts lacked credibility and was not believed is therefore a testament to the powerful influence of the religious turmoil of the time. While Grace was unable to secure convictions due to magisterial disdain for Catholic priests, a few years later, in Leicestershire, a young boy called John Smith became (statistically speaking) one of the most successful witch-hunters in English history before Matthew Hopkins. What makes this title even more significant is that it came in direct opposition to King James' efforts to quell Smith's witch-hunting endeavours.

The 'Boy of Leicester': John Smith

The account of John Smith provides a fascinating insight into perhaps one of the longest child demoniac cases since English witchcraft trials begun. Smith was only four- or five-years old when he provided depositions against 'Randall and other witches' around 1607/1608.[51] While this case did not result in any convictions, at four or five, Smith appears to be the youngest child to give evidence in an English witchcraft case.[52] Smith's role as an accuser resurfaced in 1616 when he was thirteen- or fourteen-years old; the outcome of this later trial proved to be much more devastating than the earlier ones. It is unclear whether he was suffering as a demoniac for the nine or ten years between his first stint as an accuser and this second bout; the evidence is inconclusive.[53] Unfortunately for the historian, the Assize records for the Midland Circuit do not survive for this period.[54] This is the most likely reason why Smith's case has not been discussed in much detail outside of G. L. Kittredge's 1911 article. Most of the information historians have about Smith comes from three sources. The most contemporary to the event is a letter from Robert

Heyrick to his brother Sir William dated from July 1616. There are also two later sources that Kittridge stated are less reliable due to their distance from the event but nonetheless appear to give valuable details about the case.

John Smith, like the Throckmorton girls, came from a wealthy family and it is highly likely he heard about their case twenty-seven years previously. This is evidenced by the fact that in Robert Heyrick's letter to his brother Sir William, he mentioned that the accused witches (nine in total) were forced to come to Smith when he was in his fits:

> ...and then they were charged to speak certain words ... as thus: "I such a one charge the horse, that I be a witch, that thou come forth of the child" and another by her spirits to do the like ... if any of them would speak a word contrary to that charm, he should be mightily tormented; but if she would speak as he had first directed them, at the end of the last he would fall out of his fit...[55]

This scenario is almost identical to the 'formula' the Throckmorton girls devised twenty-seven years earlier that they made the accused Samuels family say to bring them out of their fits.[56] The villages of Warboys and Husbands Bosworth in Leicestershire are geographically close to one another, and it is highly unlikely that the similarity of John Smith's 'formula' and that of the Throckmorton girls was a coincidence. The more probable answer is that Smith read or heard about the Throckmorton case and mimicked their behaviour, recognising their case as a believable and successful instance of bewitchment. Consequently, John Smith's case (though the details are not as rich as the Throckmorton's) illustrated a further example of children learning from one another.

John Smith's display as a demoniac eventuated in the execution of the nine women he accused as witches, demonstrating that the techniques he learnt from the Throckmorton girls were successful in persuading those around him of the validity of his bewitchment. For the young Smith, this was not the end of his witch-finding endeavours, and he continued to have fits after the nine women were executed on 18 July 1616. Due to Smith's accusations, six more women were imprisoned, awaiting trial at the autumn Assize. Smith's power and influence ruled without restraint, and it seemed these women would soon face the same fate as the nine women before them. However, Smith was eventually forced to face King James to prove the validity of his bewitchment.

Almost exactly a month after the execution of the nine women, King James visited Leicester in the course of a royal progress.[57] King James' reputation for being a staunch witch-hunter may have been overexaggerated by recent scholarship, but he did pride himself in being able to identify counterfeit demoniacs.[58] When the King heard of John Smith's fits, he demanded the boy be presented to him whereupon we are told by a later source that Smith, 'possibly daunted at his [the King's] presence or terrified by his words ... began to faulter so as the King discovered a fallacy'.[59] King James, being satisfied he had found another counterfeit demoniac, sent the boy back to Lambeth for further proof that he dissembled. Apparently, Smith was made to repeat his 'tricks' often times a day.[60] Perhaps more important is the admission that Smith performed these 'tricks' in the first place 'to prevent a whipping and to avoid going to school'.[61] Smith's motivation, if the sources are to be believed, provides valuable insight into why some children acted as demoniacs.

King James' determination to expose counterfeit demoniacs does not reflect a disbelief in witchcraft or demonic possession. In fact, King James believed he had been the target of witches' malice when the ship carrying him and his new wife Anne was almost shipwrecked on his crossing from Denmark to England in 1590. James' rooting out of fraudulent demoniacs, then, is best interpreted in terms of seeking to find the *real* victims of witchcraft. Fraudulent demoniacs threatened the authenticity and validity of the witchcraft phenomena as a whole; while it has been established that James' reputation as a witch-hunting king may have been overstated, he did create a new Witchcraft Act in 1604 and his book *Demonologie* was influential in both England and his native Scotland. Counterfeit demoniacs called into question his belief system and his new harsher laws to punish it. James may have said barely anything about children in *Daemonologie*, but he may have understood the cultural significance of children's relationship with the spiritual world. Through his work of exposing fraudulent cases like Gunter and Smith, he sought to maintain control of the invisible world; though even as the King, he would find this objective difficult to achieve.

According to notable lawyer and politician Frederick Inderwick, even after King James discovered Smith's imposture, Justice Winch and Serjeant Crew tried and hanged the six accused witches.[62] Inderwick went on to state that the judge was discredited for having allowed the case to be tried, as it was considered so 'impertinent an invasion of the King's prerogative'.[63] The Calendar of State Papers also noted that Justice Winch and Serjeant Crew were 'disgrace[d]' for hanging 'supposed witches' after the King had discovered the imposture of Smith.[64] Whether the witches were hanged by some magisterial error cannot be known. If they were hanged because the judge was convinced of their guilt based on the accusation of the fraudulent Smith, it would further reinforce the powerful role children played in witchcraft trials. It seemed the King of England himself could not sway the minds of the prosecutors once denunciations had been made. Both interpretations, though, remain speculative and unfortunately, John Smith disappears from the historical record after his spectacular witch-hunting career that spanned almost ten years and culminated in the deaths of at least fifteen people in only two trials. By all accounts, John Smith is one of the most successful and yet, underappreciated witch-hunters in English history.

John Smith straddled the natural and supernatural worlds, using his insight and knowledge to denounce those who he believed (or otherwise wanted to believe) bewitched him. At the same time, Smith was caught between the credulous justices of Leicester and a sceptical King. To the six witches who were executed after John Smith's imposture had been 'discovered' by King James, it mattered little that Smith was not believed by the King as he had been believed by the local authorities in Leicester. That the King of England could not abate the wave of destruction bought on by a thirteen-year-old boy is a testament to the power children still had in witchcraft trials despite official scepticism. While some children like Jennet Device and John Smith were successful witch-hunters, other children struggled to maintain credibility. For example, in 1620, four years after the Leicester trials, a twelve-year-old boy named William Perry faced similar challenges as Grace Sowerbutts had eight years previously. Though he displayed all the classic signs of bewitchment, Perry's credibility as a demoniac wavered because of the discovery that he too had been influenced by Catholic priests.

The 'Boy of Bilson': William Perry

Historian Anna French noted that William Perry's possession was a 'Catholic saga' but described how he was visited by both Catholic and Protestant exorcists in the hope of alleviating his sufferings.[65] Both Catholics and Protestants wrote an account about the young boy. However, the Catholic version of events now only exists entirely within the Protestant source and its strong anti-Catholic prejudice – evidenced by the first forty-four pages of warnings against 'Popish exorcising of unclean spirits' – must be noted. This includes any possible omissions the Protestant author made to the Catholic treatise.[66]

Another element to note is the suggestion by Ronald Seth that William Perry knew about the story of William Sommers, one of John Darrell's infamous demoniacs.[67] However, Seth referred to Sommers in his text as 'The Boy of Burton' which is undoubtedly Thomas Darling seeing as he lived in Burton-Upon-Trent. William Sommers was known as 'The Boy of Nottingham' for the same reason, so it is safe to assume that Seth meant Thomas Darling in this instance. While a tenuous suggestion, there are elements in Perry's story that give the impression that he knew about Darling's possession twenty-three years previously. For example, their stories of how they both came to be possessed are very similar. In Darling's account, he became distressed after Alice Goodridge exchanged ill-meaning words with him upon meeting her in the woods. Similarly, William Perry claimed that his possession began when Joan Cocke cursed him for not giving her 'the good time of day' after seeing her on his way home from school.[68] Both were chance encounters with older, estranged women and both boys became bewitched when they had vexatious words spoken over them after allegedly not showing due respect. Hence, it is possible to claim that Perry formulated his bewitchment story after learning about Darling's account, but without more evidence, this remains conjecture.

According to the Catholic account of Perry's possession, Perry complained of being pricked 'to the very heart' after meeting Joan Cocke on his way home from school and languished for 'some days' and had 'extreme fits'.[69] The Catholic author described how Perry's parents sought help from Catholic priests to ease the sufferings of Perry; after ascertaining there were three devils inside the boy, the author endeavoured to discover whether 'he were possessed or obsessed', a distinction no other demoniac case makes so clearly.[70] The two Catholic priests then used Catholic relics such as holy water and oil on Perry to help him talk and walk. In their absence, after drinking the 'blessed water' Perry vomited 'pins, wool, knotted thread, thrums, rosemary, walnut leaves and feathers'.[71] Over the next few days, Perry vomited eleven pins and a folded-up knitting needle. Apparently, the only comment the Catholic priest made to Perry's parents about this was that he was glad Perry was voiding these objects in their absence as it proves, 'it was no collusion of us'.[72] Alas, Perry's creative allotriophagy went without the accolades he might have wanted, so he sought to extend greater control over the Catholic priests who sought to take charge of the young boy. Perry told the priests that he 'would not hear us' and would not tell them anything other than '[Joan Cocke] would make an end of him'. He began to lash out at the Catholics around him, calling them: 'roughish p'.[73] Then, as if by some miracle, Perry became 'perfectly himself' after inhaling Frankincense smoke, claiming that 'he saw his enemies tormented'.[74] Perry delighted in his newfound deliverance saying that he would become a Catholic, entreating his parents and siblings to do the same.[75] That may have been the end of William Perry's account, according to the Catholic priest, had 'many Puritans' not come to visit the boy.[76]

Perry was doubtlessly aware of the religious turmoil at the time and, unsurprisingly, became grievously tormented by the Devil when the Puritans visited him, saying the Devil afflicted him in the shape of a blackbird. This is the same allegory seven-year-old Annis Dowsing used to describe her mother's demonic familiar in the infamous second Chelmsford trials in 1579.[77] The arrival of the Puritans to Perry's bedside had a disastrous effect on his spiritual well-being. His condition deteriorated until the priest postulated that perhaps the cause of his bewitchment was a 'lack of belief' on the part of his parents.[78] The priest tried to convert them without any success and concluded his account by lamenting how Perry's parents decided to go to witches for help. The priest, for his part, stated that he 'would not mingle

God and the devil together' and so left the family to their 'bad resolution ... desiring that all may succeed to God's glory'.[79]

The rest of William Perry's account detailed how the authorities discovered he was a counterfeit; this included two examinations of Perry explaining why he became a demoniac, as well as detailing (allegedly from his own perspective) his time with the Catholic priests. Such rich information is uncommon in witchcraft/demoniac cases. While biases, influences and pressures on Perry must be noted, it is significant that historians have this insight into why and how Perry transformed himself into a demoniac, as well as a different perspective into his unsuccessful time with the Catholic priests. The author started by claiming that, at first, there were two symptoms that gave Perry high levels of credibility. While Perry showed many of the classic symptoms of bewitchment and possession, the swollen throat, the groaning and moaning, etc., the two most convincing symptoms were his ability to identify Joan Cocke out of a crowd as the one who bewitched him (an experiment that was conducted at the Stafford Assize to test the validity of his bewitchment), as well as his revulsion at John 1:1.[80] According to the author, 'thousands' came to see Perry 'in which plight he continued many months', but luckily for the accused witch Joan Cocke, when it came time for her trial at the Assize, suspicion was raised only against Perry.

Sir Peter Warburton was the presiding judge over the Stafford Assize which was held on 10 August 1620. He was clearly a witchcraft sceptic and argued against the 'idleness of such fantastical delusions', finding Joan Cocke not guilty.[81] As for William Perry's, he was committed to 'the care and (if it might so be) the cure' of the Bishop of Coventry and Lichfield.[82] Perry managed to keep suspicions at bay for a month before people started to doubt the credibility of his spiritual torments. Those around him began to suspect Perry counterfeited since his pulse remained 'easy and equal' even in his strongest fits, combined with his 'quiet rest and sleep' and his 'clear complexion'.[83] This gave those around Perry the impression that he was not vexed with evil spirits like he had led them to believe. It is impressive that at twelve-years old, Perry was able to maintain his performance without wavering in his conviction that he was bewitched. While the judges did not believe his accusation of witchcraft against Joan Cocke, they did not outright deny he was a demonic or accuse him of simulating his fits. Furthermore, through going to Catholics, Puritans and witches for assistance, Perry clearly had the acceptance and support of his family, as well as those around him who simply did not know what to do with the troubled young boy.

The means by which Perry was found to be faking his fits was a stroke of ingenuity on the part of the Bishop. The discovery led to Perry's admissions of his motivations and perspective which give valuable insight into his role as a mediator of the spiritual world. It began when Perry's father came to visit him and earnestly asked the Bishop whether his son was possessed or not, particularly as Perry had grievous fits at the hearing of the words of John 1:1. At this point, the author observed that Perry's father was 'an honest husbandman ... innocent and ignorant of any practice in his child' which gave all the accountability and, more importantly, agency to Perry for the simulation of his fits.[84] In the afternoon of the same day, the Bishop decided to conduct an experiment to test the validity of Perry's possession. Upon asking for the Greek text the Bishop told Perry:

> ...Boy it is either thou, or the devil, that abhors those words of the Gospel [John 1:1] and if it be the devil, he (being so ancient a scholar as of almost six thousand years standing) knows and understands all languages in the world so that he cannot but know when I recite the same sentence in the Gospel out of the Greek text. But if it be yourself, then art thou an execrable wretch who plays the devils part...[85]

The Bishop then read two verses of the Gospel of John in Greek. The first was the tenth verse which Perry, thinking it was the first verse, fell into 'the passion of a trance'.[86] The second passage the Bishop read was the first verse and Perry, thinking it was not the same text, showed no sign of trouble: 'by this means was his notable fraud, in a manner, fully discovered'.[87] In a remarkable display that attempted to reverse elder authorial control, Perry remained defiant in attempting to prove his possession was real, stating that he was troubled by the sight of two mice. In normal circumstances, the Bishop demonstrating his theological authority should have ended Perry's obvious fraudulent behaviour. However, Perry, building and learning from the traditions of children who went before him had carved out a place for himself in the invisible world and was not going to relinquish it easily.

After the Bishop's discovery, Perry was sent home to his father's house where he complained of 'extreme sickness' in his belly; when he passed urine it came out as 'black as ink'.[88] After three days of passing black urine, Perry's imposture was discovered again when someone spied on him to watch how he might be making black urine. Perry mixed ink with his urine and then 'nimbly convey[ed] the inkhome into a private place'.[89] That a twelve-year-old boy would be so desperate to regain his preternatural credibility by inserting ink into his urethra is a testament to the cultural significance of this role. After an 'earnest but loving exhortation' was made to the boy, Perry broke down into tears and made two full confessions as well as private and public acknowledgements.[90]

Upon being asked who taught him to counterfeit his fits, Perry explained that he met an old man near his house called Thomas who taught him how to fake his fits so that he did not have to go to school. These details are puzzling for historians, who are left to wonder whether Thomas was a real person, or whether Perry simply provided the adults around him with a patsy and he had instead simply learnt this behaviour from word of mouth or gossip. It has already been suggested that Perry had some familiarity with the case of Thomas Darling. The old man Perry described as having a 'grey beard' and 'russet apparel', who carried glasses and pots on his back, certainly sounded eccentric but one must question whether this was another of Perry's clever tactics of deception.[91] With regard to accusing Joan Cocke as a witch, Perry explained that he 'was once minded' to make his own image in clay and put it into her house 'for the better proof of her bewitching me'.[92] That a young boy had the knowledge and determination to go to such lengths to convince a court of law that a woman bewitched him by planting evidence at her house is a display of sophisticated malice, well beyond what most adults were contributing to other witchcraft trials.

After Perry's admission of motivation and his plan to incriminate Joan Cocke, he provided his perspective of his encounter with the Catholic priests. Perry's account and the one given in the Catholic version presented earlier in the treatise appear to align in most of the details. However, Perry's clear anti-Catholic sentiment provided more details of explicit 'Popish' behaviour and omitted any of the glorifying of Catholicism he was said to have done in the Catholic version. These discrepancies are not unsurprising, given the nature and biases of both accounts, but Perry's perspective is a unique point of view from a child who had convinced three priests of his diabolical torments for no other apparent reason than liking the attention and not wanting to go to school.[93] After his confessions and public acknowledgments, Perry went to trial at the Summer Assize in Stafford on 26 July 1621. One of the judges, Peter Warburton, was the same judge who cleared Joan Cocke a year earlier; now, he presided over the trial of Perry on charges of blasphemy and false accusations of witchcraft. The outcome of the trial is not overly clear, but it seemed as if Perry threw himself on the mercy of the judges and Joan Cocke who was also there, craving their pardon and her forgiveness. Without direct evidence to the contrary, it seemed as if he escaped without punishment.[94]

At only twelve-years old, William Perry was the youngest English child to face charges of simulating demonic fits and falsely accusing someone of witchcraft. Anne Gunter was the first to face legal judgement within the Star Chamber in 1606 at the age of twenty but she admitted she was forced into her fits by her father.[95] In only fifteen years, from the Gunter trial to Perry's, the role of children shifted markedly. Children took bolder steps to solidify their place in the invisible world. As William Perry demonstrated, even when those in authority challenged their position (as the Bishop had) they remained steadfast until Perry stood alone in the courtroom to face the consequences of his actions. It seemed that children understood the repercussions of losing one's status as a seer into the supernatural world; it was so culturally and religiously significant it was tantamount to a form of social suicide. William Perry explained as much when he was asked, after he 'saw himself half discovered [as a fraud]' whether he thought to himself 'some bodily mischief?' Perry responded: 'The devil had stolen my heart so that I cared not to hang myself and had purposed to do so one night but that I was watched and [was] hindered.'[96]

Although William Perry's account provided rich and insightful details into the role of children in witch-hunting, his story is not covered in-depth by most scholars, or at best, it is often passed over in brief detail. Even when authors do discuss William Perry, they are unsure how much agency to ascribe to him, noting that he seemed unwilling to accept responsibility for his actions: 'Perry's imaginative desire [was] to lay blame everywhere but upon himself'.[97] Yet, the same historians also acknowledged Perry's sophisticated ability in masterfully playing the part of the demoniac, noting that between the priests and the many people who came to see him: '[Perry]... cleverly directed ... starred and, along with the other participants was a co-writer of the script.'[98] For children who wanted to maintain their role, being believed was the most crucial part of their performance. For Grace Sowerbutts and William Perry, suspicions surrounding their credibility were sparked by their involvement with Catholic priests which was fuelled by anti-Popish sentiments. These cases also represent the importance and political uses of religious confessionalism at the time.[99] The ripples of the Darrell Controversy were still being felt by the clergy and magistrates who now had greater suspicions about demoniacs. Lastly, King James' influence also made it more difficult for children trying to assert their spiritual authority. King James' success in discovering imposters helped fuel clerical and magisterial scepticism and as C. L'Estrange suggested, witchcraft trials were actually at their peak at the height of Elizabeth's reign, not James.[100] This suggests that the role of children in witchcraft trials was also waning. However, evidence shows that children after Perry were just as persistent in accusing witches and using their role for their own means, despite a rise in official scepticism. For example, two years after William Perry, Katherine Malpas and her immediate family were summoned to the Star Chamber to face charges on simulating bewitchment for the purposes of procuring money.

'To gain and get money': Katherine Malpas

In 1622, Thomas Saunders, his wife Elizabeth and their daughter Katherine Malpas Senior were examined in the Star Chamber in Westminster for having 'procured and incited Katherine Malpas the younger ... to counterfeit and feign herself to be bewitched and possessed ... and to counterfeit and feign certain strange fits and trances... .'[101] It is impossible to determine how old Katherine Malpas was when she was under scrutiny by the Star Chamber, the notes from the Attorney General simply describe her as a 'young maiden'.[102] This combined with the fact that she was unmarried and still reliant on her extended family for support means that she would fit the cultural status of a child.

Brian Levack noted that the Essex Assize prosecuted Katherine for counterfeiting her fits, stating that she was placed in the stocks and committed to a house of correction for eight months. However, this seems to be the fate of Katherine's co-accused Anne Godfrey.[103] There is no evidence to suggest that Katherine herself faced any legal punishment for her imposture. Like Anne Gunter's case sixteen years previously, Katherine's case in the Star Chamber caught the attention of King James and her case is particularly rich in detail. As she was not formally charged, Katherine is not directly questioned in the interrogatories, although she was informally interrogated by King James. However, fascinating details about her level of participation in the affair are stated by her family who were forced to face one of the highest courts in England.

Elizabeth Saunders admitted that she devised the plan '...for the better maintenance of the aforesaid Katherine Malpas the younger and her mother ... not for any other intent or purpose'.[104] Thomas Saunders – while his answers waivered in consistency – claimed that while he was initially furious with his granddaughter, once he saw 'persons of quality' giving money to her out of pity, it seemed he was happy to comply with the scheme.[105] The fact that a family concocted such a plan for no other reason other than to make money was not unheard of in early modern times, but it adds valuable insight into the roles that children played and their motivations for doing so.[106]

According to Elizabeth Saunders, Katherine's fits began two years earlier in December 1620. Apparently, Katherine would

> have a rising up in her stomach to the bigness of a half penny loaf and would beat her head against the wainscot [wall] and would shrug up her shoulders and would make her bones to crackle within her skin and sometimes her mouth would be drawn on one side....[107]

While Elizabeth may have been instrumental in Katherine's debut as a demoniac, the evidence shows that Katherine used her own creativity to embellish her fits. The interrogatories from the Star Chamber indicated that Katherine would 'cast away any Bible or prayer book that was offered or given unto her to read', which is in line with traditional demoniac behaviour.[108] Elizabeth Saunders staunchly denied having taught Katherine this, claiming 'that she did not nor any other to her knowledge persuade or direct the aforesaid Katherine Malpas to fling or cast away any Bible or prayer book that was given unto her...'.[109] This demonstrated how Katherine asserted her own agency in her status as a demoniac, to the extent where Thomas Saunders and Katherine Malpas Senior claimed that they did not know Katherine faked her fits until well into 1620. When they eventually found out about her imposture, they repeatedly refuted the claim that Katherine was taught by her grandmother, insisting that she had taught herself. Perhaps this claim attempted to lessen the guilt felt by Elizabeth, but it is also likely that both Thomas Saunders and Katherine Malpas Senior understood the cultural significance of young Katherine's supernatural insight and were not surprised when she made the demonic performance her own; Katherine clearly did this when she added repulsion to holy books to her repertoire.

Elizabeth Saunders claimed that news about Katherine's possession spread through the parish within three weeks.[110] As was hoped by the family, multitudes of people came to see Katherine in her fits and Thomas Saunders was reportedly very strict in ensuring that no one saw her without paying admission. For example, Thomas admitted that persons 'should not be admitted unto her without giving money or promising to give…'.[111] In order to keep up the façade that Katherine was truly possessed, Katherine Malpas Senior petitioned the Bishop of London for a license to hire a preacher to pray with her daughter in an attempt to quell the spiritual disturbance inside her.[112] The need for a license was a requirement after the Darrell Controversy which ended in the instigation of Canon 74. This forbade any type of dispossessions without special permission from the Bishop. While some historians have claimed that the only licence of this kind to ever pass seal was given in the case of Thomas Harrison in 1604, the Bishop of London granted Katherine Malpas' family permission to have two vicars and a parish lector to pray over their daughter.[113] It is immensely curious that scholars have overlooked the fact that this license was granted. Anglican clergy were not overly sympathetic to prayer and fasting as a means to dispossess children as they saw it as Puritan religious propaganda. Since it had only been eighteen years since the Canon had been established, why even two licences were issued remains puzzling, given the uproar stirred up by the controversy that John Darrell and his ilk caused the Anglican clergy in the late sixteenth-century. Either the bishops were becoming lenient on matters of dispossession – which seemed unlikely since attitudes did not change fundamentally until 1975 – or they seemed to understand the cultural significance of dispossession to lay people.[114] In granting licenses to allow the use of prayer and fasting in a few cases of demonic possessions, the clergy were seen to give the people what they wanted: physical manifestations for the purpose of alleviating faith-based torments. That children were the centre of both licenses being granted is a testament to the influence and importance of their role as actors within these faith-based tribulations.

As Katherine's fits continued, suspicions she was faking her fits began to circulate. Katherine accused Elizabeth Hedlyn and Goodwife White of bewitching her.[115] In a further demonstration of her own autonomy, the accusations against Hedlyn and White appeared to come from no one but young Katherine herself. Thomas Saunders admitted that he had to ask a smith who lived in Plaistow where Hedlyn lived and neither Elizabeth Saunders or Katherine Malpas Senior said anything about instructing or directing Katherine to accuse the women of witchcraft.[116] Conversely, it appeared that Katherine knew Goodwife White, for when she accused her, White came to visit Katherine. After she was confronted, Katherine withdrew her accusation, claiming she had been mistaken.[117] However, Katherine persisted in her denunciation of Hedlyn, claiming that she had come to her in the likeness of a brown dog, a white cat and, unusually, as a swarm of bees.[118] The inception of this money making plan might not have come from Katherine initially, but the evidence suggests it was her ideas and skill that enabled the scheme to work for almost a year.

References to Katherine's agency proliferate through parts of the interrogatories. For example, when asked whether it was Katherine's idea to beat the walls of her room, Katherine Malpas Senior replied:

> ...that the aforesaid Katherine Malpas in her fits did of herself and her own according beat the walls of her room where she lay ... but does not think that she was so taught to say by anyone neither can this defendant conceive that she was so taught or instructed...[119]

Elizabeth Saunders concurred with Katherine's mother, stating that the younger Katherine beat the walls: 'from herself without any advice or instruction of any person'.[120] While these may seem like trivial actions and accusations, they were clearly sufficient to secure the validity of both Katherine's fits and the accusation of witchcraft against Hedlyn. However, the whole affair soon crumbled when Thomas Saunders sought assistance from a woman called Anne Godfrey.

In order to make the witchcraft accusation against Hedlyn more believable, Thomas Saunders went to Anne Godfrey (who had recently been ill) and persuaded her that her illness was caused by Hedlyn's witchcraft.[121] The intention behind this was clear: the more people who accused Hedlyn of witchcraft, the more credible Katherine's fits seemed in the eyes of those who paid to see her.[122] Thomas apparently convinced Godfrey to make a formal complaint against Hedlyn at the July Assize. However, the plan backfired and an indictment survives against Godfrey herself for pretending to be bewitched and maliciously accusing someone of a felony.[123] With Anne convicted, Katherine's bewitchment was also compromised, and she came under increasing scrutiny, ending in her being summoned by the King where she and Elizabeth Saunders confessed all. Thus, the three adults were forced to answer questions from the Attorney General, though, unfortunately, no record of the verdict of the Star Chamber has survived.

Katherine Malpas' case – while an explicit demonstration of fraud – does not diminish her role. Katherine's ability to embellish her fits and attempt to make them more credible by adding well-known aspects of demonic possession was a remarkable display of creativity. The fact that her imposture was discovered only when Godfrey's accusation of Hedlyn backfired is a testament to Katherine's performance as a demoniac; suspicions arose, but it is unclear how long she may have continued to enjoy credibility had Godfrey not become involved. While the individual consequences of Katherine's case are uncertain (outside of Godfrey's punishment), the broader implications meant another blow to the validity of child demonic possession and bewitchment cases. Though magisterial and clerical scepticism rose after these infamous impostures were discovered, the cultural, social and religious significance of children as mediators of the spiritual world did not dissipate entirely. In fact, the second Lancashire witchcraft trials of 1634 were a disturbing demonstration of the lingering power and influence of children.

More Witchcraft in Lancashire: Edmund Robinson and the 1634 Witchcraft Trials

The main account detailing the 1634 Lancashire witchcraft trials, that were instigated by eleven-year-old Edmund Robinson, comes from John Webster's work which was published forty-three years after the beginning of the event. Although they were published well after the events, Webster was an eye-witness to most of Robinson's antics as he was a curate at the church in Kildwick where Edmund visited at one point to 'discover witches'.[124] Furthermore, Webster stated that at the time of his writing he had access to original documents including the examinations of Edmund, which the magistrates involved encouraged him to include in his work.[125] Another source that is relevant to the Robinson case is the Calendar of State Papers which revealed fascinating details, including how Edmund devised his story and his motivation for doing so. Edmund Robinson's case represents a historical quagmire for the historian; he was believed by most of the locals, clerics and magistrates of the town, who imprisoned approximately nineteen people, culminating in at least seventeen convictions.[126] However, according to a later source, the judge 'respited the convicts' and reported the case to King Charles I where Edmund's imposture was eventually discovered.[127] This is roughly the extent of information acknowledged by secondary sources when Edmund's case is mentioned at all. Yet, this only scratches the surface of information and value that Edmund Robinson's case reveals about the role of children in witchcraft trials.[128]

Edmund Robinson was examined on 10 February 1633 in front of two Justices of the Peace (one of whom, John Starkie, had been a young demoniac thirty-six years earlier).[129] Edmund stated that his neighbour, Henry Parker, desired him to collect some 'bulloes', which he did.[130] After going to a field, Edmund came across two greyhounds. Noting that no one followed them,

Edmund decided to take the greyhounds and attempted to hunt with them. When the dogs refused 'he being very angry took them ... tied them to a little bush at the next hedge and with a switch ... he beat them'.[131] After Edmund beat the greyhounds, he claimed the black one turned into Dickenson's Wife and the brown one turned into a 'little boy' who Edmund claimed he did not know.[132] After becoming afraid Edmund claimed he tried to run away but Dickenson's wife offered him 'a piece of silver' for his silence whereby he refused saying 'nay thou art a witch'.[133] Dickenson's wife then pulled 'a thing like unto a bridle' from her pocket and put it on the little boy and he then turned into a white horse.[134] This is the first reference in English witchcraft trials to a bridle being placed on someone causing them to turn into a horse and be ridden, but this motif arose later in Anne Armstrong's case in 1673 and again in New England as late as 1768; it is not unlikely they learnt about this idea from Edmund's highly publicised case.[135]

According to Edmund, when he and the two witches got to a house called 'Hoarstones', Edmund admitted that a 'young woman' – whom he did not know gave him – 'flesh and bread upon a trencher and drink in a glass' which he tasted. Interestingly, no witchcraft accusations were made against Edmund, who clearly partook in the diabolical activities.[136] Edmund then followed some of the witches into a barn where he saw six people pulling on ropes where: 'there came into this informer's sight flesh smoking, butter in lumps, and milk as it were flying from the said ropes'.[137] Edmund claimed that he attempted to run home but got into an altercation with those from the barn who chased him.[138] At the end of his examination, Edmund gave nineteen names of those who were at the Hoarstones gathering. Significantly, one of those names was Jennet Device, the same woman who twenty-one years earlier was central in the first set of Pendle witchcraft trials. Jennet Device, now aged around thirty, found no safety in the invisible world as Edmund Robinson used similar tactics Device used in 1612 to now successfully denounce her as a witch. As a nine-year old, Jennet Device was lauded for her accusations against alleged witches at the Malkin Tower meeting. Now, without her status as a child, Jennet's presence at Edmund's Hoarstones meeting was not interpreted as one of an innocent bystander, but as a malevolent witch; the only element that changed was the role she was seen to have played. As a child, she had the capacity to see into the invisible world, to be able to observe and report on the activities of witches; as an adult, Jennet Device could only be guilty.

After the judge 'respited' the convicted witches – seventeen in total – and referred the case to the King, four of them were remitted to the Bishop of Chester. One of the four, Margaret Johnson (who was never even accused by Edmund) made a full confession stating that while she was not at Hoarstones the day that Edmund was, she was there on other nights.[139] Margaret admitted that the Devil did 'abuse and defile her body by committing wicked uncleanness together'.[140] Why Margaret felt pressured to confess even though she was not named by Edmund is unclear; it could be that she felt genuinely guilty of some inward transgression or perhaps she really did believe she consorted with Satan and her conscience became too heavy after accusations of witchcraft came to light.[141] With regard to those that Edmund did accuse as witches, the reality might have been more sinister.

From the records kept at the Calendar of State Papers, it appears as if Edmund and his father – who at some point became an accomplice in his fraud – blackmailed people for money or else they would accuse them as witches. For example, Mary Fisher stated:

> that if Dickenson would have given the accuser Robinson 40s [forty shillings] before the arraignment, neither he nor his son ... would have said anything against her; but when she advised her husband to give nothing, Robinson said he had no malice to any but her.[142]

Francis Dickenson later confirmed this story around June 1634 after she was questioned by the Bishop.[143] It seemed that the money-making plan that Katherine Malpas' family employed had become more sophisticated by the time Edmund Robinson and his father devised a similar idea. Rather than charging people to see the possessed child – which took a mental and physical toll on them – the Robinson family simply extorted people. If they could not or did not pay, Edmund was ready to claim they were at the Hoarstones gathering. The evidence is unclear as to whose idea it was to implement this scheme; however, it seems as if it was Edmund Robinson's father who took advantage of his son's supernatural visions. This can be pieced together from the examination of Edmund's father (also called Edmund) taken on 12 July 1634. Edmund's father stated that his son came to him last November and immediately 'gave no credit to him but sharply rebuked and corrected him' regarding his son's story of witches.[144] Nevertheless, the elder Edmund claimed that his son stuck to his story and so he believed that his son might have been 'troubled in mind' or 'imagined he had seen some vision' but claimed he 'never believed anything that the boy spoke'.[145] The elder Edmund removed any shred of guilt or responsibility from himself, claiming that he never gave any evidence against any of the accused, placing the blame for the whole affair on his eleven-year-old son.[146]

Even more astonishing is the fate of one of Edmund's accused witches, Mary Spencer. Mary was only twenty-years old when she was brought to the Bishop for questioning. She claimed that her mother and father were both condemned at the last Assize for being witches but she 'is not afraid of death for she hopes it will make an entrance for her into heaven'.[147] Being the daughter of two executed witches surely would have made Mary a prime target. Yet, it is perplexing that neither primary nor secondary sources have commented on the fact that she was an orphan and only twenty when she was accused and imprisoned; especially because she is perhaps one of the youngest people to have died following a witchcraft accusation. There appeared to be no consensus on the legal status of the accused witches following their respite from the King. Some sources claimed they were 'happily acquitted' while others stated that the accused witches may have not been released for their own protection.[148] What is clear is that due to some kind of magisterial error, ten of the accused – including Mary Spencer and Jennet Device – were still in prison in 1636.[149] Without any evidence to the contrary, it is highly likely they remained there until their deaths.[150] Including three people (possibly four) who were already dead when the Bishop came to examine them on 15 July 1634, this brings the death toll for Edmund Robinson's witchcraft affair to a total of around thirteen or fourteen people. While they may not have died on the scaffold, their imprisonment and subsequent death based on his testimony alone, serves as a powerful reminder of the influence children could still wield in matters pertaining to the supernatural. In fact, in all of Edmund's examinations, he accounted for his own agency, refusing to implicate his father. He laid out his fraud clearly and detailed his motivation and ingenuity, showing how he outsmarted his parents, the townspeople and even the judicial system.

On 10 July 1634, Edmund Robinson's first examination was taken before George Long, the Justice of the Peace for Middlesex.[151] After a brief repetition of the narrative of Edmund's original story, he stated '...that all that tale is false and feigned and has no truth at all but only as he has heard tales and reports made by women, so he framed his tale out of his own invention'.[152] Firstly, this statement highlights the significance of gossip and rumour as Edmund admitted that he conjured his story using ideas from 'tales and reports' he heard from women. Edmund continued to outline why he made up the story in the first place, stating that his mother wanted him to spin wool and fetch home her cattle. Rather than doing this, Edmund went and played with other children: 'fearing his father or mother would beat him' he made up the story 'for an excuse'.[153] Edmund's revelation that his parents would beat him if he admitted to not fulfilling their requests might reflect an abusive household, which appears to be a pattern in children who created witchcraft stories/accusations.[154] It was a way to excuse themselves or their behaviour through a medium which was culturally understood. Edmund's tale of witches at Hoarstones likely saved him a beating for playing with other children rather than doing his chores; his father, whether he believed his son's story or not, then seized the opportunity to make money from his son's 'ability' to 'discover' witches by blackmailing people. Edmund was examined a second time six days later and revealed more details on how he concocted his witchcraft story, giving more insight into how gossip and rumour influenced his witchcraft accusations and how his own agency fuelled his motivations.

When Edmund was asked why he accused certain people as witches – including Jennet Device – he stated that he had heard neighbours talk of:

> ...a witch feast that was kept at Mocking [Malkin] Tower in Pendle Forest about twenty years since to which feast divers witches came and many were apprehended and executed at Lancaster ... thereupon he framed those tales concerning the persons aforesaid because he heard the neighbours repute them for witches.[155]

Notwithstanding, Edmund was quick not to implicate anyone else in the formation of his story, '...nobody was ever acquainted with any part of his fiction or invention nor did anybody ever advise him but it merely proceeded out of his own brain'.[156] He further denies that anyone forced him to make the 'declaration'.[157] Edmund concluded by stating that at first he invented the story as an excuse but 'perceiving that many folks gave ear to him he grew confident in it more and more'.[158] As an eleven-year old, Edmund's ownership of his accountability is remarkable. While he did not appear to show remorse for his actions per se, his refusal to implicate anyone else may reveal that Edmund knew that no one but himself had the capability to create, control and conduct a trial of witches based purely on a story he invented. This appears to be related to the fact that no one else in his immediate circle held the same unique status he did in the supernatural realm. Edmund Robinson was a child who was believed by his neighbours and by the jury; by the time the judge and the King intervened, and Edmund was found to be an imposter, three people had already died in prison and one more was dying. By 1636 ten more were still languishing in prison and there is little reason to believe they were ever released. The consequences for children who were believed but then found to be frauds often came too late for those who had been falsely accused as witches. Edmund Robinson's case is a poignant reminder that while scepticism triumphed in numerous cases before, a belief in witchcraft and children's ability to identify it could, under the right circumstances, prevail.

The Civil War Interlude

The onset of the English Civil War in 1642 saw unprecedented social, political and religious upheaval which disrupted the normal functioning of everyday life, including the Assize trials.[159] While trials were still held, the political and military chaos meant that anomalies developed more freely than ever before. The starkest example of this were the infamous Matthew

Hopkins-led witchcraft trials in East Anglia between 1645 and 1647.[160] Not only did Hopkins and his assistant John Stearne implement harsher tactics, such as leading questions, sleep deprivation and the swimming test to aid their interrogations, their success as witch-hunters marked an extraordinary place in the history of English witch-hunting. Within two years, around 300 witches were arraigned and some 100 were executed in Essex and Suffolk. As Wallace Notestein stated: 'Even if [these figures] approach correctness' a remarkable determination can be made.[161] Hopkins and Stearne, in only two years' time, sent more witches to the gallows than any other magisterial court in England in the previous 160 years.[162]

Significantly though, while Hopkins and Stearne employed more torture tactics in their witch-hunting investigations, there is little mention of children in their two-year career. When children are mentioned, they reflect the same attitudes seen in works like the *Malleus Maleficarum*: children were simply innocent victims of the witches' malice.[163] It is curious that children do not feature in the East Anglia trials, but this could be because Hopkins and Stearne did not need to involve children to obtain accusations or information. Rather than turning to the invisible world, Hopkins and Stearne used the temporal one; through using physical torture and psychological manipulation, the self-titled Witch Finder General gained the information he wanted. However, the success of Hopkins and Stearne did not occur in a vacuum, nor should it be assumed that their arrival into every village or town was celebrated. Opposition did filter through different courts against Hopkins and Stearne, particularly with regard to their interrogation methods. Yet, the chaos of the Civil War bought them enough time so when the last court session renewed against them in 1647, both men had retired from their witch-hunting endeavours.[164]

The Hopkins and Stearne era represented a remarkable surge of witch-hunting in England and while children featured little in their proceedings, witchcraft trials that involved children co-existed with the East Anglia trials; both occurred simultaneously throughout the turbulent period of the Civil War. The following three examples perfectly encapsulate changing but persistent role of children in witchcraft trials throughout this period. The first example, from Devon in 1645, described how a fifteen-year-old boy called Joseph Buxford was visited by the Devil after refusing to be bound as an apprentice to a local weaver.[165] Joseph's story was deeply rooted within the context of the Civil War. For example, the treatise described 'how the Devil carried him up in the air and showed him the torments of Hell and some of the Cavalieres there…'.[166]

In Northumberland of the same year, the children of George Muschamp – though particularly his eleven-year-old daughter Margaret – became bewitched through the supposed malice of John Hutton, Dorothy Swinow and others.

While this source is challenging to decipher, as it is written in both the third and first person, the story is particularly unique as some scholars believe it is the only story of bewitchment whose authorship is attributable to a woman, although other historians disagree.[167] Margaret's symptoms aligned with other bewitchment signs that were demonstrated by other children in preceding years. For example, just like the Throckmorton children, when Margaret woke out of her fits she did not remember anything she said or did while she was in them.[168] In a similar way to William Perry, Margaret vomited 'a piece of fir-stick full of crooked pins' as well as 'stones, coals, brick, lead, straw, quills full of pins ... straw full of pins, tow and virginal wire, all full of pins...'.[169] John Hutton died in prison and the pamphlet ends somewhat abruptly with a warrant for the apprehension of Dorothy Swinow; her fate is unknown.

One last example involved a young girl called Elizabeth Parkson in Yorkshire in 1650. The accused in this instance was a widow named Ann Wagg who was 'suspected to be a witch' by her neighbours for at least three years.[170] This is evidenced by the fact that the information Francis Torratt gave on Elizabeth's behalf concerned an incident that occurred three years prior to 1650.[171] According to the information Francis gave, Ann stood in the church doorway one Sunday and 'uttered no words' but 'frowned upon the said maid' whereupon Elizabeth presently fell sick.[172] That night, Elizabeth cried out that she could see a cat and complained that the wind in her throat 'was stopped'.[173] This invocation of a malicious glance or 'evil eye' was not an uncommon weapon of the witch. In fact, Thomas Cooper, an orthodox Protestant clergyman, mentioned it in his work *The Mystery of Witchcraft* where he stated: 'though it be conceited ... the witch by her looks may affect these things [bodies and minds]'.[174] The fate of the accused in this instance also remains unknown. That children persisted as preternatural agents within the unparalleled chaos of the Civil War is a testament to how entrenched their role had become, despite obvious shifts in their society's priorities.

Even before the Civil War, children's role in witchcraft trials had become tenuous due to high-scale fraudulent cases such as Katherine Malpas. However, cases like Edmund Robinson's proved that the capacity to believe children remained and could still have devastating consequences. The conclusion of the Civil War and the period of parliamentary rule known as the Interregnum irreparably changed the political and social functioning of England. Yet, children were still tenacious mediators of the spiritual world, demonstrating that their role in witchcraft trials remained powerful and influential. Though the scepticism of the previous years continued, and the aftershocks of the Civil War were still being felt, children continued to take centre stage in witchcraft trials.

'If she denies it, I shall be ill again': Elizabeth Mallory

Elizabeth Mallory's story, while separated from the Throckmorton children's account by sixty-seven years, provides a fascinating indication of how learnt behaviour or 'traditions' were perpetuated by bewitched children. In 1656 in Yorkshire, Elizabeth Mallory, a fourteen-year-old girl from a prominent and wealthy family 'languished' without the use of her limbs for twelve weeks.[175] Elizabeth saw apparitions of a woman named Mary Waide and called out that she was a cat sitting on the window sill.[176] Like the Throckmorton girls, Elizabeth used spectral evidence against Mary Waide, telling those around her that she was being attacked by invisible manifestations of the woman no one else saw. Similar to other bewitched children, Elizabeth vomited '... blotting paper full of pins and thread tied about ... a lump of tow with pins and thread tied about it and a piece of wool and pins in it and ... two feathers and a stick', but Elizabeth added a more ingenious layer to the voiding of foreign objects.[177] When she was asked about some of the items, Elizabeth claimed she had seen them in the hands of Mary Waide, insinuating that Waide had been the one to put them inside her using her witchcraft. A very similar tactic was used in the Salem trials thirty-six years later when Sarah Nurse testified that she saw Sarah Bibber '...pull out pins out of her [purse] and h[o]ld them between her fingers and clasp her hands round her knees and then she cried out that goody Nurse pricked her'.[178]

Elizabeth continued in her denunciation of Mary who was pressured to come and see her. Apparently, she asked for Elizabeth's forgiveness and admitted she 'had done her wrong' whereupon Elizabeth was well.[179] However, upon leaving, Mary denied afflicting the young girl and Elizabeth claimed 'if she denies it, I shall be ill again'.[180] Elizabeth then resumed her fits as before, stating that she would not be well until Mary confessed or 'was carried before a justice and punished.'[181] The control Elizabeth attempted to exert over Mary was clearly reminiscent of what the Throckmorton girls had done to the Samuels family years earlier. Elizabeth then implicated Mary's husband William Waide who refused to see Elizabeth after she had sent for him 'to ask forgiveness and to repeat some words after her'.[182] This too echoes the 'formula' the Throckmorton girls devised for the Samuels family to recite. Furthermore, just as Elizabeth claimed that the items she vomited were seen in the hands of Mary, she also claimed that the pins she vomited in the presence of Anne Brown were 'the said pins in the hands of William Waide'.[183] The document ended with both the Waides being imprisoned for bewitching Elizabeth; their fate is unknown.

Elizabeth Mallory's story reflected many of the same themes the Throckmorton girls established years earlier, including attempting to get adults to say formulaic responses to ease her fits and seeing apparitions of the accused. Elizabeth also cleverly told those around her that the objects she vomited were not random but were in fact objects that belonged to the accused. Elizabeth Mallory's case demonstrates that despite the scepticism that arose throughout the reign of King James I and Charles I, as well as the turmoil of the Civil War, children still maintained a prominent position in witchcraft trials. Their status as supernatural agents endured into the Restoration of the Monarch in 1660; the learnt behaviour and traditions in cases previously had been continued, developed and expanded on. In fact, in one of the last English witchcraft trials that resulted in execution, children were again the linchpin of evidence that sent the accused to their deaths.

The 'touch test': Deborah and Elizabeth Pacy

The trial of Rose Cullender and Amy Duny at Bury St Edmunds provides valuable information pertaining to the role of children in witchcraft trials but also represents one of the most perplexing miscarriages of justice in English witch-hunting history. Even the date of the trial has been the subject of debate for historians. For example, James Sharpe claimed the trial occurred in 1662 whereas C. L'Estrange Ewen stated that it occurred in March 1664.[184] The latter seems to be confirmed by the primary source which claimed that the events occurred in 1664.[185] However, the date is only the first curiosity of this trial which began with, and was spurred on by, young children; even the author of the treatise declared that his motivation for publishing the account was to show the 'integrity' of the presiding judge Matthew Hale because of the current 'controversy' of the times.[186] Thus, his bias against the accused should not be overlooked.

The treatise concerning the trial is not set out chronologically but rather, centres around what crimes both Cullender and Duny had allegedly done to the children. The treatise then discussed the crimes the women supposedly committed against adults before outlining the findings of the jury. The fact that the document focused more on the crimes committed against the children, rather than the adults, possibly reflected their importance in the proceedings. Several children became embroiled in this case but it was the actions of Elizabeth and Deborah Pacy which are the most relevant. The Pacy sisters show how attitudes appeared – in this case – to return to an intrinsic belief in children's accusations.

Elizabeth Pacy was described as eleven-years old and her younger sister Deborah was said to be nine. The circumstances surrounding how and why they first accused Amy Duny of bewitching them is unclear; the treatise simply stated that Duny had a long-standing reputation as a witch.[187] When Elizabeth was at the Assize, she was 'senseless' until the judge forced Duny to touch her. Suddenly, Elizabeth leapt up and scratched Duny's face until blood came, showing the longevity of 'scratching', though Elizabeth's torments only worsened.[188] Similar to Duny, it is unclear why the girls included Rose

Cullender in their accusations but in a recurring theme, when the children claimed to see apparitions of Cullender attacking them, they correctly described what she was wearing as a way to validate their fits.[189] To test the authenticity of their vomiting up of pins, all of their clothes were left unpinned and Margaret Arnold, the girls' aunt, testified that 'the children afterwards raised at several times ... thirty pins in her presence'.[190] This tactic was also used later in the Salem witchcraft trials.[191] It may seem obvious that the children simply knew where the pins were kept or had a secret supply of them. However, to be able to stay one step ahead of the adults by finding ways to 'prove' their integrity is a level of ingenuity that exceeded the expectations of typical eleven- and nine-year olds.

At the trial, it was said there were 'some experiments' made against the bewitched children to test the validity of their claims but the 'touch test' yielded the most significant results. Rose Cullender was made to touch one of the Pacy girls (which one is not specified) who was blindfolded. The girl shrieked in a grievous fit and the same results occurred when Amy Duny touched the girl.[192] The judge was then persuaded to have the girl blindfolded again and have someone else touch her; she produced the exact same response as when the accused witches touched her, 'whereupon the gentlemen returned, openly protesting, that they did believe the whole transaction of this business was a mere imposture'.[193] However, Samuel Pacy, father of the two girls, made the convoluted argument 'that possibly the maid might be deceived by the suspicion that the witch touched her when she did not'.[194] This appeared to change the minds of those in court and the author of the treatise made a significant appeal to believe the children, which appeared reminiscent of earlier trials when evidence from children was considered more important as children were innocent and thought incapable of lying. His statement is worth repeating in full as it reflects how, in ninety-nine years since the first witchcraft trial that involved a child, attitudes appeared to return to accepting the sanctity of children's accusations:

> for, say they it is not possible that any should counterfeit such distempers, being accompanied with such various circumstances, much less children, and for so long time, and yet undiscovered by their parents and relations. For no man can suppose that they should all conspire together (being out of several families and as they affirm no way related one to the other and scarce of familiar acquaintance) to do an act of this nature whereby no benefit or advantage could rebound to any of the parties but a guilty conscience for perjuring themselves in taking the lives of two poor simple women away and there appears no malice in this case.[195]

The jury found both women guilty of all thirteen indictments in half an hour and it was reported that all but one afflicted child became instantly well when the conviction was delivered.[196] Amy Duny and Rose Cullender were executed on 17 March; the treatise noted 'they confessed nothing'.[197] The 1664 Bury St Edmunds trial is a stark reminder of the influence and control children maintained despite the ebb and flow of credibility. Although it was Samuel Pacy who raised the puzzling question, which made the court rethink the conclusion of the experiment, it was the status of the children themselves that made his statement believable; the sanctity of the child's evidence, the belief that they would not lie for there was no malice, was inherently a belief in children themselves. Children were the agents of the spiritual world and Samuel Pacy simply pointed it out.

The role of children in witchcraft trials during this period represents an imperfect dichotomy. Children's credibility fluctuated between those who were believed, those who were not believed and those who were a mixture of both; by the end of the seventeenth century, the cultural significance of children as preternatural actors appeared to triumph over scepticism. The Bury St Edmunds trial reflected a significant moment in English witch-hunting. Though the conclusion of the experiment and the execution of Cullender and Duny might seem like a complex and gross miscarriage of justice, the impression it made on wider society was lasting. This case was explicitly mentioned in Cotton Mather's *Wonders of the Invisible World* and it is highly likely it affected the behaviour of the accusatory girls in the Salem witchcraft trials as the 'touch test' became one of the most frequent experiments used by the judges in 1692.[198] Children's involvement in witchcraft trials in New England and the transmission of ideas from across the Atlantic pre-dated the infamous Salem trials by forty-four years. Children in New English witchcraft trials were first passive victims of the witches' malice, like those described in the *Malleus Maleficarum*. Their role developed quickly, and in an incredibly short amount of time, children played a dominant and pervasive role in witchcraft trials. What is more significant is the amount of evidence that demonstrates that New English children mimicked behaviour from children in English witchcraft trials. Once they became more prevalent in witchcraft trials in New England, children began to learn and build on their own learnt behaviour and traditions from local cases. Overall, the agency and influence of children in English and New English witchcraft trials are evident and the trajectory of their roles, while not the same, ended in similar devastating consequences.

Notes

1 The 1612 Pendle witchcraft trials are specified as there was witchcraft in 1634 which will be discussed further on.

2 Philip C. Almond, *The Lancashire Witches: A Chronicle of Sorcery and Death on Pendle Hill* (London and New York: Bloomsbury Academic, 2012), p. 13.

3 Thomas Potts, *The Wonderful Discoverie of Witches in the Countie of Lancaster...*, 2nd edn. (London: Printed by W. Stansby, 1613), sig. B2v. On the Pendle area's historic reputation see: Philip C. Almond, *The Lancashire Witches: A Chronicle of Sorcery and Death on Pendle Hill* (London and New York: Bloomsbury Academic, 2012), p. 7; Wolfgang Behringer's book on Bavarian witchcraft trials argued that by 1600 most Protestants regarded witch-hunting as a Catholic preoccupation. See Wolfgang Behringer, *Witchcraft Persecutions in Bavaria: Popular Magic, Religious Zealotry and Reason of State in Early Modern Europe* (Cambridge: Cambridge University Press, 1997).

4 Thomas Potts, *The Wonderful Discoverie of Witches in the Countie of Lancaster...*, 2nd edn. (London: Printed by W. Stansby, 1613), sig. Sv.

5 Thomas Potts, *The Wonderful Discoverie of Witches in the Countie of Lancaster...*, 2nd edn. (London: Printed by W. Stansby, 1613).

6 Thomas Potts, *The Wonderful Discoverie of Witches in the Countie of Lancaster...*, 2nd edn. (London: Printed by W. Stansby, 1613), sig. R4v-R4r.

7 Thomas Potts, *The Wonderful Discoverie of Witches in the Countie of Lancaster...*, 2nd edn. (London: Printed by W. Stansby, 1613), sig. Sr.

8 Marion Gibson, *Reading Witchcraft: Stories of Early English Witches* (London and New York: Routledge, 1999), p. 4.

9 Thomas Potts, *The Wonderful Discoverie of Witches in the Countie of Lancaster...*, 2nd edn. (London: Printed by W. Stansby, 1613), sig. R3v.

10 Thomas Potts, *The Wonderful Discoverie of Witches in the Countie of Lancaster...*, 2nd edn. (London: Printed by W. Stansby, 1613), sig. Er.

11 Thomas Potts, *The Wonderful Discoverie of Witches in the Countie of Lancaster...*, 2nd edn. (London: Printed by W. Stansby, 1613), sig. C3r.

12 Thomas Potts, *The Wonderful Discoverie of Witches in the Countie of Lancaster...*, 2nd edn. (London: Printed by W. Stansby, 1613); Philip C. Almond, *The Lancashire Witches: A Chronicle of Sorcery and Death on Pendle Hill* (London and New York: Bloomsbury Academic, 2012), pp. xvi–xvii. Covell was a gaoler, magistrate and sometimes Lancaster mayor. Lister was an enemy of accused witch Jennet Preston.

13 Ronald Seth, *Children Against Witches* (London: Robert Hale, 1969), p. 13 and Rossell Hope Robbins, *The Encyclopedia of Witchcraft and Demonology* (New York: Girard & Stewart, 1959), p. 298.

14 Thomas Potts, *The Wonderful Discoverie of Witches in the Countie of Lancaster...*, 2nd edn. (London: Printed by W. Stansby, 1613), sig. E2r.

15 Thomas Potts, *The Wonderful Discoverie of Witches in the Countie of Lancaster...*, 2nd edn. (London: Printed by W. Stansby, 1613), sig. Er.

16 Ronald Seth, *Children Against Witches* (London: Robert Hale, 1969), p. 11.

17 Thomas Potts, *The Wonderful Discoverie of Witches in the Countie of Lancaster...*, 2nd edn. (London: Printed by W. Stansby, 1613), sig. F2r.

18 Thomas Potts, *The Wonderful Discoverie of Witches in the Countie of Lancaster...*, 2nd edn. (London: Printed by W. Stansby, 1613), sig. F3v.

19 Thomas Potts, *The Wonderful Discoverie of Witches in the Countie of Lancaster...*, 2nd edn. (London: Printed by W. Stansby, 1613), sig. Gv.

20 Thomas Potts, *The Wonderful Discoverie of Witches in the Countie of Lancaster...*, 2nd edn. (London: Printed by W. Stansby, 1613), sig. Gv-Gr.

21 On the Sellys boys see above, Chapter 2, W. W., *A True and Just Recorde of the information, Examination and Confession of all the Witches...* (London: Imprinted by Thomas Dawson, 1582), sig. D1v.
22 Thomas Potts, *The Wonderful Discoverie of Witches in the Countie of Lancaster...*, 2nd edn. (London: Printed by W. Stansby, 1613), sig. Gr.
23 Thomas Potts, *The Wonderful Discoverie of Witches in the Countie of Lancaster...*, 2nd edn. (London: Printed by W. Stansby, 1613), sig. G2v.
24 Thomas Potts, *The Wonderful Discoverie of Witches in the Countie of Lancaster...*, 2nd edn. (London: Printed by W. Stansby, 1613).
25 Ronald Seth, *Children Against Witches* (London: Robert Hale, 1969), p. 92.
26 Thomas Potts, *The Wonderful Discoverie of Witches in the Countie of Lancaster...*, 2nd edn. (London: Printed by W. Stansby, 1613), sig. G4v-G4r.
27 Thomas Potts, *The Wonderful Discoverie of Witches in the Countie of Lancaster...*, 2nd edn. (London: Printed by W. Stansby, 1613), sig. G4r.
28 Thomas Potts, *The Wonderful Discoverie of Witches in the Countie of Lancaster...*, 2nd edn. (London: Printed by W. Stansby, 1613), sig. H4r.
29 Thomas Potts, *The Wonderful Discoverie of Witches in the Countie of Lancaster...*, 2nd edn. (London: Printed by W. Stansby, 1613), sig. Iv.
30 Thomas Potts, *The Wonderful Discoverie of Witches in the Countie of Lancaster...*, 2nd edn. (London: Printed by W. Stansby, 1613), sig. Iv-Ir.
31 On Boguet, see above, Chapter 2.
32 Thomas Potts, *The Wonderful Discoverie of Witches in the Countie of Lancaster...*, 2nd edn. (London: Printed by W. Stansby, 1613), sig. P2v–P2r.
33 Thomas Potts, *The Wonderful Discoverie of Witches in the Countie of Lancaster...*, 2nd edn. (London: Printed by W. Stansby, 1613), sig. P2r.
34 Thomas Potts, *The Wonderful Discoverie of Witches in the Countie of Lancaster...*, 2nd edn. (London: Printed by W. Stansby, 1613).
35 Thomas Potts, *The Wonderful Discoverie of Witches in the Countie of Lancaster...*, 2nd edn. (London: Printed by W. Stansby, 1613), sig. P3v.
36 Thomas Potts, *The Wonderful Discoverie of Witches in the Countie of Lancaster...*, 2nd edn. (London: Printed by W. Stansby, 1613), sig. Q3v–Q3r.
37 Thomas Potts, *The Wonderful Discoverie of Witches in the Countie of Lancaster...*, 2nd edn. (London: Printed by W. Stansby, 1613), sig. L4v.
38 Thomas Potts, *The Wonderful Discoverie of Witches in the Countie of Lancaster...*, 2nd edn. (London: Printed by W. Stansby, 1613), sig. Lv.
39 Thomas Potts, *The Wonderful Discoverie of Witches in the Countie of Lancaster...*, 2nd edn. (London: Printed by W. Stansby, 1613), sig. Lr.
40 Walshman was a neighbour of Sowerbutts.
41 Thomas Potts, *The Wonderful Discoverie of Witches in the Countie of Lancaster...*, 2nd edn. (London: Printed by W. Stansby, 1613), sig. L2r.
42 Thomas Potts, *The Wonderful Discoverie of Witches in the Countie of Lancaster...*, 2nd edn. (London: Printed by W. Stansby, 1613).
43 Thomas Potts, *The Wonderful Discoverie of Witches in the Countie of Lancaster...*, 2nd edn. (London: Printed by W. Stansby, 1613).
44 Thomas Potts, *The Wonderful Discoverie of Witches in the Countie of Lancaster...*, 2nd edn. (London: Printed by W. Stansby, 1613), sig. L3v.
45 Thomas Potts, *The Wonderful Discoverie of Witches in the Countie of Lancaster...*, 2nd edn. (London: Printed by W. Stansby, 1613).

46 Thomas Potts, *The Wonderful Discoverie of Witches in the Countie of Lancaster…*, 2nd edn. (London: Printed by W. Stansby, 1613).
47 This is the 1585: *Act Against Jesuits and Seminarists*, 27 Eliz. Cap. 2. In *Documents Illustrative of English Church History*, eds., Henry Gee and William John Harvey (New York: Macmillan, 1896), pp. 485–492.
48 Thomas Potts, *The Wonderful Discoverie of Witches in the Countie of Lancaster…*, 2nd edn. (London: Printed by W. Stansby, 1613), sig. M2v-M3v.
49 Some Jesuits, like Martin Delrio, were also in the forefront of promoting belief in diabolical witch stories and anti-Protestant propaganda. See Gary K. Waite, *Heresy, Magic and Witchcraft in Early Modern Europe* (Basingstoke: Palgrave Macmillan Publishers, 2003), p. 108.
50 Thomas Potts, *The Wonderful Discoverie of Witches in the Countie of Lancaster…*, 2nd edn. (London: Printed by W. Stansby, 1613), sig. M4r.
51 Historical Manuscripts Commission, *Twelfth Report, Appendix, Part IV: The Manuscripts of His Grace the Duke of Rutland, G.C.B.* vol. 1 (preserved at Belvoir Castle, 1888), p. 422.
52 G. L. Kittredge, "King James I and 'The Devil Is an Ass" *Modern Philology* 9 (No. 2, 1911), p. 200.
53 G. L. Kittredge, "King James I and 'The Devil Is an Ass" *Modern Philology* 9 (No. 2, 1911), p. 199. Kittredge postulates as much based on the fact that John Smith died unmarried at aged forty; John Nichols, *The History and Antiquities of the County of Leicester*, vol. 2, part 2 (London: printed by and for the author, 1798), p. 185.
54 Peter Elmer, *Witchcraft, Witch-Hunting, and Politics in Early Modern England* (Oxford: Oxford University Press, 2016), p. 67.
55 Reprint of a letter from Robert Heyrick to his brother Sir William, dated 18 July 1616 in G. L. Kittredge, "King James I and 'The Devil Is an Ass" *Modern Philology* 9 (No. 2, 1911), pp. 197–198.
56 The Throckmorton formula was: 'As I am a witch, and consenting to the death of Lady Cromwell, so I charge thee to depart and to let her come forth of her fit, you should presently be well' Anon., *The Most Strange and Admirable Discoverie of Three Witches of Warboys…* (London: printed by the Widow Orwin for Thomas Man and John Winnington, 1593), sig. J6v.
57 G. L. Kittredge, "King James I and 'The Devil Is an Ass" *Modern Philology* 9 (No. 2, 1911), p. 201.
58 Like he did when he discovered Anne Gunter as a fraud in 1604. For interpretations that see King James as a devout witch-hunter see Tracy Borman, *Witches: A Tale of Sorcery, Scandal and Seduction* (London: Jonathan Cape, 2013), p. 28; Malcolm Gaskill, *Witchfinders: A Seventeenth-Century English Tragedy* (London: John Murray Publishers, 2005), p. 30, and Brian Levack, *The Witch Hunt in Early Modern Europe*, 4th edn. (London and New York: Routledge, 2016), pp. 88–89. For a view that sees King James as more moderate in his witch-hunting efforts see Deborah Willis, *Malevolent Nurture: Witch-Hunting and Maternal Power in Early Modern England* (Ithaca and London: Cornell University Press, 1995), pp. 124–125.
59 Francis Osborne, *The Works of Francis Osborne…*, 7th edn. (London: Printed for R.D, 1673), p. 553.

60 Francis Osborne, *The Works of Francis Osborne...*, 7th edn. (London: Printed for R.D, 1673).
61 Francis Osborne, *The Works of Francis Osborne...*, 7th edn. (London: Printed for R.D, 1673).
62 Frederick Andrew Inderwick, *Side-lights on the Stuarts*, 2nd edn. (London: Sampson Low, Marston, Searle and Rivington, 1891), p. 150.
63 Frederick Andrew Inderwick, *Side-lights on the Stuarts*, 2nd edn. (London: Sampson Low, Marston, Searle and Rivington, 1891).
64 *Calendar of State Papers, Domestic Series, of the Reign of James I 1611-1618*, ed., Mary Anne Everett Green (Nendeln: Kraus Reprint Ltd, 1967), p. 398.
65 Anna French, *Children of Wrath: Possession, Prophecy and the Young in Early Modern England* (Oxford and New York: Routledge, 2016), p. 98.
66 R. B., *The Boy of Bilson: or, A True Discovery of the Late Notorious Impostures of a Certain Romish Priests...* (London: Imprinted by Felix Kingston for William Barret, 1622), sig. A4r.
67 Ronald Seth, *Children Against Witches* (London: Robert Hale, 1969), p. 158.
68 R. B., *The Boy of Bilson: or, A True Discovery of the Late Notorious Impostures of a Certain Romish Priests...* (London: Imprinted by Felix Kingston for William Barret, 1622), sig. H2v; John Webster, *The Displaying of Supposed Witchcraft...* (London: printed by J.M, 1677), p. 274.
69 R. B., *The Boy of Bilson: or, A True Discovery of the Late Notorious Impostures of Certain Romish Priests...* (London: Imprinted by Felix Kingston for William Barret, 1622), sig. H2v.
70 R. B., *The Boy of Bilson: or, A True Discovery of the Late Notorious Impostures of a Certain Romish Priests...* (London: Imprinted by Felix Kingston for William Barret, 1622), sig. H2r.
71 R. B., *The Boy of Bilson: or, A True Discovery of the Late Notorious Impostures of a Certain Romish Priests...* (London: Imprinted by Felix Kingston for William Barret, 1622), sig. H3v. Thrums are loose threads/end pieces that are cast away from looms or knitting.
72 R. B., *The Boy of Bilson: or, A True Discovery of the Late Notorious Impostures of a Certain Romish Priests...* (London: Imprinted by Felix Kingston for William Barret, 1622), sig. H3v–H3r.
73 R. B., *The Boy of Bilson: or, A True Discovery of the Late Notorious Impostures of a Certain Romish Priests...* (London: Imprinted by Felix Kingston for William Barret, 1622), sig. H3r. The inclusion of the letter 'p' is interesting as it may simply indicate the word 'priests' or it may have been censorship of a curse word Perry had used, such as the work 'prick.' The term 'prick', used in a derogatory sense, has origins that date back to the fifteenth century so it is not impossible to imagine that Perry used this term in his outburst. See Jonathon Green, *The Vulgar Tongue: Green's History of Slang* (Oxford: Oxford University Press, 2015), p. 24.
74 R. B., *The Boy of Bilson: or, A True Discovery of the Late Notorious Impostures of a Certain Romish Priests...* (London: Imprinted by Felix Kingston for William Barret, 1622), sig. H3r-H4v.
75 R. B., *The Boy of Bilson: or, A True Discovery of the Late Notorious Impostures of a Certain Romish Priests...* (London: Imprinted by Felix Kingston for William Barret, 1622), sig. H4v.

76 R. B., *The Boy of Bilson: or, A True Discovery of the Late Notorious Impostures of a Certain Romish Priests...* (London: Imprinted by Felix Kingston for William Barret, 1622).

77 W. W., *A True and Just Recorde of the information, Examination and Confession of all the Witches...* (London: Imprinted by Thomas Dawson, 1582), sig. F4v. By the time the witchcraft outbreak reached the Puritans of the New World in Salem, the blackbird became a yellow bird. See Bernard Rosenthal, ed., *Records of the Salem Witch-Hunt* (New York: Cambridge University Press, 2009), docs. 3, 6, 7, 16, 17, 18, 21, 180, 345, 428, 504, 516, 519.

78 R. B., *The Boy of Bilson: or, A True Discovery of the Late Notorious Impostures of a Certain Romish Priests...* (London: Imprinted by Felix Kingston for William Barret, 1622), sig. Iv.

79 R. B., *The Boy of Bilson: or, A True Discovery of the Late Notorious Impostures of a Certain Romish Priests...* (London: Imprinted by Felix Kingston for William Barret, 1622), sig. I2v.

80 R. B., *The Boy of Bilson: or, A True Discovery of the Late Notorious Impostures of a Certain Romish Priests...* (London: Imprinted by Felix Kingston for William Barret, 1622), sig. I3v.

81 R. B., *The Boy of Bilson: or, A True Discovery of the Late Notorious Impostures of a Certain Romish Priests...* (London: Imprinted by Felix Kingston for William Barret, 1622), sig. I3r, and C. L' Estrange Ewen, *Witchcraft and Demonism: A Concise Account Derived from Sworn Depositions and Confessions Obtained in the Courts of England and Wales* (London: Heath Cranton Limited, 1933), p. 237.

82 R. B., *The Boy of Bilson: or, A True Discovery of the Late Notorious Impostures of a Certain Romish Priests...* (London: Imprinted by Felix Kingston for William Barret, 1622), sig. I3v.

83 R. B., *The Boy of Bilson: or, A True Discovery of the Late Notorious Impostures of a Certain Romish Priests...* (London: Imprinted by Felix Kingston for William Barret, 1622).

84 R. B., *The Boy of Bilson: or, A True Discovery of the Late Notorious Impostures of a Certain Romish Priests...* (London: Imprinted by Felix Kingston for William Barret, 1622), sig. I4v.

85 R. B., *The Boy of Bilson: or, A True Discovery of the Late Notorious Impostures of a Certain Romish Priests...* (London: Imprinted by Felix Kingston for William Barret, 1622), sig. I4v-I4r.

86 R. B., *The Boy of Bilson: or, A True Discovery of the Late Notorious Impostures of a Certain Romish Priests...* (London: Imprinted by Felix Kingston for William Barret, 1622), sig. I4r.

87 R. B., *The Boy of Bilson: or, A True Discovery of the Late Notorious Impostures of a Certain Romish Priests...* (London: Imprinted by Felix Kingston for William Barret, 1622).

88 R. B., *The Boy of Bilson: or, A True Discovery of the Late Notorious Impostures of a Certain Romish Priests...* (London: Imprinted by Felix Kingston for William Barret, 1622), sig. Kv.

89 R. B., *The Boy of Bilson: or, A True Discovery of the Late Notorious Impostures of a Certain Romish Priests...* (London: Imprinted by Felix Kingston for William Barret, 1622).

90 R. B., *The Boy of Bilson: or, A True Discovery of the Late Notorious Impostures of a Certain Romish Priests…* (London: Imprinted by Felix Kingston for William Barret, 1622).
91 R. B., *The Boy of Bilson: or, A True Discovery of the Late Notorious Impostures of a Certain Romish Priests…* (London: Imprinted by Felix Kingston for William Barret, 1622), sig. Kr.
92 R. B., *The Boy of Bilson: or, A True Discovery of the Late Notorious Impostures of a Certain Romish Priests…* (London: Imprinted by Felix Kingston for William Barret, 1622), sig. K2v.
93 R. B., *The Boy of Bilson: or, A True Discovery of the Late Notorious Impostures of a Certain Romish Priests…* (London: Imprinted by Felix Kingston for William Barret, 1622), sig. L2v.
94 R. B., *The Boy of Bilson: or, A True Discovery of the Late Notorious Impostures of a Certain Romish Priests…* (London: Imprinted by Felix Kingston for William Barret, 1622), sig. L3v.
95 James Sharpe, *The Bewitching of Anne Gunter, A Horrible and True Story of Deception, Witchcraft, Murder, and the King of England* (New York: Routledge, 2001), p. xii.
96 R. B., *The Boy of Bilson: or, A True Discovery of the Late Notorious Impostures of a Certain Romish Priests…* (London: Imprinted by Felix Kingston for William Barret, 1622), sig. L2v.
97 Philip Almond, *Demonic Possession and Exorcism in Early Modern England: Contemporary Texts and their Cultural Contexts* (Cambridge: Cambridge University Press, 2004), p. 332.
98 Philip Almond, *Demonic Possession and Exorcism in Early Modern England: Contemporary Texts and their Cultural Contexts* (Cambridge: Cambridge University Press, 2004).
99 Peter Elmer, *Witchcraft, Witch-Hunting, and Politics in Early Modern England* (Oxford: Oxford University Press, 2016), pp. 7–8.
100 C. L' Estrange Ewen, *Witchcraft and Demonism: A Concise Account Derived from Sworn Depositions and Confessions Obtained in the Courts of England and Wales* (London: Heath Cranton Limited, 1933), p. 112. It should be noted that this is with reference to the Home Circuit for which most of the sources are extant. In the counties of Chester and Middlesex, the persecution of witches did not reach its height until later. Complete records for other circuits have unfortunately not survived.
101 STAC 8/ 32/ 13 f. 18r. Any reference to Katherine Malpas will be to Katherine Malpas the younger unless otherwise specified.
102 STAC 8/ 32/ 13 f. 18r.
103 Brian P. Levack, *The Devil Within: Possession and Exorcism in the Christian West* (New Haven and London: Yale University Press, 2013), p. 26 and Richard Raiswell, 'Faking It: A Case of Counterfeit Possession in the Reign of James I' *Renaissance and Reformation* 23 (No. 3, 1999), pp. 44 and 48.
104 STAC 8/ 32/ 13 f. 12r, q.14.
105 STAC 8/ 32/ 13 f. 16r.
106 See for example the cases of Edmund Robinson in John Webster, *The Displaying of Supposed Witchcraft…* (London: printed by J. M., 1677), p. 277; *Calendar of*

State Papers, Domestic Series, of the Reign of Charles I 1634-1635 (London: Great Britain Public Record Office, 1864), pp. 78 and 144; Sarah Williams in Samuel Harsnett, *A Declaration of Egregious Popish Impostures…* (London: printed by James Roberts, 1603), p. 182; also mentioned within Richard Bernard, *A Guide to Grand-jury Men Divided into Two Books…* (London: printed by Felix Kingston for Ed. Blackmore, 1627), pp. 35–38.

107 STAC 8/ 32/ 13 f. 10v, q.4. A half penny loaf would roughly equate to the size of modern-day round sourdough loaf.

108 STAC 8/ 32/ 12 f. 11v, q. 12.

109 STAC 8/ 32/ 12 f. 11v, q. 12.

110 STAC 8/ 32/ 13 f. 12r. q.14.

111 STAC 8/ 32/ 13 f. 3v. q. 17.

112 STAC 8/ 32/ 13 f. 6r. q. 16.

113 Francis Hutchinson, *An Historical Essay Concerning Witchcraft: With Observations Upon Matters of Fact…* (London: printed for R. Knaplock, 1718), p. 210 and Kathleen R. Sands, *Demonic Possession in Elizabethan England* (Westport: Praeger, 2004), p. 195.

114 Francis Young, *A History of Anglican Exorcism: Deliverance and Demonology in Church Ritual* (New York and London: Bloomsbury Publishing, 2018), p. 180.

115 STAC 8/ 32/ 13 f. 9r. q. 18 and STAC 8/ 32/ 13 f. 9r. q. 22.

116 STAC 8/ 32/ 13 f. 7v. q. 21.

117 STAC 8/ 32/ 13 f. 6v. q. 18.

118 STAC 8/ 32/ 13 f. 6v. q. 18; Seeing the witch as a swarm of bees was unusual for the English context, however, in 1545 the residents of Saint-Julien-de-Maurienne in France attempted to sue a plague of flies for destroying a vineyard. See Darren Oldridge, *Strange Histories: The Trial of the Pig, The Walking Dead and Other Matters of Fact from the Medieval and Renaissance Worlds* (London and New York: Routledge, 2007), p. 69. For other examples of animals being tried as criminals see Thomas A. Fudgé, *Medieval Religion and its Anxieties: History and Mystery in the* Other *Middle Ages* (New York: Palgrave Macmillan, 2016), pp. 14–50.

119 STAC 8/ 32/ 13 f. 2r. q. 7.

120 STAC 8/ 32/ 13 f. 10v. q. 7.

121 STAC 8/ 32/ 13 f. 9r. q. 19.

122 STAC 8/ 32/ 13 f. 9r. q. 19.

123 ASSI 35/ 63/ 7.

124 John Webster, *The Displaying of Supposed Witchcraft…* (London: printed by J. M., 1677), p. 277.

125 John Webster, *The Displaying of Supposed Witchcraft…* (London: printed by J. M., 1677), p. 346.

126 John Webster, *The Displaying of Supposed Witchcraft…* (London: printed by J. M., 1677), p. 348; Notestein stated that historians cannot be certain of how many people were imprisoned as a result of Robinson's testimony. Provided here is the approximate number of nineteen as this was how many people Robinson named in his accusations. Wallace Notestein, *A History of Witchcraft in England, From 1558 to 1718* (Baltimore: The American Historical Association, 1911), p. 119.

127 Thomas Dunham Whitaker, *An History of the Original Parish of Whalley, and Honor of Clitheroe, in the Counties of Lancaster and York* (London: Nichols and Son, 1818), p. 215.
128 See for example Peter Elmer, *Witchcraft, Witch-Hunting, and Politics in Early Modern England* (Oxford: Oxford University Press, 2016), pp. 249–250 and James Sharpe, *Instruments of Darkness: Witchcraft in Early Modern England* (Philadelphia: University of Pennsylvania Press, 1997), pp. 78 and 164.
129 John Webster, *The Displaying of Supposed Witchcraft…* (London: printed by J.M, 1677), p. 346. The bewitchment of John Starkie and his siblings, who were also dispossessed by John Darrell, can be seen in John Darrell, *A True Narration of the Strange and Grievous Vexation by the Devil of Seven Persons in Lancashire* (London: publisher unknown, 1600).
130 John Webster, *The Displaying of Supposed Witchcraft…* (London: printed by J.M, 1677), p. 346. Bulloes are a type of wild plum.
131 John Webster, *The Displaying of Supposed Witchcraft…* (London: printed by J.M, 1677), A switch is another word for rod.
132 John Webster, *The Displaying of Supposed Witchcraft…* (London: printed by J.M, 1677).
133 John Webster, *The Displaying of Supposed Witchcraft…* (London: printed by J.M, 1677).
134 John Webster, *The Displaying of Supposed Witchcraft…* (London: printed by J.M, 1677).
135 ASSI 45/ 10/ 3/ 34, 36, 40, 43–44 and J. Hammond Trumbull, ed., *The Memorial History of Hartford County Connecticut 1633-1884*, vol. 2 (Boston: Edward L. Osgood Publisher, 1886), p. 51.
136 John Webster, *The Displaying of Supposed Witchcraft…* (London: printed by J.M, 1677), p. 347.
137 John Webster, *The Displaying of Supposed Witchcraft…* (London: printed by J.M, 1677).
138 John Webster, *The Displaying of Supposed Witchcraft…* (London: printed by J.M, 1677).
139 Thomas Dunham Whitaker, *An History of the Original Parish of Whalley, and Honor of Clitheroe, in the Counties of Lancaster and York* (London: Nichols and Son, 1818), p. 216.
140 Thomas Dunham Whitaker, *An History of the Original Parish of Whalley, and Honor of Clitheroe, in the Counties of Lancaster and York* (London: Nichols and Son, 1818).
141 For a useful discussion on the internal pressures that may cause women to voluntarily confess to witchcraft see Louise Jackson, 'Witches, Wives and Mothers' in *The Witchcraft Reader*, ed., Darren Oldridge, 3rd edn. (London and New York: Routledge, 2019), pp. 347–360.
142 *Calendar of State Papers, Domestic Series, of the Reign of Charles I 1634-1635* (London: Great Britain Public Record Office, 1864), p. 78.
143 *Calendar of State Papers, Domestic Series, of the Reign of Charles I 1634-1635* (London: Great Britain Public Record Office, 1864), pp. 78 and 98.
144 *Calendar of State Papers, Domestic Series, of the Reign of Charles I 1634-1635* (London: Great Britain Public Record Office, 1864), p. 144. Any mention to Edmund Robinson will refer to the younger Edmund unless otherwise stated.

145 *Calendar of State Papers, Domestic Series, of the Reign of Charles I 1634-1635* (London: Great Britain Public Record Office, 1864).
146 *Calendar of State Papers, Domestic Series, of the Reign of Charles I 1634-1635* (London: Great Britain Public Record Office, 1864).
147 *Calendar of State Papers, Domestic Series, of the Reign of Charles I 1634-1635* (London: Great Britain Public Record Office, 1864), p. 79.
148 Rossell Hope Robbins, *The Encyclopedia of Witchcraft and Demonology* (London: Girard and Stewart, 1959), p. 382 and Samuel R. Gardiner, *History of England from the Accession of James I to the Outbreak of the Civil War 1603-1642*, vol. VII, 1629-1635 (London, New York and Bombay: Longmans, Green and Co. 1899), p. 326
149 Susan Maria Ffarington, 'The Farington Papers. The Shrievalty of William Ffarington, Esq; a.d. 1636; Documents relating to Civil War...' in *Remains Historical and Literary Connected with the Palatine Counties of Lancaster and Chester*, The Chetham Society, vol. 39 (Worden: Printed for the Chetham Society, 1856), p. 27.
150 Herbert Berry, 'The Globe Bewitched and "El Hombre Fiel", *Medieval & Renaissance Drama in England* 1 (1984), p. 229.
151 *Calendar of State Papers, Domestic Series, of the Reign of Charles I 1634-1635* (London: Great Britain Public Record Office, 1864), p. 141.
152 *Calendar of State Papers, Domestic Series, of the Reign of Charles I 1634-1635* (London: Great Britain Public Record Office, 1864).
153 *Calendar of State Papers, Domestic Series, of the Reign of Charles I 1634-1635* (London: Great Britain Public Record Office, 1864).
154 See the cases of Mildred Norrington, Henry and John Sellys in the St Osyth trial (discussed in Chapter 2), as well as Jennet Device explored above.
155 *Calendar of State Papers, Domestic Series, of the Reign of Charles I 1634-1635* (London: Great Britain Public Record Office, 1864), p. 152.
156 *Calendar of State Papers, Domestic Series, of the Reign of Charles I 1634-1635* (London: Great Britain Public Record Office, 1864).
157 *Calendar of State Papers, Domestic Series, of the Reign of Charles I 1634-1635* (London: Great Britain Public Record Office, 1864), pp. 152–153.
158 *Calendar of State Papers, Domestic Series, of the Reign of Charles I 1634-1635* (London: Great Britain Public Record Office, 1864), p. 153.
159 J. S. Cockburn, *A History of English Assizes 1558-1714* (Cambridge: Cambridge University Press, 1972), p. 241.
160 Malcolm Gaskill, *Witchfinders: A Seventeenth-Century English Tragedy* (London: John Murray Publishers, 2005), p. 13.
161 Wallace Notestein, *A History of Witchcraft in England, From 1558 to 1718* (Baltimore: The American Historical Association, 1911), p. 151.
162 Wallace Notestein, *A History of Witchcraft in England, From 1558 to 1718* (Baltimore: The American Historical Association, 1911).
163 Matthew Hopkins, *The Discovery of Witches...* (Norfolk, published by Matthew Hopkins, 1647), unpaginated: answer to question 6.
164 Wallace Notestein, *A History of Witchcraft in England, From 1558 to 1718* (Baltimore: The American Historical Association, 1911), p. 149.
165 Anon, *A True and Strange Relation of a Boy who was Entertained by the Devil to be a Servant to Him...* (London: Printed by J. H, 1645), p. 2.

166 Anon, *A True and Strange Relation of a Boy who was Entertained by the Devil to be a Servant to Him...* (London: Printed by J. H, 1645), title page.
167 Philip Almond, *Demonic Possession and Exorcism in Early Modern England: Contemporary Texts and their Cultural Contexts* (Cambridge: Cambridge University Press, 2004), p. 358; Diane Purkiss, 'Invasions: Prophecy and Bewitchment in the Case of Margaret Muschamp' *Tulsa Studies in Women's Literature* 17 (No 2, 1998), p. 235 stated that the source was written by Margaret's mother; Wallace Notestein, *A History of Witchcraft in England, From 1558 to 1718* (Baltimore: The American Historical Association, 1911), p. 282 claimed it was written by a friend of Margaret's mother.
168 Mary Moor, *Wonderfull newes from the North. Or, A True Relation of the Sad and Grievous Torments Inflicted Upon the Bodies of Three Children of Mr. George Muschamp...* (London: Printed by T.H,. 1650), p. 1.
169 Mary Moor, *Wonderfull newes from the North. Or, A True Relation of the Sad and Grievous Torments Inflicted Upon the Bodies of Three Children of Mr. George Muschamp...* (London: Printed by T.H,. 1650), p. 16.
170 J. Charles Cox, *Three Centuries of Derbyshire Annals as Illustrated by the Records of the Quarter Sessions of the County of Derby from Queen Elizabeth to Queen Victoria*, vol. 2 (London: Bemrose and Sons, 1890), p. 89.
171 J. Charles Cox, *Three Centuries of Derbyshire Annals as Illustrated by the Records of the Quarter Sessions of the County of Derby from Queen Elizabeth to Queen Victoria*, vol. 2 (London: Bemrose and Sons, 1890).
172 J. Charles Cox, *Three Centuries of Derbyshire Annals as Illustrated by the Records of the Quarter Sessions of the County of Derby from Queen Elizabeth to Queen Victoria*, vol. 2 (London: Bemrose and Sons, 1890).
173 J. Charles Cox, *Three Centuries of Derbyshire Annals as Illustrated by the Records of the Quarter Sessions of the County of Derby from Queen Elizabeth to Queen Victoria*, vol. 2 (London: Bemrose and Sons, 1890).
174 Thomas Cooper, *The Mystery of Witchcraft: Discovering the Truth, Nature, Occasions, Growth and Power thereof...* (London: printed by Nicholas Okes, 1617), p. 163.
175 ASSI 45/ 5/ 3/ f. 132.
176 ASSI 45/ 5/ 3/ f. 132.
177 ASSI 45/ 5/ 3/ f. 132.
178 Bernard Rosenthal, ed., *Records of the Salem Witch-Hunt* (New York: Cambridge University Press, 2009), doc. 366.
179 ASSI 45/ 5/ 3/ f. 132.
180 ASSI 45/ 5/ 3/ f. 132.
181 ASSI 45/ 5/ 3/ f. 132.
182 The Publications of the Surtees Society, *Depositions from The Castle of York relating to offences Committed in The Northern Counties in the Seventeenth Century*, vol. 40 (London: 1840), p. 78.
183 ASSI 45/ 5/ 3/ f. 133.
184 James Sharpe, *Instruments of Darkness: Witchcraft in Early Modern England* (Philadelphia: University of Pennsylvania Press, 1997), p. 224 and C. L' Estrange Ewen, *Witchcraft and Demonism: A Concise Account Derived from Sworn*

Depositions and Confessions Obtained in the Courts of England and Wales (London: Heath Cranton Limited, 1933), p. 347.
185 This date also appears to be confirmed by other historians such as Wallace Notestein see Wallace Notestein, *A History of Witchcraft in England, From 1558 to 1718* (Baltimore: The American Historical Association, 1911), p. 367.
186 Anon, *A Tryal of Witches, at the Assizes Held at Bury St. Edmunds for the County of Suffolk, on the Tenth Day of March, 1664, before Sir Matthew Hale Kt., then the Lord Chief Baron of His Majesties Court of Exchequer* (London: printed for William Shrewsbery, 1682), p. i.
187 Anon, *A Tryal of Witches, at the Assizes Held at Bury St. Edmunds for the County of Suffolk, on the Tenth Day of March, 1664, before Sir Matthew Hale Kt., then the Lord Chief Baron of His Majesties Court of Exchequer* (London: printed for William Shrewsbery, 1682), p. 4.
188 Anon, *A Tryal of Witches, at the Assizes Held at Bury St. Edmunds for the County of Suffolk, on the Tenth Day of March, 1664, before Sir Matthew Hale Kt., then the Lord Chief Baron of His Majesties Court of Exchequer* (London: printed for William Shrewsbery, 1682), p. 13.
189 Anon, *A Tryal of Witches, at the Assizes Held at Bury St. Edmunds for the County of Suffolk, on the Tenth Day of March, 1664, before Sir Matthew Hale Kt., then the Lord Chief Baron of His Majesties Court of Exchequer* (London: printed for William Shrewsbery, 1682), p. 20.
190 Anon, *A Tryal of Witches, at the Assizes Held at Bury St. Edmunds for the County of Suffolk, on the Tenth Day of March, 1664, before Sir Matthew Hale Kt., then the Lord Chief Baron of His Majesties Court of Exchequer* (London: printed for William Shrewsbery, 1682), pp. 24–25.
191 Rosenthal, *Records,* docs. 16 and 18.
192 Anon, *A Tryal of Witches, at the Assizes Held at Bury St. Edmunds for the County of Suffolk, on the Tenth Day of March, 1664, before Sir Matthew Hale Kt., then the Lord Chief Baron of His Majesties Court of Exchequer* (London: printed for William Shrewsbery, 1682), pp. 43–45
193 Anon, *A Tryal of Witches, at the Assizes Held at Bury St. Edmunds for the County of Suffolk, on the Tenth Day of March, 1664, before Sir Matthew Hale Kt., then the Lord Chief Baron of His Majesties Court of Exchequer* (London: printed for William Shrewsbery, 1682), p. 45.
194 Anon, *A Tryal of Witches, at the Assizes Held at Bury St. Edmunds for the County of Suffolk, on the Tenth Day of March, 1664, before Sir Matthew Hale Kt., then the Lord Chief Baron of His Majesties Court of Exchequer* (London: printed for William Shrewsbery, 1682).
195 Anon, *A Tryal of Witches, at the Assizes Held at Bury St. Edmunds for the County of Suffolk, on the Tenth Day of March, 1664, before Sir Matthew Hale Kt., then the Lord Chief Baron of His Majesties Court of Exchequer* (London: printed for William Shrewsbery, 1682), p. 47.
196 Anon, *A Tryal of Witches, at the Assizes Held at Bury St. Edmunds for the County of Suffolk, on the Tenth Day of March, 1664, before Sir Matthew Hale Kt., then the Lord Chief Baron of His Majesties Court of Exchequer* (London: printed for William Shrewsbery, 1682), p. 56–57.

197 Anon, *A Tryal of Witches, at the Assizes Held at Bury St. Edmunds for the County of Suffolk, on the Tenth Day of March, 1664, before Sir Matthew Hale Kt., then the Lord Chief Baron of His Majesties Court of Exchequer* (London: printed for William Shrewsbery, 1682), p. 59.

198 Cotton Mather, *The Wonders of the Invisible World: being an account of the tryals of several witches lately executed in New England...* (London: John Russell Smith, 1862 [originally published 1692]), p. 119.

5

1648–1688, THE NEW ENGLISH CHILDREN THAT SET THE SCENE AND THE CHILDREN THAT SHOOK THE ADULT WORLD

In early 1630, aboard the *Arabella*, John Winthrop delivered a passionate sermon to those making their way to the New World, stating:

> the eyes of all people are upon us; so that if we shall deal falsely with our God in this work we have undertaken and so cause him to withdraw his present help from us, we shall be made a story and a by-word through the world.[1]

Indeed, the story of Massachusetts Bay has been told countless times; the first formal history of the colony was published only twenty-five years after the original landing, and generations of historians since have offered their perspective of those 'remarkable times'.[2] The English Puritans who arrived in New England were embarking on a new, dangerous and bold mission that was fraught with external and internal challenges from its inception. While it is beyond the scope of this work to delve deep into the surrounding context of the early settlement phase of colonial America, it is essential to establish some contextual characteristics of the early New Englanders.

After outlining the basic contextual features of the New World and the Puritans who settled it, this chapter focuses on Massachusetts, Connecticut and New Hampshire where witchcraft cases predominated in the New World.[3] Yet, it must be noted that while all proceedings were recorded, most trial records have disappeared, which hampers an in-depth analysis of many of New England's witch trials.[4] According to David D. Hall, there were no convictions for witchcraft in Rhode Island and relatively few persecutions in New York, Pennsylvania and Virginia.[5] Notwithstanding, the first recorded witchcraft accusation documented in the New World did come from the

DOI: 10.4324/9781003685319-6

colony of Virginia in 1626. Amongst other accusations, this case involved a young, unnamed girl who was threatened by a woman called Goodwife Wright, who told her that if she did not bring in the lightwood, 'she would make her dance stark naked'.[6] While this case did go to court, there is no record of any judiciary punishment against Wright.[7] However, this very early example demonstrates that ideas about witchcraft were at least circulating in the New World by the time Winthrop and other Puritans settled in Massachusetts.

Much of the information about the early settlers is shrouded in obscurity; records are few, and thus historians have to piece together an understanding of the goals and strategies of the leaders who left England in the 1630s to form a new Godly Commonwealth in the New World.[8] The first important characteristic about these early settlers is that they were inherently English and thought of themselves as such.[9] The men and women who came to the New World attempted to complete the Reformation by setting up a 'city upon a hill' for Christendom that Old England could admire and perhaps emulate.[10] According to Perry Miller's *New England Mind* – which still remains prominent in 'the settlement culture of New England's' scholarship – the New World provided the 'ideal laboratory' for a Godly community to be established that was free from English, Anglican control.[11] Miller emphasised the intellectual strength of these ventures, stressing the 'majesty and coherence' of Puritan thought.[12] Of course, there have been criticisms from scholars who have argued for more pluralistic or polyvocal forces behind the settlement and growth of New England, but all agree that religion – particularly Puritanism – was a defining factor in the establishment and growth of the infant colony.[13]

It is important to note that the Puritan mission, indeed, the colony itself, was constantly under threat by wars with the Indians and harsh winters which often led to starvation.[14] Even when the settlers became more established in the New World, internal difficulties arose which threatened the ideal of Puritan hegemony. This included the influx of Quakers in the mid-1650s and the Half-Way Covenant in 1662 which allowed baptised but unconverted parents to present their children for baptism.[15] Conversion experiences were required before one could gain church membership, but they were becoming less common amongst the second-generation colonists.[16] Hence, the Half-Way Covenant was thought of as a solution to this issue. The Half-Way Covenant was highly controversial and permanently diluted the idea of maintaining Puritan dominance throughout the colony.[17] For those who had come to the New World in pursuit of establishing a Godly Commonwealth, the abandonment of the Puritan mission alluded not just to social change but societal extinction. It is unsurprising then, given the challenges early New Englanders faced, that witchcraft accusations arose. Puritans were no strangers to witchcraft lore and beliefs, and the 1626 witchcraft case in Virginia demonstrated this in the New World.[18] Witchcraft confessions confirmed belief in the Devil and thus in God and helped establish religious and moral norms. Another important characteristic to note about New England revolves around its charter and its legal status, which affected not only its existence as a colony but also how it was able to prosecute witchcraft trials.

Few details are known regarding the precise arrangements of the first charter; however, the bare narrative reveals much about 'the practical temper which lay below the surface of Puritan idealism'.[19] The first charter, granted by King Charles I in 1629, served as a title to land in New England and operated as their fundamental constitution. This document provided the government of Massachusetts Bay with its only legal claim for almost sixty years.[20] The charter itself was quite liberal in that it stipulated that the colony could make its own laws, only requiring that they did not conflict with English laws.[21] Yet, New England's statutes did not have time to 'mature gracefully' like the common law of England. Hence, the laws of the colony contained a mix of Puritan ideals of discipline (taken from the Old Testament), as well as traditional safeguards (taken from English law).[22] Furthermore, the Puritans who travelled from England were not overly skilled in jurisprudence, and developing laws for New England took several years. In 1641 a brief bill of rights, known since as the Body of Liberties was passed by the General Court, and in 1648 a comprehensive code of law was officially adopted.[23]

Unlike England, New England did not have an Assize system but rather three levels of courts which existed in Massachusetts and, with slight variations, in Connecticut and New Haven.[24] The lowest level of court was the local magistrate, who was someone empowered by the governor to hear and decide on certain kinds of cases. The second level of county courts was where several magistrates conducted trials and decided verdicts. It was often these kinds of courts where people accused others of being witches. Where evidence seemed credible, a county court referred a case of witchcraft to the highest court. The highest court, the Court of Assistants, was where a grand jury was summoned to issue an indictment, and a trial by jury followed. The Assistants (or magistrates) could accept or overturn the verdict. In general (with few exceptions), the people being examined or tried were not represented by attorneys.[25]

The laws and court system of New England were not only a code to protect the inhabitants of the Puritan colony but also 'an attempt to spell out the dimensions of the New English way'.[26] The colonists had to grapple with what was old in the process of starting new: 'by accepting the Bible as their spiritual parentage, England as their political parentage, and a trading company as their economic parentage, the colonists of the Bay owed their corporate identity to a wide assortment of elements'.[27] Throughout this process, the Puritans, in a harsh land with unfamiliar faces and unforeseen challenges, must have found the idea of implementing their mission somewhat challenging. Nevertheless, by attempting to define what they *were*, the Puritans also attempted to seek new ways of measuring what they were *not*. Increasingly, they looked for signs and shapes of the Devil – their dark and looming adversary – as one of the surest ways of proving their own identity as a community and as an individual. It did not take long before the Devil infected the Godly Commonwealth, and the first detailed execution for witchcraft in New England was in Charlestown, Massachusetts, in 1648, the same year the Body of Liberties was passed.[28] As with the first documented case in Old England, children featured prominently in this case, demonstrating that the agents of the invisible world had found their place in this new 'city upon a hill'.

Although their law systems were different, it is useful to make a comparison between Old and New English witch-hunting, while making allowances in differences in population, time period and an overall lack of complete data. The English county of Essex, being one of the areas with the most complete data, can provide a standard measure. James Sharpe found that over the span of 120 years, about 650 people were indicted for witchcraft, resulting in at least seventy-four executions.[29] For the whole of England, C. L'Estrange Ewen estimated that there were just under 1000 executions.[30] Sharpe, revisiting these numbers, concluded that there were likely 1000 indictments and 300 executions for the whole of England during the witch-hunting period.[31] Considering New England's contribution to witchcraft history – chronologically speaking – came relatively late, the infant English colony can be thought of as being as active, if not, 'probably a good deal more so' in finding and persecuting witches than Old England.[32] In only forty years, the role of children in New English witchcraft trials developed from silent victims, to children who had the ability to affect judicial outcomes using their spectral knowledge. It is clear, then, with the sources available, that children played an active and persistent role in both English and New English cases from the first to the last documented early modern witchcraft trials.

'A malignant touch': Margaret Jones

The first detailed case of witchcraft in New England involved a woman named Margaret Jones who was a healer, possibly a cunning woman and, according to John Winthrop, a fortune teller. The details surrounding her case are sparse, but Winthrop provided some information about her in his journal which provides valuable insight into beliefs about witchcraft that were circulating around this time, as well as the role children played in it. In his journal, Winthrop outlined the evidence against Jones in numeric order (numbering six in total), but it is the first and last of these accusations that are particularly relevant. The first accusation, and possibly the most damning against her, was that Jones 'was found to have such a malignant touch' that men, women and children were taken sick or have other 'violent pains' if she 'stroked or touched [them] with any affection or displeasure'.[33] Having an evil touch was a typical example of *maleficium*, and the clarification that Jones' intention apparently did not matter – that she could have touched someone lovingly or violently with the same end result – was meant to add fear and terror to her characterisation as a witch.

The last accusation against Jones claimed that while in prison,

> in the clear daylight, there was seen in her arms, she sitting on the floor and her clothes up … a little child, which ran from her into another room and the officer following it, it vanished. The like child was seen in two other places, to which she had relation; and one maid that saw it, fell sick upon it….[34]

Firstly, that multiple people testified to seeing an apparition of a child is striking in that they may have been either mad or lying, or they were (or had been) convinced they saw something they did not. Regardless, seeing a child must have been a poignant image as children's liminal status was well understood in the New World just as it had been in the Old. Hence, it may have further strengthened Jones' reputation as a witch if multiple people saw her with a figure of an invisible child with her in her prison cell. Furthermore, the two references to Jones having 'relation' to the child are ambiguous; it could either mean the child was related to her, or perhaps Winthrop was suggesting she had sexual relations with it. That Jones was accused of being in her prison cell with 'her clothes up' may be a reference to her suckling the child. One of the earlier accusations against Jones was that a 'teat' was found in her 'secret parts' that looked like it had been 'newly sucked'.[35] This was discovered under duress during a 'forced search'.[36]

Of course, it is highly dubious the child existed, but if multiple people attested to seeing an incorporeal child, as well as seeing a sucked teat in Jones' private parts, it is somewhat unsurprising to concoct a story about how she might have suckled the child from within her prison cell. Thus, the child in this instance becomes a demonic figure, a protégé of the witch.[37] Margaret Jones, one of the first witches in New England, was thus convicted of harming good, innocent Puritan children with her malignant touch, but perhaps was also thought to have fed and nurtured invisible, demonic children with her body. Instances of invisible (and almost certainly demonic) children were also mentioned in Old England, such as Edmund Robinson's story which had only occurred fourteen years previously.[38] An invisible 'black' child was also purportedly seen by the Throckmorton children in the infamous Witches of Warboys case in 1589.[39] Yet, references to seeing invisible children can be traced back to Katherine Wright's case in 1586,

Derbyshire, when she became afraid at the sight of a 'child without feet'.[40] It is possible these cases were known to the newly arrived English Puritans who settled in the New World, but whether they directly inspired the invisible child in this narrative remains speculative. One of the last important elements to note in Margaret Jones' case is the court order that she be watched – just like Matthew Hopkins had done to accused witches in East Anglia around the same time – to procure evidence.[41] It is likely that it was during these long nights of watching Margaret Jones that the invisible child appeared; she was executed a month later on 15 June 1648.

Children as Victims: 1651 Parsons and Kendall Cases

The next two witchcraft cases in New England that involved children occurred in 1651 in Springfield and Cambridge, Massachusetts. The first revolved around a couple called Mary and Hugh Parsons. Their case is rich in detail with thirty-five of their neighbours providing depositions to the magistrates against Hugh.[42] The case itself is highly convoluted; Mary accused her husband Hugh of witchcraft but was then herself accused, only to be found guilty of infanticide. It is unclear whether her execution went ahead.[43] The information given in the depositions against Hugh Parsons is just as challenging to interpret as it included details pertaining to an alleged magic pudding, an imaginary dog, a missing trowel and an enchanted beer tap.[44] However, one of the most noteworthy accusations against Hugh was his involvement in the supposed bewitchment of the children of Reverend George Moxon.[45]

The two young girls, Martha and Rebekah, fell ill after their father and Hugh Parsons had a dispute about Hugh's building of Moxon's chimney.[46] Interestingly, it was not Moxon that first made the accusation but Hugh's wife, Mary, who would be his chief accuser. In the opening of the deposition about the Moxon girls, the document reads: 'your wife [Mary] says that she suspects you may be the cause of all the evil that is befallen to Mr Moxon's children…'.[47] Mary's procurement of Moxon as an accuser against her husband may have been an attempt to strengthen her own accusations of witchcraft against Hugh. George Moxon was the first pastor of Springfield and one of its largest property holders, a graduate of Cambridge and a former representative to the General Court.[48] Hence, Moxon's opinions would have likely found a receptive hearing amongst society. The reason why Mary Parsons attempted to rally such people against her husband alludes to marital difficulties being at the core of this particular witch-hunt.[49] Certainly, other details emerged later in the case which seemed to support this view. For example, Mary and Hugh were apparently always quarrelling, and Mary testified that her husband once attempted to throw a block of wood at her head.[50] Yet, suspicions about Hugh's character – and therefore his possible affiliation with the Devil – arose not because of his relationship with his wife but because of the relationship with his deceased child.

It soon became apparent that Reverend Moxon, while he supported the accusation against Hugh, was not as fervent in his pursuit of Hugh as Mary would have liked. Thus, Mary Parsons took a different approach, realising that a bewitchment accusation would work best if she used her *own* children. Mary claimed that part of the reason she suspected her husband to be a witch was because he did not grieve the loss of their child. Mary had not kept this thought to herself either, telling the magistrates: 'I have spoken of it to him and to other folks together above forty times'.[51] Predictably, many in the community expressed confusion as to why Hugh did not show outward concern or grief for his deceased child; something Hugh attributed to wanting to show respect for his wife as she was 'of the weak condition', simply stating that he was grieving privately.[52] However, to Mary and others, not mourning openly for his child was proof that Hugh had bewitched the child to death. Part of the evidence admitted into court included when Mary spoke 'very harsh things against him before his face' regarding the death of the child, and in response, Hugh simply ignored her, stating that he was used to her abuse.[53] Remarkably, it was objected that if Hugh was innocent about the death of his child, 'he would have reproved her speeches'.[54] Hugh Parsons was found guilty of witchcraft and sentenced to death.

Although a number of – albeit unusual – accusations were laid against him, it was the accusations of causing harm against children that were the most damning, as it was a demonstration of direct *maleficia*. However, when Hugh's case came to the General Court, they overturned the verdict and he fled to Rhode Island.[55] Although the children's role in this case appears passive, it was not coincidental. Mary likely knew that an accusation of harming children was the best way to secure a conviction against her husband. By involving the pastor, a wealthy gentleman whose opinions were deeply considered, as well as adding accusations concerning the welfare of her own children, Mary mounted a damning case against Hugh's character. Other than the invisible demonic child Margaret Jones was seen with, children played the role of the innocent, almost sanctified victim that the *Malleus Maleficarum* had made them out to be almost 165 years earlier.[56] They were easy targets of the witches' malice, but more specifically, they also represented the hope and continuation of the Puritan mission in the New World.

This pattern continued in another witchcraft trial in 1651 in Cambridge, Massachusetts, which was a much briefer affair than the trial of Mary and Hugh Parsons. According to John Hale, whose *A Modest Enquiry* is the only source that mentions this case, an unnamed nurse accused Mistress Kendall of bewitching to death the child of Goodman Gennings.[57] According to Hale, the court took this evidence 'among others' and Mistress Kendall was found guilty and executed; it was reported that Goodman Gennings knew nothing about the proceedings. Unfortunately, too late for Kendall, when Goodman Gennings found out about the execution, he claimed he never suspected her to be a witch and thought the child died of exposure to the cold as a consequence of the aforementioned nurse's neglect. In an ironic twist of fate, the nurse was put into prison for adultery and died awaiting trial.[58]

Thomas O'Malley, who undertook extensive research on this case, is 'strongly of the opinion that the Kendall case never existed', and Hale simply added it to embellish his book.[59] Whether the account was fictional or not does not detract from what it represented. The significance of this story showed that the nurse was astute enough to blame her own negligence on Mistress Kendall and accuse her of bewitching the child to death, securing a conviction and thus absolving her own guilt. Hence, this case helps affirm that the role of children in these early cases was that they could be weaponised by those wishing to effectively denounce someone as a witch. Mary Parsons knew it, and John Hale clearly knew it too as the story of Mistress Kendall, real or not, appeared to go unchallenged for over 200 years. However, the role of children in New English witchcraft trials drastically shifted in only two years after these cases, ushering in a new wave of agency that only became stronger and more refined over the next forty years until it culminated in the devastating Salem trials.

'Look how she lies...': The Goodyear and Lamberton Children

Elizabeth Godman was a widow living in the house of Deputy Governor Stephen Goodyear in New Haven, 1653.[60] Godman was charged with the usual accusations of witchcraft such as causing the sickness of animals and having magical abilities, such as knowing what others had said.[61] Yet, it is the information given by Goodyear's daughters Hannah and Sellevant that is of particular interest, as it represented an increased involvement of children in witchcraft trials. According to their father, who testified in court on their behalf, Hannah and Sellevant were sleeping in the chamber under Elizabeth Godman when they were 'awakened with a great fumbling at the chamber door'.[62] The girls, clearly terrified, listened in the darkness as they heard something 'which jumbled at the other end of the room and about the trunk'.[63] Hannah called for her father, but he did not hear 'which made her more afraid'.[64] Clothes were then allegedly pulled off their bed 'two or three times' whereby Hannah called for her father 'so loud as was thought [it] might be heard to the meeting-house'.[65] When Mr Goodyear eventually came to the aid of the girls, he immediately went to Elizabeth Godman and asked 'why she disturbed the family?' After stalling with a few different answers, Elizabeth curiously stated that she was looking for two grapes she had dropped so that the mice did not play with them.[66]

Firstly, it is striking that Mr Goodyear immediately suspected Elizabeth Godman as the person who disturbed the house, instantly believing the girls' fright to be genuine. Secondly, Mr Goodyear seemed to instantly accept that the sounds might have been supernatural or malevolent in nature, evidenced by the fact that this information was admitted in court as further proof that Elizabeth Godman was a witch. Indeed, the final sentence after this story was recounted in court was that: '[the] courts apprehension renders her more suspicious [as a witch.]'[67] While they did not testify personally, the information that Sellevant and Hannah Goodyear provided was a key demonstration that children's testimony was thought of as important in witchcraft cases, even if the girls were merely frightened by unidentifiable sounds in their room. The fact the girls' fear was interpreted as Elizabeth Godman's invisible witchery marked a poignant shift with regards to the extent of agency and credibility children had been given thus far in New English witchcraft trials.

Further evidence of this came when Elizabeth Godman attempted to rebuke some of the allegations being made about her. According to Godman, she accused Hannah and Elizabeth Lamberton of making claims that Godman: 'lay for some[one] to suck her' when she lay down on a bed to rest one day.[68] When Godman layed down, Hannah and Elizabeth Lamberton mocked Godman: 'look how she lies, she lies as if somebody was to suck her'.[69] Not long after, Godman lost her patience and threatened Hannah. Two days later, Hannah began having 'dreadful' fits where she was 'pinched and heard a hideous noise and was in strange manner sweating and burning [sometimes] cold and full of pain yet she shrieked out'.[70] Although Godman brought up this incident in the hope that the court might see how she was being defamed, it provides valuable insight into how children interpreted their world around them through the prism of witchcraft beliefs. Perhaps more importantly, it also demonstrates how children were not afraid to reproach adults for seeming to conform to these beliefs. Godman claimed that she had only laid down on the bed and removed some of her clothes because it was hot but was successfully baited by the two girls who thought she looked like she was about to suckle a demonic familiar.

The source material does not offer a clear indication on how this information affected the court's opinion of Elizabeth Godman. However, the verdict shows that this admonition did not weigh favourably for Godman like she had hoped. The court stated that while the evidence against Godman was not sufficient 'to take away her life', she was barred from visiting neighbours where she might 'give offence' and was released pending her 'good behaviour'.[71] From this case, it is evident that in an incredibly short amount of time, New English children extended their role from passive victims to those ready to make bolder accusations, weaponising their knowledge of the invisible world. This was demonstrated dramatically in the largest witch-hunt in mid-seventeenth-century New England: the 1662 Hartford witchcraft trials.

'If I could go myself I would': The 1662 Hartford Witchcraft Trials

Despite being the largest witch-hunt New England faced in the middle of the seventeenth century, the origins of the 1662 Hartford witch trials remain 'obscure'.[72] Even expert historians, such as David D. Hall, appear to have recorded the timeline of events in an incorrect order.[73] While this case illuminates fascinating details pertaining to the role of children, historians such as John Demos have skimmed over them, referring to their case as simply involving: 'the death of an eight-year old child [and] the fits and delusions of an adolescent girl…'.[74] Richard Godbeer was also brief in his mention of the children in this case, referring to one of the two significant children in this affair only twice in his book.[75] However, historians do know more details about these children, and a thorough examination of the available source material reveals their unprecedented levels of agency and influence, culminating in a community torn apart.

Trouble began in the spring of 1662 when eight-year-old Elizabeth Kelly ventured into the house of Goody Ayres who offered her some hot broth.[76] After accepting some, the child began to immediately complain that her stomach hurt, but her father testified that he did not suspect Goody Ayres, thinking that Elizabeth's stomach hurt simply because the broth was too hot for her.[77] However, that night, while Elizabeth slept in bed with her father, she woke up in the middle of the night crying: 'Father, father help me, help me, Goodwife Ayres is upon me, she chokes me, she kneels on my belly, she will break my bowels, she pinches me, she will make me black and blue…'.[78] Unlike the Goodyear's father, Elizabeth's father's immediate response was not one of comfort but of dismissal, telling Elizabeth to quiet down as to not wake her mother sleeping in another room. Moments later, Elizabeth renewed her cries, 'with greater violence than before against Goodwife Ayres'.[79] Elizabeth's father finally took her into her mother's bed in the hope the young girl would find relief, but Elizabeth's rage at Goody Ayres was unrelenting: 'Oh! Father set on the great furnace and scald her, get the broad axe and chop off her head…'.[80] It seems remarkable, without any explicit instigation from her parents or outside sources, that an eight-year-old girl unleashed such violent threatenings upon a woman much her senior; staunch in her own beliefs, it seemed, that Goody Ayres bewitched her through the hot broth she ate.

A few days later, Elizabeth's mother and a few other women in the village (including Rebecca Greensmith, who would later become a central figure in the witch narrative) gathered around the sick child. When Goody Ayres came in to visit, Elizabeth immediately asked her: 'why do you torment me and prick me?' This demonstration of boldness well above her usual social standing did not go unnoticed by those in present company. Before Ayres could answer, one of the women standing by rebuked the child stating, 'you must not speak against Goody Ayres, she comes in love to see you'.[81] However, Elizabeth's mother later testified that Goody Ayres blackmailed Elizabeth, allegedly telling the child:

> Betty why do you speak so much against me [?] I will be even with you for it before you die but if you will say no more of me I will give you a fine lace for your dressing.[82]

Despite her deteriorating health, Elizabeth took no notice of either warning against slandering Goody Ayres, for that night she cried out even louder against her. This time, she questioned her father's ability as an authoritative adult figure, who had the legal and social standing she did not, to do something about her alleged attacker:

> Father why do you not go to the magistrates and get them to punish Goody Ayres [?] Pray father go to the magistrates and if I could go myself I would complain to them of her how she misuses me....[83]

Elizabeth Kelly died the next night, her last words were: 'Goody Ayres chokes me'.[84]

The bold statement Elizabeth made to her father claiming that she would go to the courts to pursue justice if she could is reminiscent of others made by children in England who claimed that they would have greased the wheels of justice themselves. An early example is seen in the Throckmorton case in 1589 where Joan Throckmorton somewhat disturbingly said that she would 'blow the coals' of the pyre for the accused Samuels family.[85] Another example from Old England, slightly more contemporary to the Hartford trial, revolved around an unnamed boy from Worcester in 1649. After being scared by an old woman in the woods, the young boy saw her later 'amongst other poor people...supping up a mess of hot pottage'.[86] Taking justice into his own hands, he 'ran furiously upon her and threw her pottage in her face and offered some other violence at her'. Rather than helping the poor woman, those witnessing joined in, 'suspecting that she had done him some hurt'. She was then committed to prison for witchcraft, and her fate remains unknown. Whether or not Elizabeth Kelly had familiarity with these cases is immaterial to the significance it represents. Its reoccurrence in England and New England over decades demonstrated that some children were not afraid to announce their desire to be proactively involved in the judicial process. What is more, while these examples are explicit in nature, there are dozens more examples in aforementioned cases that show children's implicit desire to be involved in witchcraft trials.[87] Elizabeth Kelly's frustration that she could not simply bring her grievance to the magistrates herself is a significant reminder of how children could be the driving force in witch prosecutions. Indeed, even in death, Elizabeth's body helped spur on her accusations against Goody Ayres, by initiating the first autopsy in America to be conducted in response to a witchcraft allegation.[88]

Elizabeth Kelly had been dead for five days when Doctor Bray Rossiter of Guilford was sent to examine the girl.[89] Doctor Rossiter made six observations about the body concluding that the cause of death was 'preternatural'.[90] One of the observations Doctor Rossiter made about Elizabeth's body was that 'there was the appearance of pure fresh blood in the backside of the arm'.[91] This remark is intriguing because a few days before the autopsy some neighbours also examined the body. When Goody Ayres was brought in, she stood near Elizabeth's arm and, when the girl's sleeve was ripped open, witnesses testified to seeing strange bruises up her arms 'as if they had been bruised or beaten'.[92] Elizabeth had said on the first night she was troubled that Goody Ayres would 'make me black and blue'. Surely, the connection must not have been far from Elizabeth's father's mind as he testified to seeing a 'reddish tawny great spot' on the side of Elizabeth's face where Goody Ayres stood during the examination of the body.[93] Now that the doctor noted the marks on Elizabeth's arms and affirmed that the cause of death was preternatural, Goody Ayres must have felt nervous about her fate. Fearing the worst, Goody Ayres and her husband fled, leaving behind their eight-year-old son John Ayres.[94] All the Ayres' land and possessions were sold to satisfy their bond to the colony and their debts. Their son was apprenticed to James Ensign to learn the cooper's trade. It is important for historians to also consider how this young boy's life was completely uprooted due to witchcraft allegations made about his family. Unfortunately, nothing else is known about him.

With Elizabeth Kelly dead and both the Ayres fleeing before formal legal action could be made against them, one might think the proceedings would have dissipated. However, before the Ayres left town, they fuelled witchcraft allegations themselves and had an (unsuccessful) suit of slander brought against them by Nathaniel Greensmith for calling his wife Rebecca Greensmith a witch.[95] The growing hostility and tension saw accusations come from another source: an afflicted twenty-one-year-old girl called Ann Cole.[96] Increase Mather referred to Ann as a person of 'real piety and integrity' but claimed that the Devil 'express[ed] things' with her tongue that she was unaware of when she came out of her fits.[97] In her fits, Ann stated that the witches would 'afflict her body, spoil her name [and] hinder her marriage' which gives valuable insight into what could be considered to be real fears of adolescent girls at this time.[98] Ann began to name witches in her fits, including Rebecca Greensmith, Elizabeth Seager and Judith Varlet. As pressure mounted and the accused were rounded up, Ann's accusations became more elaborate. She started speaking in a 'Dutch tone', and an unnamed Dutch man and woman who lived nearby were forced to undergo the swimming test.[99] Mather himself deplored this 'superstitious' experiment, but its implementation may give further credence to the community's belief that Ann's ramblings signalled an insight into the supernatural world where, to them, she accurately identified witches.[100] Certainly, John Whiting's letter to Increase Mather indicated that Ann's 'amazing' imitation of the Dutch language was thought to be 'impossible', strongly implying that Ann's ability to do it was a demonically inspired sign of the Dutch couple's guilt. Whiting seemed so impressed, he did not even mention the torture of the swimming test.[101] After no legal action was found against the Dutch couple, they too fled.

Ann's fits worsened and a special day of prayer was kept for her. Whiting stated that the noise and motions she made were so terrible 'a godly person fainted under the appearance of it'.[102] Whether it was this external pressure or otherwise, Rebecca Greensmith, now in prison, made a full confession incriminating her husband and Goody Ayres who had been at the origins of this witch-hunt.[103] Rebecca testified that the Devil came to her at Christmas, admitting that she and all the witches had a 'merry meeting' with him at a place near her house. She also claimed that the Devil had 'frequent use of her body' and admitted that it brought 'delight to her'.[104] Though her husband did 'not acknowledge himself guilty' both the Greensmiths, Mary Sanford and Mary Barnes, were executed.[105] Although Judith Varlet was set free, Elizabeth Seager faced renewed attempts at condemnation for the next four years. Amongst other things, one of the pieces of evidence against Elizabeth Seager involved her dismissal of Ann Cole's bewitchment, which she apparently called 'a great deal of hodgepodge'.[106] This demonstrates that the community clearly accepted Ann's bewitchment as genuine, and scepticism seemed to be solid enough grounds to accuse one of witchcraft. When the court dismissed the witchcraft allegations, Seager was accused of adultery, which was also ultimately unsuccessful. Accused of witchcraft for a third time, Seager was finally convicted in 1665, but a year later a special Court of Assistants released her, and she, unsurprisingly, fled to Rhode Island.[107]

Ann Cole's health was restored after the execution of the four convicted witches, and Whiting noted that she 'remains maintaining her integrity'.[108] Unlike other bewitched children, further details about Ann's life can be traced after her time as an accuser, which adds rich and important details to these neglected historical actors. In 1668, the court sold Nathaniel and Rebecca Greensmith's house to a man called Andrew Benton. Ann Cole later married him, and they raised their twelve children in the house of two of her former victims, marking a somewhat morbid conclusion to one of Connecticut's largest witch-hunts.[109]

The 1662 Hartford witch trials represented a significant development for the role of children in New English witchcraft trials. Rather than being passive and relatively silent victims, eight-year-old Elizabeth Kelly was not afraid to call out not just Goody Ayres as her tormentor, but also her own father for not seeking justice for her. When Elizabeth's voice was silenced by her death, her body provided further evidence, prompting Goody Ayres to flee. It is likely Ann Cole then saw an opportunity and, through her demonic fits, was able to further convince the community of an infestation of witches, leading to a total of four executions. The two children involved in this case were not afraid to use their words (and their bodies) to mediate between the natural and supernatural worlds, identifying witches and wreaking havoc in the community. It is clear through the judicial process, the fear that consumed those that left their homes, as well as the witness statements testifying to Coles' behaviour, that Elizabeth Kelly and Ann Coles were believed; their role as witchcraft identifiers was secured. Both children showed unprecedented levels of agency and boldness in their accusations, rising above their usual social status in order to pursue them. The court's willingness to execute four of those deemed responsible demonstrated an acceptance of this behaviour, setting a dangerous precedent for the future of the colony.

After the Hartford trials, there was a lull in executions for witchcraft, possibly because these trials were such a traumatic event; both official and popular pressure for witch-hunts simply quietened down. For example, the number of accusations dropped from an average of four or five persons each year between 1647 and 1663 to just over three persons per year during the next twenty-four years.[110] Of these seventy-five people, only twelve were bound over to higher courts for trial, and only three of these people were convicted, but none were executed.[111] It is likely that the end of the Puritan rule and the 1660 Restoration of the Stuart monarch in England influenced New England's official responses to witchcraft accusations, as popular beliefs about witchcraft became increasingly under attack by English intellectuals.[112] Yet, it would be mistaken to assume that witches were not still the subject of fear and hatred in their community. In fact, children only grew more intense in their denunciation of witches, proving that their calamitous connection between the visible and invisible worlds was only just beginning to be realised.

'It is too late for me': Elizabeth Knap

Although there were sporadic cases after the Hartford trial, the next key case occurred in Groton, Massachusetts, in 1671 and concerned a sixteen-year-old girl called Elizabeth Knap. Elizabeth's case was dutifully recorded by Samuel Willard, the presiding minister of Groton at the time, who wrote an account of Knap's bewitchment in a letter to Increase Mather.[113] Elizabeth came to live with Willard sometime during the preceding summer as a maidservant. In October of 1671, for reasons that are unclear, Elizabeth Knap began having strange fits.[114] At the outset of his treatise, Willard described how Elizabeth suddenly 'burst forth into immoderate and extravagant laughter' which was a persistent theme amongst English demoniacs.[115] On 30 October, Elizabeth's fits grew worse and she complained of pain in her breast, legs and throat. Those around her questioned her integrity wondering: 'whether she was in earnest or dissembled'.[116] Notably, suspicions about whether Elizabeth was a counterfeit seemed to revolve around her character as a person, rather than her status as a child. Thus, the debate about Elizabeth's afflictions was not about whether she had the ability to interact with the supernatural world but whether it was really happening to *her*. This is evidenced by her conflicting statements, confessions and then retractions that appear throughout Willard's narrative as he desperately tried to ascertain the truth from Elizabeth.

After the onset of her fits, Willard noted that 'divers' persons observed Elizabeth 'in a strange frame...sometimes weeping, sometimes laughing and many foolish and apish gestures'.[117] Elizabeth also attested to seeing the apparitions of two people in the cellar. Still, those around her 'took [her] for a fancy', so Elizabeth became more intense in her displays of possession in an attempt to secure validity. One night, she was taken with a 'violent fit' and 'raising the whole family', she attempted to throw herself into the fire; so powerful were her bodily agitations that three or four people struggled to hold her down.[118] Willard noted that she was tormented in this way for a number of days: 'violent also in roarings and screamings, representing a dark resemblance of hellish torments'.[119] It was at this point that Elizabeth accused a woman in town as a witch, claiming she was the one who tormented her, but Willard did not release her name, stating that the woman was 'of sincere uprightness before God'.[120] Nonetheless, an experiment similar to those used in England was conducted where the accused woman was brought in to see Elizabeth, and the girl was apparently able to discern the witch's touch from anyone else's in the room despite having her eyes closed. To this point, it seemed that Elizabeth's bewitchment story followed the well-worn path of other demoniacs who came before her. She displayed many of the typical symptoms that she may have learnt from others and named a local woman as a witch who she suspected of tormenting her. However, Willard stated, 'God was pleased to vindicate...and justify the innocent' for after the woman prayed with all of them, Elizabeth confessed that 'Satan had deluded her' and never complained of the woman afterwards. Elizabeth's fits continued, whereupon 'divers' people came to see 'these amazing fits'. Elizabeth's denunciation of a local woman as a witch was not believed, but she would not give up her role as a demoniac so easily.

What makes Elizabeth Knap's story remarkable amongst other bewitched children is how closely she walked between the natural and preternatural worlds. Seemingly unsatisfied with her role as a victim of bewitchment, Elizabeth began to tell people that the Devil came to her and offered her a treaty of a covenant, a book written in blood with the names of others. In exchange, the Devil promised her things that 'suited her youthful fancy' such as: 'money, silks, fine clothes, ease from labour [and] to show her the whole world'.[121] Admissions like these are important insights into the minds of adolescent girls at the time which tells historians much about their wants and desires; it might also give insight into the motivating factors for why children like Elizabeth became demoniacs, for while most of her ambitions were far-fetched, other demoniacs like Katherine Malpas (1622) did make money from charging admission to view her demonically inspired performances.[122]

Elizabeth then detailed her 'temptations' which were disturbingly sinister for a sixteen-year-old girl. Elizabeth was tempted to murder her parents, her neighbours, their children (especially the youngest), and Samuel Willard and oftentimes wanted to 'murder herself'. John Demos attributed these flashes of destructive impulse to 'Satanic agency', but it is difficult to understand Elizabeth's meaning, other than deducing that she was clearly a troubled girl who used the medium of the spiritual world to speak to those around her, using it (rightly or wrongly) to gain the attention of Willard and those in her community.[123]

As the town's pastor and head of the household Elizabeth lived in, Willard likely felt compelled to ease her sufferings. However, he soon realised that discovering the truth of Elizabeth's condition was challenging. After Elizabeth admitted that the Devil came to her with a covenant and a book marred with blood, he 'pressed' her to declare whether or not she signed the book.[124] Finally, Elizabeth stated that she had not but continued to discuss her meetings with Satan and lament her many sins. In early November 1671, a doctor was called and diagnosed Elizabeth's malady as 'natural', so she was sent home. Yet, even Willard himself expressed little hope that the Devil had left her, 'because she remained under such extreme senselessness of her own estate'.[125] It seemed Elizabeth would not let a formal diagnosis from a doctor prevent her supernatural fits, and she now confessed that she had consented to travelling with the Devil. Incredibly, when the same doctor was brought in, he now claimed that Elizabeth's fits were 'diabolical' and refused to see her.[126] Ministers were called to pray for Elizabeth, and like other demoniacs, such as the Starkie children (1597) and Thomas Harrison (1604), she made animal noises, bleating like a calf and barking like a dog.[127]

In early December, Elizabeth tried a second time to accuse a neighbour (again, Willard did not release her name) of being a witch and tormenting her. Elizabeth claimed she saw a dog with a woman's head go up the chimney, and for the next two days, Willard described how Elizabeth complained of being beaten, scratched and strangled by this invisible witch.[128] Similar again to other demoniacs, Elizabeth stated if the accused witch was apprehended she would be well. However, when the woman was brought to her, she was 'violently handled and lamentably tortured'. Yet, Elizabeth's credibility clearly wavered as Willard noted: 'but having experience of [her] former actings, we made nothing of it'.[129] Willard did not detail how but noted that this second woman was cleared because Elizabeth made 'two mistakes'. Consequently,

Elizabeth never made any more accusations of witchcraft as her integrity had well and truly been diminished.[130] However, she still had a captivated audience willing to hear her stories about her discourses with the Devil and found that Willard was still interested – although increasingly exhausted – about whether or not she had made a pact with Satan. Elizabeth may not have mastered the interaction society accepted that she had with the invisible world, but she at least had the astuteness – or perhaps the desperation – to maintain a hold of it.

Finally, on 8 December, Elizabeth confessed to making a covenant with the Devil. She explained to Willard how the Devil appeared to her 'in the habit of an old man' and asked for some blood which she consented to. She explained how Satan gave her a knife, and she cut her finger whereupon the Devil told her to write her name in his book. She answered that she could not write, but he told her that he would direct her hand. The Devil then took a stick, dipped it in blood and Elizabeth wrote her name with the Devil's help. Elizabeth agreed to serve the Devil for one year, then he would serve her for the remainder of the time, and then he would make her a witch.[131] This confession appears to be the most explicit covenant made between a child and the Devil in early modern England or New England. It seems remarkable that Willard left Elizabeth in this state and promised to visit her again the next day, rather than apprehending her as a witch. He left no indication as to whether he simply did not believe her or thought she was mad, but the inference is certainly there. Nevertheless, Willard seemed plagued with genuine concern about her condition and the state of her soul, perhaps wanting to rescue her from the Devil's snare, rather than punish her. Unfortunately for Willard, the next day, he noted that he found Elizabeth's 'tears had dried up and her senses stupefied [and he] could get nothing from her…'.[132]

Only two days later, Elizabeth sent for Willard and the despondent minister wrote: 'immediately with tears [she] told me that she had belied the Devil in saying she had given him of her blood and professed that the most of the apparitions she had spoken of were but fantasies'.[133] Elizabeth begged Willard to believe her, whereupon he told Elizabeth (somewhat unsurprisingly), that if she could tell him something that made sense, considering she had told 'so many lies and untruths' he would believe her. With a captivated audience once more, Elizabeth divulged another story about how the Devil sometimes visited her because she was 'discontent' with life.[134] That night, Elizabeth grew violent again, spitting in the faces of those around her and striking those who held her. Elizabeth then verbally abused those in the room, calling Willard a 'great black rogue', using her demonic possession as an outlet to vent expressions, frustrations and blasphemies she dared not speak otherwise.[135] Willard noted that Elizabeth's fits grew worse the more attention she received: 'she is observed always to fall into her fits when any strangers go to visit her, and the more go the more violent are her fits'.[136] Elizabeth's two attempts to accuse local women as witches failed, and many questioned her credibility. Nevertheless, Elizabeth created an environment where her fluctuations of demonic flashes were 'entertaining' enough to fascinate the neighbours, as well as Willard who she seemed to crave attention from the most. In this way, Elizabeth demonstrated that the power and control were surreptitiously in her hands.

On 11 January, Elizabeth called for Willard again and regaled to him with former details such as disowning a covenant with Satan and declared that the occasion of her fits was her discontentment with her own life. Elizabeth stated that although 'the devil had power of her body, she hoped he should not of her soul' and 'that she was sometimes disposed to do mischief'.[137] Willard made no comment on this admonition and seemed frankly overwhelmed by Elizabeth's bewitchment. However, her statements do provide insights into how Elizabeth might have interpreted her own psychology, including her motivations for acting bewitched, as well as perhaps admitting that she counterfeited (at least some of it) for attention or for 'mischief'. Willard's exasperation at Elizabeth's demonic disturbances is evidenced by his anti-climactic final statements regarding her when he simply stated that she was in a weeping fit and sent for Willard, but could not speak to him, whereby 'she continues speechless to this instant'.[138] Willard ended his account with a series of questions regarding Elizabeth's affliction, postulating questions such as whether the Devil really spoke to her. He provided comments rather than answers, suggesting that while Elizabeth was beyond his help, she would either be delivered by God or would be his martyr:

> charity would hope the best, love would also fear the worse, but th[i]s much is clear, she is an object of pity, and I desire all that hear of her would be compassionate for her forlorn state. She is (I question not) a subject of hope and therefore all means ought to be used for her recovery. She is a monument of divine severity and the Lord grant that all that see or hear, may fear and tremble.[139]

In fact, two years after Elizabeth's torments, Willard preached a series of jeremiadic sermons, later published in a large volume.[140] One of the three sermons in this volume was in direct response to Elizabeth's bewitchment as Willard called out to the village of Groton stating: 'God hath in his wisdom singled out this poor town…to dispense such an amazing Providence in …let us look upon ourselves to be set up as a *Beacon Upon a Hill…*'.[141] The language used here is nearly identical to that used by John Winthrop aboard the *Arabella* on his way to settle the New World more than forty years earlier when he called on his fellow Puritans to think of the new Godly Commonwealth as a 'city upon a hill'. Outside of providing fodder for Willard's sermons, Elizabeth Knap's story provides illuminating details pertaining to the role of children in New English witch-hunting.

John Demos attempted to psychoanalyse Elizabeth Knap, and while some of his theories – such as claiming that Elizabeth had repressed sexual tension between herself and Willard – may be wanting of evidence, other arguments are more persuasive.[142] For example, Demos claimed that 'exhibitionism, dependency [and] rage' were amongst the 'leading forces fuelling Knap's 'illness', which is perhaps a more accurate summary of Elizabeth's mental state; however, all remain speculative.[143] Demos' psychoanalysis of Elizabeth is a helpful reconstruction of what may have been happening in the sixteen-year-old girl's mind. However, it somewhat removes Elizabeth from the period in which she lived, which was deeply religious. To talk of Freud and Oedipal complexes would have meant nothing to a girl living in 1671.[144] Elizabeth Knap, whether she was psychologically ill or not, interpreted her world and her existence within it using mediums which she understood: Christian elements of bewitchment, possession and sin. In venting her frustrations about her life and telling stories and lies about the Devil, Elizabeth attempted to explain perceptions she had of herself and of her world. In acting bewitched, Elizabeth followed in the footsteps of dozens of children that went before her, subverting her social status in order to speak blasphemies she could never get away with otherwise as well as receiving notoriety, and most importantly it seemed, gaining attention. The fact that her two accusations of witchcraft against local women failed simply meant she was not very good at it; her habit of spreading lies and storytelling meant that she failed to gain the credibility she needed to formulate a successful career as an accuser.

Furthermore, it is noteworthy that Elizabeth was never indicted for witchcraft though she appeared to make multiple confessions to having familiarity with Satan. Whether Willard did not believe her or was simply unmotivated to bring her to court is unclear. Perhaps, in this instance, Elizabeth's young age protected her from judicial retribution. As stated earlier, her suspect credibility seemed to waver not because those around her doubted that children had any connection to the invisible world; they merely questioned whether Elizabeth did. This opinion is unsurprising given her frequent retractions, her lies and storytelling which ended in Willard merely giving up, relying on God's grace to deliver her. However troubled Elizabeth was psychologically, for three months she captured the attention of Groton and certainly maintained integrity long enough until Willard handed her over to the mercy of God.

Finally, one of Demos' conclusions was that Elizabeth Knap had many symptoms consistent with 'narcissism', and it is difficult to dismiss this amid the evidence of her wanting constant attention and spreading what appeared to be deliberate lies.[145] Despite her failures and ultimate pity she won from Samuel Willard, Elizabeth Knap occupied the space between worlds, never quite letting those around her know just how close she was to the Devil. Though her accusations of witchcraft failed, people struggled to deny she was demonically influenced. When a doctor initially diagnosed her symptoms as being 'natural', it did not take long for Elizabeth to change his mind and re-diagnose her as being bewitched. Furthermore, Elizabeth's details of the covenant offered by Satan, the signing of the book and other stories she told of him reveal a remarkable understanding of witchcraft lore for a sixteen-year-old. Straddling the supernatural and the natural spheres, Elizabeth demonstrated that children still held the reins of influence. This would become abundantly clear during the witchcraft trial of Goody Glover in Boston of 1688, which was initiated and continued by the possession of the Goodwin children. This case was the first trial to end in execution since the infamous Hartford trials of 1662.[146]

'Food for faith': The Goodwin Children

The case of the Goodwin children has not gained the same level of attention as the Salem witchcraft trials that occurred shortly after it, though the demonic possessions of John Goodwin's four children were a critical source of inspiration for the bewitched Salem accusers. Despite its significance, the trial of Goody (or Goodwife) Glover is plagued by errors that persist in the scholarship. For example, Goody Glover's first name is erroneously given as 'Mary' or 'Ann' by multiple historical sources despite no primary evidence to support either of these assertions.[147] Apart from the insight it provides to the Salem trials, the trial of Goody Glover is critical in understanding the role of children in New English witchcraft trials as it represented a reinvigoration of the court's pursuit in trying witches. As mentioned earlier, the qualitative data reflects a decline in witchcraft persecutions, and indeed, there were no executions between the Hartford trials of 1662 and 1688. Yet, as Elizabeth Knap's case demonstrated, it was not just the courts who appeared reluctant to prosecute witches, as the clergy was also hesitant to fan the flames of witchcraft accusations due to changes in their responsibility in extracting confessions. Furthermore, as Knap's case indicated, there was an aura of suspicion as perceptions of whether accusers could accurately identify witches wavered.[148]

The reasons why the Goodwin case marked a resurgence in witch-hunting in New England cannot be definitively accounted for, but two major factors – King Philip's War in 1675 and the revocation of Massachusetts' charter in 1684 – would have contributed to a collective feeling that Satan had resumed his assault on the Godly Commonwealth. King Philip's War, also known as the First Indian War, spanned fourteen months between 1675 and 1676.[149] On 20 June 1675, the execution of three Wampanoag warriors incited a group of Indians to attack the English settlement at

Swansea.[150] The details of the battles need not be exhausted here, but what is important to note is that by the time the war ended, a total of thirteen frontier towns had been totally destroyed, while a further six were partially burnt.[151] 500 of the colony's 5000 males of draft age were killed or captured, as well as many women and children.[152] King Philip's War has thus been described as America's bloodiest and deadliest war in its history, relative to population.[153] It was a complete disaster for the colony, especially for its ruling class. Many of the men who were looked up to as the leaders and protectors of Massachusetts later sat as magistrates in court. The significance of this detail lies in the implicit connection with the terrible occurrences befalling the colony in the late 1600s, the ruling classes' inability to deal with them adequately, and consequently their fervour in persecuting witches in the late seventeenth century. The men who failed to protect the colony from Indians attempted to shift the blame and responsibility for their own insufficient defence of the colony onto the invisible world which, in turn, abetted the Goodwin children's assertions that they suffered from it. Therefore, it is plausible that the court was willing to believe in the reputed witches' guilt, largely because the magistrates themselves wanted to believe that they were not guilty of causing New England's woes.

The loss of Massachusetts' charter in June 1684 was a further devastating blow to the legitimacy of New England and its associated mission. A new charter was not signed until 1691, and while it recognised Massachusetts as a province of the British Empire, it required 'that the political boundaries of Massachusetts be reconstituted to include previously disenfranchised religious groups', including Quakers and Anglicans. This permanently diluted the idea of Puritan hegemony in the New World.[154] The interlude of the period without a charter can be described as being nothing short of chaotic for those living in the New World.[155] Like most of the unfortunate incidents that befell the colony, the loss of the charter was interpreted in spiritual terms as a moral and sinful failing. In fact, the way that Puritan ministers dealt with disasters began to change. There was a growing emphasis on 'spiritual corruption and moral deficiency'.[156] The disasters faced by the colony were viewed less as a call for collective atonement and more as a punishment for collective sin. Thus, the success of a sermon being delivered by the end of the seventeenth century could be measured by its vividness in portraying impending doom.[157] Early modern society understood that the visible world was intrinsically attached to the invisible one, providing an intriguing yet frighteningly unknown aspect to everyday life. Ministers used their positions to try to make sense of both worlds, chastising their community for their collective sinful failings which enabled the Devil, both physically and spiritually, to wreak havoc on their society. Hence, to those living in the late 1680s, it became increasingly apparent that the Devil had begun to lay waste to New England; this was the context where the Goodwin children began to have fits in the summer of 1688.

The story of the Goodwin children comes solely from Cotton Mather's treatise titled *Memorable Providences: Relating to Witchcrafts and Possessions*.... Mather wrote the account with his own knowledge as an eyewitness to the events as well as 'undoubted information' he received from neighbours.[158] More than simply wanting to outline the case of the Goodwin children, Mather's motives for writing the treatise were clear in the section to the reader:

> there is both a God and a Devil and witchcraft [;] there is no outward affliction but what God may and sometimes doth permit Satan to trouble his people withall [and] the malice of Satan and his instruments is very great against the children of God...[159]

These statements were affirmed by the signatures of other ministers, including Samuel Willard, the leading minister in Elizabeth Knap's case, who may have now held stronger views on possession as a result of the Goodwin children's more persuasive performances. In his work, Mather explicitly mentioned English authors like Joseph Glanvill, Richard Baxter and Henry More, hoping that his work might emulate theirs: 'I said, let me also run after them...go then my little book, as a lackey to the more elaborate essays of those learned men. Go tell mankind that there are devils and witches...'.[160] This connection between English and New English witchcraft may only be represented through one man, but Cotton Mather was a wealthy, influential minister in the colony, and if his perception of English demonologists was not only well-known but also positive, it is likely others too had similar ideas and opinions. It is also likely that the Goodwin children heard about English witchcraft trials and possibly even extracts from works like Glanvill's or More's through growing up in Mather's church. This may have shaped and affected their behaviour as themes and patterns from cases in Old England were expressed in the Goodwin children's demonic torments.

Mather claimed that four of John Goodwin's six children became bewitched though they had 'enjoyed a religious education' and were in constant employment to 'deliver them from the temptation... [of] idleness...'.[161] Although their names and some of their ages are not given, Hall identified the four bewitched children as: Martha (thirteen), John (eleven), Mercy (seven) and Benjamin (five).[162] The outbreak started in the summer of 1688 when Martha noticed some missing linen and 'examined' their washerwoman, suspecting that she had stolen it for possible use in witchcraft.[163] The laundress was the daughter of a woman named Goody Glover who Mather claimed was an 'ignorant and scandalous old woman'.[164] When Glover heard of Martha's inquest about the linen, she, in her daughter's defence, 'bestowed very bad language upon the girl' which immediately sent Martha into 'strange fits'.[165] Mather was quick to assure the reader that the nature of the fits was beyond those of epilepsy or catalepsy, and it was not long before three of Martha's siblings shared her symptoms. Indeed, a physician was called in and 'concluded nothing but [a] hellish witchcraft could be the [origin] of these maladies'.[166] Mather then described their symptoms, which were archetypal of other bewitched/demonically possessed children: 'sometimes they would be deaf, sometimes dumb, and sometimes blind...one while their tongues would be drawn down their throats, another while they would be pulled out upon their chins to a prodigious length...'.[167] Many 'superstitious proposals' were made to the family to attempt to ease the sufferings of the children, but Mather confirmed that only 'prayers and tears' were useful weapons to oppose the Devil.[168] Apparently, the youngest child was delivered in this way, but the other three children were still violently taken with fits until the magistrates apprehended Goody Glover.

Mather admitted that while John Goodwin had 'no proof' Glover had done any hurt to his children, the magistrates committed her to gaol based on two reasons: she could not properly answer whether she believed in God and although it was repeated to her many times, she also could not correctly recite the Lord's Prayer.[169] One explanation that may shed insight into this comes from Goody Glover's trial where it is revealed that she was Irish, and English appeared to be her second language. Hence, interpreters had to be used to allow communication between the bench and the bar.[170] During the trial, a search warrant was issued, and several poppets made of rags stuffed with goat's hair were brought into court. When these were shown to Glover, she apparently acknowledged them, stating that she would wet her finger and stroke the poppets to 'torment the objects of her malice'.[171] At this stage, the Goodwin children were brought in as physical evidence and an experiment was conducted to further test Glover's guilt. When the children were brought in, Glover was made to hold one of the poppets, whereupon the children fell into 'sad fits' in front of the whole assembly.[172] Demonstrating their fits in front of the courtroom whenever Glover handled the poppets was an effective way to secure Glover's conviction and showed the control and influence the young children had over the fate of the old woman. The judges repeated this several times before concluding that Glover was either mad and had deluded herself to be a witch, or she was guilty and deserved to die. After five or six physicians examined her and concluded she was '*compos mentis*', Goody Glover was sentenced to death.[173]

Goody Glover was executed a few days later, stating that the Goodwin children would not be 'relieved by her death, for others had a hand in it as well as she'.[174] Predictably, the children's fits grew worse after the execution of Glover and Mather made the distinction that their fits now seemed to be from a possession by evil spirits rather than 'demonstrations of an enchantment' now that Glover was dead.[175] This, however, did not seem to align with the narrative the children were attempting to portray, as they continued to complain of spectral attacks from women in the village. Eleven-year-old John named one 'ignorant' woman, but Mather, like Willard, did not expose her name, claiming that he should be 'tender in such relations'.[176] Even though Mather did not encourage further witchcraft accusations, the fact that the young children attempted to shift the narrative themselves demonstrated a level of autonomy and influence well beyond their usual social standing. Moreover, despite Mather not facilitating further judicial processes against the children's accused witches, the children would not be silent; in fact, they grew more restless.

Similar to Elizabeth Knap, the children tried to do 'mischief both to themselves and others'.[177] Like many demonically possessed children, they found pleasure and laughed at the most mundane events such as, 'the tearing or dirtying of a garment, the falling of a cup [or] the breaking of a glass'.[178] Another similar pattern to other demonically possessed children was the revulsion towards the Bible and prayers, with Mather lamenting that 'no good thing must then be endured near those children'.[179] The children were also more astute than other demoniacs like William Perry, for it seemed that when Bible verses were read out in Latin, Greek or Hebrew, those in the room were convinced that the children could understand what was being said though the children were not formally skilled in those languages.[180]

Other themes appear from the Goodwin children which give the impression that they either knew of or heard of earlier English trials. For example, the eldest girl, Martha, explained how she sometimes rode an 'invisible horse' that was brought to her by 'her company'. Martha claimed her eyes remained closed for she said, 'they say I am a tell-tale and therefore they will not let me see them'.[181] This remark from Martha is a fascinating reminder that even in the invisible world – that the children themselves helped build and shape – there appeared to be rules. Perhaps Martha signalled that accusing Goody Glover meant that she had overstepped these rules and was being punished by not being allowed to see the others in the 'company'. The horse motif had been used in England in the cases of Thomas Rabbet (1582), John Smith (1616), Helen and Elizabeth Fairfax (1622), Edmund Robinson (1634), Joseph Buxford (1645), Margaret Muschamp (1645) and Anne Armstrong (1673).[182] Most of these cases were highly publicised, and it has already been established that Mather was well versed in many English treatises, so it is likely that Martha had at least heard of some of these cases and sought to emulate them. Furthermore, when Martha was asked who was in 'her company' she claimed she did not know, whereupon Mather told her to describe what clothes they were wearing, which was another commonly used experiment in England.[183] It is unclear whether Mather was attempting to identify the witches just to keep their names secret, or if the Goodwin children were succeeding in arousing more panic. Regardless, they had asserted more control over the unfolding situation.[184]

After Mather took Martha to live with him to try and ease her torments, Martha's discussions with the spirits became more in-depth. She used them – like the Throckmorton children did – to ask how many fits she would have and when they would be. Martha also appeared to use these secret conversations as an opportunity to set her own bedtime, telling Mather that the spirits would kill her unless he allowed her to stay up until ten o'clock.[185] While seeming like a trivial matter, it is important to recognise how children used their connection to the spiritual world for their own wants and desires, even if that was only to stay up late. The story of the Goodwin children concluded rather anti-climactically when weeks of prayer led the invisible adversaries to simply 'retire'.[186] Small bouts of revisitations by demons were noted, but overall the children were said to have been delivered.

In a relatively short time frame of only forty years, the role of children in New English witchcraft trials developed substantially. In early trials, children were usually voiceless victims of the witches' malice, primarily used as weapons by adults to facilitate accusations. The role of children quickly expanded and their trajectory followed a similar path to that of England where children became more actively involved in judicial proceedings. After the bold statements made by the Goodyear and Lamberton children, it was in the 1662 Hartford witchcraft trials where children used their status as preternatural agents to identify and denounce witches. However, the bewitchment of Elizabeth Knap demonstrated the tenuous position of some children as her credibility wavered. Though the Goodwin case in 1688 was a triumph for children's authority in matters pertaining to the supernatural world. The transmission of ideas from across the Atlantic and from within New England itself helped children to build and foster their bewitchment narratives into believable accusations of witchcraft. The role of children in New English trials, then, had gone from passive victims to children who had the power to affect judicial proceedings and outcomes using their spectral sight.

In the case of the Goodwin children, Cotton Mather added an afterword from the father of the children who provided a brief summation of the saga in his own words to bolster the authenticity of Mather's account. The children's father, John Goodwin, described the whole affair as 'food for faith', relating him and his family's struggles to Job, noting how grateful he was for the power of prayer in delivering his family from the snares of the Devil.[187] However, if John Goodwin thought that 'no one's affliction was like mine' and that his house was 'made a den for devil's' he (and indeed no one) was ready for Satan's ultimate assault on the colony which germinated over the winter of 1692 in Salem Village.[188]

Notes

1 John Winthrop, 'A Model of Christian Charity', *Winthrop Papers*, vol. 2 (Boston: The Massachusetts Historical Society, 1931), p. 295.
2 Kai T. Erikson, *Wayward Puritans: A Study in the Sociology of Deviance* (New York, John Wiley & Sons, 1966), p. ix.
3 John Demos, *Entertaining Satan: Witchcraft and the Culture of Early New England* (Oxford: Oxford University Press, 2004), p. 11.
4 John Demos, *Entertaining Satan: Witchcraft and the Culture of Early New England* (Oxford: Oxford University Press, 2004).
5 David D. Hall, *Witch-Hunting in Seventeenth-Century New England: A Documentary History 1638-1693* (Boston: Northeastern University Press, 1999), p. 15.
6 H. R. McIlwaine, ed., *Minutes of the Council and General Court of Colonial Virginia, 1622-1632, 1670-1676 with Notes and Excerpts from Original Council and General Court Records into 1683, Now Lost* (Richmond: publisher unknown, 1924), p. 112.
7 H. R. McIlwaine, ed., *Minutes of the Council and General Court of Colonial Virginia, 1622-1632, 1670-1676 with Notes and Excerpts from Original Council and General Court Records into 1683, Now Lost* (Richmond: publisher unknown, 1924), p. 114.
8 John Demos, *The Enemy Within: A Short History of Witch-Hunting* (New York: Penguin Group, 2008), p. 80.
9 Charles M. Andrews, *Our Earliest Colonial Settlements: Their Diversities or Origin and Later Characteristics* (Ithaca: Cornell University Press, 1961), p. iii.
10 Michael McGiffert, 'American Puritan Studies in the 1960s' *The William and Mary Quarterly* 27 (No. 1, 1970), p. 38 and Winthrop, 'A Model of Christian Charity'. p. 295.
11 Bryce Traister, *American Literature and The New Puritan Studies* (New York: Cambridge University Press, 2017), p. 1, and Perry Miller, *The New England Mind: From Colony to Province* (Cambridge: Harvard University Press, 1953), p. x.
12 Perry Miller, *Orthodoxy in Massachusetts, 1630-1650* (Boston: Harvard University Press, 1959), p. xx.
13 For those who argue for a more pluralistic or polyvocal approach, see Janice Knight, *Orthodoxies in Massachusetts: Rereading American Puritanism* (Cambridge, MA: Harvard University Press, 1994) and Catherine Albanese, *A Republic of Mind and Spirit: A Cultural History of American Metaphysical Religion* (New Haven: Yale University Press, 2007).
14 Ronald P. Dufour, *Colonial America* (New York: West Publishing Company, 1994), p. 120.
15 Mary Beth Norton, *In the Devil's Snare: The Salem Witchcraft Crisis of 1692* (New York: Vintage Books, 2002), p. 18, and Richard Weisman, *Witchcraft, Magic, and Religion in 17th Century Massachusetts* (Amherst: The University of Massachusetts Press, 1984), p. 124.
16 Philip Greven, *The Protestant Temperament: Patterns of Child-Rearing, Religious Experience, and the Self in Early America* (New York: Alfred A. Knopf, 1977), p. 64, stated that conversion experiences or 'new birth' was less of a transformation and more of a fulfillment that they had become children of God. It was a breaking

and subjecting of their personal wills by surrendering to the omnipotent power and authority of God.

17 Richard Weisman, *Witchcraft, Magic, and Religion in 17th Century Massachusetts* (Amherst: The University of Massachusetts Press, 1984), p. 124.
18 Peter Elmer, *Witchcraft, Witch-Hunting, and Politics in Early Modern England* (Oxford: Oxford University Press, 2016), p. 10.
19 Kai T. Erikson, *Wayward Puritans: A Study in the Sociology of Deviance* (New York, John Wiley & Sons, 1966), p. 37.
20 Kai T. Erikson, *Wayward Puritans: A Study in the Sociology of Deviance* (New York, John Wiley & Sons, 1966), p. 38.
21 Barbara Moe, *The Charter of the Massachusetts Bay Colony: A Primary Source Investigation into the 1629 Charter* (New York: Rosen Publishing Group, 2003), p. 41.
22 Kai T. Erikson, *Wayward Puritans: A Study in the Sociology of Deviance* (New York, John Wiley & Sons, 1966), p. 54.
23 Kai T. Erikson, *Wayward Puritans: A Study in the Sociology of Deviance* (New York, John Wiley & Sons, 1966), p. 62.
24 David D. Hall, *Witch-Hunting in Seventeenth-Century New England: A Documentary History 1638-1693* (Boston: Northeastern University Press, 1999), p. 11; Connecticut and New Haven were separate colonies until the 1662 charter from King Charles II united them.
25 David D. Hall, *Witch-Hunting in Seventeenth-Century New England: A Documentary History 1638-1693* (Boston: Northeastern University Press, 1999).
26 Edmund S. Morgan, *The Puritan Dilemma: The Story of John Winthrop* (Boston: Little Brown & Co., 1958), p. 170.
27 Kai T. Erikson, *Wayward Puritans: A Study in the Sociology of Deviance* (New York, John Wiley & Sons, 1966), p. 64.
28 James Kendal Hosmer, ed., *Winthrop's Journal: History of New England, 1630-1649*, vol. 2 (New York: Charles Scribner's Sons, 1908), p. 323; the first person to be executed for witchcraft in New England was Alice Young in Hartford, Connecticut, a year earlier in 1647; however, other than these details, nothing else is known about her case. David D. Hall, *Witch-Hunting in Seventeenth-Century New England: A Documentary History 1638-1693* (Boston: Northeastern University Press, 1999), p. 21.
29 James Sharpe, ed., 'Introduction' in Alan Macfarlane, *Witchcraft in Tudor and Stuart England: A Regional and Comparative Study*, 2nd edn. (Oxford: Routledge, 1999), pp. 57–60.
30 C. L'Estrange Ewen, *Witch Hunting and Witch Trials* (London: Kegan Paul, Trench, Trubner and Co., 1929), p. 112.
31 James Sharpe, ed., 'Introduction' in Alan Macfarlane, *Witchcraft in Tudor and Stuart England: A Regional and Comparative Study*, 2nd edn. (Oxford: Routledge, 1999), p. 61.
32 John Demos, *Entertaining Satan: Witchcraft and the Culture of Early New England* (Oxford: Oxford University Press, 2004), p. 12.
33 James Kendal Hosmer, ed., *Winthrop's Journal: History of New England, 1630-1649*, vol. 2 (New York: Charles Scribner's Sons, 1908), vol. 2, p. 344.
34 James Kendal Hosmer, ed., *Winthrop's Journal: History of New England, 1630-1649*, vol. 2 (New York: Charles Scribner's Sons, 1908).

35 James Kendal Hosmer, ed., *Winthrop's Journal: History of New England, 1630-1649*, vol. 2 (New York: Charles Scribner's Sons, 1908).
36 James Kendal Hosmer, ed., *Winthrop's Journal: History of New England, 1630-1649*, vol. 2 (New York: Charles Scribner's Sons, 1908).
37 See Deborah Willis, *Malevolent Nurture: Witch-Hunting and Maternal Power in Early Modern England* (Ithaca and London: Cornell University Press, 1995), p. 34, onwards for the idea that the witch's familiar became the substitute for the 'earthly children they no longer have to care for' (p. 34). In this way, the witch can be seen as the inverse or 'monstrous' mother.
38 John Webster, *The Displaying of Supposed Witchcraft…* (London: printed by J. M., 1677), p. 346.
39 Anon., *The Most Strange and Admirable Discoverie of three Witches of Warboys…* (London: printed by the Widow Orwin for Thomas Man and John Winnington, 1593), sig. D5v.
40 Samuel Harsnett, *A Discovery of the Fraudulent Practices of John Darrell…* (London: Imprinted by John Wolfe, 1599), p. 127.
41 David D. Hall, *Witch-Hunting in Seventeenth-Century New England: A Documentary History 1638-1693* (Boston: Northeastern University Press, 1999), p. 22.
42 David D. Hall, *Witch-Hunting in Seventeenth-Century New England: A Documentary History 1638-1693* (Boston: Northeastern University Press, 1999), p. 29. First names will be used in the discussion of the Parson's case to distinguish between Hugh and Mary Parsons.
43 *Records of the Governor and Company of the Massachusetts Bay in New England*, ed., Nathaniel B. Shurtleff, vol. 4, part 1 (Boston: from the press of William White, 1854), pp. 47–48. The verdict stated that Mary was found guilty by her own confession of infanticide and stated that she would be executed; however, a marginal note claimed that she was reprieved sixteen days later on 29 May 1651. Richard Godbeer, *The Devil's Dominion: Magic and Religion in Early New England* (New York: Cambridge University Press, 1992), p. 235, claimed that Mary Parsons was acquitted.
44 'Appendix No. I. Examination of Hugh Parsons of Springfield on a Charge of Witchcraft, and The Testimonies Given against Him, before Mr. William Pynchon, at Springfield, 1651', in *Annals of Witchcraft in New England and Elsewhere in the United States from Their First Settlement* ed., Samuel G. Drake (Boston: W. Elliot Woodward, 1869), pp. 219–258.
45 J. Franklin Jameson, ed., *Edward Johnson's Wonder-Working Providence: 1628-1651* (New York: Charles Scribner's Sons, 1910), p. 237.
46 'Appendix No. I. Examination of Hugh Parsons of Springfield on a Charge of Witchcraft, and The Testimonies Given against Him, before Mr. William Pynchon, at Springfield, 1651', in *Annals of Witchcraft in New England and Elsewhere in the United States from Their First Settlement* ed., Samuel G. Drake (Boston: W. Elliot Woodward, 1869), pp. 227–229, and *Records of the Governor and Company of the Massachusetts Bay in New England*, ed. Nathaniel B. Shurtleff, vol. 4, part 1 (Boston: from the press of William White, 1854), vol. 4, part 1, p. 47.
47 David D. Hall, *Witch-Hunting in Seventeenth-Century New England: A Documentary History 1638-1693* (Boston: Northeastern University Press, 1999), p. 37.

48 John Demos, *Entertaining Satan: Witchcraft and the Culture of Early New England* (Oxford: Oxford University Press, 2004), p. 290.
49 'Appendix No. I. Examination of Hugh Parsons of Springfield on a Charge of Witchcraft, and The Testimonies Given against Him, before Mr. William Pynchon, at Springfield, 1651', in *Annals of Witchcraft in New England and Elsewhere in the United States from Their First Settlement,* ed. Samuel G. Drake (Boston: W. Elliot Woodward, 1869), p. 227
50 'Appendix No. I. Examination of Hugh Parsons of Springfield on a Charge of Witchcraft, and The Testimonies Given against Him, before Mr. William Pynchon, at Springfield, 1651', in *Annals of Witchcraft in New England and Elsewhere in the United States from Their First Settlement,* ed. Samuel G. Drake (Boston: W. Elliot Woodward, 1869), p. 234.
51 'Appendix No. I. Examination of Hugh Parsons of Springfield on a Charge of Witchcraft, and The Testimonies Given against Him, before Mr. William Pynchon, at Springfield, 1651', in *Annals of Witchcraft in New England and Elsewhere in the United States from Their First Settlement,* ed. Samuel G. Drake (Boston: W. Elliot Woodward, 1869), p. 235.
52 'Appendix No. I. Examination of Hugh Parsons of Springfield on a Charge of Witchcraft, and The Testimonies Given against Him, before Mr. William Pynchon, at Springfield, 1651', in *Annals of Witchcraft in New England and Elsewhere in the United States from Their First Settlement,* ed. Samuel G. Drake (Boston: W. Elliot Woodward, 1869).
53 'Appendix No. I. Examination of Hugh Parsons of Springfield on a Charge of Witchcraft, and The Testimonies Given against Him, before Mr. William Pynchon, at Springfield, 1651', in *Annals of Witchcraft in New England and Elsewhere in the United States from Their First Settlement,* ed. Samuel G. Drake (Boston: W. Elliot Woodward, 1869), p. 236.
54 'Appendix No. I. Examination of Hugh Parsons of Springfield on a Charge of Witchcraft, and The Testimonies Given against Him, before Mr. William Pynchon, at Springfield, 1651', in *Annals of Witchcraft in New England and Elsewhere in the United States from Their First Settlement,* ed. Samuel G. Drake (Boston: W. Elliot Woodward, 1869).
55 John Demos, *The Enemy Within: A Short History of Witch-Hunting* (New York: Penguin Group, 2008), p. 107.
56 Christopher S. Mackay, *The Hammer of Witches: A Complete Translation of the Malleus Maleficarum* (Cambridge, Cambridge University Press, 2009), p. 115.
57 John Hale, *A Modest Inquiry and How Persons Guilty of that Crime may be Convicted…* (Boston, B. Green and J. Alten, 1702), p. 18; David D. Hall, *Witch-Hunting in Seventeenth-Century New England: A Documentary History 1638-1693* (Boston: Northeastern University Press, 1999), p. 24, claimed that Kendall's first name was Elizabeth; Richard Godbeer, *The Devil's Dominion: Magic and Religion in Early New England* (New York: Cambridge University Press, 1992), p. 235, also claimed that Kendall's first name was Elizabeth but stated that her execution date was 1647. Neither Hall or Godbeer specify the evidence used to support their assertions.
58 John Hale, *A Modest Inquiry and How Persons Guilty of that Crime may be Convicted…* (Boston, B. Green and J. Alten, 1702), p. 19.

59 Thomas O'Malley, 'Gallows Hill: The Ancient Place of Execution' in *The Cambridge Historical Society: Publications XVII Proceedings for the Years 1923 and 1924* (Cambridge: published by the Society, 1931), p. 50. O'Malley's reasoning for believing the case never existed centres around the fact that the names given in Hale's account do not match the genealogical records for Cambridge at the time of the alleged witchcraft trial.

60 David D. Hall, *Witch-Hunting in Seventeenth-Century New England: A Documentary History 1638-1693* (Boston: Northeastern University Press, 1999), p. 61.

61 Charles J. Hoadly, *Records of the Colony or Jurisdiction of New Haven from May 1653 to the Union* (Hartford: Printed by Case, Lockwood and Company, 1858), pp. 29–36.

62 'New Haven Town Records: 1649–1662' in *New Haven Colony Historical Society: Ancient Town Records*, ed. Franklin Bowditch Dexter, vol. 1 (New Haven: printed for the Society, 1917), p. 251.

63 'New Haven Town Records: 1649–1662' in *New Haven Colony Historical Society: Ancient Town Records*, ed. Franklin Bowditch Dexter, vol. 1 (New Haven: printed for the Society, 1917).

64 'New Haven Town Records: 1649–1662' in *New Haven Colony Historical Society: Ancient Town Records*, ed. Franklin Bowditch Dexter, vol. 1 (New Haven: printed for the Society, 1917).

65 'New Haven Town Records: 1649–1662' in *New Haven Colony Historical Society: Ancient Town Records*, ed. Franklin Bowditch Dexter, vol. 1 (New Haven: printed for the Society, 1917).

66 'New Haven Town Records: 1649–1662' in *New Haven Colony Historical Society: Ancient Town Records*, ed. Franklin Bowditch Dexter, vol. 1 (New Haven: printed for the Society, 1917)., p. 252.

67 'New Haven Town Records: 1649–1662' in *New Haven Colony Historical Society: Ancient Town Records*, ed. Franklin Bowditch Dexter, vol. 1 (New Haven: printed for the Society, 1917).

68 Charles J. Hoadly, *Records of the Colony or Jurisdiction of New Haven from May 1653 to the Union* (Hartford: Printed by Case, Lockwood and Company, 1858), p. 34.

69 Charles J. Hoadly, *Records of the Colony or Jurisdiction of New Haven from May 1653 to the Union* (Hartford: Printed by Case, Lockwood and Company, 1858).

70 Charles J. Hoadly, *Records of the Colony or Jurisdiction of New Haven from May 1653 to the Union* (Hartford: Printed by Case, Lockwood and Company, 1858).

71 Charles J. Hoadly, *Records of the Colony or Jurisdiction of New Haven from May 1653 to the Union* (Hartford: Printed by Case, Lockwood and Company, 1858), p. 152.

72 Carol. F. Karlsen, *The Devil in the Shape of a Woman: Witchcraft in Colonial New England* (New York: W. W. Norton & Company, 1987), p. 24.

73 David D. Hall, *Witch-Hunting in Seventeenth-Century New England: A Documentary History 1638-1693* (Boston: Northeastern University Press, 1999), p. 147.

74 John Demos, *Entertaining Satan: Witchcraft and the Culture of Early New England* (Oxford: Oxford University Press, 2004), p. 351.

75 Richard Godbeer, *The Devil's Dominion: Magic and Religion in Early New England* (New York: Cambridge University Press, 1992), p. 107 and p. 115.
76 'Testimony of John and Bethia Kelly', *Samuel Wyllys Papers*, accession number MS 342, box 1, folder 7, 13 May 1662, sig. W–W6r. Access via Brown University Library online: https://repository.library.brown.edu/studio/item/bdr:211529/.
77 'Testimony of John and Bethia Kelly', *Samuel Wyllys Papers*, accession number MS 342, box 1, folder 7, 13 May 1662. Access via Brown University Library online: https://repository.library.brown.edu/studio/item/bdr:211529/.
78 'Testimony of John and Bethia Kelly', *Samuel Wyllys Papers*, accession number MS 342, box 1, folder 7, 13 May 1662. Access via Brown University Library online: https://repository.library.brown.edu/studio/item/bdr:211529/.
79 'Testimony of John and Bethia Kelly', *Samuel Wyllys Papers*, accession number MS 342, box 1, folder 7, 13 May 1662. Access via Brown University Library online: https://repository.library.brown.edu/studio/item/bdr:211529/.
80 'Testimony of John and Bethia Kelly', *Samuel Wyllys Papers*, accession number MS 342, box 1, folder 7, 13 May 1662. Access via Brown University Library online: https://repository.library.brown.edu/studio/item/bdr:211529/.
81 'Testimony of John and Bethia Kelly', *Samuel Wyllys Papers*, accession number MS 342, box 1, folder 7, 13 May 1662. Access via Brown University Library online: https://repository.library.brown.edu/studio/item/bdr:211529/.
82 'Testimony of John and Bethia Kelly', *Samuel Wyllys Papers*, accession number MS 342, box 1, folder 7, 13 May 1662, sig. W–W6v. Access via Brown University Library online: https://repository.library.brown.edu/studio/item/bdr:211529/.
83 'Testimony of John and Bethia Kelly', *Samuel Wyllys Papers*, accession number MS 342, box 1, folder 7, 13 May 1662. Access via Brown University Library online: https://repository.library.brown.edu/studio/item/bdr:211529/.
84 'Testimony of John and Bethia Kelly', *Samuel Wyllys Papers*, accession number MS 342, box 1, folder 7, 13 May 1662. Access via Brown University Library online: https://repository.library.brown.edu/studio/item/bdr:211529/.
85 Anon., *The Most Strange and Admirable Discoverie of Three Witches of Warboys…* (London: printed by the Widow Orwin for Thomas Man and John Winnington, 1593), sig. E1v.
86 Anon., *A Collection of Modern Relations of Matter of Fact Concerning Witches and Witchcraft…* (London: printed for John Harris, 1693), pp. 50–51.
87 For examples where implicit desires and motivations to be involved in witch-hunts can be ascertained, see cases such as Elizabeth Mallory, Jennet Device, Katherine Malpas, Edmund Robinson and William Perry discussed in Chapter 4.
88 R. G. Tomlinson, *Witchcraft Trials of Connecticut: The First Comprehensive, Documented History of Witchcraft Trials in Colonial Connecticut* (Hartford: The Bond Press, 1978), p. 30.
89 R. G. Tomlinson, *Witchcraft Trials of Connecticut: The First Comprehensive, Documented History of Witchcraft Trials in Colonial Connecticut* (Hartford: The Bond Press, 1978).
90 'Testimony of Dr Rossiter on death of Kelly's child', *Samuel Wyllys Papers*, accession number MS 341, box, 1, folder 6, 31 March 1662, sig. W–W5v-r, access via Brown University Library online. https://repository.library.brown.edu/studio/item/bdr:211562/

91 'Testimony of Dr Rossiter on death of Kelly's child', *Samuel Wyllys Papers*, accession number MS 341, box, 1, folder 6, 31 March 1662, access via Brown University Library online. https://repository.library.brown.edu/studio/item/bdr:211562/.

92 'Testimony of Dr Rossiter on death of Kelly's child', *Samuel Wyllys Papers*, accession number MS 341, box, 1, folder 6, 31 March 1662, access via Brown University Library online. https://repository.library.brown.edu/studio/item/bdr:211562/.

93 David D. Hall, *Witch-Hunting in Seventeenth-Century New England: A Documentary History 1638-1693* (Boston: Northeastern University Press, 1999), p. 154.

94 R. G. Tomlinson, *Witchcraft Trials of Connecticut: The First Comprehensive, Documented History of Witchcraft Trials in Colonial Connecticut* (Hartford: The Bond Press, 1978), p. 31.

95 R. G. Tomlinson, *Witchcraft Trials of Connecticut: The First Comprehensive, Documented History of Witchcraft Trials in Colonial Connecticut* (Hartford: The Bond Press, 1978).

96 Frank T. Cole, *The Early Genealogies of the Cole Families in America* (Columbus: P. Ann & Adair, 1887), p. 21, and Anon., 'Ann Benton (Cole)', Geni, www.geni.com/people/Anne-Benton/ date accessed, 15 January 2024.

97 Increase Mather, 'An Essay for the Recording of Illustrious Providences' in *Narratives of the Witchcraft Cases 1648-1706*, ed. George Lincoln Burr (New York: Charles Scribner's Sons, 1914), p. 18.

98 John Whiting, 'Letter from John Whiting to Increase Mather' in *Collections of the Massachusetts Historical Society*, vol. 8, fourth series (Boston: published for the Society, 1868), p. 467. In a similar way to Ann Cole, a twenty-five-year-old French woman named Marthe Brossier became demonically possessed when she feared her marital prospects were dismal. See Sarah Ferber, *Demonic Possession and Exorcism in Early Modern France* (London and New York: Routledge, 2004), pp. 40–59, and Anita M. Walker and Edmund H. Dickerman, '"A Woman under the Influence": A Case of Alleged Possession in Sixteenth-Century France', *The Sixteenth Century Journal* 22 (No. 3, 1991), pp. 534–554.

99 Increase Mather, 'An Essay for the Recording of Illustrious Providences' in *Narratives of the Witchcraft Cases 1648-1706*, ed. George Lincoln Burr (New York: Charles Scribner's Sons, 1914), p. 21.

100 Increase Mather, 'An Essay for the Recording of Illustrious Providences' in *Narratives of the Witchcraft Cases 1648-1706*, ed. George Lincoln Burr (New York: Charles Scribner's Sons, 1914).

101 John Whiting, 'Letter from John Whiting to Increase Mather' in *Collections of the Massachusetts Historical Society*, vol. 8, fourth series (Boston: published for the Society, 1868), pp. 467–468.

102 John Whiting, 'Letter from John Whiting to Increase Mather' in *Collections of the Massachusetts Historical Society*, vol. 8, fourth series (Boston: published for the Society, 1868), p. 468.

103 R. G. Tomlinson, *Witchcraft Trials of Connecticut: The First Comprehensive, Documented History of Witchcraft Trials in Colonial Connecticut* (Hartford: The Bond Press, 1978), p. 35.

104 John Whiting, 'Letter from John Whiting to Increase Mather' in *Collections of the Massachusetts Historical Society*, vol. 8, fourth series (Boston: published for the Society, 1868), p. 468.
105 Mather, 'An Essay for the Recording of Illustrious Providences', p. 21 and Tomlinson, *Witchcraft Trials of Connecticut*, pp. 31 and p. 35. Unfortunately, little is known regarding the details surrounding the two executed Marys.
106 'Testimony of Goodwife Garrett against Elizabeth Seager', *Samuel Wyllys Papers,* accession number MS 340, box 1, folder 5, sig. W–W4r, access via Brown University Library online. https://repository.library.brown.edu/studio/item/bdr:211539/.
107 Carol. F. Karlsen, *The Devil in the Shape of a Woman: Witchcraft in Colonial New England* (New York: W. W. Norton & Company, 1987), p. 26.
108 John Whiting, 'Letter from John Whiting to Increase Mather' in *Collections of the Massachusetts Historical Society*, vol. 8, fourth series (Boston: published for the Society, 1868), p. 469.
109 R. G. Tomlinson, *Witchcraft Trials of Connecticut: The First Comprehensive, Documented History of Witchcraft Trials in Colonial Connecticut* (Hartford: The Bond Press, 1978), p. 40. Eight of the children were from Benton's previous marriage.
110 Carol. F. Karlsen, *The Devil in the Shape of a Woman: Witchcraft in Colonial New England* (New York: W. W. Norton & Company, 1987), p. 29.
111 Carol. F. Karlsen, *The Devil in the Shape of a Woman: Witchcraft in Colonial New England* (New York: W. W. Norton & Company, 1987).
112 Carol. F. Karlsen, *The Devil in the Shape of a Woman: Witchcraft in Colonial New England* (New York: W. W. Norton & Company, 1987), p. 30.
113 Samuel Willard, 'A Brief Account of a Strange and Unusual Providence of God Befallen to Elizabeth Knap of Groton' in *Groton in The Witchcraft Times*, ed. Samuel A. Green (Cambridge: John Wilson and Son, 1883), p. 5.
114 John Demos, *Entertaining Satan: Witchcraft and the Culture of Early New England* (Oxford: Oxford University Press, 2004), p. 100.
115 See cases such as Alexander Nyndge (1573), the Throckmorton girls (1589), William Sommers (1597), the children of Nicholas Starkie (1597), Marmaduke Jackson (1601), Helen Fairfax (1622) and James Barrow (1664). Relevant source material includes Edward Nyndge, *A True and Fearful Vexation of One Alexander Nyndge...* (London: imprinted for W. B, 1615), p. 4; Anon., *The Most Strange and Admirable Discoverie of three Witches of Warboys...* (London: printed by the Widow Orwin for Thomas Man and John Winnington, 1593), sig. Cv; Anon., *A Briefe Narration of the Possession, Dispossession and Repossession of William Sommers...* (Amsterdam: publisher unknown, 1598), im. 14, 15 and 18; George More, *A True Discourse Concerning the Certain Possession and Dispossession of 7 Persons in One Familie in Lancashire...* (Middelburg: printed by Richard Schilders, 1660), p. 52; BL, Add. MSS, 32496, f. 42v; Edward Fairfax, *A Discourse of Witchcraft as It Was Acted in the Family of Mr Edward Fairfax...*, communicated by R. M. Milnes, 1621, in *Miscellanies of the Philobiblon Society*, vol. 5 (London: printed by Charles Whittingham, 1858–1859), pp. 113, 185, 261, 276, 283–284 and 298; John Barrow, *The*

Lord's Arm Stretched Out in an Answer of Prayer... (London: published by John Barrow, 1664), p. 14.
116 Samuel Willard, 'A Brief Account of a Strange and Unusual Providence of God Befallen to Elizabeth Knap of Groton' in *Groton in The Witchcraft Times*, ed. Samuel A. Green (Cambridge: John Wilson and Son, 1883), p. 7.
117 Samuel Willard, 'A Brief Account of a Strange and Unusual Providence of God Befallen to Elizabeth Knap of Groton' in *Groton in The Witchcraft Times*, ed. Samuel A. Green (Cambridge: John Wilson and Son, 1883).
118 Samuel Willard, 'A Brief Account of a Strange and Unusual Providence of God Befallen to Elizabeth Knap of Groton' in *Groton in The Witchcraft Times*, ed. Samuel A. Green (Cambridge: John Wilson and Son, 1883).
119 Samuel Willard, 'A Brief Account of a Strange and Unusual Providence of God Befallen to Elizabeth Knap of Groton' in *Groton in The Witchcraft Times*, ed. Samuel A. Green (Cambridge: John Wilson and Son, 1883).
120 Samuel Willard, 'A Brief Account of a Strange and Unusual Providence of God Befallen to Elizabeth Knap of Groton' in *Groton in The Witchcraft Times*, ed. Samuel A. Green (Cambridge: John Wilson and Son, 1883), p. 8.
121 Samuel Willard, 'A Brief Account of a Strange and Unusual Providence of God Befallen to Elizabeth Knap of Groton' in *Groton in The Witchcraft Times*, ed. Samuel A. Green (Cambridge: John Wilson and Son, 1883).
122 STAC 8/32/13, 12r, q. 14.
123 John Demos, *Entertaining Satan: Witchcraft and the Culture of Early New England* (Oxford: Oxford University Press, 2004), p. 100.
124 Samuel Willard, 'A Brief Account of a Strange and Unusual Providence of God Befallen to Elizabeth Knap of Groton' in *Groton in The Witchcraft Times*, ed. Samuel A. Green (Cambridge: John Wilson and Son, 1883), p. 8.
125 Samuel Willard, 'A Brief Account of a Strange and Unusual Providence of God Befallen to Elizabeth Knap of Groton' in *Groton in The Witchcraft Times*, ed. Samuel A. Green (Cambridge: John Wilson and Son, 1883), p. 10.
126 Samuel Willard, 'A Brief Account of a Strange and Unusual Providence of God Befallen to Elizabeth Knap of Groton' in *Groton in The Witchcraft Times*, ed. Samuel A. Green (Cambridge: John Wilson and Son, 1883), p. 11.
127 See George More, *A True Discourse Concerning the Certain Possession and Dispossession of 7 Persons in One Familie in Lancashire*... (Middelburg: printed by Richard Schilders, 1660), p. 15, and William Hinde, *A Faithfull Remonstrance of the Holy Life and Happy Death of John Bruen*... (London: printed by R.B. for Philemon Stephens and Christopher Meredith, 1641), p. 141.
128 Samuel Willard, 'A Brief Account of a Strange and Unusual Providence of God Befallen to Elizabeth Knap of Groton' in *Groton in The Witchcraft Times*, ed. Samuel A. Green (Cambridge: John Wilson and Son, 1883), p. 13.
129 Samuel Willard, 'A Brief Account of a Strange and Unusual Providence of God Befallen to Elizabeth Knap of Groton' in *Groton in The Witchcraft Times*, ed. Samuel A. Green (Cambridge: John Wilson and Son, 1883).
130 Samuel Willard, 'A Brief Account of a Strange and Unusual Providence of God Befallen to Elizabeth Knap of Groton' in *Groton in The Witchcraft Times*, ed. Samuel A. Green (Cambridge: John Wilson and Son, 1883), p. 14.
131 Samuel Willard, 'A Brief Account of a Strange and Unusual Providence of God Befallen to Elizabeth Knap of Groton' in *Groton in The Witchcraft Times*, ed. Samuel A. Green (Cambridge: John Wilson and Son, 1883).

132 Samuel Willard, 'A Brief Account of a Strange and Unusual Providence of God Befallen to Elizabeth Knap of Groton' in *Groton in The Witchcraft Times*, ed. Samuel A. Green (Cambridge: John Wilson and Son, 1883), pp. 15–16.
133 Samuel Willard, 'A Brief Account of a Strange and Unusual Providence of God Befallen to Elizabeth Knap of Groton' in *Groton in The Witchcraft Times*, ed. Samuel A. Green (Cambridge: John Wilson and Son, 1883), p. 16.
134 Samuel Willard, 'A Brief Account of a Strange and Unusual Providence of God Befallen to Elizabeth Knap of Groton' in *Groton in The Witchcraft Times*, ed. Samuel A. Green (Cambridge: John Wilson and Son, 1883).
135 Samuel Willard, 'A Brief Account of a Strange and Unusual Providence of God Befallen to Elizabeth Knap of Groton' in *Groton in The Witchcraft Times*, ed. Samuel A. Green (Cambridge: John Wilson and Son, 1883), p. 17; Anita M. Walker and Edmund H. Dickerman explored a similar concept in their article which looked at the demonic possession of a young, French Ursuline nun called Madeleine de la Palud, who accused her former confessor Louis Gaufridy of seducing her and taking her to Sabbats. The young girl and her confessor apparently had 'many familiarities and liberties' (p. 7) between them, but when Madeleine returned to the Ursulines she, 'fused consent to her sexual encounter with Gaufridy with consent to the devil'. Like Knap, Madeleine's possession exonerated her, and her accusations of witchcraft against Gaufridy allowed her to express any harbouring feelings of resentment or guilt (p. 8). See Anita M. Walker and Edmund H. Dickerman, 'A Notorious Woman: Possession, Witchcraft and Sexuality in Seventeenth Century Provence', *Historical Reflections* 27 (No.1, 2001), pp. 1–26.
136 Samuel Willard, 'A Brief Account of a Strange and Unusual Providence of God Befallen to Elizabeth Knap of Groton' in *Groton in The Witchcraft Times*, ed. Samuel A. Green (Cambridge: John Wilson and Son, 1883), p. 19.
137 Samuel Willard, 'A Brief Account of a Strange and Unusual Providence of God Befallen to Elizabeth Knap of Groton' in *Groton in The Witchcraft Times*, ed. Samuel A. Green (Cambridge: John Wilson and Son, 1883).
138 Samuel Willard, 'A Brief Account of a Strange and Unusual Providence of God Befallen to Elizabeth Knap of Groton' in *Groton in The Witchcraft Times*, ed. Samuel A. Green (Cambridge: John Wilson and Son, 1883), p. 20. 'This instant' being 15 January according to Willard's narrative.
139 Samuel Willard, 'A Brief Account of a Strange and Unusual Providence of God Befallen to Elizabeth Knap of Groton' in *Groton in The Witchcraft Times*, ed. Samuel A. Green (Cambridge: John Wilson and Son, 1883), p. 21.
140 Perry Miller in *The New England Mind: The Seventeenth Century* (New York: The Macmillan Company, 1939), p. 29. Miller coined the term 'jeremiad' to describe these types of sermons that appeared towards the end of the seventeenth century. These sermons were characterised by viewing disasters as the physical manifestations (and punishment) of the collective sin of the colony.
141 Samuel Willard, *Useful Instructions for a Professing People in Times of great Security and Degeneracy…* (Cambridge: printed by Samuel Green, 1673), pp. 32–33. Italics in the original.
142 John Demos, *Entertaining Satan: Witchcraft and the Culture of Early New England* (Oxford: Oxford University Press, 2004), p. 121.
143 John Demos, *Entertaining Satan: Witchcraft and the Culture of Early New England* (Oxford: Oxford University Press, 2004), p. 119.

144 John Demos, *Entertaining Satan: Witchcraft and the Culture of Early New England* (Oxford: Oxford University Press, 2004).
145 John Demos, *Entertaining Satan: Witchcraft and the Culture of Early New England* (Oxford: Oxford University Press, 2004), p. 120.
146 John Demos, *Entertaining Satan: Witchcraft and the Culture of Early New England* (Oxford: Oxford University Press, 2004), p. 409.
147 Bernard Rosenthal, ed., *Records of the Salem Witch-Hunt* (New York: Cambridge University Press, 2009), p. 15; for scholars who have mistakenly claimed that Goody Glover's first name was either Mary or Ann, see David D. Hall, *Witch-Hunting in Seventeenth-Century New England: A Documentary History 1638-1693* (Boston: Northeastern University Press, 1999), p. 265; Erika Gasser, *Vexed with Devils: Manhood and Witchcraft in Old and New England* (New York: New York University Press, 2017), p. 95; Francis Hill, *A Delusion of Satan* (Cambridge: Da Capo Press, 1997), p. 18, and Benjamin C. Ray, *Satan & Salem: The Witch-Hunt Crisis of 1692* (Charlottesville: University of Virginia Press, 2015), p. 27.
148 Carol. F. Karlsen, *The Devil in the Shape of a Woman: Witchcraft in Colonial New England* (New York: W. W. Norton & Company, 1987), p. 31.
149 King Philip's War is named after Metacomet, the Wampanoag chief who adopted the name Philip because of the friendly relations between his father Massasoit, and the Mayflower Pilgrims. Metacomet was the main leader of these attacks.
150 Francis J. Bremer, *The Puritan Experiment: New England Society from Bradford to Edwards* (New York: St Martin's Press, 1976), p. 153.
151 Francis J. Bremer, *The Puritan Experiment: New England Society from Bradford to Edwards* (New York: St Martin's Press, 1976), p. 154.
152 Francis J. Bremer, *The Puritan Experiment: New England Society from Bradford to Edwards* (New York: St Martin's Press, 1976).
153 James David Drake, *King Philip's War: Civil War in New England 1675-1676* (Boston: University of Massachusetts Press, 1999), p. 4.
154 Richard Weisman, *Witchcraft, Magic, and Religion in 17th Century Massachusetts* (Amherst: The University of Massachusetts Press, 1984), p. 124.
155 Emerson W. Baker, *A Storm of Witchcraft: The Salem Trials and the American Experiment* (Oxford: Oxford University Press, 2015), p. 43.
156 Weisman, *Witchcraft, Magic, and Religion in 17th Century Massachusetts*, p. 123.
157 Richard B. Trask, *The Devil Hath Been Raised: A Documentary History of the Salem Village Witchcraft Outbreak of 1692* (Danvers: Phoenix Publishing, 1992), p. 110.
158 Cotton Mather, *Memorable Providences, Relating to Witchcrafts and Possessions...* (Boston: sold by Joseph Brunning, 1689), p. i.
159 Cotton Mather, *Memorable Providences, Relating to Witchcrafts and Possessions...* (Boston: sold by Joseph Brunning, 1689), p. iii.
160 Cotton Mather, *Memorable Providences, Relating to Witchcrafts and Possessions...* (Boston: sold by Joseph Brunning, 1689), p. iv.
161 Cotton Mather, *Memorable Providences, Relating to Witchcrafts and Possessions...* (Boston: sold by Joseph Brunning, 1689), p. 1.
162 David D. Hall, *Witch-Hunting in Seventeenth-Century New England: A Documentary History 1638-1693* (Boston: Northeastern University Press, 1999), p. 265.

163 Cotton Mather, *Memorable Providences, Relating to Witchcrafts and Possessions*... (Boston: sold by Joseph Brunning, 1689), p. 2.
164 Cotton Mather, *Memorable Providences, Relating to Witchcrafts and Possessions*... (Boston: sold by Joseph Brunning, 1689), p. 3.
165 Cotton Mather, *Memorable Providences, Relating to Witchcrafts and Possessions*... (Boston: sold by Joseph Brunning, 1689).
166 Cotton Mather, *Memorable Providences, Relating to Witchcrafts and Possessions*... (Boston: sold by Joseph Brunning, 1689).
167 Cotton Mather, *Memorable Providences, Relating to Witchcrafts and Possessions*... (Boston: sold by Joseph Brunning, 1689), p. 4.
168 Cotton Mather, *Memorable Providences, Relating to Witchcrafts and Possessions*... (Boston: sold by Joseph Brunning, 1689), p. 5.
169 Cotton Mather, *Memorable Providences, Relating to Witchcrafts and Possessions*... (Boston: sold by Joseph Brunning, 1689), pp. 6–7.
170 Mather, *Memorable Providences*, p. 7; Richard Godbeer, *The Devil's Dominion: Magic and Religion in Early New England* (New York: Cambridge University Press, 1992), p. 189, stated that Glover was an Irish Catholic which could also highlight another reason for the author's inclusion of this statement, highlighting Protestant polemics against Catholics.
171 Cotton Mather, *Memorable Providences, Relating to Witchcrafts and Possessions*... (Boston: sold by Joseph Brunning, 1689), p. 8.
172 Cotton Mather, *Memorable Providences, Relating to Witchcrafts and Possessions*... (Boston: sold by Joseph Brunning, 1689).
173 Cotton Mather, *Memorable Providences, Relating to Witchcrafts and Possessions*... (Boston: sold by Joseph Brunning, 1689), p. 9.
174 Cotton Mather, *Memorable Providences, Relating to Witchcrafts and Possessions*... (Boston: sold by Joseph Brunning, 1689).
175 Cotton Mather, *Memorable Providences, Relating to Witchcrafts and Possessions*... (Boston: sold by Joseph Brunning, 1689), p. 12.
176 Cotton Mather, *Memorable Providences, Relating to Witchcrafts and Possessions*... (Boston: sold by Joseph Brunning, 1689), p. 13.
177 Cotton Mather, *Memorable Providences, Relating to Witchcrafts and Possessions*... (Boston: sold by Joseph Brunning, 1689), p. 15.
178 Cotton Mather, *Memorable Providences, Relating to Witchcrafts and Possessions*... (Boston: sold by Joseph Brunning, 1689), p. 16.
179 Cotton Mather, *Memorable Providences, Relating to Witchcrafts and Possessions*... (Boston: sold by Joseph Brunning, 1689), p. 18.
180 Cotton Mather, *Memorable Providences, Relating to Witchcrafts and Possessions*... (Boston: sold by Joseph Brunning, 1689), p. 34.
181 Cotton Mather, *Memorable Providences, Relating to Witchcrafts and Possessions*... (Boston: sold by Joseph Brunning, 1689), p. 25.
182 W. W., *A True and Just Recorde of the information, Examination and Confession of all the Witches*... (London: Imprinted by Thomas Dawson, 1582), sig. A6v–A6r; Reprint of a letter from Robert Heyrick to his brother Sir William, dated 18 July 1616 in G. L. Kittredge, 'King James I and "The Devil Is an Ass'", *Modern Philology* 9 (No. 2, 1911), p. 4 and p. 6; Edward Fairfax, *A Discourse of Witchcraft as It Was Acted in the Family of Mr Edward Fairfax*..., communicated by R. M. Milnes, 1621, in *Miscellanies of the Philobiblon*

Society, vol. 5 (London: printed by Charles Whittingham, 1858–1859), pp. 51–52; John Webster, *The Displaying of Supposed Witchcraft*... (London: printed by J. M., 1677), pp. 346–347; Anon., *A True and Strange Relation of a Boy, Who Was Entertained by the Devil to Be a Servant to Him*.... (London: Printed by J.H, 1645), p. 4; Mary Moor, *Wonderfull Newes from the North. Or, A True Relation of the Sad and Grievous Torments Inflicted upon the Bodies of Three Children of Mr. George Muschamp*... (London: printed by T.H., 1650), p. 5; ASSI 45/10/3/34, 36, 40, 43–44, sig. 34r.

183 Fairfax, *A Discourse of Witchcraft*, p. 139; ASSI 45/10/3/34, 36, 40, 43–44, sig. 34r; C. L' Estrange Ewen, *Witchcraft and Demonism: A Concise Account Derived from Sworn Depositions and Confessions Obtained in the Courts of England and Wales* (London: Heath Cranton Limited, 1933), p. 375; Thomas Albridge, *The Prevalence of Prayer*... (London: printed for S. Popping, 1717), p. 16.

184 Cotton Mather, *Memorable Providences, Relating to Witchcrafts and Possessions*... (Boston: sold by Joseph Brunning, 1689), p. 27.

185 Cotton Mather, *Memorable Providences, Relating to Witchcrafts and Possessions*... (Boston: sold by Joseph Brunning, 1689), pp. 31–31.

186 Cotton Mather, *Memorable Providences, Relating to Witchcrafts and Possessions*... (Boston: sold by Joseph Brunning, 1689), p. 43.

187 Cotton Mather, *Memorable Providences, Relating to Witchcrafts and Possessions*... (Boston: sold by Joseph Brunning, 1689), p. 49.

188 Cotton Mather, *Memorable Providences, Relating to Witchcrafts and Possessions*... (Boston: sold by Joseph Brunning, 1689), p. 47.

6

1692, THE CHILDREN WHO DEVASTATED NEW ENGLAND

John Demos estimated that at the end of the seventeenth century, the total number of witchcraft cases in New England was ninety-three, with sixteen witches being put to death.[1] After the Salem trials, this number exploded to a total of 234 cases and thirty-four executed witches.[2] In the history of witch-hunting in New England, then, the Salem witchcraft trials represent a significant anomaly. The deviation from caution and restraint shown in previous trials by judges and clergy, combined with a large group of young accusers, became a dangerous mix for a colony plagued by disasters, death and destruction. There is, of course, no monocausal answer for why the Salem witchcraft trials erupted in the winter of 1692, but an outline of the contextual factors affecting Salem Village may help explain why witchcraft accusations flourished on an unprecedented level. The breadth of sources available allows for an in-depth analysis into the various and multifaceted roles children played throughout the nine-month saga.[3] Children were accused as witches or voluntarily confessed to being so; others appeared to be stage-managed by invested adults to secure convictions (like in the St Osyth trials); yet others used their power and influence to subvert the desires of the magistrates and seek vengeance for real or imagined slights against them or their community.

Indeed, the Salem witchcraft trials embody one of the richest collections of sources available for historians seeking to understand the role of children in early modern witchcraft trials. Even when attitudes towards the trials became unpopular, the so-called Salem girls were not accused of malice but were simply thought to have been deceived by Satan. Few questioned whether they had insight into the invisible world or whether their role had been genuine; they simply argued that the girls had been tricked by the greatest

DOI: 10.4324/9781003685319-7

trickster of them all: the Devil. To best understand how this developed, it is first essential to outline the basic narrative of the Salem trials before turning to the immediate context leading to the biggest witch trial in colonial North American history.

In the early months of 1692, Betty Parris and Abigail Williams (the nine-year-old daughter and eleven-year-old niece, respectively, of the then Salem minister, Samuel Parris) began experiencing strange fits.[4] This behaviour was described by contemporary observer John Hale:

> these children were bitten and pinched by invisible agents; their arms, necks and backs turned this way and that way, and returned back again, so it was impossible for them to do of themselves, and beyond the power of any epileptic fits, or natural disease to effect. Sometimes they were taken dumb their mouths stopped, their throats choked, their limbs wracked and tormented so as might move [a] heart of stone.[5]

When no medical diagnosis was found and prayers and fasting did not relieve their torments, the children were said to be 'under the evil hand'.[6] Eventually, the girls named three women as their tormentors.[7] The first three people Betty and Abigail accused were Tituba (Parris' slave from the West Indies), Sarah Osborne (a beggar of ill repute) and Sarah Good (another beggar with an unsavoury reputation). Over the next few months, more people (mostly but not all young girls) joined the afflicted or Salem girls in experiencing fits and tortures from the invisible world. The most noteworthy of these will be introduced in slightly more detail as these core accusers help form the basis on which much of this discussion is predicated.

Ann Putnam Junior, who was approximately thirteen years old in 1692, was the eldest daughter of Ann Putnam Senior and Thomas Putnam who were a wealthy and influential family; she was also one of the most tenacious accusers. Mary Warren, about twenty years old, was a refugee from the Maine frontier and lived as a maidservant in the house of John and Elizabeth Proctor. Abigail Hobbs was about fifteen and was also a refugee from the Maine frontier. Susannah Shelden, about eighteen, was another refugee from Maine. Elizabeth Hubbard, about seventeen years old, was a servant in the house of the physician Dr William Griggs. Mercy Lewis was also about seventeen years old and was a servant in Thomas Putnam's house. Mary Walcott, also seventeen, was the niece of Ann Putnam Senior. There were, of course, other girls, women and even men who accused people during the witch-hunt; however, scholars usually agree that these girls, including Abigail Williams, comprised the most central group of the afflicted. Betty Parris, although previously mentioned, is not usually considered in the core group of accusers, as she disappeared from the judiciary record early in the trials after making initial accusations.[8]

While the group of afflicted girls grew, the accusations they made began to spiral out of control, and by May, over 100 people were in prison. No one was tried until the new Governor, William Phips, arrived with Massachusetts' new charter. On 26 May, Phips established the court of Oyer and Terminer to try the accused witches waiting in gaol. Bridget Bishop was the first to hang on 2 June. After the court next sat in July, Rebecca Nurse, Sarah Good, Elizabeth How, Susannah Martin and Sarah Wilds were executed. An ex-minister of Salem (George Burroughs), along with George Jacobs Senior, Martha Carrier, John Procter and John Willard, was the next to be hanged on 19 August. Sensing the urgency of the crisis, the court quickly sat again in September, and on the 22nd of that month, Mary Esty, Martha Corey, Mary Parker, Alice Parker, Ann Pudeator, Wilmot Redd, Margaret Scott and Samuel Wardwell Senior were executed. Giles Corey was pressed to death a few days before for refusing to enter a plea. By the end of October 1692, and under pressure from an ever-growing resentful community, Governor Phips dissolved the court of Oyer and Terminer, but not before twenty-five people had died (including five that perished in gaol awaiting trial).

This narrative has been thoroughly explored by historians who generally agree on the bare details of what transpired over those tumultuous months in 1692. However, the role that children played within these trials has only just begun to be realised by the scholarship who are usually divided over whether they were 'mad' or 'bad'. Children played an essential role in the instigation and continuation of the Salem witchcraft trials; more than that, some children thrived as agents of the invisible world, others were terrified of it, but all manipulated it and were manipulated by it. To understand this, it is imperative to first outline the immediate context of Salem Village before the 1692 witchcraft trials.

Demographics, Death and Destruction

In his seminal work, *The Devil Hath Been Raised*, Richard Trask noted 'obvious gaps within the surviving records', which makes analysing the demographics of Salem Village prior to 1692 challenging.[9] Notwithstanding, Trask provided brief details of the demographics of Salem during 1692 which assists in understanding how life may have looked immediately before the trials. Understanding the dynamics of Salem Village before the witch trials is integral for interpreting its later struggles.

In 1692, Salem Village comprised of approximately 525 to 550 people.[10] 60% were engaged in farming, while an additional 9% combined both agriculture and trade. Forty-five households – which constituted 75% of the population – had about six people per household, which may reflect how quickly rumours or information spread during the trials as many people could have heard the same information at the same time.[11] Of the total population in 1692, 31% of people were married, which might be connected to the fact that Salem had a relatively young population; almost 50% of inhabitants were under the age of sixteen.[12] Information for at least nine servants survives with various ages and ethnic backgrounds being noted, which is useful in contemplating the variety of different cultures that may have impacted Salem's homes.[13] Lastly, Salem had complex familial relationships as fifteen family names represented 62% of the entire population.[14] This factor should not be forgotten when assessing the interfamilial disputes and tensions that were evident throughout the witchcraft trials.

Contrary to the assertion E.J. Kent made that 'there is no evidence' of a society immersed in a state of panic, there are many examples demonstrating that Salem Village, and indeed Massachusetts, in general, was consumed by chaos at the end of the seventeenth century.[15] With regard to disease, even though New England seemed to fare slightly better than Europe because of its low population density and better food supply, 'epidemic disorders visited death and destruction upon the American colonies with relentless regularity'.[16] For example, due to its contagious nature, smallpox ravaged New England.[17] Colonists were highly aware of its prevalence because of its 'extremely fatal and…loathsome nature'.[18]

In 1690, a smallpox outbreak occurred in Andover, a town approximately seventeen miles away from Salem. Andover was highly important to the witchcraft trials, particularly in the latter half of 1692.[19] The smallpox outbreak killed at least ten people, although multiple authors confirmed that gossip added an additional three deaths to this number.[20] It is widely believed that before this time, Andover had not been introduced to the disease. The outbreak of this disease has direct relevance to the Salem trials that occurred two years later, as it was thought that Martha Carrier – who was executed for witchcraft on 19 August – was responsible for introducing the virus into the Andover community. This, alongside an innate fear of the disease, can be seen in the town records of Andover:

> your sister Carrier and some of her small children are smitten with the contagious disease the smallpox and some have been so inconsiderate as to think that the care of them belongs to the selectmen of Andover which [it] does not…only take care that they do not spread the distemper with wicked carelessness which we are afraid they have already done.[21]

The selectmen of Andover also issued a warrant to the constable to ensure that the Carrier family did not spread the disease or visit the public meetinghouse.[22] Therefore, it can be seen how disease – particularly smallpox – affected the community both physically and mentally, as the indignant attitude towards Martha Carrier for her part in spreading smallpox permanently tainted her reputation. This reputation possibly helps explain why Carrier was the first person from Andover to be arrested on charges of witchcraft following accusations by the Salem girls in 1692.

High mortality rates were another factor that greatly impacted life. Exact mortality rates, like epidemic rates, are inconclusive as records are either incomplete or unavailable. However, some quantitative data can be deduced which may help to give further indication of a struggling community. For example, Salem records show that out of every 1000 births, only 202 males and 313 females survived.[23] Sources indicate that Salem particularly struggled with high infant mortality rates due to its comparatively more 'urban' condition compared to other, more inland or agricultural towns.[24] Outside of these factors, there were other reasons why Cotton Mather referred to the 1690s as the *Decennium Luctuosum* or the 'sorrowful decade'.[25]

Disease and high mortality rates were not the only factors that made life in New England difficult in the late seventeenth century. This period was also greatly affected by what is now known as the Little Ice Age, which affected most of the world between the sixteenth and mid-nineteenth centuries.[26] In the northern hemisphere, the overall temperature dropped by almost one degree celsius.[27] To give two examples of the significance and extent of the Little Ice Age, records indicate that floating ice appeared in Lake Superior in June 1608 and the River Thames in London froze over no fewer than eleven times during the seventeenth century.[28] With regard to New England specifically, sources confirmed that the colony struggled with extreme weather, which often led to famines.[29] In 1696, 1697 and 1698 there were dramatic food shortages as a result of several years of short harvest, causing the price of food, such as wheat and maize, to almost double.[30] In his diary, Cotton Mather described this period as 'the terrible famine' and took to fasting so that he might 'procure food for my distressed neighbours'.[31] In Samuel Sewall's diary, between 1676 and 1699, Sewall makes over sixty-six references to the 'extraordinary cold' and the 'very severe winter of snow and a continuance of cold weather'.[32] The Wabanaki tribe took advantage of this cold weather and fought a series of wars in the form of raids on New England villages to further deplete crucial food supplies.[33] While their physical exteriors were laid open to ferocious weather, disease and war, the children in Salem Village lay at the epicentre of a spiritual battle. Not only did Salem's minister, Samuel Parris, constantly warn his parishioners of Satan's unrelenting attacks, but Parris himself became a contentious figure within his own church, heightening fears surrounding the inevitability of Satan's assault.

Contention and Conflict in the Congregation at Salem Village

The turmoil Salem Village endured regarding its spiritual stability even before Samuel Parris became their minister in 1689 is key to understanding why his appointment and ministerial stay in the Village were met with intense bitterness and animosity.[34] Such feelings of resentment and spiritual unrest in the Salem community prior to the witchcraft outbreak provide perspective when attempting to understand the role of children in the Salem trials; it was Parris' household, after all, where the Devil first came.

In 1666 and 1670, Salem Village petitioned Salem Town multiple times asking permission to hire their own minister so they would not have to travel elsewhere to attend church.[35] They were granted this in 1672, but they were not allowed to bestow church membership nor offer the sacraments to those who attended. Salem Village remained in this frustrating and awkward position for the next seventeen years.[36] At the same time, division broke out between two of Salem's biggest families, the Porters and the Putnams, which only exacerbated feelings of hostility.[37] The effects of the opposition regarding Salem's ministers are clear, as Salem Village's first minister, James Bayley, wrote a letter to the Village's inhabitants venting his frustration that they had questioned his qualifications, his work and even his invitation to preach at the Village.[38] Bayley left the Village in 1680 after only eight years of preaching there.[39] After Bayley, Salem Village had two more ministers before Parris arrived. George Burroughs arrived in November 1680 and left in 1683, and Deodat Lawson arrived in January 1684 before leaving in 1687.[40] All men left their positions in bitter and unhappy circumstances.[41] Circulating through three ministers in fifteen years was highly unusual as ministers were usually in their positions for life.[42] This uncommon occurrence was doubtlessly felt by Salem's inhabitants as they expressed in a letter in 1695: 'we have had three ministers removed already and by every removal our differences have been rather aggravated'.[43] In fact, during the witchcraft trials, William Baker Senior's examination claimed that the Devil came first to Salem due to differences between their ministers.[44] Thus, Salem Village's inherent difficulties in resolving their internal conflicts exasperated their inhabitants; this came to a climax during Samuel Parris' appointment.

Parris believed his call was commerce, not the ministry, but accepted Salem's offer to become their minister after writing a lengthy eight-point document detailing his conditions. Two of the eight conditions concerned a salary of sixty pounds a year with firewood being given to Parris 'in yearly, freely'.[45] As enumerated earlier, Salem Village inhabitants had existing resentment surrounding their new minister's appointment. On 17 May 1689, a full-scale negotiation was set down between Parris and the Salem community with regard to his request for free firewood. The only extant record of this meeting came from Parris himself in a court deposition in 1697 where he described the villagers' unease about his demand for free firewood, stating that Salem lacked the land to easily supply the minister's request.[46] Parris recounted that 'after much agitation' it was agreed the villagers would instead increase his salary by an extra six pounds to account for firewood.[47] While seeming like a trivial episode, this event was the beginning of long and unresolved tensions between Parris and his congregation.

When Parris was ordained as Salem's minister on 19 November 1689, he opened his sermon with Joshua 5:9, 'this day I have rolled away the reproach of Egypt from off you'.[48] Parris was clearly alluding to Salem's struggle in prior years to hold on to a ministerial candidate until his arrival. While this sermon invited harmony and peace at last, the tone of Parris' subsequent sermons reflected his evolving disappointment with his new church while Parris' own actions strengthened feelings of indignation against him. As Parris made obtaining church membership increasingly difficult, he also chose to remain in the minority of Puritan churches by rejecting the so-called Half-Way Covenant. Perhaps unsurprisingly, by 1691, three-fourths of adult villagers had not become church members.[49] Hence, the factionalism evident before his arrival was made worse by these actions, and Parris became increasingly frustrated with the lack of loyalty within his congregation. The congregation itself also seemed dissatisfied with Parris, and this can be seen in their refusal to pay his salary in full after his first two years at the Village.[50]

Parris' retaliation in response to this was reflected in his inflammatory sermons which not only ascribed to the jeremiad genre typical of the late 1680s, but also chastised his embittered congregation for their lack of devotion to him.[51] For example, on 3 January 1692, Parris' sermons discussed how the 'church is separated from the world' and 'it is the main drift of the Devil to pull it all down'.[52] This description can be seen to allude to Parris' detractors in Salem Village. A month later, in his sermon on 14 February, Parris stated, 'the Lord said unto my Lord, sit thou at my right hand until I make thine enemies thy footstool', emphasising the distinction between those who supported him and those who did not.[53] Parris lamented further: 'It is a woeful piece of our corruption in an evil time when the wicked prosper and the Godly party meet with vexations by and by to cry down divine Providence as if God had forsaken the Earth'.[54] In this, Parris claimed that support for him was not merely a choice of alignment, but a choice between God and the Devil. Parris continued his provocative preaching after the witchcraft outbreak occurred, further strengthening the factionalism and fear that were already inflamed within his community.

On 27 March 1692, only weeks after the witchcraft episode began, Parris delivered a sermon called: 'Christ knows how many Devils there are in his churches, and who they are'.[55] The title of this sermon was undoubtedly an allusion to John 6:70, 'Jesus answered them, "have I not chosen you twelve, and one of you is a Devil!"' The thrust of this sermon further denounced people in Parris' congregation as he greatly emphasised the fact that there were both saints and devils in his own church. On spectral evidence, Parris doubted that God allowed the Devil to use the shapes of innocent persons to afflict others and drew particular attention to those who did not support the witchcraft accusations stating: 'a slanderer or an accuser of the godly' was a 'certain sin' that could make a person 'more devilish'.[56]

In the backdrop of these sermons, one event in particular arose that Parris used to blame the witchcraft outbreak on. This allowed him to shift the blame from himself and his provocative preaching, as he undoubtedly felt embarrassed and frustrated that the Devil first came to his door. Mary Sibley was a church member who devised to bake a 'witch cake' to reveal the identities of the persons bewitching Parris' daughter Betty and his niece Abigail Williams.[57] While it was Sibley's idea, she instructed Parris' slave John Indian to bake it. This cake, mixed with rye and the urine of the afflicted children, was fed to a dog who somehow revealed the identities of their tormentors.[58] The idea of baking a 'witch cake' also featured in a pamphlet account of an English witchcraft trial in the case of a young boy called Abraham Swift from Yorkshire in 1683.[59] The instructions for making the cake are almost exactly the same, and while it remains conjecture, it is worth postulating whether Mary Sibley had heard about Swift's case and got the idea to make the 'witch cake' from this English account.

In the church record book, Parris described how he publicly reprimanded Sibley for instructing his 'Indian man' to make the cake, going so far as to claim that the whole episode was contained until this event: 'Nay it never break forth to any considerable light, until diabolical means was used by the making of a cake...'.[60] It is interesting to note that Robert Calef, a later commenter on the trials, also stated that the girls only began making accusations of witchcraft *after* the witch cake was made.[61] Although visibly frustrated with Sibley, Parris was likely grateful he had someone to pin the witchcraft outbreak on, diverting any blame or attention away from himself.

Samuel Parris' entrance into Salem Village as their minister was met with acrimony and resentment that only hardened the factionalism already evident before his arrival. This factionalism was implicit during the witch trials as Paul Boyer and Stephen Nissenbaum convincingly argued that the majority of the witchcraft accusations came from families that supported Parris against families who did not.[62] In fact, Richard Weisman argued that until 31 May: 'the suspicions of the afflicted cannot be clearly disentangled from those of the village groups with whom they were associated'.[63] Thus, the turmoil the inhabitants of Salem Village experienced in the late 1600s, and Samuel Parris' role in exacerbating it, should not be underestimated when analysing the direct influences on the children within Salem. It was within this context that Betty Parris and Abigail Williams, confined within the walls of Parris' parsonage and suffering together without much material or spiritual support, were first molested by the Devil.

To Be Seen and Not Heard

The environment before the witch trials begun was plagued by disasters, including physical wars from the Indians and spiritual wars incited by Samuel Parris in his quest for support and loyalty amongst his congregation. The generation the Salem girls belonged to not only had to endure growing up in this turbulent period, but they also bore the heavy burden of being blamed for the physical and spiritual failings of the colony. If the first generation were regarded as the exonerated founding fathers and the second were those who persisted against the odds to uphold that mission, the third were described as apostates who were rejected by God.[64] This can be seen in the aforementioned feelings of helplessness and despair that would have plagued the early lives of these girls. While the Salem girls were not mentioned explicitly in Parris' sermons as being responsible for their community's woes, it is possible that this was due to the fact that the first two afflicted girls were part of Parris' own family; explicitly denouncing the generation which included two of his kin would have only added to the embarrassment he undoubtedly felt as the Devil's first victim. Other members of the second generation – which included the magistrates – would have wanted to feel that they themselves were not responsible for the failings befalling the colony, so blaming the third generation was perhaps another way to alleviate their own guilt.

Historian Mary Beth Norton stated that because most of the Salem girls were young, unmarried and poor they were supposed to be 'seen and not heard'.[65] Although comprehensive biographical details of the Salem girls are either not recorded or no longer extant, a close inspection of what does survive reveals information that assists in understanding their behaviour during the witchcraft trials. As stated earlier, of the eleven core accusers, Abigail Hobbs, Mercy Lewis, Mary Warren and Susannah Shelden were all refugees from the northern frontier. Of these four, only Susannah Shelden did not work as a domestic servant, although Enders A. Robinson contended that she lived in poverty with her mother.[66] Elizabeth Hubbard was a servant in the house of William Griggs, the doctor who supposedly first diagnosed Betty's and Abigail's fits as bewitchment.[67] Hubbard, Warren and Lewis were also orphans.[68]

These girls represented the lowest rung of society and must have lived difficult and stressful lives. Apart from the overwhelming tragedies befalling the colony, it is evident from the trial documents that many of these girls who worked as domestic servants faced other trauma at the hands of their masters. For example, in a deposition by Samuel Sibley against John Proctor, Sibley stated that Proctor 'would fetch his jade home and thresh the Devil out of her' for having fits and accusing others of witchcraft.[69] Proctor later confirmed that the girl he was referring to was his servant Mary Warren.[70] Furthermore, Sibley stated that when Warren first had fits, Proctor kept her 'close to the wheel and threatened to thresh her' to stop her fits which proved successful for a time until her torments started again.[71] Whether these comments referencing abuse were faked to discredit the accused or were genuine expressions of ill-treatment remains uncertain; Proctor's verification of the girl he was referring to in his comment to Sibley suggests that these comments were genuine.

In a general sense, historian Carol Karlsen showed that most of the other Salem girls had miserable life prospects with grim marital opportunities.[72] As for the other children that became encapsulated in the Salem drama, historians know little else about them, but it can only be assumed that their lives were difficult in other ways, especially in the aftermath of the trials. For example, Dorothy Good – who was only four or five when she was accused as a witch – was committed to prison for at least seven months. Dorothy was considered 'very chargeable' having 'little to or no reason to govern herself' by her father who pleaded with the judges for restitution in 1710.[73] Thus, the Salem witch trials erupted in a society besieged by disease, unrelenting cold weather, war, jeremiads from embittered ministers and an encompassing, overwhelming feeling of hopelessness and despair. This political and religious conflict made Salem 'ripe for a witch hunt'.[74] With the immediate context established, Wendel Craker's question requires exploration: 'that the victims of [the] Salem trials suffered from malice is abundantly clear. But the question remains, whose malice?'[75]

Stage-Managing the Salem Girls

Most Salem historians argue that without the eager support of the families of the afflicted, the Salem trials may have looked very different.[76] The families of the Salem girls were intrinsically involved not only in their everyday care and supervision but also during the legal procedure of the trials.[77] For example, Thomas Putnam (Ann Putnam Junior's father) wrote more depositions for presentation to the grand jury than anyone else and had a high success rate in getting them to act against the accused. Putnam rarely received an 'ignoramus' on a document he completed, and his success rate for receiving 'true bills' was close to perfect. The idea that some girls were in some way 'stage-managed' by their families and other invested adults is an important idea that has persisted in the scholarship.[78] Therefore, determining the extent of familial manipulation on the Salem girls is integral in understanding their multifaceted role within the witchcraft trials.

There is evidence in the trial documents that the afflicted and their families colluded amongst themselves, which, in turn, influenced and manipulated the accusations and behaviour of the Salem girls. One instance of this can be seen in the frequent examples of the Salem girls' inability to correctly identify an accused person in court. The records show at least eighteen examples of instances where the afflicted girls and/or the judicial body were unable to correctly identify the person who was allegedly tormenting them.[79] This begs the question, how did the afflicted know who they accused? Speculative answers exist in the trial documents. Yet, this intriguing feature of the trials has not been comprehensively explored in the secondary literature, including by Rosenthal himself in *Records* who only simply, but importantly, noted its frequency. One example comes from a single page of Samuel Parris' notebook which is the only surviving page from this source.[80] This single page detailed fits that consumed Abigail Williams, Mary Walcott and John Indian between 4 and 12 April. This document was relinquished to the marshal as part of evidence being collected to support the case against the Proctors.[81] On 12 April, Parris provided a minute-by-minute description of the apparent spectral assaults of John Proctor and other accused witches against the aforementioned three afflicted persons.[82] From this, historians can deduce that Parris – and probably other family members of the Salem girls – kept copious notes about the behaviour of the afflicted. This demonstrates that adults involved likely had information regarding the accused persons such as dates, names and times that they could have easily provided to the Salem girls.[83]

In fact, the trial documents show that family members of the afflicted frequently had conversations outside of the courtroom which were often referenced and retold in depositions and testimonies.[84] Historians will never know the entirety or extent of these conversations, but there is evidence that some family members manipulated the Salem girls in order to coordinate their responses and reactions in court. For example, in a statement given by Samuel Nurse and John Tarbell in defence of Rebecca Nurse, they stated that during a stay at Thomas Putnam's house on 28 March, they asked him 'whether the girl that was afflicted did first speak of Goody Nurse before others mentioned her to her'.[85] Putnam replied that the girl (later in the document confirmed to be Mercy Lewis) said that she saw 'thc apparition of a pale-faced woman…but did not know her name'.[86] After Samuel Nurse and John Tarbell again asked who told her it was Rebecca Nurse, Mercy Lewis answered that it was 'Goody Putnam' who had told her. Then, Ann Putnam Senior replied that it was Mercy Lewis who had told her and so the two went back and forth accusing one another.[87] Finally, Nurse and Tarbell added: 'this was before any [were] afflicted at Thomas Putnam's besides his daughter [and] that they told his daughter it was Goody Nurse'.[88] The implication in this final comment was that both of the girls in Thomas Putnam's house did not accuse Rebecca Nurse until Thomas or Ann Putnam Senior told them to.

Indeed, silence is a key feature in the accusations of the Salem girls which seemed to reflect a level of uncertainty as to how to proceed. For example, on 10 April, Ephraim Shelden stated that while he was at Lieutenant Ingersoll's house, he heard Mercy Lewis cry out upon Goodwife Cloyce in her fit, yet when she came out of it, Lewis said that she saw no one.[89] When Shelden asked if it was Rebecca Nurse, Sarah Cloyce or Martha Corey, Lewis affirmed that she saw no one. Thus, it is highly likely that the adults surrounding the afflicted often assisted or even constructed accusations, information or evidence to support the trials. These pieces of evidence are therefore crucial in understanding the multifaceted role of the Salem girls. The adults in these situations were clearly invested in encouraging denunciations and knew that the most likely way to get successful accusations in court was to feed them to the children.

Further evidence of this can be found from the testimony of Samuel Barton and John Houghton on 5 August, the day after the aforementioned event in March regarding Rebecca Nurse. However, the two men did not admit this information into court until August for reasons that remain unclear. These men also overheard a conversation between the Putnams and the afflicted where they were being instructed on whose spectre they saw, but this time, it was about the Proctors:

> I being at Thomas Putnam's helping to tend the afflicted folks heard them talking who the children complained of and I heard them tell Mercy Lewis that she cried out of Goody Proctor and Mercy Lewis said that she did not cry out of Goody Proctor nor nobody she said she did say there she is but did not tell them who and Thomas Putnam and his wife and others told her that she cried out of Goody Proctor and Mercy Lewis said if she did it was when she was out of her head for she said she saw nobody.[90]

Not only does this statement give credibility to the claims made by Samuel Nurse and John Tarbell about the influence of Thomas and Ann Putnam Senior over the Salem girls living in their household, but it also demonstrates a level of agency exhibited by the girls. While Mercy Lewis was clearly under pressure by Thomas Putnam and Ann Putnam Senior to denounce the people they named, Lewis stood her ground in many instances and either claimed that she saw no one or denied that the person they named was the person she saw. This level of boldness from Lewis demonstrates a type of power struggle between the Salem girls and the adults with regard to who held the reins of the preternatural world. In the end, it was the Salem girls' accusations and supernatural knowledge that would be the linchpin in nearly all cases that came to court. The adults may have had a hand in who they accused, but the children ultimately controlled who and what they saw in the invisible world.

One last example that demonstrated external manipulation on the Salem girls can be seen in the examination of Martha Corey. In her examination the prosecutor asked Corey: 'how could you tell that the child was bid to observe what clothes you wore when some came to speak with you?' Corey replied that her husband had told her.[91] The prosecutors seemed fixated on this issue of clothing until Corey's unsatisfying answers forced them to change the subject. A deposition by Ezekiel Cheever and Edward Putnam from the same day clarified this matter. They claimed that Ann Putnam Junior was asked to observe the clothes that Corey wore (which was a typical experiment in English bewitchment cases).[92] As a covenant member of the church, they wanted to be certain Ann was not mistaken about the person she accused. However, Ann claimed that '[Corey] blinded her but told her that her name was Corey and she should see her no more before it was night…'.[93] When these two men visited Corey, she asked them twice: 'does she tell you what clothes I have on?' When Corey found out that Ann was unable to provide an answer, Corey 'made but little answer to this but seemed to smile as if she had showed us a pretty trick'.[94] These two documents demonstrate the external manipulation and secret conversations that permeated outside of the families of the afflicted. Corey claimed that her husband told her that Ann was supposed to know what clothes she wore. Unfortunately for Corey, this did little to prove her innocence as Ann cleverly attributed her lack of knowledge about the clothes to Corey's supernatural powers, demonstrating Ann's own level of ingenuity.

In combination with these secret conversations and stage-managing, there is evidence in the trial documents that reveal how Parris embellished some reports and even changed crucial information to reflect his belief in the guilt of the accused. A discrepancy in the trial sources is significant, given that the documents themselves are over 300 years old, as well as the likelihood that drafts and other documents might have been destroyed or otherwise lost to posterity. Therefore, historians should not assume that because only a few examples of embellishment exist, this does not necessarily mean it did not happen with more frequency. For example, two copies of the examination of Susannah Martin survive, a draft and a completed copy, both written by Parris on 2 May. In the draft version, Parris wrote: 'Elizabeth Hubbard was afflicted and then the Marshall who was by her said she pinched her hand'.[95] The strong implication was that Hubbard pinched her own hand. Possibly because the apparent fraud exhibited by Hubbard might compromise the validity of the document, Parris changed this in the completed version of Martin's examination stating: 'the Marshall said she [insinuating Martin] pinched her hands and Elizabeth Hubbard was immediately afflicted'.[96] Whether Parris was simply clarifying what he meant in the previous document or changed the narrative to make it seem as though Martin had used her supernatural powers to inflict pain on Hubbard cannot be determined with absolute certainty. However, the latter is more likely given that there was evidence of Parris corrupting evidence more than once. Take, for example, the examination of Dorcas Hoar which was also taken on 2 May. At one point in the examination, Parris claimed: 'the marshal struck and several of the bystanders testified that they saw a fly like a Millar'.[97] This is very likely a direct reference to English demonologist Joseph Glanvill's *Saducismus Triumphatus* where he wrote that 'a fly like a great Millar flew out from the place', the fly being a witch's 'familiar'.[98] Not only does this give further evidence to the idea that some of the trial records were corrupted, but it also demonstrated that Parris, like Cotton Mather, was familiar with English demonological works which could have affected the behaviour of the Salem girls.

John Alden's account of his examination on 31 May offers another clear example of one of the Salem girls being stage-managed by an anonymous man in the courtroom. The document was likely written after the event, and although written in the third person, the fact that the document ended with the addition 'per John Alden' supports the idea that the account was either written or narrated by Alden himself.[99] In the document, which survives only in Robert Calef's *More Wonders*, Alden described how he was denounced openly in court:

> the magistrates demanded of them [the Salem girls] several times, who it was of all the people in the room that hurt them? One of the accusers pointed several times at one Captain Hill, there present but spoke nothing. The same accuser had a Man standing at her back to hold her up; he [leaned] down to her ear, then she cried out, Alden, Alden, afflicted her. One of the magistrates asked her if she had ever seen Alden, she answered no, he asked how she knew it was Alden? She said, the Man told her so.[100]

While acknowledging the biases of both Calef and Alden, who were both staunch in their condemnation of the trials, this document appears to show an adult identifying Alden to a Salem girl who then denounced him to his face in court. Hence, these examples reflect a repetitive theme which suggests that at least some of the persons the Salem girls accused were due them being encouraged by invested adults. However, evidence also exists of the girls attempting to exert their own agency over accusations that were made, revealing a considerable struggle between the girls and adults. Moreover, it was not only the families that affected the behaviour of the Salem girls; no matter how influential and credible the girls were in their accusations and behaviour, this alone never could have warranted arrests or death sentences without the formal and legal support of the court. The coercion and manipulation by the magistrates then is also crucial in understanding the role of children in the Salem witchcraft trials.

'In Playful Terror'

In his legal assessment of the Salem trials, Peter Charles Hoffer postulated that the Salem witchcraft outbreak was begun by the girls 'in playful terror', implying that it started as a childish game. Hoffer argued that once the girls realised the gravity and possible consequences of their actions, they had to continue to respond to judicial and familial demands.[101] Hoffer concluded that the girls knew the wickedness of lying but persisted, and adults like Parris encouraged them, 'once they had gone public'.[102] This is only one of many differing interpretations regarding the origins of the witchcraft trials. Through analysing the trial evidence, it seems that there is a grain of truth to Hoffer's assessment. However, this idea only begins to scratch the surface behind the role of children in the Salem trials. What Hoffer did not seem to account for is just how complex, sustained and multifaceted the relationship was between the Salem girls and the judges. Using Abigail Hobbs and Mary Warren as case studies, it becomes apparent that some girls had symbiotic relationships with the judges during the trials. Hobbs and Warren appeared to exchange evidence or accusations in return for mercy in the form of legal protection. Although similar interpretations have been raised by other scholars, most have failed to discern between the accusers or give the Salem girls any considerable thought or agency to their actions, choosing rather to focus on other power dynamics or related consequential factors of the trials.[103] For example, Benjamin C. Ray claimed the girls were 'young, frightened and manipulated', whose fits were a 'theatrical display' endorsed by the magistrates and local ministers present.[104] However, Ray's idea is generalised across all the afflicted, and his removal of agency from the girls does not allow for a thorough discussion of the discursive sophistication these girls exhibited in order to keep those in power on their side.

This idea of a symbiotic relationship between some of the afflicted girls and the judges does not mean that the trials were a mass hoax or conspiracy. Nor does it mean that the girls were always content to obey the judge's demands. Furthermore, the motivation or reasoning for each of these girls cannot be assumed to be the same. Hobbs seemed to have a genuine belief in her own guilt, whereas Warren began her role as an accusatory Salem girl and found herself accused when she appeared to betray the other afflicted girls. Hence, no clear-cut formula exists to perfectly explain each of the motivations or behaviours of the two girls. Yet, an acknowledgement that some symbiotic relationship existed offers a fresh insight into the role of these particular girls which, in turn, helps to add to the varied role of this neglected but important group of Salem girls.

Another important factor to consider is how the other Salem girls responded to Hobbs' and Warrens' relationship to the judges. The other Salem girls attempted to keep their integrity by distancing themselves from these two girls. The trial documents reveal multiple instances where the other Salem girls appeared to gatekeep knowledge and insight of the invisible world from the two girls in order to uphold their own credibility and power, barring these other children access to it. Hobbs and Warren faced enormous pressure and pain through admitting complicity with the Devil in order to obtain judicial protection, but they did so in an attempt to join the ranks of the other Salem girls who had power. In this way, 'in playful terror' has a revised meaning: some Salem girls *were* playing a role in terror, not merely as wicked children but as fearful ones, struggling for a guarantee of their lives.

'I have been very wicked': Abigail Hobbs

Abigail Hobbs was the second person to confess after Tituba, and her confession on 19 April came after her indictment for acts of witchcraft committed against five of the afflicted girls.[105] Not requiring the intense questioning of the judges, fifteen-year-old Hobbs freely admitted to meeting the Devil and making a covenant with him 'three or four years ago' when she was just eleven or twelve.[106] The details Hobbs gave surrounding this event were incredibly detailed. Hobbs stated she signed the Devil's book and was contracted to serve him for four years.[107] She would have to 'hurt' Ann Putnam Junior and Mercy Lewis in exchange for 'fine clothes', which she admitted she never received.[108] Hobbs implicated others and also validated the judge's use of spectral evidence admitting that the Devil had her consent to hurt others in her spirit.[109] Hobbs also showed signs of repentance: 'I hope God will forgive me' to which the prosecutor replied, somewhat surprisingly, 'the Lord give you repentance'.[110] Still in court, Hobbs 'was taken deaf' whereby the other Salem girls responded by saying that Sarah Good and Sarah Osborne '[ran] their fingers into the examinant's ears'.[111] It is also noteworthy that none of the afflicted girls were tormented during Hobbs' examination, even expressing sympathy for her after she had left stating openly in court that 'they were very sorry for the condition this poor Abigail Hobbs was in which compassion they expressed over and over again'.[112]

Hobbs' confession, on the surface, seems akin to Elizabeth Knap's bewitchment in Groton, 1671. Indeed, both reflected delicate balancing acts of girls mediating both the spiritual and natural realms, as well as interpreting their internal struggles through the filter of demonological discourse. Unlike Knap – who never faced judicial punishment – Hobbs' examination reflected a detailed narrative that thoughtfully combined witchcraft beliefs with Hobbs' own individual experiences; this appeared to satisfy both the judges and the afflicted. In this way, Hobbs' confession was clearly effectual in winning the favour of those in power through cooperation. That is not to say that Hobbs was simply lying to appease them, although the chances of a 'deal' being struck whereby Hobbs offered a confession in return for support from the other accusers cannot be ruled out.[113] However, other, more sophisticated interpretations can be substantiated by the trial evidence that allow for a deeper appreciation of Hobbs' role in the trials.

Another way of interpreting Hobbs' confession is seeing it as an expression of *her* truth. Hobbs may have truly believed she had met the Devil and made a covenant with him. As Louise Jackson convincingly argued in her work on witch trials in seventeenth-century England, Abigail Hobbs may have been 'contextualising her own insecurities and experiences within the linguistic framework of demonology'.[114] Jackson argued that women's impulses, 'bad' thoughts and ideas were sometimes explained by an association with the Devil: 'Satan was everything you did not want to admit to'.[115] While Jackson's argument revolved around women's ideas about being 'good' wives and mothers – the witch being an inversion of these things – it is easy to extend this idea onto fifteen-year-old Hobbs.[116] Hobbs was a refugee from the Maine frontier after having escaped a Wabanaki assault in September 1689.[117] Her denunciation as a witch seemingly came as no surprise as two trial documents reveal that she was a troublesome child. For example, Priscilla Chubb testified against Hobbs stating that after a discussion about 'her wicked carriages and disobedience to her mother and father' Hobbs replied that 'she did not care what anybody said to her for she had seen the Devil and had made a covenant or bargain with him'.[118] Margaret Knight also testified against Hobbs, stating that Hobbs had told Knight her mother was not baptised whereby Hobbs 'immediately took water and sprinkled [it] in her mother's face and said she did baptise her in the name of the Father, Son and Holy Ghost'.[119] Jackson's idea of externalising guilt onto Satan is implied as Abigail's 'baptism' of her mother may reveal guilt or embarrassment that her mother had not received the first sacrament.

While only brief, these depositions reveal a non-compliant and headstrong girl who believed she had no one to fear since the Devil was on her side. This use of language might also reveal that Hobbs' feelings and insecurities manifested themselves through an easily identifiable medium: the spiritual world. Since these feelings were perceived as negative, Hobbs may have believed she had an association with Satan. Hence, believing that she was a disobedient child, adverse to society's standards of how a fifteen-year-old girl should behave, with a mother who was not baptised, Hobbs could have truly believed that she was in league with the Devil, thinking it was Satan's influence on her that made her act out against her parents. The fact that Hobbs was committed to prison for her elaborate confession, while Knap was not, is a testament to the development of witch-hunting attitudes as well as the persuasive performances of the other afflicted Salem girls.

After Hobbs' first examination, she was examined again in prison on 20 April and 12 May, which were the first recorded examinations of an accused person in prison during the Salem trials.[120] These examinations clearly reflected the judge's keen desire for information that would validate their *a priori* assumptions. Hobbs described Continental demonological features such as flying to escape examination and performing a mock 'sacrament' outside Samuel Parris' house where she and her fellow witches 'did eat of the red bread and drink of the red wine'.[121] Hobbs' knowledge of Continental aspects of witchcraft was impressive for a young girl, but her admonitions were highly significant; through validating the judge's beliefs of a witch cult in Salem, Hobbs confirmed that the children held supernatural knowledge and were permitting judges control, allowing them to glimpse into the invisible world.

Hobbs' second examination in May was much more detailed and targeted as the judges tried to build a case against Salem's former minister, George Burroughs. Burroughs did not appear in either of the April examinations of Hobbs, but the prosecutor was clearly interested in discussing his involvement in witchcraft in this examination on 12 May (which is the same day Burroughs was taken into custody over witchcraft charges). In this examination, the first recorded question was: 'Did Mr Burroughs bring you any of the poppets of his wives to stick into?'[122] The inclusion of Burroughs' first two wives is significant, as the documents reveal that there was a suspicion that he had murdered them.[123] Hobbs' responses indicated that she was unwilling to fully implicate Burroughs which seems to suggest that discussing him was not her idea. In line with aforementioned ideas of internalising her guilt, Hobbs instead seemed more interested in discussing her own culpability. After offering unclear answers on Burroughs, Hobbs eventually described how she pushed thorns into the 'likeness' of persons whom Hobbs struggled to name, although she stated that as a consequence of her actions a woman named Mary Laurence died. This admission also seems to demonstrate Hobbs' internalised guilt, as she might have really believed in her witchcraft abilities and thought that her actions against Mary, which were spurred on by 'some words' they exchanged, did eventually kill her.[124] After her reference to Mary Laurence, Hobbs was pressed on who brought the 'images' to her, to which she finally affirmed: 'It was Mr Burroughs'.[125] However, this exchange was brief, as Hobbs immediately returned to implicating herself as the prosecutor asked: 'How did you know Mr Burroughs was a witch? [Hobbs answered] I don't know, she owned again she had made two covenants with the Devil... and she confessed herself to have been a witch these six years'.[126] Clearly, Hobbs' shame was overwhelming as she could not help but constantly blame herself. The prosecutor seemed interested in Hobbs' guilt only so much as it helped build a case against Burroughs, whose persecution as a former minister of Salem Village was particularly profound.[127]

Hobbs was further examined in prison on 29 June, this time to support a charge against John Proctor. The examination was short and described an apparent incident where Proctor, being alone in 'a room' with Hobbs, told her 'that she had better to afflict than be afflicted that she should not be hanged but encouraged her to afflict Ann Putnam and persuaded her to set her hand to the book'.[128] These two instances demonstrate the symbiotic relationship between Hobbs and the judges. In exchange for information, Hobbs seemed to be offered some kind of judicial protection or mercy, or so it seemed as Hobbs was eventually sentenced to death on 17 September.[129] Why this sentence was not carried out is unclear, as others who were condemned with her were hanged only days after the sentencing.[130] The only document that survives that indicated that Hobbs received a reprieve from the Governor was a reference Phips made to 'five others who were condemned' who he had sent a reprieve for 'whereby the execution was stopped'.[131] Therefore, even though Hobbs was part of a symbiotic relationship between her and the judges, this does not mean this relationship was not plagued with doubt and suffering. As Hobbs languished in prison for a total of ten months, she must have been acutely aware of the precarious position she was in: caught between the snare of the Devil, the watchful eyes of the judges and Gallows Hill.[132]

Although Hobbs may have been in a compromised position and certainly did not have as much liberty as other Salem girls, it is still important to recognise the levels of agency she demonstrated through cooperating with the judges. Indeed, some scholars have characterised Hobbs: '… and her companions as girls rebelling against the repressive patriarchal nature of Puritan society…'.[133] It seems unlikely and slightly protofeministic to suggest that Hobbs was astute enough to be able to recognise and devise a way to dismantle the patriarchal Puritan structure. Hobbs was undoubtedly aware of her dire situation as a confessed witch, and whether she knew the extent of it or not, her cooperation proved to be in her favour. Hobbs used supernatural mediums and language she understood to externalise her feelings of guilt and shame, delicately translating this into giving the judges information they wanted. The judges, like they had done in countless trials before, took advantage of this and used Hobbs for their own purposes through building and supporting cases. Hence, whether Hobbs realised it or not, she had more influence and power in her prison cell; it was a role that likely spared her life. However, it is important to recognise that it was the other Salem girls and not just the judges that had a role in manipulating and influencing other children.

'I will tell, I will tell': Mary Warren

Mary Warren has attracted more attention than Abigail Hobbs in both popular and scholarly circles as the indecisive and implicitly more 'mad' member of the Salem girls.[134] Indeed, Warren's grievous fits and explicit acts of self-harm throughout the trials may be why she has come to be depicted as the 'subservient, naive [and] lonely girl'.[135] Warren was indicted on the same day as Hobbs. Yet, the other Salem girls fell into loud fits before Warren even reached the bar.[136] The first question Warren was asked revealed her dual role as an accused and an accuser: 'You were a little while ago an afflicted person, now you are an afflicter, how does this come to pass?'[137] Warren replied that it was attributed to 'a great mercy of God'.[138] More importantly, when Elizabeth Hubbard said that Warren 'was well', Warren replied: 'The afflicted persons did but dissemble'.[139] The word dissemble is striking as it can either mean 'to deceive' or 'to disguise'. The strong insinuation was that Warren had told the judges that the afflicted girls were frauds. The afflicted were calculated in their response and became 'grievously afflicted', exclaiming that Warren had somehow admitted her complicity with the Devil: 'Well here was just now...a tormentor in her apparition and now she owns that she ha[s] made a league with the Devil'.[140] Unsure how to respond, Warren fell down into a fit. Seizing their opportunity to maintain their credibility and control in the invisible world, the other Salem girls began interpreting Warren's fit: 'Goody Corey and Proctor and his wife came in, in their apparition and struck her [Warren] down'.[141] Warren, clearly overwhelmed, began to cry: 'Oh! I am sorry for it, I am sorry for it and wringed her hands and fell a little while into a fit again'.[142] At this point, it is unclear whether Warren was apologising for tormenting the girls or betraying them. The latter appears likely based on her subsequently joining them as an afflicted girl.

Her internal turmoil is evident throughout the trial documents as she struggled to decide whether she will accuse or be accused herself. Some phrases read as if Warren was trying to denounce the accusers crying: 'I will tell, I will tell they brought me to it...' as well as referring to Satan as a 'she' claiming: 'she saith she will kill me', which appears to be the only time in New English witchcraft trials where the Devil was referred to explicitly as a woman.[143] However, Warren was prevented from being able to discredit the authority of the Salem girls, as she was frequently impeded with fits so dreadful, she was forced to leave the room. On one of the occasions she was taken out, Warren was spoken to 'in private' by the ministers and magistrates.[144] What occurred between them is not recorded; however, upon her return, the judges had apparently accepted her confession and Warren was committed to prison. For the other Salem girls, their treatment of Mary Warren is a remarkable display of power and manipulation that erased the last major threat to their credibility, forcing Warren to withhold whatever their true intentions were. For the judges, Warren's preternatural insight became a useful weapon in the fight against the coven of witches that had infiltrated Salem Village, and they used her, like Abigail Hobbs, for information.

This can be seen in Warren's examination in prison on 20 April which was used to support the growing case against John and Elizabeth Proctor. The judges likely assumed she was the best candidate to use since Warren was their domestic servant. Warren supported claims that the Proctors were witches and also gave evidence against Giles Corey, describing in detail what his spectre was wearing when he came to attack her which, when tested, proved to be accurate.[145] How Warren knew about the clothes Corey wore when he was in a separate cell to her can only be explained in three ways: either she really had seen Corey's spectre, she was told the information beforehand or she had guessed. This examination was short, and it appeared the prosecutor was unsatisfied with Warren's information, as she was further examined in prison the following day.

Similar to the day before, Warren seemed reluctant to fully implicate the Proctors, giving as little information as she believed she could get away with. The magistrates pressed on for precise details including whether she had touched the book; she replied only with the tip of her finger. Then, they asked what she had dipped it in and she replied 'but her mouth'. Finally, they asked Warren whether it was wet and what it tasted like.[146] These back-to-back examinations, searching for specific details, support the idea that Warren was used to support the mounting case against the Proctors. Hoping to use her spectral sight, the magistrates counted on Warren to place John and Elizabeth Proctor in the invisible world, so they could be punished in the visible one.

Warren's moral integrity and perhaps mental stability seemed compromised by her stay in prison and the relentless interrogations. Despite the prosecutor's questions about the Proctors, Warren (like Abigail Hobbs) could not stop blaming herself. For example, Warren asserted that her signing of the Devil's book must have been her own voluntary act.[147] Becoming further convinced of her own guilt, Warren pondered whether she really was a witch: 'being asked whether she had not been instrumental to afflict the afflicted persons [Warren] answered no but when she heard they were afflicted in her shape she began to fear it was the Devil that hurt in her shape'.[148] Yielding to her unique role as an accused/confessed witch who also accused others, Mary Warren soon became one of the most tenacious Salem girls.

The way in which the judges used Warren can be accurately summed up in the examination of John Jackson Junior. On 27 August, John was brought before the judges who began asking him about his familiarity with Satan. Implementing an interesting approach – perhaps as a way to appease the judges by telling them what they wanted to hear – John said that he was bewitched by his aunt Elizabeth How, who had been executed almost a month earlier.[149] After a brief discussion on the nature of his bewitchment, the Salem girls pointed out that John's father was standing close by 'and bid him not [to] confess, which he owned and cried'.[150] John tried to distract the judges by continuing to talk about his aunt Elizabeth, but the judges were now curious about his father, implicating him in the questions to John: 'But you say your Aunt How and your father bewitched you, when did your father bewitch you?' John responded that his father had not bewitched him, to which the judges threatened him: 'If you will not confess, witnesses should be called in'.[151] At this point, Mary Warren was called in and was asked if John was one of the men she had seen 'the other night'. She replied that he was but then was struck down into a fit.[152] When she regained control of herself, Warren stated that John had afflicted her and she had seen him afflict others. Calling Warren in to intimidate John and provide evidence of his guilt right when he was most vulnerable was a strategy the judges used often with other Salem girls. As in other cases like the Throckmortons and the Goodwin children, the physical writings of the children and their words provided the most useful evidence against the accused. Thus, the afflicted were largely successful in giving the prosecutors evidence they themselves could not obtain.

Diabolical Lightning Rods

While there is evidence that reflects how the trials were influenced by invested adults, as well as showing how children like Abigail Hobbs and Mary Warren were manipulated and coerced by the magistrates, this does not suffice to explain the entire role of children in the Salem witchcraft trials. Despite numerous scholars' indications that the Salem girls were nothing more than helpless victims of organised hostility, other historians noticed the nuances in this argument, showing how a group of homogenous adults working towards one goal is simply not a feasible explanation:

> to interpret the conduct of the Salem trials as merely a response to the demands of any of these constituencies, however, is to overlook important differences among the popular, theological, and official orientations to the problem of witchcraft. Ultimately, the objectives of the court transcended and even conflicted with the more limited concerns of each of the groups with which it was temporarily allied.[153]

Yet, even an acceptance of some level of external manipulation does not remove the centrality of the Salem girls within the trials. The sophisticated and intricate ways they responded to external manipulation demonstrated extensive integrity and perceptiveness. Outside of the discernment shown by Hobbs and Warren, there are other examples where the Salem girls seemed to act almost independently – and sometimes at odds with – their family's and the magistrate's directions. This required the girls to exercise their own autonomy which adds to their importance as meaningful historical actors. As Kent affirms: 'The evolution of the witch-hunt, the unfolding of events day to day, and the management of their credibility within this dynamic tale of witchcraft affliction required a great deal of perspicacity on the part of the young accusers'.[154]

Even though the families of the girls and the magistrates seemed willing to believe the afflicted, there were countless attempts by family members of the accused to discredit the Salem girls. However, there is no indication of anyone successfully achieving this in 1692. In fact, it should not be forgotten how successful the Salem girls were in achieving guilty verdicts. For example, out of the nineteen people who were executed, all but three were accused by Ann Putnam Junior who was involved in the cases of sixty-nine defendants. Through examining how effective the Salem girls were in a number of key cases, it becomes clear that the Salem girls were more significant than simply being 'mad' or 'bad'; they were diabolical lightning rods and decisive shapers of the witchcraft trials. The first example of this can be seen in the case of Mary Esty.

Mary Esty – Rebecca Nurse's sister – was first examined on 22 April. The exact reasons why Esty was first accused are unclear; however, the Putnams appeared to have held a grievance against Nurse, so perhaps being her close relation evoked suspicion. Her examination is brief and the prosecutor seemed reluctant – in comparison to previous accusations – to believe in Esty's guilt, asking the Salem girls three times to confirm that this was the woman who afflicted them.[155] Upon the insistence of the girls, Esty was committed to prison. Rosenthal noted that she was released from prison on 18 May but was imprisoned two days later upon Mercy Lewis' insistence.[156] On the day Esty was re-arrested, two statements by no fewer than six men complained that Lewis was in a 'very dreadful and solemn condition', so much so that they believed 'death would have quickly followed'.[157] As Lewis was seemingly unable to speak, the men sent for Elizabeth Hubbard who 'discovered' that Esty tortured Lewis, whereby Hubbard became presently tormented as well. In order to 'save' Lewis' life, Mary Esty was apprehended and recommitted to prison.[158] Esty was eventually executed on 22 September. Essentially, Mercy Lewis almost single-handedly prevented Esty from being freed, even when the magistrates seemed content not to proceed against her. Lewis' power and influence seemed so great, she was able to convince the authorities to resume their prosecution against Esty, almost without overt support from other Salem girls who seemed willing to drop their accusations against her.[159] This can be inferred from the lack of trial documents from other Salem girls against Esty. For example, only two indictments exist against Mary Esty, and they only included the names of Mercy Lewis and Elizabeth Hubbard. In this instance, historians can speculate that these girls were working largely autonomously, which reveals that the girls used their role to denounce, persist and rid their community of their chosen target. Mary Esty's case reflects that children in the Salem trials were more than just victims of external manipulation; other trial documents reveal the extent of power and influence of the Salem girls.

The authority the Salem girls demonstrated during the trials was unusual for their age, gender and status and the fact that their impact on the trials can be easily traced through the sources is a testament to this. For example, the language used to describe the Salem girls in many of the documents often revealed how central they were in 1692. In the examinations of Mary Clark and Mary Parker (on 4 August and 22 September, respectively), it is noteworthy that the trial record was almost exclusively dedicated to the reactions and testimonies of the Salem girls, with almost no attention to the reaction of the accused or even the questions that were posed to them.[160] The exact reason for this is unclear; however, it seems to reflect the level of importance of the Salem girls.

Another example that demonstrates the centrality of the Salem girls comes from 23 May when Elizabeth Cary and her husband Nathaniel travelled to Salem Village as they felt 'disturbed' by the news that Elizabeth had been accused of witchcraft.[161] The account is preserved in Calef's *More Wonders* and is written by Nathaniel himself.[162] Nathaniel described the afflicted as being '...two girls of about ten years old and about two or three others, of about eighteen, one of the girls talked most and could discern more than the rest'.[163] Although Cary was clearly repulsed by the use of spectral evidence and other features of the trials, the power and intimidating presence of the girls was strongly represented in his account. He described how his wife was asked for her name by an unidentified Salem girl, which may highlight the fact that she probably did not know who Elizabeth was. Nathaniel asked John Hale for a private audience with the afflicted to discuss their accusations against his wife; this did not eventuate, and upon walking towards Nathaniel, a group of Salem girls fell to the floor 'like swine'.[164] Apprehension seized the room as Nathaniel stated: 'We in the room were all at a stand to see who they would cry out of'.[165] The girls cried out against Elizabeth Cary, and she was immediately taken into custody.[166] It was highly unorthodox that a man above their social status would seek the audience of the Salem girls to plead for the case of his wife's reputation and possibly her life. Nathaniel's unsuccessful attempt to dissuade the Salem girls' accusations against his wife further demonstrated their authority as preternatural agents. After Elizabeth Cary was cried out upon, there was seemingly little Nathaniel could do. Elizabeth Cary survived as her husband helped her escape gaol after which they both fled to New York. Although some denunciations may have been encouraged or even constructed by others, this does not negate the fact that the Salem girls' accusations carried considerable weight.

The essential role the Salem girls played can also be seen in the way they identified witches in Andover. The Andover phase of the trials began with Martha Carrier's arrest on 28 May, and the examination of Ann Foster resumed this phase on 16 July. John Ballard, the constable of Andover, brought two unnamed Salem girls to Andover in an attempt to ascertain who had bewitched his wife, Elizabeth.[167] There is a strong possibility that the two Salem girls were Elizabeth Hubbard and Mary Walcott as they were the only two that claimed affliction by Foster on 15 July, the day before her examination.[168] The significance of the girls' ability to communicate with the invisible world was again demonstrated, as this event with Ballard began one of the biggest phases of the Salem trials (in terms of accusations and arrests generated).

It is unlikely that Ballard coerced the girls into identifying witches in Andover, as many of the girls persisted with accusations even when they were not explicitly encouraged to do so, as in the case of Mary Esty. Furthermore, Elizabeth Hubbard – who came to Andover – seemed relentless in her involvement in the trials, as she continued to give evidence against accused witches in other jurisdictions in November 1692 when the lead prosecutors in Salem Village stopped taking depositions.[169] Mary Warren, who was perhaps initially coerced into her role, became indefatigable in her involvement in the trials, particularly in the later Andover phase when other Salem girls largely withdrew. Warren's dramatic displays of self-harm – involving the insertion of pins deep enough so she bled, as well as biting and hitting herself – persisted from May until the end of the trials. Although these actions likely reflected her mental instability, they also displayed Warren's determined attitude to not only remain involved, but also to show herself as strikingly more tormented than the other Salem girls during the proceedings.

It is important to note that it was not just the accused that the Salem girls exerted their authority over. An observer of the trials and former minister of Salem Village, Deodat Lawson, offered valuable insight into the behaviour of the afflicted which demonstrated the extent of their power. In early March, while Lawson led the meetinghouse in public prayer, many of the Salem girls began to have fits that interrupted Lawson, which he admitted was 'so unusual'.[170] Shortly afterwards Abigail Williams fearlessly demanded: '...Stand up and name your text'. After Lawson began to read, Williams remarked: 'It is a long text'. Another afflicted person also complained of the length, telling Lawson: 'Now there is enough of that'. When Lawson finished, Williams approached him and stated: 'I know no doctrine you had, if you did name one, I have forgotten it'. At the same time, Ann Putnam Junior boldly exclaimed that the witches' familiar yellow bird sat on his hat as it hung in the pulpit.[171] Lawson's comments about the girls are reminiscent of other demoniacs who also rebuked ministerial figures.[172] Outside of a few hushed remarks trying to quiet the girls, it is strongly implied by Lawson that no punishment ensued for such disrespectful behaviour.

This brazen attitude displayed by the girls towards Lawson during prayer highlights their significance as the afflicted. As seers into the invisible world, it was assumed by the magistrates – if not by many in the community – that the girls were the key to uncovering the infestation of witches. In fact, by this stage of the trials, it was becoming increasingly obvious that the prosecutors were failing to expose the accused through other means of evidence, such as finding contradictions in their stories. Relying almost completely on the fits, visions and physical reactions of the girls, the magistrates succeeded in extracting the evidence they wanted to prosecute the accused. Certainly, some of the girls were manipulated by external influencers, yet the aforementioned examples demonstrate that the role of children in these trials is complex and multifaceted. Indeed, in many instances, the Salem girls showed that they needed little to no encouragement to denounce the accused. In fact, there is evidence that some girls were motivated by a need for (real or perceived) vengeance, a word that is used in the trial documents no fewer than eleven times.

'Vengeance'

In an event as complex as Salem, there are many different motivations to consider. In fact, Bernard Rosenthal believes this task is impossible declaring: 'The dead...are beyond our reach for motivational analysis'.[173] Salem historians who have offered motivating factors for the trials often do so in a general sense, referring to communal disputes or war in the northern frontier which has been described as 'plausible but not satisfying'.[174] However, there is evidence to support the idea that the Salem girls sometimes chose their targets based on personal or communal vexations. It must be acknowledged that historians may not be able to ascertain to what extent this behaviour was of their own volition. Based on the evidence available, it seems highly likely that at least sixteen cases – eleven of which ended in execution – were directly the result of, or directly influenced by, a desire for vengeance from the Salem girls. The girls targeted alleged murderers, abusive masters and husbands and other 'easy targets' who had been accused before. The delicate ways the Salem girls used their role to intricately weave their personal and communal animosity into witchcraft accusations demonstrate their ability to influence the trials and consign many to the gallows.

Rebecca Nurse was arrested on 24 March and was the second church member to be detained after Martha Corey. Her accusation as a witch and her ensuing trial were challenging given her high social status. Yet, the trial documents reveal why the Salem girls may have sought her conviction. There is a possibility that the afflicted girls believed Nurse was responsible for the deaths of Benjamin Holton, John Fuller, Rebekah Shepard and also several Putnam children.[175] Furthermore, in a deposition by Ann Putnam Senior, she claimed: 'Six children in winding sheets which called me aunt...told me they were my sisters Bakers children of Boston and that Goody Nurse...had murdered them'.[176] Ann goes on to claim that the ghosts of her nieces and nephews told her to tell the magistrates of this 'or else they would tear me to pieces for their blood did cry for vengeance'. Whether Nurse was actually responsible for these deaths is immaterial. The Salem girls' fervent belief that she was helps explain their grievous fits and furious persecution against her. It should be noted that other Putnams showed support for Nurse, but this did little to dissuade the Salem girls or the magistrates.[177] The fact that not even other Putnams could dismantle the credibility of the Salem girls is a testament to their significance and centrality in the trials.

During her trial, Nurse was initially found not guilty to which all the afflicted 'made a hideous outcry to the amazement not only of the spectators but the court also seemed strangely surprised…'.[178] Calef stated that some of the magistrates advised the jury to reconsider their decision, whereby a guilty verdict was returned.[179] Afterwards, Nurse received a reprieve from the Governor – reflecting the magistrates' hesitation to condemn a church member – yet, after the afflicted 'renewed their dismal outcries against her', the reprieve was quickly withdrawn and she was executed on 19 July.[180] As a highly respected matron of Salem Village, Nurse's denunciation and execution – largely if not solely at the hands of the Salem girls' who were incited by cries of vengeance – ultimately reflects their power as decisive shapers of the trials. This idea is further represented in the case of George Burroughs.

As a man and a minister, George Burroughs' accusation and eventual execution seemed to shock even the Salem Village community in 1692. It was reported that many people were so moved by Burroughs' 'speech, prayer and protestation', while he stood on the gallows that, according to Calef, some believed the spectators might hinder the execution.[181] Hence, the Salem girls – and the magistrates – must have known that their case against him needed to be lengthy, detailed and damning. The motivating factors behind his accusation may be linked to no fewer than seven references in the trial documents revealing that Burroughs was thought to be a domestic abuser who murdered his first two wives. As briefly mentioned earlier, the first reference of this comes from the examination of Abigail Hobbs where the first question asked of her was: 'Did Mr Burroughs bring you any of the poppets of his wives to stick into?'[182] This question suggests that the prosecutors had reason to believe that Burroughs attempted to bewitch his wives. This suggestion becomes more obvious during Burroughs' examination on 9 May when Susannah Shelden exclaimed that two of Burroughs's wives appeared 'in their winding sheets and said that man [Burroughs] killed them'.[183] On the same day, four depositions from other Salem girls revealed more details about these alleged murders.[184] Ann Putnam Junior goes into particular detail about these events, even describing how and where Burroughs killed his first two wives whose 'blood did cry for vengeance against him'.[185] Other adults – noticeably all members of the Putnam family – affirmed these ideas by relaying memories of Burroughs being at their acquaintances where they noticed he was a 'very harsh [and] sharp man to his wife'.[186] The Salem girls' persistence against Burroughs – fuelled by a desire for vengeance – was essential in his case as their allegations of abuse and murder can be seen to directly lead to his execution. Without a confession from Burroughs, the girls became the magistrates of the invisible world, extracting evidence and testimony from the apparitions of Burroughs' alleged murder victims.

John Willard and Giles Corey also had allegations of murder lodged against them, either from the spectres of their victims or as a result of the supernatural knowledge of the girls.[187] On 3 June, Ann Putnam Junior testified against Willard stating that he '[threatened] to kill me if I would not write in his book' adding that he 'had whipped my little sister Sarah to death'.[188] Ann then gave further details specifically tying her dead sister in with her denunciation of Willard: 'after this I saw the apparition of my little sister Sarah who died when she was about six weeks old crying out for vengeance against John Willard'. Willard, like Burroughs, also had a reputation as a domestic abuser and Ann added this to her testimony claiming: 'I also saw the apparition of a woman in a winding sheet which told me she was John Willard's first wife and that John Willard had a hand in her death'. Through her role, Ann was not only able to detail real or perceived crimes against her and her community, but she was also able to tactfully communicate this information through using a medium her society understood and accepted. John Willard was executed on 22 September.

Referring to Giles Corey, Thomas Putnam wrote a letter to Samuel Sewall whereby he stated that in a nightmare, Ann Putnam Junior was visited by a man that Corey allegedly murdered by 'pressing him to death with his feet'.[189] Putnam was trying to justify Corey's death to Sewall as Sewall's diary entries indicated his disturbance over Corey's torture.[190] There was a strong implication that Putnam claimed that Corey's death was deserved, as a record from seventeen years before the 1692 trial noted that Corey was reprimanded for manslaughter over the death of a worker at his farm.[191] Corey was fined as a result but as the apparition told Ann: 'it must be done to him as it has been done to me'.[192] Thus, one can speculate that Corey's pressing on 19 September is another example of a case that was motivated by vengeance. Ann's nightmare is also interesting as she must have been told the information regarding Corey's manslaughter charges, as she would not have been alive when this incident with Corey's former worker occurred.

Although the motivations against the aforementioned persons can be ascribed to personal vexations or a desire for vengeance, other documents reveal that the Salem girls may have also targeted people who appeared to disturb the delicate fabric of their society. While it has previously been outlined how Andover residents believed Martha Carrier introduced smallpox into their community, this event also seemed to have been a motivating factor for why the Salem girls accused her. During Carrier's examination, Susannah Shelden asked: 'What could make you murder thirteen persons?'[193] Mary Walcott, Elizabeth Hubbard and Ann Putnam Junior all affirmed this and testified that they also saw thirteen ghosts before them, claiming that Carrier had killed them in Andover. The number thirteen is significant as this is the speculative number of persons killed in the smallpox outbreak of 1690 that Carrier was blamed for instigating. In fact, even Carrier's two young children, Sarah and Thomas – who were eight and ten, respectively – became convinced of their mother's guilt and claimed that she had baptised them and taught them how to be witches.[194] Therefore, a tentative link can be drawn between Carrier, the smallpox outbreak and her condemnation as a witch. This link is further exhibited by the fact that at least two people referred to her as the 'Queen of Hell', despite being a coveted church member.[195]

A similar theme of unleashing wickedness on the community can be seen in John Alden's examination where he was accused of fraternising with and assisting the enemy French and Indian nations. During his examination, one of the Salem girls reportedly called out: '…there stands Alden…he sells powder and shot to the Indians and French and lies with the Indian Squaes and has Indian Papooses'.[196] It was clear that by this stage in the war with the French and the Indians that anyone who aided them were considered traitors and – perhaps by this admission by a Salem girl – witches.

Lastly, it can be seen in the cases of at least five of the accused that their denunciations may have been motivated by former accusations or outstanding reputations as witches. For the Salem girls, the implementation of this method was that it was simply the easiest way to validate their actions and behaviour; targeting formally accused or reputed witches was usually seen as a safe bet. For example, Dorcas Hoar was a reputed fortune teller who had been practising for at least twenty years.[197] Bridget Bishop was seen to be dyeing small pieces of lace; the general consensus being that she was using it for her poppets, which was later substantiated by others who claimed they found some when working at her house.[198] In the examination of Elizabeth How, the prosecutor reminded her that she had been formally accused of witchcraft in Ipswich, where she had been a suspected as a witch for the last decade.[199] How's accusations at Ipswich had been so serious, her application to become a church member there had been rejected.[200] Sarah Good also seemed to be an easy target for the Salem girls as her reputation for being 'turbulent of spirit, spiteful and so maliciously bent' almost effortlessly manifested itself into a believable witchcraft claim.[201] Mary Warren's eventual status as a core accuser, as well as her compelling displays of self-harm, culminated in her denunciation against Abigail Soames.[202] Soames was also an easy target as she came from a persecuted Quaker family and had been in recent trouble for not attending church.[203] While it is likely the majority of the Salem girls may not have previously known about these reputations or past allegations, the impact of rumour and gossip should not be underestimated as it was the medium through which news spread.[204] Thus, it is not far-fetched to imagine how the girls could have had access to specific details about who were the easiest or – in the cases of others such as Burroughs – who were the most dangerous members of society to accuse and eradicate.

While definitive evidence clarifying the Salem girls' motivations may be unobtainable, the aforementioned examples support the argument that the Salem girls' aspirations for vengeance may have been behind some of their actions. What becomes evident throughout the trial documents is that the role of the Salem girls as mediators of the supernatural world assumed such centrality in the trials; it seemed to encroach on the leading prosecutors' ability to control the courtroom. Through listening to the ghosts of murder victims or using their spectral knowledge to elicit confessions the accused would not give, the Salem girls proved to be much more successful than the prosecutors; the magistrates were helpless in that they relied almost solely on the information that was provided to them by the Salem girls. Consequently, the girls held a significant amount of power and control over the trials. On the surface, it appears almost contradictory; some girls appeared to be manipulated and coerced, while others seemed to act almost independently. Yet, these roles are not mutually exclusive as the tapestry of Salem cannot be woven with a single thread. Indeed, these dual roles coincided with each other, ebbing and flowing throughout the trials while both remaining crucially important to the outcomes of cases. Considering the girls displayed considerable control and influence, it is vital to examine another critical element of the role of the Salem girls, which may shed light on the prosecutor's question to Rebecca Nurse during her examination: 'They accuse you of hurting them, and if you think it is unwillingly but by design you must look upon them as murderers'.[205]

'They seemed to make a jest of it': Inspiration, Integrity and the Salem Girls

In addition to asking what motivated the Salem girls, it is important to understand what may have inspired them and to what extent this affected their credibility. In fact, suspicions surrounding the credibility of the Salem girls arose ever since the Salem trials began. For example, Thomas Brattle (a merchant and scholar) wrote to an unidentified clerical correspondent in October 1692 describing the girls as 'possessed' and 'nonsensical', stating that he did not understand why the magistrates gave credence to what they said: 'I am sure they lie, at least speak falsely if they say so'.[206] When examining the trial documents, it becomes clear that the most obvious source of inspiration for the Salem girls came from the case of Goody Glover from Boston which occurred only four years earlier.[207]

The case of Goody Glover survives only in Cotton Mather's book *Memorable Providences*. Mather was an active observer of the trial and was instrumental in its containment. The comparisons between the Glover case and the Salem episode cannot be overstated. Their similarities were apparent to those involved in the Salem crisis, as John Hale observed: 'I will not enlarge in the description of their cruel sufferings because they were in all things afflicted as bad as John Goodwin's children at Boston, in the year 1688'.[208] It began much in the same way as Salem when four of John Goodwin's children showed symptoms of being bewitched. Like Salem, the most ferocious accuser in this case was a thirteen-year-old girl. The language used to describe the fits of the Goodwin children was incredibly like those Hale used to describe the Salem girls: 'sometimes they would be deaf, sometimes dumb, and sometimes blind, and often, all this at once. One while their tongues would be drawn down their throats, another while they would be pulled out upon their chins to a prodigious length'.[209] The eldest Goodwin girl (Martha) was described as being 'indisposed in her health', which was similar to the symptoms expressed by girls like Mercy Lewis when she complained of Mary Esty.[210] Other symptoms such as trying to burn or drown themselves can also be seen in both trials, as well as spiritual attacks manifesting themselves as physical marks. For example, in the Goodwin case, the children complained of being struck with cudgels (short sticks) and Mather described seeing red marks upon their backs.[211] The Salem girls complained of similar attacks, as seen with Ann Putnam Junior and Mary Warren when they claimed that spectres had bitten them whereupon they showed bite marks on their wrists.[212] In the Goodwin case, as with the Salem girls, when Glover was named as their tormentor the Goodwin children all appeared in court screaming about 'blows they could not bear' before the judges and 'the whole assembly'.[213] The Goodwin children also struggled to describe who they saw in the spectral attacks, which the Salem girls almost perfected during their later courtroom appearances. Finally, in a similar manner to how the Salem girls disrupted Deodat Lawson during his sermon, the Goodwin children interrupted Mather during prayer, which he described as an 'odd thing'.[214]

However, one of the biggest differences between the two trials came when Mather refused to name the other persons the children complained of: '…for we should be tender in such relations, lest we wrong the reputation of the innocent by stories not enough enquired into'.[215] Mather also took Martha Goodwin into his personal care, after which her symptoms slowly improved. Glover was committed to prison and executed, but through Mather's persistence of maintaining confidentiality, the trial died with her, though it is significant to note how Mather's personal attitudes towards witch-hunting changed four years later in the Salem trials where he played much more of an incendiary role. Although Frances Hill argued 'there is no reason to think they [the Salem girls] consciously imitated them [the Goodwin children]', her alternative argument is less convincing, claiming that the girls were merely suggestible: 'hysterical symptoms are catching'.[216] While the symptoms and behaviour of the Goodwin children and the Salem girls could be considered a mere coincidence, the almost identical language and behaviour exhibited in the evidence suggests that it was not. It is highly possible the Salem girls copied the behaviour of the Goodwin children as they represented believable and successful notions of what it meant to be afflicted. The probability of the girls being instructed or encouraged to behave like the Goodwin children by others cannot be ruled out, yet a lack of primary evidence limits this to conjecture. If the girls were copying the behaviour of the Goodwin children, this would have certainly affected their credibility throughout the trials.

In addition to the Goodwin case, there were frequent references to themes from the Swedish witch trials. This element could have also reflected a level of fraudulent behaviour on the behalf of the Salem girls, as they may have been simply relaying information they were told or heard about regarding these trials to bolster their credibility. Themes disclosed in the Salem documents like a crowned hat, being baptised by the Devil and dancing after a meal with Satan, were all prominent features of the Swedish trials, which were explicitly referenced by Cotton Mather in his *Wonders of the Invisible World*.[217] References to these trials were not always mentioned by the Salem girls, but it is important to consider that the inclusion of these well-known witchcraft elements may be another example of how the girls manifested their knowledge of other witchcraft trials to validate their behaviour. Outside of these sources of inspiration – which might have inhibited their integrity if it could have been proved the afflicted were being coached – other sources of inspiration seemed to come from the imaginations of the Salem girls themselves, showing just how close they walked between the visible and invisible worlds.

The trial documents indicate that relatives of the accused knew that one of the most effective ways to protect their family was to try and discredit the reputation of the Salem girls. They understood how important the girls were to the judicial proceedings and knew that without their credibility, their accusations were worthless and the trials would end. Hence, there are no fewer than six documents that give damaging testimony against the characters of Elizabeth Hubbard, Mercy Lewis, Susannah Shelden and Abigail Williams.[218] For example, Robert Moulton Senior testified that Shelden often contradicted herself and got her stories of witchcraft mixed up.[219] Hubbard was accused of telling lies, but it was the claim from Clement Coldrum that revealed an intriguing insight into the minds of the afflicted girls.[220] Coldrum claimed that on a journey from the meetinghouse, where he was set to take Hubbard home, she asked if he could ride faster 'for the woods were full of Devils'.[221] After some time, Hubbard stated that they could slow down for they had outridden them. Coldrum then asked her if she was not afraid of the Devil: '[she] answered me no, she could discourse with the Devil as well as with me'.[222] This mentality – which was also seen with Abigail Hobbs – might indicate that the girls believed there was implicit power in holding correspondence with the Devil. Further evidence of this can be seen in the testimony of Joseph Hutchinson against Abigail Williams when he claimed: 'I asked her if she was not afraid to see the Devil, she said at the first she was and did go from him, but now she was not afraid and could talk with him as well as she could with me'.[223]

What is clear from these documents is that the families of the accused attempted to discredit the accusers by implying they were untrustworthy liars and, most importantly, that they were familiar with Satan, implying they might be witches themselves. However, it is clear that the families of the afflicted, as well as the judges, saw the inverse as true: that their status as preternatural agents made them particularly useful witch-hunters. In some instances, the petitions in support of the accused did slow down the trials, but eventually none succeeded in dismantling the integrity of the Salem girls. Of course, the magistrate's willingness to believe the Salem girls played a key part in their centrality, yet the courtroom may have remained empty if not for the persistence of the girls who used the framework of witchcraft accusations to (frequently) achieve their own ends.

'A Great Delusion of Satan'

The various and intricate reasons why the Salem trials ended somewhat abruptly at the end of 1692 cannot be exhaustively explored here. Two of the most important factors appear to be the court's inability to effectively and prudently manage the trials as well as the community's growing resentment of the witchcraft affair in general. After the last executions in September, many members of the community were distressed and pondered whether justice had been miscarried. In a few short months, over a hundred people had been imprisoned, and at least twenty-five had died, either as a result of execution, torture or languishing in gaol. The idea that many of the executed victims were innocent began to circulate, and the basis of using spectral evidence was crumbling. Rather than admitting that they had murdered innocent people, there was a growing belief that Satan had simply tricked them all.

Governor Phips clearly encapsulated this sentiment in a letter to the Earl of Nottingham dated 21 February1693:

> The stop put to the first method of proceedings hath dissipated the black cloud that threatened this province with destruction for whereas this delusion of the Devil did spread and its dismal effects touched the lives and estates of many of their majesty's subjects...'.[224]

Consequently, support for the girls began to evaporate. Instead of being described as 'pined, consumed wasted and tormented', the girls were labelled as being under 'diabolical molestations', while Francis Dane went so far as to call his own daughter 'simplish'.[225] No longer were the girls' fits seen as afflictions from witches, as the growing consensus was that 'the Devil deluded them'.[226] However, it must be acknowledged that this change of attitude appears to be a consequence of the trials declining, rather than the sole cause of it.

While subsequent authors like Brattle and Calef were scathing in their opinions of the Salem girls, the general attitude in the immediate aftermath of the trials was that the girls had not been conniving or malicious but were deceived by Satan. The reason for this was likely connected to self-preservation for the shattered community, as they struggled to make amends with what had happened. Convincing themselves that the girls were merely duped by Satan was certainly easier than admitting they were massively culpable in the tragic loss of life. This fact should not be understated as Salem, as a community, remains unparalleled in the history of witch-hunting, certainly in the Anglophone world, in terms of the outpouring of public confession and compensation for its victims in the aftermath of the trials.[227] Furthermore, there is evidence that suggests the Salem girls escaped the trials unpunished, even after the trials became unpopular. For example, Abigail Hobbs received compensation for the duress she experienced throughout the trials despite being a confessor and an accuser.[228] Mary Lacey Junior was found not guilty in January 1693 despite also being a confessor and a key accuser in the Andover phase of the trials.[229] Compensation and a not-guilty verdict for two young confessed witches is a testament to the acceptance and understanding of the role they played despite a deteriorating tolerance for the witchcraft trials within the community.

Other than a small number of trial documents such as these, historians have few sources that illustrate what life was like for the Salem girls after the trials ended, as most disappear from the historical record. Although the historical basis for this statement has not been established, Marilynne K. Roach argued that the girls led difficult lives after the trials: '...some were fined for fornication and another was excommunicated from her church for adultery...'.[230] Roach also stated that Mary Warren's name appeared on a gaol bill from December 1693; after that, any reference to her disappears.[231] Emerson Baker further substantiated the claim that the girls led problematic lives, stating that Susannah Shelden was made to appear in court in 1694 and was described as a person of 'evil fame'.[232] Perhaps the most valuable piece of evidence is an apology from a then twenty-seven-year-old Ann Putnam Junior in 1706. Ann never left Salem Village and her apology was read aloud to the congregation by the new minister Joseph Green in an attempt to gain church membership:

> I desire to be humbled before God ... that I, then being in my childhood ... be made an instrument for the accusing of several persons...whereby their lives were taken away from them, whom now I have just grounds and good reason to believe they were innocent persons; and that it was a great

> delusion of Satan that deceived me in that sad time, whereby I justly fear I have been instrumental, with others, though ignorantly and unwittingly, to bring upon myself and this land the guilt of innocent blood; though what was said or done by me against any person I can truly and uprightly say, before God and man, I did it not out of any anger, malice, or ill-will... for I had no such thing against one of them; but what I did was ignorantly, being deluded by Satan.[233]

Ann's apology provides fascinating insight into how she viewed and perhaps reconciled her behaviour during the witch trials, clearly expressing belief that Satan manipulated her. However, it is clear that Ann was careful to marshal adverbs of limitation to qualify her guilt, using the word 'instrument' three times. Thus, the extent of Ann's sincerity is ambiguous, as the new minister doubtlessly assisted her in the construction of this apology which she needed to successfully join the church and re-enter society. Historians will never know if Ann was truly apologetic; perhaps she was simply saying the right things at the right time as she had done in 1692. Whatever the fate of the other girls post-1692, what can be inferred from the comments pertaining to Shelden, Warren and Ann Putnam Junior is that their lives were likely plagued by a constant reminder of the trials they so intrinsically influenced.

Notes

1 John Demos, *Entertaining Satan: Witchcraft and the Culture of Early New England* (Oxford: Oxford University Press, 2004), p. 11.
2 John Demos, *Entertaining Satan: Witchcraft and the Culture of Early New England* (Oxford: Oxford University Press, 2004).
3 Trials continued into 1693 with the establishment of the new Superior Court of Judicature but all ended in either acquittals or reprieves. Bernard Rosenthal, ed., *Records of the Salem Witch-Hunt* (New York: Cambridge University Press, 2009), p. 20.
4 The term 'niece' meant kinswoman and was not necessarily used in our contemporary sense of a blood relative. The exact relationship between Samuel Parris and Abigail Williams has never been established. Bernard Rosenthal, ed., *Records of the Salem Witch-Hunt* (New York: Cambridge University Press, 2009), p. 15.
5 John Hale, *A Modest Inquiry and How Persons Guilty of that Crime may be Convicted...* (Boston: B. Green and J. Alten, 1702), p. 24.
6 John Hale, *A Modest Inquiry and How Persons Guilty of that Crime May be Convicted...* (Boston: B. Green and J. Alten, 1702).
7 John Hale, *A Modest Inquiry and How Persons Guilty of that Crime may be Convicted...* (Boston: B. Green and J. Alten, 1702), p. 26.
8 Whether Betty removed herself from the group of accusers or was removed by some external influence is unclear. However, there is evidence that Samuel Parris actively attempted to remove his daughter from the group. This can be seen in

doc. 207 in *Records* where Parris originally had Betty Parris as the complainant in a deposition against Sarah Good, Sarah Osborne and Tituba but later crossed out her name and wrote Abigail Williams instead. Why and when Parris made this change is unclear. Rosenthal noted that the original draft was likely written before 25 March. Bernard Rosenthal, ed., *Records of the Salem Witch-Hunt* (New York: Cambridge University Press, 2009), p. 315.

9 Richard Trask, *The Devil Hath Been Raised: A Documentary History of the Salem Village Witchcraft Outbreak of 1692* (Danvers: Phoenix Publishing, 1992), pp. 121–123.

10 Richard Trask, *The Devil Hath Been Raised: A Documentary History of the Salem Village Witchcraft Outbreak of 1692* (Danvers: Phoenix Publishing, 1992), p. 122.

11 Richard Trask, *The Devil Hath Been Raised: A Documentary History of the Salem Village Witchcraft Outbreak of 1692* (Danvers: Phoenix Publishing, 1992).

12 Richard Trask, *The Devil Hath Been Raised: A Documentary History of the Salem Village Witchcraft Outbreak of 1692* (Danvers: Phoenix Publishing, 1992), p. 123.

13 Richard Trask, *The Devil Hath Been Raised: A Documentary History of the Salem Village Witchcraft Outbreak of 1692* (Danvers: Phoenix Publishing, 1992), p. 122.

14 Richard Trask, *The Devil Hath Been Raised: A Documentary History of the Salem Village Witchcraft Outbreak of 1692* (Danvers: Phoenix Publishing, 1992), p. 123.

15 E. J. Kent, 'Salem Girls (1692): Problems of Gender and Agency' in *Religion, the Supernatural and Visual Culture in Early Modern Europe: an album amicorum for Charles Zika*, eds., Jennifer Spinks and Dagmar Eichberger (Leiden: Brill, 2015), p. 79.

16 Barbara J. Louge, 'In Pursuit of Prosperity: Disease and Death in Massachusetts Commercial Port, 1660-1850' *Journal of Social History* 25 (No. 2, 1991), p. 312, and John Duffy, *Epidemics in Colonial America* (Baton Rouge: Louisiana State University Press, 1953), p. 5.

17 Barbara J. Louge, 'In Pursuit of Prosperity: Disease and Death in Massachusetts Commercial Port, 1660-1850' *Journal of Social History* 25 (No. 2, 1991), p. 312, and John Duffy, *Epidemics in Colonial America* (Baton Rouge: Louisiana State University Press, 1953), p. 313.

18 John Duffy, *Epidemics in Colonial America* (Baton Rouge: Louisiana State University Press, 1953), p. 238.

19 Richard Hite, *In the Shadow of Salem: The Andover Witch Hunt of 1692* (Yardley: Westholme Publishing, 2018), p. 34.

20 Anon., *Vital Records of Andover, Massachusetts, to the End of the Year 1849*, vol. 2 (Topsfield: Topsfield Historical Society, 1912), pp. 375–376.

21 Sarah Loring Bailey, *Historical Sketches of Andover: Comprising the Present Towns of North Andover and Andover Massachusetts* (Boston: Mifflin and Company, 1880), p. 220.

22 Sarah Loring Bailey, *Historical Sketches of Andover: Comprising the Present Towns of North Andover and Andover Massachusetts* (Boston: Mifflin and Company, 1880), p. 221.

23 Stephen J. Kunitz, 'Mortality Change in America, 1620–1920', *Human Biology* 56 (No. 3, 1984), p. 563.
24 Barbara J. Louge, 'In Pursuit of Prosperity: Disease and Death in Massachusetts Commercial Port, 1660-1850' *Journal of Social History* 25 (No. 2, 1991), p. 312, and John Duffy, *Epidemics in Colonial America* (Baton Rouge: Louisiana State University Press, 1953), p. 325.
25 Kathleen Kennedy, 'On Writing the History of So Much Grief: Cotton Mather's *Decennium Luctuosum* and the Trauma of Colonial History' *The Eighteenth Century* 58 (No. 2, 2017), p. 219.
26 Sam White, *A Cold Welcome: The Little Ice Age and Europe's Encounter with North America* (Cambridge, MA: Harvard University Press, 2017), pp. 3–4.
27 Michael E. Mann, 'Little Ice Age' in *Encyclopedia of Global Environmental Change*, eds., Michael C. MacCracken and John S. Perry, vol. 1 (2002), p. 504.
28 H. H. Lamb, *Climate History and the Modern World* (London: Psychology Press, 1995), pp. 241 and 230.
29 Karen Ordahl Kupperman, 'Climate and Mystery of the Wilderness in Seventeenth-Century New England', *Seventeenth Century New England* 63 (1984), p. 36.
30 Karen Ordahl Kupperman, 'Climate and Mystery of the Wilderness in Seventeenth-Century New England', *Seventeenth Century New England* 63 (1984).
31 Cotton Mather, 'Diary entry 18th of April 1696' in *Diary of Cotton Mather 1681-1708* (Boston: The Plympton Press, 1708), p. 192.
32 Samuel Sewall, 'Diary of Samuel Sewall 1674-1729. Vol. I. 1674-1700', diary entry 25 January 1687 and diary entry 28 February 1681, respectively, in *Collections of the Massachusetts Historical Society*, vol. 5, fifth series (Boston: published by the society, 1877), pp. 12, 13, 21, 24, 32, 37, 40, 42, 49, 86, 107, 114, 116, 117, 118, 157, 166, 197, 198, 207, 246, 337, 338, 340, 354, 370, 397, 438, 442, 448, 450, 452, 461, 466, 467, 468, 471, 473, 479, 488 and 507.
33 Thomas Wickman, 'Winters Embittered with Hardships": Severe Cold, Wabanaki Power, and English Adjustments, 1690-1710' *The William and Mary Quarterly* 72 (No. 1, 2015), p. 58.
34 Paul Boyer and Stephen Nissenbaum, *Salem Possessed: The Social Origins of Witchcraft* (Cambridge and London: Harvard University Press, 1974), p. 154.
35 Larry Gragg, *A Quest for Security: The Life of Samuel Parris 1653-1720* (Greenwood: Greenwood Press, 1990), pp. 41–42.
36 Larry Gragg, *A Quest for Security: The Life of Samuel Parris 1653-1720* (Greenwood: Greenwood Press, 1990), p. 42.
37 Larry Gragg, *A Quest for Security: The Life of Samuel Parris 1653-1720* (Greenwood: Greenwood Press, 1990), p. 43.
38 Larry Gragg, *A Quest for Security: The Life of Samuel Parris 1653-1720* (Greenwood: Greenwood Press, 1990), p. 43.
39 Paul Boyer and Stephen Nissenbaum, *Salem Possessed: The Social Origins of Witchcraft* (Cambridge and London: Harvard University Press, 1974), p. 45.
40 Marilynne K. Roach, *The Salem Witch Trials: A Day-By-Day Chronicle of a Community Under Siege* (Lanham: Cooper Square Press, 2002), pp. xxix-xxxiii.
41 Marilynne K. Roach, *The Salem Witch Trials: A Day-By-Day Chronicle of a Community Under Siege* (Lanham: Cooper Square Press, 2002).
42 Marilynne K. Roach, *The Salem Witch Trials: A Day-By-Day Chronicle of a Community Under Siege* (Lanham: Cooper Square Press, 2002), p. xxxvi.

43 Paul Boyer and Stephen Nissenbaum, *Salem-Village Witchcraft: A Documentary Record of Local Conflict in Colonial New England* (Belmont: Wadsworth Publishing Co., 1972), p. 262.
44 Bernard Rosenthal, ed., *Records of the Salem Witch-Hunt* (New York: Cambridge University Press, 2009), doc. 525.
45 Charles W. Upham. *Salem Witchcraft with an Account of Salem Village and a History of Opinions on Witchcraft and Kindred Subjects*, vol. 1 (Boston: Wiggin and Lunt, 1867), p. 289.
46 Samuel Fowler, 'An Account of the Life and Character of the Rev. Samuel Parris, of Salem Village, and of his Connection with the Witchcraft Delusion of 1692' in *The Witchcraft Delusion in New England*, ed. Samuel G. Drake, vol. 3 (Roxbury: Munsell, 1866), pp. 200–201.
47 Samuel Fowler, 'An Account of the Life and Character of the Rev. Samuel Parris, of Salem Village, and of his Connection with the Witchcraft Delusion of 1692' in *The Witchcraft Delusion in New England*, ed. Samuel G. Drake, vol. 3 (Roxbury: Munsell, 1866), p. 200.
48 Samuel Parris, 'Sermon from 19th November 1689', in *The Sermon Notebook of Samuel Parris, 1689-1694*, eds. James F. Cooper Jr and Kenneth P. Minkema (Boston: The Colonial Society of Massachusetts, 1993), p. 38. Like most ministers, Parris put his sermon text and notes, if not the entire sermon, into volumes such as these. However, it must be noted that this text is not the full sermon as it was delivered in 1692, and much that Parris said went unrecorded. Other notes regarding his sermons are described as 'loose papers' and are no longer extant.
49 Mary Beth Norton, *In The Devil's Snare: The Salem Witchcraft Crisis of 1692* (New York: Vintage Books, 2002), p. 18. As stated in the previous chapter, the so-called 'Halfway Covenant' permitted the baptism of infants born to parents who had both been baptised but who had not formally joined the church. Parris' rejection of this meant that only infants who had at least one parent as a formal church member were allowed to be baptised. This exclusionary attitude to this much sought-after sacrament heightened tensions between the community and Parris.
50 Larry Gragg, *A Quest for Security: The Life of Samuel Parris 1653-1720* (Greenwood: Greenwood Press, 1990), p. 87.
51 Perry Miller in *The New England Mind: The Seventeenth Century* (New York: The Macmillan Company, 1939), p. 29.
52 Samuel Parris, 'Sermon from 3rd of January 1691', in *The Sermon Notebook of Samuel Parris*, p. 184.
53 Samuel Parris, 'Sermon from 3rd of January 1691', in *The Sermon Notebook of Samuel Parris*, p. 185.
54 Samuel Parris, 'Sermon from 3rd of January 1691', in *The Sermon Notebook of Samuel Parris*, p. 186.
55 Samuel Parris, 'Christ Knows How Many Devils There Are in His Churches, and Who They Are', 27 March 1692 in Richard Trask, *The Devil Hath Been Raised: A Documentary History of the Salem Village Witchcraft Outbreak of 1692* (Danvers: Phoenix Publishing, 1992), pp. 110–114. The details of this sermon come from a 291-page sermon book that Parris compiled between 1689 and 1694.

56 Samuel Parris, 'Christ Knows How Many Devils There Are in His Churches, and Who They Are', 27 March 1692 in Richard Trask, *The Devil Hath Been Raised: A Documentary History of the Salem Village Witchcraft Outbreak of 1692* (Danvers: Phoenix Publishing, 1992), p. 114.
57 Samuel Parris, 'Parris Records the Witchcraft Outbreak in the Church Record Book', 27 March 1692 in Richard Trask, *The Devil Hath Been Raised: A Documentary History of the Salem Village Witchcraft Outbreak of 1692* (Danvers: Phoenix Publishing, 1992), p. 116.
58 Samuel Parris, 'Parris Records the Witchcraft Outbreak in the Church Record Book', 27 March 1692 in Richard Trask, *The Devil Hath Been Raised: A Documentary History of the Salem Village Witchcraft Outbreak of 1692* (Danvers: Phoenix Publishing, 1992).
59 J. Horsfall Turner, ed. *Rev. Oliver Heywood, 1630-1702: His Autobiography, Diaries, Anecdote and Event Books Illustrating the General and Family History of Yorkshire and Lancashire*, vol. 4 (Bingley: printed for the editor, 1885), pp. 53–54.
60 Samuel Parris, 'Parris Records the Witchcraft Outbreak in the Church Record Book', 27 March 1692 in Richard Trask, *The Devil Hath Been Raised: A Documentary History of the Salem Village Witchcraft Outbreak of 1692* (Danvers: Phoenix Publishing, 1992), p. 116.
61 Robert Calef, *More Wonders of the Invisible World: Or the Wonders of the Invisible World Displayed in Five Parts* (Boston: Cushing & Appleton, 1700), p. 189. Robert Calef was a merchant in Boston whose *More Wonders* is a direct response to Cotton Mather's *Wonders of the Invisible World*. Calef's work is plainly anti-Mather and anti-witch trials and while he did not physically attend any of the trials, he did have direct access to trial documents and letters which can be validated by cross-examining his work with the primary sources. Therefore, his work may be taken as generally credible and reliable.
62 Paul Boyer and Stephen Nissenbaum, *Salem Possessed: The Social Origins of Witchcraft* (Cambridge and London: Harvard University Press, 1974), p. 185.
63 Richard Weisman, *Witchcraft, Magic, and Religion in 17th Century Massachusetts* (Amherst: The University of Massachusetts Press, 1984), p. 142.
64 E. J. Kent, 'Salem Girls (1692): Problems of Gender and Agency' in *Religion, the Supernatural and Visual Culture in Early Modern Europe: an album amicorum for Charles Zika*, eds., Jennifer Spinks and Dagmar Eichberger (Leiden: Brill, 2015), p. 76.
65 Mary Beth Norton, *In The Devil's Snare: The Salem Witchcraft Crisis of 1692* (New York: Vintage Books, 2002), p. 10.
66 Enders A. Robinson, *The Devil Discovered: Salem Witchcraft of 1692* (New York: Hippocrene Books, 1991), p. 124.
67 Secondary sources generally assume that Griggs was the doctor called upon by Parris to diagnose the children in his household yet no primary source confirms this identification.
68 Emerson W. Baker, *A Storm of Witchcraft: The Salem Trials and the American Experience* (New York: Oxford University Press, 2015), p. 101.
69 Bernard Rosenthal, ed., *Records of the Salem Witch-Hunt* (New York: Cambridge University Press, 2009), doc. 501. The word 'jade' was used as a derogatory term to denote severe disapproval or rejection by God.

70 Bernard Rosenthal, ed., *Records of the Salem Witch-Hunt* (New York: Cambridge University Press, 2009), p. 538.
71 Bernard Rosenthal, ed., *Records of the Salem Witch-Hunt* (New York: Cambridge University Press, 2009).
72 Carol F. Karlsen, *The Devil in the Shape of a Woman: Witchcraft in Colonial New England* (New York: W. W. Norton & Company, 1987), pp. 227–228.
73 Bernard Rosenthal, ed., *Records of the Salem Witch-Hunt* (New York: Cambridge University Press, 2009), doc. 907.
74 Emerson W. Baker, *A Storm of Witchcraft: The Salem Trials and the American Experience* (New York: Oxford University Press, 2015), p. 10.
75 Wendel D. Craker, 'Spectral Evidence, Non-Spectral Acts of Witchcraft, and Confession at Salem in 1692' *The Historical Journal* 40 (No. 2, 1997), p. 350.
76 Benjamin C. Ray, *Satan & Salem: The Witch-Hunt Crisis of 1692* (Charlottesville and London: University of Virginia Press, 2015), pp. 46 and 65; Emerson W. Baker, *A Storm of Witchcraft: The Salem Trials and the American Experience* (New York: Oxford University Press, 2015), pp. 98 and 164; Paul Boyer and Stephen Nissenbaum, *Salem Possessed: The Social Origins of Witchcraft* (Cambridge and London: Harvard University Press, 1974), p. 2; Bernard Rosenthal, *Salem Story: Reading the Witch Trials of* 1692 (Cambridge: Cambridge University Press, 1993), p.121; Enders A. Robinson, *The Devil Discovered: Salem Witchcraft of 1692* (New York: Hippocrene Books, 1991), pp. 102, 109 and 111; Richard Weisman, *Witchcraft, Magic, and Religion in 17th Century Massachusetts* (Amherst: The University of Massachusetts Press, 1984), pp. 134–135; Mary Beth Norton, *In The Devil's Snare: The Salem Witchcraft Crisis of 1692* (New York: Vintage Books, 2002), pp. 72–73; Carol F. Karlsen, *The Devil in the Shape of a Woman: Witchcraft in Colonial New England* (New York: W. W. Norton & Company, 1987), p. 222; Peter Charles Hoffer, *The Salem Witchcraft Trials: A Legal History* (Lawrence: University Press of Kansas, 1997), p. 50, and Peter Charles Hoffer, *The Devil's Disciples: Makers of the Salem Witchcraft Trials* (Baltimore: The John Hopkins University Press, 1996), pp. 60–61.
77 Bernard Rosenthal, ed., *Records of the Salem Witch-Hunt* (New York: Cambridge University Press, 2009), p. 30.
78 Emerson W. Baker, *A Storm of Witchcraft: The Salem Trials and the American Experience* (New York: Oxford University Press, 2015), p. 115, and Benjamin C. Ray, *Satan & Salem: The Witch-Hunt Crisis of 1692* (Charlottesville and London: University of Virginia Press, 2015), p. 65.
79 An instance of the afflicted girls being unable to identify or members of the judicial body being unable to correctly spell the name of an accused person is seen in the following documents: Bernard Rosenthal, ed., *Records of the Salem Witch-Hunt* (New York: Cambridge University Press, 2009), docs. 22, 35, 39, 48, 63, 79, 83, 92, 93, 94, 120, 151, 203, 219, 221, 230, 247, 268 and 428.
80 Mary Beth Norton, *In The Devil's Snare: The Salem Witchcraft Crisis of 1692* (New York: Vintage Books, 2002), p. 343.
81 Mary Beth Norton, *In The Devil's Snare: The Salem Witchcraft Crisis of 1692* (New York: Vintage Books, 2002).
82 'John Proctor', *The Salem Witchcraft Papers: Verbatim Transcripts of the Legal Documents of the Salem Witchcraft Outbreak of 1692*, eds. Paul Boyer and Stephen Nissenbaum, vol. 2 (New York: Da Capo Press, 1977), pp. 677–678.

83 With regard to mistakes in the trial record by members of the acting judicial body, one reason for the numerous misspellings or misnaming of the accused could be due to the relatively lowly status of women. Misspellings could also be the result of the scribe mishearing or simply not knowing the name of the accused as many of them were from communities outside Salem Village.
84 See for example Bernard Rosenthal, ed., *Records of the Salem Witch-Hunt* (New York: Cambridge University Press, 2009), doc. 103.
85 Bernard Rosenthal, ed., *Records of the Salem Witch-Hunt* (New York: Cambridge University Press, 2009), doc. 35.
86 Bernard Rosenthal, ed., *Records of the Salem Witch-Hunt* (New York: Cambridge University Press, 2009).
87 Bernard Rosenthal, ed., *Records of the Salem Witch-Hunt* (New York: Cambridge University Press, 2009).
88 Bernard Rosenthal, ed., *Records of the Salem Witch-Hunt* (New York: Cambridge University Press, 2009).
89 Bernard Rosenthal, ed., *Records of the Salem Witch-Hunt* (New York: Cambridge University Press, 2009), doc. 48.
90 Bernard Rosenthal, ed., *Records of the Salem Witch-Hunt* (New York: Cambridge University Press, 2009), doc. 499.
91 Bernard Rosenthal, ed., *Records of the Salem Witch-Hunt* (New York: Cambridge University Press, 2009), doc. 16.
92 Edward Fairfax, *A Discourse of Witchcraft as It Was Acted in the Family of Mr Edward Fairfax...*, communicated by R. M. Milnes, 1621, in *Miscellanies of the Philobiblon Society*, vol. 5 (London: printed by Charles Whittingham, 1858–1859), p. 139; ASSI 45/10/3/34, 36, 40, 43–44, sig. 34r; C. L' Estrange Ewen, *Witchcraft and Demonism: A Concise Account Derived from Sworn Depositions and Confessions Obtained in the Courts of England and Wales* (London: Heath Cranton Limited, 1933), p. 375; Thomas Albridge, *The Prevalency of Prayer...* (London: printed for S. Popping, 1717), p. 16.
93 Bernard Rosenthal, ed., *Records of the Salem Witch-Hunt* (New York: Cambridge University Press, 2009), doc. 18.
94 Bernard Rosenthal, ed., *Records of the Salem Witch-Hunt* (New York: Cambridge University Press, 2009).
95 Bernard Rosenthal, ed., *Records of the Salem Witch Hunt* (New York: Cambridge University Press, 2009), doc. 104.
96 Bernard Rosenthal, ed., *Records of the Salem Witch-Hunt* (New York: Cambridge University Press, 2009), doc. 105.
97 Bernard Rosenthal, ed., *Records of the Salem Witch-Hunt* (New York: Cambridge University Press, 2009), doc. 103.
98 Joseph Glanvill, *Saducismus Triumphatus or a Full and Plain Evidence Concerning Witches and Apparitions* (London: printed for J. Collins, 1681), p. 144.
99 Bernard Rosenthal, ed., *Records of the Salem Witch-Hunt* (New York: Cambridge University Press, 2009), p. 335.
100 Bernard Rosenthal, ed., *Records of the Salem Witch-Hunt* (New York: Cambridge University Press, 2009), doc. 234.
101 Peter Charles Hoffer, *The Salem Witchcraft Trials: A Legal History* (Lawrence: University Press of Kansas, 1997), p. 49.

102 Peter Charles Hoffer, *The Salem Witchcraft Trials: A Legal History* (Lawrence: University Press of Kansas, 1997).
103 See Paul Boyer and Stephen Nissenbaum, *Salem Possessed: The Social Origins of Witchcraft* (Cambridge and London: Harvard University Press, 1974), p. 2; Robinson, *The Devil Discovered*, p. 4; Weisman, *Witchcraft, Magic, and Religion in 17th Century Massachusetts*, pp. 134–135, and Mary Beth Norton, *In The Devil's Snare: The Salem Witchcraft Crisis of 1692* (New York: Vintage Books, 2002), pp. 56–57.
104 Benjamin C. Ray, *Satan & Salem: The Witch-Hunt Crisis of 1692* (Charlottesville and London: University of Virginia Press, 2015), p. 59.
105 Bernard Rosenthal, ed., *Records of the Salem Witch-Hunt* (New York: Cambridge University Press, 2009), doc. 67.
106 Bernard Rosenthal, ed., *Records of the Salem Witch-Hunt* (New York: Cambridge University Press, 2009), p. 945.
107 Bernard Rosenthal, ed., *Records of the Salem Witch-Hunt* (New York: Cambridge University Press, 2009), doc. 67.
108 Bernard Rosenthal, ed., *Records of the Salem Witch-Hunt* (New York: Cambridge University Press, 2009).
109 Bernard Rosenthal, ed., *Records of the Salem Witch-Hunt* (New York: Cambridge University Press, 2009).
110 Bernard Rosenthal, ed., *Records of the Salem Witch-Hunt* (New York: Cambridge University Press, 2009).
111 Bernard Rosenthal, ed., *Records of the Salem Witch-Hunt* (New York: Cambridge University Press, 2009).
112 Bernard Rosenthal, ed., *Records of the Salem Witch-Hunt* (New York: Cambridge University Press, 2009). Instances of the afflicted not being tortured by the accused person's spectre during their examinations after that person confessed became a standard theme throughout the trials after this first instance with Hobbs.
113 Bernard Rosenthal, *Salem Story: Reading the Witch Trials of* 1692 (Cambridge: Cambridge University Press, 1993), p. 43.
114 Louise Jackson, 'Witches, Wives and Mothers: Witchcraft persecution and women's confessions in seventeenth-century England' in *The Witchcraft Reader*, ed. Darren Oldridge, 3rd edn. (London: Routledge, 219), p. 348.
115 Louise Jackson, 'Witches, Wives and Mothers: Witchcraft persecution and women's confessions in seventeenth-century England' in *The Witchcraft Reader*, ed. Darren Oldridge, 3rd edn. (London: Routledge, 219), p. 351.
116 Louise Jackson, 'Witches, Wives and Mothers: Witchcraft persecution and women's confessions in seventeenth-century England' in *The Witchcraft Reader*, ed. Darren Oldridge, 3rd edn. (London: Routledge, 219), p. 350.
117 Mary Beth Norton, *In The Devil's Snare: The Salem Witchcraft Crisis of 1692* (New York: Vintage Books, 2002), p. 119.
118 Bernard Rosenthal, ed., *Records of the Salem Witch-Hunt* (New York: Cambridge University Press, 2009), doc. 68.
119 Bernard Rosenthal, ed., *Records of the Salem Witch-Hunt* (New York: Cambridge University Press, 2009), doc. 70. Hobbs was referring to her own mother in this instance.
120 Bernard Rosenthal, ed., *Records of the Salem Witch-Hunt* (New York: Cambridge University Press, 2009), p. 237.

121 Bernard Rosenthal, ed., *Records of the Salem Witch-Hunt* (New York: Cambridge University Press, 2009), doc. 77.
122 Bernard Rosenthal, ed., *Records of the Salem Witch-Hunt* (New York: Cambridge University Press, 2009). Burroughs' significance can be seen in the way the scribe wrote a 'B' in the left margin as his name recurs throughout the document (Bernard Rosenthal, ed., *Records of the Salem Witch-Hunt* (New York: Cambridge University Press, 2009), p. 199). Burroughs played a massively complex and significant role as the 'leader' of the so-called Sabbat during the trials. See doc. 95.
123 Bernard Rosenthal, ed., *Records of the Salem Witch-Hunt* (New York: Cambridge University Press, 2009), doc. 120.
124 Bernard Rosenthal, ed., *Records of the Salem Witch-Hunt* (New York: Cambridge University Press, 2009), doc. 77.
125 Bernard Rosenthal, ed., *Records of the Salem Witch-Hunt* (New York: Cambridge University Press, 2009).
126 Bernard Rosenthal, ed., *Records of the Salem Witch-Hunt* (New York: Cambridge University Press, 2009).
127 Bernard Rosenthal, *Salem Story: Reading the Witch Trials of* 1692 (Cambridge: Cambridge University Press, 1993), p. 108.
128 Bernard Rosenthal, ed., *Records of the Salem Witch-Hunt* (New York: Cambridge University Press, 2009), doc. 344.
129 Bernard Rosenthal, ed., *Records of the Salem Witch-Hunt* (New York: Cambridge University Press, 2009), p. 664. No primary document is given, but Abigail and eight others were sentenced to death on 17 September.
130 The reference in Bernard Rosenthal, ed., *Records of the Salem Witch-Hunt* (New York: Cambridge University Press, 2009), p. 664, stated that nine people, including Abigail, were sentenced to death yet only four of those named – Mary Parker, Wilmot Redd, Margaret Scott and Samuel Wardwell – were hanged on 22 September.
131 Bernard Rosenthal, ed., *Records of the Salem Witch-Hunt* (New York: Cambridge University Press, 2009), doc. 836. Rosenthal noted (p. 811) that Abigail Hobbs was very likely one of the five condemned then reprieved persons as she was included in a summary of amounts requested (doc. 930) after the writing of this letter by Phips to the Earl of Nottingham. However, a definite list of the five persons remains elusive.
132 Bernard Rosenthal, ed., *Records of the Salem Witch-Hunt* (New York: Cambridge University Press, 2009), doc. 912.
133 Emerson W. Baker, *A Storm of Witchcraft: The Salem Trials and the American Experience* (New York: Oxford University Press, 2015), p. 103.
134 For a popular perception of Mary Warren, see Arthur Miller, *The Crucible* (London: Penguin Group, 1953); Benjamin C. Ray, *Satan & Salem: The Witch-Hunt Crisis of 1692* (Charlottesville and London: University of Virginia Press, 2015), p. 59; Chadwick Hansen, *Witchcraft at Salem* (New York: George Braziller Inc., 1969), p. 53; Richard Weisman, *Witchcraft, Magic, and Religion in 17th Century Massachusetts* (Amherst: The University of Massachusetts Press, 1984), p. 144.
135 Arthur Miller, *The Crucible* (London: Penguin Group, 1953), act one, p. 18.

136 Bernard Rosenthal, ed., *Records of the Salem Witch-Hunt* (New York: Cambridge University Press, 2009), doc. 75
137 Bernard Rosenthal, ed., *Records of the Salem Witch-Hunt* (New York: Cambridge University Press, 2009).
138 Bernard Rosenthal, ed., *Records of the Salem Witch-Hunt* (New York: Cambridge University Press, 2009).
139 Bernard Rosenthal, ed., *Records of the Salem Witch-Hunt* (New York: Cambridge University Press, 2009).
140 Bernard Rosenthal, ed., *Records of the Salem Witch-Hunt* (New York: Cambridge University Press, 2009).
141 Bernard Rosenthal, ed., *Records of the Salem Witch-Hunt* (New York: Cambridge University Press, 2009).
142 Bernard Rosenthal, ed., *Records of the Salem Witch-Hunt* (New York: Cambridge University Press, 2009).
143 Bernard Rosenthal, ed., *Records of the Salem Witch-Hunt* (New York: Cambridge University Press, 2009).
144 Bernard Rosenthal, ed., *Records of the Salem Witch-Hunt* (New York: Cambridge University Press, 2009).
145 Bernard Rosenthal, ed., *Records of the Salem Witch-Hunt* (New York: Cambridge University Press, 2009), doc. 78.
146 Bernard Rosenthal, ed., *Records of the Salem Witch-Hunt* (New York: Cambridge University Press, 2009), doc. 80.
147 Bernard Rosenthal, ed., *Records of the Salem Witch-Hunt* (New York: Cambridge University Press, 2009).
148 Bernard Rosenthal, ed., *Records of the Salem Witch-Hunt* (New York: Cambridge University Press, 2009).
149 Bernard Rosenthal, ed., *Records of the Salem Witch-Hunt* (New York: Cambridge University Press, 2009), doc. 520.
150 Bernard Rosenthal, ed., *Records of the Salem Witch-Hunt* (New York: Cambridge University Press, 2009).
151 Bernard Rosenthal, ed., *Records of the Salem Witch-Hunt* (New York: Cambridge University Press, 2009).
152 Bernard Rosenthal, ed., *Records of the Salem Witch-Hunt* (New York: Cambridge University Press, 2009).
153 Richard Weisman, *Witchcraft, Magic, and Religion in 17th Century Massachusetts* (Amherst: The University of Massachusetts Press, 1984), p. 133.
154 E. J. Kent, 'Salem Girls (1692): Problems of Gender and Agency' in *Religion, the Supernatural and Visual Culture in Early Modern Europe: an album amicorum for Charles Zika*, eds., Jennifer Spinks and Dagmar Eichberger (Leiden: Brill, 2015), p. 78
155 Bernard Rosenthal, ed., *Records of the Salem Witch-Hunt* (New York: Cambridge University Press, 2009), doc. 86.
156 Bernard Rosenthal, ed., *Records of the Salem Witch-Hunt* (New York: Cambridge University Press, 2009), p. 209.
157 Bernard Rosenthal, ed., *Records of the Salem Witch-Hunt* (New York: Cambridge University Press, 2009), docs. 191 and 192, respectively.
158 Bernard Rosenthal, ed., *Records of the Salem Witch-Hunt* (New York: Cambridge University Press, 2009),

159 Bernard Rosenthal, ed., *Records of the Salem Witch-Hunt* (New York: Cambridge University Press, 2009), docs. 459 and 460, respectively.
160 Bernard Rosenthal, ed., *Records of the Salem Witch-Hunt* (New York: Cambridge University Press, 2009), docs. 469 and 540, respectively.
161 Bernard Rosenthal, ed., *Records of the Salem Witch-Hunt* (New York: Cambridge University Press, 2009), doc. 203.
162 Bernard Rosenthal, ed., *Records of the Salem Witch-Hunt* (New York: Cambridge University Press, 2009), p. 311.
163 Bernard Rosenthal, ed., *Records of the Salem Witch-Hunt* (New York: Cambridge University Press, 2009), doc. 203. This appears similar to the Great Northern Witch Trial in Sweden (1668–1678) where, in one parish, 20% of the child witnesses who were most active were responsible for about half of all the charges made. Bengt Ankarloo, 'Sweden: The Mass Burnings' in *Early Modern European Witchcraft: Centres and Peripheries*, eds., Bengt Ankarloo and Gustav Henningsen (New York: Oxford University Press, 1993), p. 303.
164 Bernard Rosenthal, ed., *Records of the Salem Witch-Hunt* (New York: Cambridge University Press, 2009), p. 311.
165 Bernard Rosenthal, ed., *Records of the Salem Witch-Hunt* (New York: Cambridge University Press, 2009).
166 Bernard Rosenthal, ed., *Records of the Salem Witch-Hunt* (New York: Cambridge University Press, 2009), p. 311.
167 Bernard Rosenthal, ed., *Records of the Salem Witch-Hunt* (New York: Cambridge University Press, 2009), doc. 749. In this document, Mary Osgood, Mary Tyler, Deliverance Dale, Abigail Williams, Sarah Wilson Sr and Hannah Tyler stated how the Andover phase of the trials started: '…John Ballard, of Andover, his wife being sick at the same time, he, either from himself or by the advice of others, fetched two of the persons, called the afflicted persons, from Salem Village to Andover, which was the beginning of that dreadful calamity that befell us in Andover'.
168 Bernard Rosenthal, ed., *Records of the Salem Witch-Hunt* (New York: Cambridge University Press, 2009), docs. 615 and 616, respectively.
169 Bernard Rosenthal, ed., *Records of the Salem Witch-Hunt* (New York: Cambridge University Press, 2009), doc. 707.
170 Deodat Lawson, *A Brief and True Narrative of Some Remarkable Passages Relating to Sundry Persons Afflicted of Witchcraft…* (Boston: Benjamin Harris, 1692), p. 3.
171 Deodat Lawson, *A Brief and True Narrative of Some Remarkable Passages Relating to Sundry Persons Afflicted of Witchcraft…* (Boston: Benjamin Harris, 1692), p. 4; The witch's familiar yellow bird was a common motif throughout the duration of the trials appearing in docs. 3, 6, 7, 16, 17, 18, 21, 180, 345, 428, 504, 516, 519.
172 See for example R. B., *The boy of Bilson: or, A true discovery of the late notorious impostures of a certain Romish priests…* (London: Imprinted by Felix Kingston for William Barret, 1622), sig. H3r; Mather, *Memorable Providences*, p. 111, and Samuel Willard, 'A brief account of a strange and unusual Providence of God befallen to Elizabeth Knap of Groton' in *Groton in The Witchcraft Times*, ed. Samuel A. Green (Cambridge: John Wilson and Son, 1883), p. 16.

173 Bernard Rosenthal, *Salem Story: Reading the Witch Trials of* 1692 (Cambridge: Cambridge University Press, 1993), p. 40.
174 Bernard Rosenthal, *Salem Story: Reading the Witch Trials of* 1692 (Cambridge: Cambridge University Press, 1993), p. 4; see for example Paul Boyer and Stephen Nissenbaum, *Salem Possessed: The Social Origins of Witchcraft* (Cambridge and London: Harvard University Press, 1974), passim, for the former idea and Mary Beth Norton, *In The Devil's Snare: The Salem Witchcraft Crisis of 1692* (New York: Vintage Books, 2002), passim, for the later.
175 Bernard Rosenthal, ed., *Records of the Salem Witch-Hunt* (New York: Cambridge University Press, 2009), docs. 267 and 362.
176 Bernard Rosenthal, ed., *Records of the Salem Witch-Hunt* (New York: Cambridge University Press, 2009), doc. 267.
177 Bernard Rosenthal, ed., *Records of the Salem Witch-Hunt* (New York: Cambridge University Press, 2009), docs. 372 and 373.
178 Robert Calef, *More Wonders of the Invisible World: Or the Wonders of the Invisible World Displayed in Five Parts* (Boston: Cushing & Appleton, 1700), p. 209.
179 Robert Calef, *More Wonders of the Invisible World: Or the Wonders of the Invisible World Displayed in Five Parts* (Boston: Cushing & Appleton, 1700).
180 Robert Calef, *More Wonders of the Invisible World: Or the Wonders of the Invisible World Displayed in Five Parts* (Boston: Cushing & Appleton, 1700), p. 212. Calef does not specify when the reprieve came and when it was withdrawn.
181 Samuel Sewall, 'Diary entry 19th of August' in *Collections of the Massachusetts Historical Society*, p. 363, and Robert Calef, *More Wonders of the Invisible World: Or the Wonders of the Invisible World Displayed in Five Parts* (Boston: Cushing & Appleton, 1700), p. 213.
182 Bernard Rosenthal, ed., *Records of the Salem Witch-Hunt* (New York: Cambridge University Press, 2009), doc. 77.
183 Bernard Rosenthal, ed., *Records of the Salem Witch-Hunt* (New York: Cambridge University Press, 2009), doc. 120.
184 Bernard Rosenthal, ed., *Records of the Salem Witch-Hunt* (New York: Cambridge University Press, 2009), docs. 124, 125, 128 and 129.
185 Bernard Rosenthal, ed., *Records of the Salem Witch-Hunt* (New York: Cambridge University Press, 2009), doc. 125.
186 Bernard Rosenthal, ed., *Records of the Salem Witch-Hunt* (New York: Cambridge University Press, 2009), doc. 126.
187 Bernard Rosenthal, ed., *Records of the Salem Witch-Hunt* (New York: Cambridge University Press, 2009), docs. 185 and 673, respectively.
188 Bernard Rosenthal, ed., *Records of the Salem Witch-Hunt* (New York: Cambridge University Press, 2009), doc. 185
189 Cotton Mather, *Wonders of the Invisible World: Being an Account of the Tryals of Several Witches Lately Executed in New England* (London: John Russell Smith, 1862), p. 166.
190 Samuel Sewall, 'Diary entry 19th of September 1692' in *Collections of the Massachusetts Historical Society*, p. 364.
191 Harriet S. Tapley, *Records and Files of the Quarterly Court of Essex County*, ed. George Francis Dow, Essex Institute, vol. 6 (Essex County, published by the Institute, 1917), p. 191.

192 Bernard Rosenthal, ed., *Records of the Salem Witch-Hunt* (New York: Cambridge University Press, 2009), doc. 673.
193 Bernard Rosenthal, ed., *Records of the Salem Witch-Hunt* (New York: Cambridge University Press, 2009), doc. 235.
194 Bernard Rosenthal, ed., *Records of the Salem Witch-Hunt* (New York: Cambridge University Press, 2009), docs. 503 and 504, respectively.
195 Bernard Rosenthal, ed., *Records of the Salem Witch-Hunt* (New York: Cambridge University Press, 2009), doc. 425, and Cotton Mather, *Wonders of the Invisible World: Being an Account of the Tryals of Several Witches Lately Executed in New England* (London: John Russell Smith, 1862), p. 159.
196 Bernard Rosenthal, ed., *Records of the Salem Witch-Hunt* (New York: Cambridge University Press, 2009), doc. 234.
197 Bernard Rosenthal, ed., *Records of the Salem Witch-Hunt* (New York: Cambridge University Press, 2009), docs. 557, 558 and 560.
198 Bernard Rosenthal, ed., *Records of the Salem Witch-Hunt* (New York: Cambridge University Press, 2009), docs. 279 and 280.
199 Bernard Rosenthal, ed., *Records of the Salem Witch-Hunt* (New York: Cambridge University Press, 2009), doc. 241, and Mary Beth Norton, *In The Devil's Snare: The Salem Witchcraft Crisis of 1692* (New York: Vintage Books, 2002), pp. 183–184.
200 Mary Beth Norton, *In The Devil's Snare: The Salem Witchcraft Crisis of 1692* (New York: Vintage Books, 2002), p. 184.
201 Bernard Rosenthal, ed., *Records of the Salem Witch-Hunt* (New York: Cambridge University Press, 2009), doc. 352.
202 Bernard Rosenthal, ed., *Records of the Salem Witch-Hunt* (New York: Cambridge University Press, 2009), doc. 150.
203 Bernard Rosenthal, ed., *Records of the Salem Witch-Hunt* (New York: Cambridge University Press, 2009), p. 265.
204 Mary Beth Norton, *In The Devil's Snare: The Salem Witchcraft Crisis of 1692* (New York: Vintage Books, 2002), p. 6
205 Bernard Rosenthal, ed., *Records of the Salem Witch-Hunt* (New York: Cambridge University Press, 2009), doc. 28.
206 Thomas Brattle, 'Letter', Boston, 1692 in *Narratives of the Witchcraft Cases 1648 1706*, ed. George Lincoln Burr (New York: Charles Scribner's Sons, 1914), pp. 172 and 188.
207 The details of this trial were described in the previous chapter, and therefore only relevant details will be repeated here.
208 John Hale, *A Modest Inquiry and How Persons Guilty of that Crime may be Convicted*... (Boston: B. Green and J. Alten, 1702), p. 25.
209 Cotton Mather, *Memorable Providences, Relating to Witchcrafts and Possessions* ... (Boston: sold by Joseph Brunning, 1689), p. 101.
210 John Hale, *A Modest Inquiry and How Persons Guilty of that Crime may be Convicted*... (Boston: B. Green and J. Alten, 1702), p. 25.
211 Cotton Mather, *Memorable Providences, Relating to Witchcrafts and Possessions* ... (Boston: sold by Joseph Brunning, 1689), p. 101.
212 Bernard Rosenthal, ed., *Records of the Salem Witch-Hunt* (New York: Cambridge University Press, 2009), docs. 32 and 150, respectively.

213 Cotton Mather, *Memorable Providences, Relating to Witchcrafts and Possessions...* (Boston: sold by Joseph Brunning, 1689), p. 104.
214 Cotton Mather, *Memorable Providences, Relating to Witchcrafts and Possessions...* (Boston: sold by Joseph Brunning, 1689), p. 114.
215 Cotton Mather, *Memorable Providences, Relating to Witchcrafts and Possessions...* (Boston: sold by Joseph Brunning, 1689), 107.
216 Frances Hill, *A Delusion of Satan* (Boston: De Capo Press, 1995), p. 23.
217 Bernard Rosenthal, ed., *Records of the Salem Witch-Hunt* (New York: Cambridge University Press, 2009), docs. 179, 424, 535; Cotton Mather, *Wonders of the Invisible World: Being an Account of the Tryals of Several Witches Lately Executed in New England* (London: John Russell Smith, 1862), pp. 167–172; for recent scholarship on Swedish witchcraft trials, see Jari Eilola, 'Interpreting Children's Blåkulla Stories in Sweden (1675)' in *Demonology and Witch-Hunting in Early Modern Europe*, eds. Julian Goodare, Rita Voltmer and Live Helene Willumsen (Oxford and New York: Routledge, 2020).
218 Bernard Rosenthal, ed., *Records of the Salem Witch-Hunt* (New York: Cambridge University Press, 2009), doc. 369, is a fragmentary account appearing to discredit Mercy Lewis. Although the exact substance of the document is mostly lost, it appears to claim that Lewis spoke 'many untruths'.
219 Bernard Rosenthal, ed., *Records of the Salem Witch-Hunt* (New York: Cambridge University Press, 2009), doc. 370.
220 Bernard Rosenthal, ed., *Records of the Salem Witch-Hunt* (New York: Cambridge University Press, 2009), doc. 368.
221 Bernard Rosenthal, ed., *Records of the Salem Witch-Hunt* (New York: Cambridge University Press, 2009), doc. 293.
222 Bernard Rosenthal, ed., *Records of the Salem Witch-Hunt* (New York: Cambridge University Press, 2009).
223 Bernard Rosenthal, ed., *Records of the Salem Witch-Hunt* (New York: Cambridge University Press, 2009), doc. 371.
224 Bernard Rosenthal, ed., *Records of the Salem Witch-Hunt* (New York: Cambridge University Press, 2009), doc. 836.
225 Bernard Rosenthal, ed., *Records of the Salem Witch-Hunt* (New York: Cambridge University Press, 2009), docs. 313, 878 and 745, respectively.
226 Bernard Rosenthal, ed., *Records of the Salem Witch-Hunt* (New York: Cambridge University Press, 2009), doc. 822.
227 George Lyman Kittredge, *Witchcraft in Old and New England* (New York: Russell & Russell, 1929), p. 365.
228 Bernard Rosenthal, ed., *Records of the Salem Witch-Hunt* (New York: Cambridge University Press, 2009), doc. 952
229 Bernard Rosenthal, ed., *Records of the Salem Witch-Hunt* (New York: Cambridge University Press, 2009), doc. 822.
230 Marilynne K. Roach, *Six Women of Salem: The Untold Story of The Accused and Their Accusers in the Salem Witch Trials* (Philadelphia: De Capo Press, 2013), p. 396.
231 Marilynne K. Roach, *Six Women of Salem: The Untold Story of The Accused and Their Accusers in the Salem Witch Trials* (Philadelphia: De Capo Press, 2013), p. 397.

232 Emerson W. Baker, *A Storm of Witchcraft: The Salem Trials and the American Experience* (New York: Oxford University Press, 2015), p. 109.
233 'Danvers Church Records, August 25th 1706' in *The New England Historical and Genealogical Register*, ed. Samuel G. Drake, vol. 12 (Boston: H. W. Dutton and Son, 1858), p. 246.

CONCLUSION

1692 and Beyond, The Children That Tried Anything

Throughout the period of witch-hunting in England and New England, children played a central and often essential role in the trials. In early modern society, children were seen as both a threat and a promise, caught between infancy and adulthood. Children were more susceptible to the Devil but also could be seen as inherently innocent. This unique status saw children almost completely monopolise the position of the demoniac in England and New England. The role of demoniac was usually conflated with being bewitched, and it is the role of accuser that most children played in English and New English witch trials. However, an in-depth analysis of the primary sources revealed that children sometimes became the objects of witchcraft accusations. While children retained a lowly social status in the early modern world, their religious position was given much more credence in matters pertaining to the spiritual world. The period of witch-hunting demonstrated that children used and often were used as weapons of judicial and clerical power to obtain information about the accused that otherwise could not be procured. Children used their preternatural insight for a multitude of different reasons: to get attention, to avoid going to school, to gain money, to rid society of despised persons or simply because they were told to do so by invested adults.

The implications of this insight on the study of witch-hunting as a broader phenomenon are endless. While in recent scholarship, infamous trials are often used as case studies, others are mentioned only in passing, yet the influence and impact children commanded in English and New English witchcraft trials is still underrepresented in witch-hunting scholarship. The sheer number of cases involving children, on both sides of the Atlantic, has hitherto not been adequately appreciated.[1]

DOI: 10.4324/9781003685319-8

This research revealed that children played a discernible and pervasive role from the first to the last documented early modern witchcraft trial in both England and New England in spite of turbulent social and political changes, sceptical beliefs and eventually the end of the witch-hunts. Consequently, the ramifications of this study on the phenomenon of early modern witch-hunting are numerous. For example, this study demonstrated that the role of children in English and New English court cases was more widespread and varied than previously thought. As a result, those wishing to undertake further studies in early modern law should not undervalue the preponderance and influence of children. Through redefining the parameters of age by cultural status, rather than just numerical means, a more diverse group of children could be studied, allowing for an innovative interpretive lens through which to examine well-researched as well as un-explored cases. In this way, this work focussed solely on the role of children in witchcraft trials, going beyond infamous case studies or those caught up in the John Darrell Controversy. This approach offered fresh insight into the multifaceted roles children played, not just as the victims of witches' malice but also as historical actors that gained greater agency in supernatural encounters over time.

Before 1589, children played a multitude of roles in witchcraft trials. In 1566, Agnes Brown was involved in the first documented witchcraft trial where a child was permitted to give evidence against another child, Joan Waterhouse. Joan's tactics of guilt minimisation may have helped spare her life, but the imprisonment of Thomas Lever as a conjuror's assistant in 1579 reflected the growing culpability of children in matters pertaining to the spiritual world. Rachel Pinder and Agnes Briggs were the first notable cases of fraud in this period. However, the first set of Chelmsford trials (1579), the St Osyth trials (1582) and the second set of Chelmsford trials (1589) demonstrated the increasing influence and power of children when it was allowed to develop freely.

By 1589, the infamous Throckmorton case brought bewitchment and demonic possession to the higher social estates where they asserted unprecedented levels of authority over the persecuted Samuels family. The John Darrell Controversy further heightened the significance of children as they became the epicentre of ecclesiastical and political debates surrounding the efficacy of exorcism. Through their involvement in these affairs, children like Thomas Darling and Mary Glover demonstrated their own religious affiliations, despite outright hostility from Anglican clergy who sought to gatekeep insight of the invisible world. As a result of the wave of official scepticism brought on by Darrell and the imposters discovered by King James, children's credibility as preternatural agents wavered and many struggled to assert themselves as believable demoniacs or accusers. Even so, the idea that children were successful mediators of the spiritual realm persisted, and by the Bury St Edmunds trial in 1662, it appeared that the sanctity of children's evidence prevailed.

This idea persisted in New England where children were first passive victims, used as weapons and tools by adults to bolster accusations of witchcraft. By 1653, children quickly became bolder in their denunciations of adults. This is clear in the 1662 Hartford witchcraft trials where Elizabeth Kelly and Ann Cole instigated and spurred on one of Connecticut's largest witch-hunts. While Elizabeth Knap's accusations of witchcraft in 1671 against two local women were not believed, she nonetheless captured her community's attention for three months through her stories of her familiarity with Satan. Additionally, the bewitchment of the Goodwin children in 1688 and the Salem witchcraft trials of 1692 represent an almost complete acceptance of the authority of children as preternatural agents. While there were sceptics, particularly during the Salem trials, no one successfully managed to dismantle the credibility of the Salem girls in 1692. That the role of children was able to develop from passive victims to active influences of witchcraft trials in forty-four years (from 1648 to 1692) is a testament to the cultural and religiously significant position they held in early modern society.

There are, moreover, broader ramifications such as understanding the conflict between Catholicism and Protestantism in this time, as children played a much larger role in theological and ecclesiastical affairs in England than has been given due credit. Furthermore, rather than being one-dimensional, children were often seen as independent agents of community moral control. Through a comparative analysis between England and New England, the power of learnt behaviour and the transmission of ideas between children enhanced their authority and influence in matters pertaining to the preternatural world. This type of comparative analysis could be easily rendered in other geographical locations and timeframes where children played a dominant role in witchcraft trials.

It must be acknowledged that there were many more trials that involved children that were not able to be elaborated on.[2] Hence, research on the role of children in witchcraft trials has only scarcely begun. These trials could be analysed using the chronological framework implemented throughout this work; however, a thematic approach or one which seeks to incorporate a smaller number of cases or trials would add value to our knowledge of these cases. For example, one important theme was the perception of the desires and fears of young girls. This could be ascertained in the cases of Ann Cole, Abigail Hobbs and Elizabeth Knap.[3] An in-depth analysis on this element would add immense value to our understanding of early modern adolescent girls. Through this close examination of the role of children in English and New English witchcraft trials, historians can gain a better understanding of children and childhood more broadly, including their fears, desires, motivations and imaginations within the early modern belief system.

Through using modern phenomena as a means to inform and compare, such as the example of the McMartin preschool trials in the introduction, it could be argued that children never relinquished their hold as mediums of the immaterial world. Hence, the significance of children in the witch-hunting phenomena has broader ramifications not only historically but currently.

The role children played in early modern English and New English witchcraft trials continued to be significant at the turn of the seventeenth century despite the sharp decline in judicial and popular attitudes towards witch-hunting.[4] Not only did children maintain their role, but they continued to expand and develop it into the 1700s. For instance, despite the outpouring of grief at the conclusion of the Salem witchcraft trials in late 1692, this did not end witch-hunting in New England. Similarly, though the last execution in England for witchcraft (in a case that involved children) occurred in 1662, the last witchcraft trial in England during the early modern era occurred fifty years later in 1712. That children were central in the first and last witchcraft trials in both of these jurisdictions reflects their integral role in the functioning and continuation of witch-hunting. Lastly, juxtapositioning the role of early modern children in witch-hunting and children against the so-called 'Satanic Panic' of the 1980s and 1990s reveals a disturbing parallel. This reminds us of the lasting significance of children within alleged invisible crimes as well as parental fears. With the new chronological framework outlined in this study, revealing how children's role in witchcraft trials was not only important and changed over time, one can better understand and appreciate witchcraft cases that occurred in England and New England post-1692; a brief survey of a few later cases illustrates this.

'What will be the issue of these troubles, God only knows...'

The significance of children in matters pertaining to the unseen world did not cease to become important – either to them or to their society – in 1692. Certainly, the courts were becoming more sceptical and increasingly hesitant to condemn people for witchcraft. However, children continued to try anything to retain their meaningful status as supernatural agents as seen in a small selection of trials that occurred post-1692. These cases provide valuable insights about broader themes and concepts explored throughout this work. Firstly, this study demonstrated not only that the transmission of ideas or learnt behaviour occurred within England, as well as across the Atlantic, but that mimicking behaviour of other demoniacs was a powerful and often successful way of proving one's bewitchment. Secondly, children's roles in witchcraft trials were varied and not merely restricted to being accusers or victims. Thirdly, an in-depth study of children in witchcraft trials provides clues about their inner desires, fears, imagination and motivations. That these themes are demonstrated in some trials that occurred well into the eighteenth century demonstrates the longevity and significance of children in preternatural affairs. The first key case overlapped with the Salem trials and concerned a seventeen-year-old girl called Mercy Short.

The bewitchment of Mercy Short from Boston provides insight into the role children continued to play in witchcraft trials after the Salem episode. Short's bewitchment was also directly tied to English witchcraft beliefs. Short's bewitchment narrative was recorded by Cotton Mather who, like in the case of the Goodwin children, featured heavily in Short's case. Short was a seventeen-year-old maidservant who, in the summer of 1692, was asked by her mistress to go on an errand to the prison where many accused witches were committed.[5] One of the accused, later identified as Sarah Good, asked her for some tobacco whereupon Short threw 'shavings' at her stating, 'that's tobacco good enough for you'.[6] Good responded with some 'ill words' against the girl, and Short fell into grievous fits as a result. After fasting for twelve days, Short recovered until she found herself 'variously tortured and harassed by evil spirits' that November.[7] Short displayed the typical characteristics of a demoniac, including revulsion at Godly objects to the extent where, at one point, Short went 'flying upon' Mather while he was praying, tearing a page out of his Bible.[8]

A feature that makes Short's bewitchment more interesting was Mather's discernment that although Short 'had no sort of acquaintance with histories of what has happened elsewhere', he noted that 'the Devil that visited her was just of the same stature, feature and complexion with what the histories of the witchcraft beyond [the] sea ascribe unto him'.[9] Mather continued: 'although she could be no other than utterly ignorant of what the European Books relate concerning such matters, nevertheless the voice of these demons was exactly such as you shall read in Glanvill's collections and elsewhere'.[10] Whether this was Mather's own bias regarding Short's perceptions and descriptions of the invisible world is difficult to ascertain. What is remarkable about Mather's perspicacity is what it may reflect about the extent of Short's insight about other witchcraft trials or beliefs and how she may have used this knowledge to inform her own bewitchment narrative.

The last known witchcraft trial in New England occurred in Wallingford, Connecticut, against a woman called Winifred Benham and her twelve-year-old daughter of the same name in 1697. According to Robert Calef, the elder Benham was accused by 'some children that pretended to have spectral sight'.[11] The accusatory children in this instance were all from wealthy and influential families who claimed that the apparitions of Winifred Benham Senior and Junior 'frequently and sorely afflicted…their bodies'.[12] According to Calef, Winifred Senior was searched for witches' teats and was made to endure the swimming test; it is unclear whether the younger Winifred was also forced to undergo such measures, but both were bound to appear in court that October to face charges of witchcraft.[13] The elder Benham was also excommunicated by the minister Wallingford.[14] The Court of Assistants, held in October of 1697, returned a grand jury verdict of 'ignoramus', meaning there was insufficient evidence to proceed against them.[15] However, after both Benhams were freed, Calef noted that complaints were renewed against them, perhaps an indication of local dissatisfaction of the court's inability to deal with the accused witches. Consequently, the Benhams fled to New York.[16] The fact that five years after Salem, a small group of young accusers successfully brought a mother and daughter to trial on spectral evidence alone demonstrated the tenacity of children in witchcraft beliefs and judicial procedure. Witchcraft trials may have ended in 1697, but there is evidence that children still played a key role in witchcraft trials in New England well into the eighteenth century.

In 1768, a girl called Norton declared that she was bewitched by her aunt who had 'often put a bridle upon her and driven her through the air to Albany where great witch-meetings were held'.[17] The pastor, Elder Wildman, took her to his house 'that he might exorcise her'.[18] The pastor invited some people to come to his house to pray with him, and people claimed that they were tormented by unseen hands 'pinching them, sticking red-hot pins into their flesh and bringing strange maladies upon them'.[19] What became of Norton is not recorded. What is fascinating about this brief account is how it echoed themes recorded in witchcraft trials decades earlier. The motif of having a bridle put on and being ridden was seen in Edmund Robinson's case in Lancashire in 1634, as well as Anne Armstrong's account in Northumberland in 1673.[20] While mere coincidences are possible, it is dubious that young Norton was able to come up with such a specific motif on her own. What is more likely is that Norton heard about one of these English cases and decided to weave this information into her own bewitchment narrative more than 100 years after it was first described. The transmission, persistence and relaying of such motifs and traditions within the sphere of acting bewitched was a powerful part of the role of children in witchcraft trials; that it seemed to continue to cross the Atlantic for more than 100 years is a poignant display of the central role of children in witch-hunting. In Old England, even as witchcraft trials sharply decreased at the end of the seventeenth century, some children appeared to try anything to stay active and relevant as mediators of the preternatural world.

In Kent in 1698, fifteen-year-old Mary Clarke was brought to the Assize on charges of witchcraft. She readily confessed to meeting the Devil who had given her an apple and in exchange she promised to serve him her whole life. Two weeks after this encounter, Clarke further admitted that the Devil came to her again and asked her to murder the Earl of Winchelsea. Clarke asked him how to do it, and the Devil gave her a poppet whereby she stuck five pins in its side. Clarke was an illegitimate child, bound as an apprentice to one Widow Reeve who admitted that she was in 'great hopes she had been clear of her' when Clarke had been taken away by the Constable to be examined.[21] Trouble began for Clarke when bricks and other objects seemingly started to fly around the house while she and other women were washing. Upon mounting pressure from those around her, who suspected her as a witch, she admitted to familiarity with Satan, 'begging for her God's sake to pardon her'.[22] Similar to Elizabeth Knap and Abigail Hobbs, Mary Clarke seemed to genuinely believe in her supernatural powers and could not stop incriminating herself.

Clarke was a bastard child who was clearly unwanted by her Dame; Clarke's belief she could consort with Satan and her guilt at being found out may be a genuine reflection of the manifestation of her internalised shame and emotional turmoil. Clarke even went so far as to take people to the place where the poppet was supposed to be, digging through the dirt on her hands and knees; however, she could not find it. Clarke was bound over to the Assize on 21 March and admitted to everything the judge asked her. The judge, unwilling to prosecute her, commanded Clarke to say her prayers and serve her Dame 'and so let her go taking no...further notice of these matters'.[23] At only fifteen, Mary Clarke's denunciation, imprisonment and trial by her own confession at the end of the seventeenth century have been curiously overlooked by historians. Yet, it reveals captivating insights into the role of children in early modern English witchcraft trials. In the same year, Elizabeth Noel further demonstrated that children played roles in witchcraft outside of the victim or the accuser; she also dabbled in the dark arts.

Elizabeth Noel was described both as an 'ordinary cook maid' and 'that conjuring maid' in a letter from Charles Seward to the Archbishop of York who wished to know the details of the matter. In 1698, Seward witnessed Noel draw:

> some rude lines upon a piece of white paper and then held it behind a big bellied glass (like those wherein flowers are commonly put) filled full of water and after some inward commotions of her mind, her lips not seemingly to stir, she would be up in the glass the effigies of any person who was desired of her to be shown.[24]

According to Seward, Noel showed King Charles II in a green satin suit but was unable to show Oliver Cromwell, whom the audience gathered wanted to see. Seward goes on to explain that people 'frequently' came to see Noel to know their fortunes which caused her mistress 'to put her away'.[25] The letter concluded with Seward noting that he did not know what became of Noel and that she 'could not be persuaded' to name the person who taught her 'such tricks'.[26] This brief account provides fascinating details demonstrating that children still engaged with the supernatural world, not just as accusers but as consorts to magic, just as Thomas Lever had been accused of in 1579.

Moreover, the fact that people allegedly came to see Noel 'frequently' to use her services indicated a popular demand for a connection to the preternatural world; Noel, though only an ordinary cook maid, was thought to be able to provide that connection. Children still maintained their position as accusers in witchcraft trials, and Anne Thorn was a star witness in one of the last recorded witchcraft trials in England.

In 1712 Jane Wenham of Hertfordshire became one of the last convicted witches in England. The main source of evidence against her surrounded her apparent bewitchment of Anne Thorn, a sixteen-year-old girl, who was a domestic servant to one Mr Gardiner.[27] As Thorn sat by the fire one night (her knee recently being set after an accident the night before) she was found on the floor, mostly naked with a parcel of twigs and leaves bundled up in her apron. When the apron was opened, Thorn began to cry out 'I am ruined and undone' telling her master that 'her mind ran upon Jane Wenham'.[28] Those around Thorn eventually procured a warrant for Wenham, and she was brought to Thorn who cried against her 'you are a [bastard] woman, you have ruined me' and flew at her, scratching her face so violently 'that the noise of her nails seemed to all that were present as if she were scratched against a [wall.]'[29] This demonstrates two themes: the persistence in the tradition of scratching the witch and Thorn's boldness to use such language against an elderly woman. This reflects the pertinacity of children in witchcraft lore but also the subversion of the normal social order. Subverting the social order was a consistent theme in the role of children in witchcraft trials and was perhaps one of the key reasons why children became involved in supernatural affairs. From Joan Throckmorton rebuking adults for not watching Agnes Samuels closely enough, to William Perry calling a priest a 'roughish p', children used their status to blaspheme, lash out and assert authority in ways that were usually far out of reach.[30]

Wenham was eventually found guilty but quickly received a reprieve from the sceptical judge. However, she was moved to a different town for her own protection. Thorn's account showed that popular notions of witchcraft (and the role children played in it) were still deeply entrenched by the eighteenth century. Thorn's case also reveals elements of child's fears and frustrations, as Thorn's want for agency is clear in her furious need to scratch Wenham. In a final example, Elizabeth Hicks' case highlights how children could be more than just victims or accusers; Hicks' case also represents another overall theme in this work: how children, in this period, could be both loved and feared.[31]

Elizabeth Hicks was described as being nine years old from Huntingdonshire in 1716 when she admitted to her father that her mother taught her how to be a witch. Her father, Edmund Hick, described how his only daughter was 'the apple of his eye' but was saddened to hear that both his wife and daughter were witches.[32] His wife, Mary Hicks, was described as vexing her neighbours and making them vomit 'pins and needles and having a clay image which she would...represent any person she had a mind to torment'.[33] The account has themes consistent with Continental witchcraft beliefs when Elizabeth was described as being able to sink ships by '...getting a basin of water and some soap, [pulling] her stocking from her left leg, and making lather with it in the water, as the lather rose...a violent storm arose with it...'.[34]

Convinced of his daughter's guilt, Edmund Hicks presented both his wife and daughter to Justice Wilmot where they both confessed; they were committed to prison and on 20 July 1716 they both received the death sentence. Nine days later while standing on the scaffold, Elizabeth apologised 'for what mischiefs she had done any body' whereupon the ladder 'being over-turned, they were both hanged'.[35]

Wallace Notestein believed this account is 'wholly fictitious' which is likely why this case is rarely mentioned in secondary sources.[36] Yet, C. L' Estrange Ewen believed that the names were likely accurate and 'it is very probable that there is a sub-stratum of truth in the story' but the convictions and executions, however, were 'journalistic invention'.[37] Regardless of the level of truth behind the story of Elizabeth Hicks, there is still immense value in the account. That someone thought to write an account (real or not) of a nine-year-old girl who had been taught to use witchcraft by her mother, to use poppets and to lay waste to ships, may reveal popular perceptions about witchcraft and the long-standing role of children within it. An emotive tale of how a father turned in his only daughter who, in turn, gave a moving speech before being executed for witchcraft had the didactic purpose of telling its intended audience that witchcraft still existed, noting that anyone could be guilty. Though the witch-hunts ended and the Acts were eventually repealed, children were still seen to hold power and control in the unseeable world, sometimes with devastating results.

Notes

1 For some recent examples examining the role of children in witch trials on the Continent, see Lu Ann Homza, *Village Infernos and Witches' Advocates: Witch-Hunting in Navarre, 1608–1614* (University Park: The Pennsylvania State University Press, 2022), and Jari Eilola, 'Interpreting Children's Blåkulla Stories in Sweden (1675)' in *Demonology and Witch-Hunting in Early Modern Europe*, eds. Julian Goodare, Rita Voltmer, Live Helene Willumsen (London and New York: Routledge, 2020).

2 See Appendix A and Appendix B.

3 John Whiting, 'Letter from John Whiting to Increase Mather' in *Collections of the Massachusetts Historical Society*, vol. 8, fourth series (Boston: published for the Society, 1868), p. 467; Bernard Rosenthal, ed., *Records of the Salem Witch-Hunt* (New York: Cambridge University Press, 2009), doc. 67; Samuel Willard, 'A brief account of a strange and unusual Providence of God befallen to Elizabeth

Knap of Groton' in *Groton in The Witchcraft Times*, ed. Samuel A. Green (Cambridge: John Wilson and Son, 1883), p. 8.

4 John Demos, *Entertaining Satan: Witchcraft and the Culture of Early New England* (Oxford: Oxford University Press, 2004), p. 13.

5 Carol. F. Karlsen, *The Devil in the Shape of a Woman: Witchcraft in Colonial New England* (New York: W. W. Norton & Company, 1987), p. 233.

6 Cotton Mather, 'A Brand Pluck'd Out of the Burning', 1693 in *Narratives of the Witchcraft Cases 1648-1706*, ed. George Lincoln Burr (New York: Charles Scribner's Sons, 1914), pp. 259–260.

7 Cotton Mather, 'A Brand Pluck'd Out of the Burning', 1693 in *Narratives of the Witchcraft Cases 1648-1706*, ed. George Lincoln Burr (New York: Charles Scribner's Sons, 1914), p. 260.

8 Cotton Mather, 'A Brand Pluck'd Out of the Burning', 1693 in *Narratives of the Witchcraft Cases 1648-1706*, ed. George Lincoln Burr (New York: Charles Scribner's Sons, 1914).

9 Cotton Mather, 'A Brand Pluck'd Out of the Burning', 1693 in *Narratives of the Witchcraft Cases 1648-1706*, ed. George Lincoln Burr (New York: Charles Scribner's Sons, 1914), p. 261.

10 Cotton Mather, 'A Brand Pluck'd Out of the Burning', 1693 in *Narratives of the Witchcraft Cases 1648-1706*, ed. George Lincoln Burr (New York: Charles Scribner's Sons, 1914), p. 262.

11 Robert Calef, *More Wonders of the Invisible World: or the wonders of the invisible world displayed in five parts* (Boston: Cushing & Appleton, 1700), p. 232.

12 Donald Lines Jacobus, ed., *New Haven Genealogical Magazine*, vol. 4, no. 3 (New York: Clarence D. Smile, 1927), pp. 956–957.

13 Richard Godbeer, *The Devil's Dominion: Magic and Religion in Early New England* (New York: Cambridge University Press, 1992), pp. 173–174.

14 Robert Calef, *More Wonders of the Invisible World: Or the Wonders of the Invisible World Displayed in Five Parts* (Boston: Cushing & Appleton, 1700), p. 232.

15 C. Bancroft Gillespie and George Munson Curtis, *An Historic Record and Pictorial Description of the Town of Meriden, Connecticut* (Meriden: Journal Publishing Company, 1906), p. 259.

16 Robert Calef, *More Wonders of the Invisible World: Or the Wonders of the Invisible World Displayed in Five Parts* (Boston: Cushing & Appleton, 1700), p. 233.

17 J. Hammond Trumbull, ed., *The Memorial History of Hartford County Connecticut 1633-1884*, vol. 2 (Boston: Edward L. Osgood Publisher, 1886), p. 51.

18 J. Hammond Trumbull, ed., *The Memorial History of Hartford County Connecticut 1633-1884*, vol. 2 (Boston: Edward L. Osgood Publisher, 1886).

19 J. Hammond Trumbull, ed., *The Memorial History of Hartford County Connecticut 1633-1884*, vol. 2 (Boston: Edward L. Osgood Publisher, 1886).

20 See John Webster, *The Displaying of Supposed Witchcraft…* (London: printed by J. M., 1677), pp. 346–347 and ASSI 45/10/3/34, 36, 40, 43–44.

21 Thomas James, *A Faithful Narrative of the Strange Disturbances Which Now in Several Houses but Most Remarkable in Two Houses in Ashford in Kent With What Befell Mary Clarke…* (Ashford: T.J., 1698), p. 15.

22 Thomas James, *A Faithful Narrative of the Strange Disturbances Which Now in Several Houses but Most Remarkable in Two Houses in Ashford in Kent With What Befell Mary Clarke...* (Ashford: T.J., 1698), p. 21.
23 Thomas James, *A Faithful Narrative of the Strange Disturbances Which Now in Several Houses but Most Remarkable in Two Houses in Ashford in Kent With What Befell Mary Clarke...* (Ashford: T.J., 1698).
24 GRO, D3549/6/2/4 Y9.
25 GRO, D3549/6/2/4 Y9.
26 GRO, D3549/6/2/4 Y9.
27 Anon., *A Full and Impartial Account of the Discovery of Sorcery and Witchcraft, Practis'd by Jane Wenham...*', 3rd edn. (London: printed for E. Curll, 1712), p. 3.
28 Anon., *A Full and Impartial Account of the Discovery of Sorcery and Witchcraft, Practis'd by Jane Wenham...*', 3rd edn. (London: printed for E. Curll, 1712).
29 Anon., *A Full and Impartial Account of the Discovery of Sorcery and Witchcraft, Practis'd by Jane Wenham...*', 3rd edn. (London: printed for E. Curll, 1712), p. 10.
30 Anon., *The Most Strange and Admirable Discoverie of Three Witches of Warboys...* (London: printed by the Widow Orwin for Thomas Man and John Winnington, 1593), sig. H6v and R. B., *The Boy of Bilson: Or, A True Discovery of the Late Notorious Impostures of a Certain Romish Priests...* (London: Imprinted by Felix Kingston for William Barret, 1622), sig. H3r.
31 'Fear' as an overarching concept is innate to witchcraft. This sentiment is expressed by Robin Briggs: 'Witchcraft may therefore be a phenomenon we are predisposed to suspect, a psychic potential we cannot help carrying round within ourselves as part of our long-term inheritance.' Robin Briggs, *Witches and Neighbours: The Social and Cultural Context of European Witchcraft,* 2nd edn. (Malden: Blackwell Publishing, 2002), p. 342.
32 Anon., *The Whole Trial and Examination of Mrs Mary Hicks and Her Daughter Elizabeth...* (London: printed by W. Matthews, 1716), p. 2.
33 Anon., *The Whole Trial and Examination of Mrs Mary Hicks and Her Daughter Elizabeth...* (London: printed by W. Matthews, 1716), p. 3.
34 Anon., *The Whole Trial and Examination of Mrs Mary Hicks and Her Daughter Elizabeth...* (London: printed by W. Matthews, 1716), p. 6.
35 Anon., *The Whole Trial and Examination of Mrs Mary Hicks and Her Daughter Elizabeth...* (London: printed by W. Matthews, 1716), pp. 7–8.
36 Wallace Notestein, *A History of Witchcraft in England from 1558-1718* (Washington D.C.: The American Historical Association, 1911), pp. 297–302.
37 C. L'Estrange Ewen, *Witchcraft and Demonism: A Concise Account Derived from Sworn Depositions and Confessions Obtained in the Courts of England and Wales* (London: Heath Cranton Limited, 1933), p. 461.

EPILOGUE

'The Sacrosanct Accusation'

The parallels between the role of children in early modern English and New English witch-hunting and themes surrounding the 'Satanic Panic' in the 1980s and 1990s in Britain, Canada, New Zealand, and America are easily identifiable. As seen in the aforementioned case of the McMartin preschool, children are readily believed despite questionable evidence with regard to particular crimes, especially pertaining to the ritual sexual abuse of children.[1] There is no shortage of modern-day examples; the focus here will be on the 1990 Rochdale case and the 1987 Kelly Michaels' case. These cases reflect our perpetuating instinct to protect children from heinous and often hidden crimes. Unfortunately, like the early modern witchcraft trials, this instinct can be distorted and manipulated in the pursuit of justice for these 'extraordinary crimes'.

The Rochdale case began in Middleton, 1990, after a seven year old boy named Daniel Wilson told his teachers he had dreamt of ghosts.[2] As a result of being alerted to 'satanic indicators', social services were called and they quickly believed they had uncovered a group of Devil worshippers.[3] Soon after, twenty children were taken from their families and placed in interim care; some did not see their parents again for another ten years. The allegations levelled against the parents included wearing 'strange costumes', drugging their children and chaining them in cages.[4] However, social services found no evidence of any ritual sexual abuse. The following year the case reached the High Court. Justice Douglas Brown ruled there had been a 'gross breach of good practice' by Rochdale social services and ordered that most of the children be returned to their homes.[5] Cases such as these perpetuate because the significance of these cases lies not so much in their 'numbers' but in the extreme nature of the acts being alleged and the horror they evoked.[6]

DOI: 10.4324/9781003685319-9

In a similar case, Kelly Michaels was convicted and served five years in prison for comparable accusations in 1987 while she worked as a teacher in Wee Care Nursery School in Maplewood, New Jersey. After a child made a comment about having his temperature taken with a rectal thermometer, Michaels was indicted for 235 counts of sexual offences against children. When a journalist asked one of the prosecutors about some of the inconsistencies in the evidence, such as how the children could be hurt with knives without leaving marks, the prosecutor responded: 'what is there left to know? The jury has spoken. She's convicted'.[7] Michaels was eventually released after five years in prison after it was found that the methods in which the information was elicited from the children needed to be 'reliable enough to warrant admission'.[8] However, the almost unquestioned response to believe the children against 'the most hated woman in the state' harkens back to early modern times when witchcraft was the most feared crime and where children were believed despite dubious, even impossible evidence.[9]

As liminal actors – not infants but not quite adults – children held a unique place in society. Their role in the early modern English and New English witch-hunts provides a captivating but also terrifying glimpse into how children used and were used to facilitate accusations of witchcraft; others sometimes becoming ensnared in the process themselves. Children's connection to the supernatural world made them believable vessels whereby accusations of witchcraft proliferated through English and New English courts. There was, of course, scepticism, particularly from King James who endeavoured to root out counterfeit demoniacs. That children persisted in the face of such high-level scepticism reflects their tenacity, as well as their societies' appetite for a medium through which to deal with the problem of witchcraft.

This research demonstrated that children were often central to the initiation and functioning of witchcraft cases. Forever walking the fine line between the preternatural and natural worlds, their role and its significance in society ebbed and flowed with the political, social and religious turmoil at the time. Yet, children remained prevalent in witchcraft trials well into the eighteenth century. In the moral panics of the 1980s and 1990s, children again assumed centre stage using their imagination to attest to things only they saw, to the detriment and destruction of dozens of lives. The investigators who questioned them became the new 'witch-hunters', which makes this area of research all the more relevant both historically and currently. In the early modern era, children were often stripped of their autonomy; preferred to be seen and not heard. In witchcraft scholarship, children are often sidelined and relegated to the margins of historiography. This study places children back on centre stage and demonstrates that they truly were agents of the invisible world.

Notes

1 Of course, this does not pertain to all crimes against children which doubtlessly occur; this section alludes to crimes that fall within the area of dubious evidence during the moral panic era.
2 Paul Lewis, '"Satanic abuse" Case Families Sue Council for Negligence', *The Guardian*, 12 January 2006, n.p.
3 Paul Lewis, '"Satanic Abuse" Case Families Sue Council for Negligence', *The Guardian*, 12 January 2006.
4 Micahel Salter and Selda Dagistanli, 'Cultures of Abuse: "Sex Grooming", Organised Abuse and Race in Rochdale, UK', *International Journal for Crime, Justice and Social Democracy* 4 (No. 2, 2015), p. 51.
5 Damon Wilkinson, 'Satanic Panic on a Greater Manchester Council Estate: The Long Shadow Cast by the "Ritual Abuse" Scandal', *Manchester Evening News*, 14 March 2021, n.p.
6 J. S. La Fontaine, *Speak of the Devil: Tales of Satanic Abuse in Contemporary England* (Cambridge: Cambridge University Press, 1998), p. 58.
7 Dorothy Rabinowitz, 'No Crueller Tyranny: The Sacrosanct Accusation', *Opinion Journal from the Wall Street Journal,* 28 April 2003, n.p.
8 E. Nieves, 'Prosecutors Drop Charges in Abuse Case from Mid-80s', *The New York Times*, 3 December 1994, n.p.
9 Dorothy Rabinowitz, 'No Crueller Tyranny: The Sacrosanct Accusation', *Opinion Journal from the Wall Street Journal,* 28 April 2003, n.p.

APPENDIX A

Catalogue of Children in English Witchcraft Trials

Appendix A catalogues 109 cases of children in English witchcraft cases where their involvement was meaningful or influential. As stated in the introduction, there are doubtlessly hundreds more cases that involved children – particularly as victims – but this catalogue reflects the substantial impact children had in English witchcraft trials through a vast geographical and chronological time period.

Most of the cases have archival repositories, but some are found only through secondary source material, so archival information is non-applicable. Furthermore, most of the treatises/pamphlets are available online through the Early English Books Online (EEBO) database, and the sources that are available this way have been identified.

Catalogue of Children in English Witchcraft Trials

Name	*Date*	*Place*	*Primary Sources*	*Repository*
Agnes Brown and Joan Waterhouse	1566	Essex	'The Examination and Confession of Certain Witches at Chelmsford in the County of Essex' (EEBO)	Lambeth Palace Library
Sarah Caldwell	1567	Surrey	PRO ASSI 10/3/	The National Archives, London
Alexander Nyndge	1573	Herringswell, Suffolk	'A True and Fearful Vexation of one Alexander Nyndge…' (1615) (EEBO) and 'A Book Declaring the Fearful Vexation of one Alexander Nyndge…' (1573) (EEBO)	British Library
Agnes Briggs and Rachel Pindar	1574	London	'The Disclosing of a Late Counterfeited Possession…' (EEBO); Webster, 'The Displaying of Supposed Witchcraft…' (EEBO)	British Library
Mildred Norrington	1575	Westwell, Kent	Reginald Scot's 'A Discovery of Witchcraft' pp. 72–73 Harsnett's 'A Discovery of the Fraudulent Practices of John Darrell', p. 16 (AEEBO); Richard Bernard 'A Guide to Grand-Jurymen…' (EEBO) p. 33	British Library
Son of Ellen Smith	1579	Essex	'A Detection of Damnable Driftes…' (EEBO); Ewen, *WD*, pp. 149–152	British Library
Inclusions of children	1579	Windsor	'A Rehearsal Both Strange and True…' (EEBO); Richard Galis, 'A Brief treatise containing the most strange…' (EEBO)	British Library and Bodleian Library respectively
Thomas Lever	1579	Ipswich, Essex	Ewen, *WD*, references the *Acts of the Privy Council* volumes 11 p, 370 and vol. 12, p. 102, as including/mentioning Lever	*Acts of the Privy Council* volumes 11 and 12 available online

(*Continued*)

Catalogue of Children in English Witchcraft Trials

Name	*Date*	*Place*	*Primary Sources*	*Repository*
Thomas Kempe (and others)	1582	St. Osyth, Essex	'A True and Just Record of the Information, Examination and Confession…' (EEBO); PRO, ASSI 35/24/1/18, 21–9, 36	British Library and the National Archives, London
Katherine Wright	1586	Derbyshire	Harsnett, 'A Discovery of the Fraudulent Practices of John Darrell' (AEEBO); Darrell, 'A Detection of that Sinful…' (EEBO); Darrell, 'The Triall of Maist. Dorrell or a Collection of Defences against Allegations…' (EEBO)	British Library
Sarah Williams	1586	Denham, Buckinghamshire	Harsnett, 'Declaration of Popish Impostures' (EEBO) pp. 75, 191 and 202	British Library
Two boys against their mothers: Advice and Margaret Cunny as well as their grandmother Joan Cunny	1589	Stisted, Essex	'The Apprehension and Confession of Three Notorious Witches.' (EEBO); Ewen, *WD*, pp. 166–168; Ewen, WH, pp. 163–166	Lambeth Palace Library
Throckmorton Children	1589	Warboys, Huntingdonshire	'The Most Strange and Admirable Discovery of the Three Witches of Warboys' (EEBO)	Norris Museum, Bodleian library, British Library
Thomas Darling 'The Boy of Burton'	1596	Burton Upon Trent	'The Most Wonderful and True Story…' (EEBO); 'A Detection of that Sinful…'(EEBO); 'A Discovery of the Fraudulent…' (AEEBO)	'The MW and TS' in Lambeth Palace Library; 'A Detect' in British Library; 'A Discovery of the Fraud' in British Library

William Sommers 'The Boy of Nottingham'	1597	Nottingham	'A Brief Narration of the Possession, Dispossession and Repossession of William Sommers…' (EEBO) and in Almond p. 244 onwards; 'A Brief Apology Proving the Possession of William Sommers' (EEBO); 'A True Narration of the Strange and Grievous Vexation by the Devil…..'; The much shorter and slightly amended version of this account is: 'A True Relation of the Grievous Handling of William Sommers' (EEBO) and Harsnett's 'Discovery of the Fraudulent Practices of John Darrell' (AEEBO).	'A Brief Narration' in Bodleian Library (Oxford) and the British Library. Appears at reel 213 (Bodleian) and reel 1035 (British Library)
The Children of Nicholas Starchie/ Starkie	1597	Lancashire	Darrell, 'A True Narration of the Strange and Grievous Vexation by the Devil of Seven Persons in Lancashire' (EEBO); More, 'A True Discourse Concerning the Certain Possession…' (AEEBO and EEBO); Harsnett, 'A Discovery of the Fraudulent Practices of John Darrell' (AEEBO)	'A True Narration…' in British Library, 'A True Discourse…' in Bodleian library, 'A True Discovery' in Bodleian library and British Library
Mary Couper/Cowper/ Cooper	1597	Leicester	'A Discovery of the Fraudulent…' (AEEBO); 'A Detection of that Sinful…' (EEBO)	Both in British Library
The children of Mr Nayler and other children	1599	London	'The Triall of Maist. Dorrell, or a Collection of Defences…' (EBBO) pp. 99–103	British Library
Joanne Jorden	1599	Stradbrook, Suffolk	Contained within: 'The Triall of Maist. Dorrell…'	British Library
Marmaduke Jackson	1601	Bishop Burton, Yorkshire	BL, Add. MSS, 32496, f. 42v	British Library

(*Continued*)

Catalogue of Children in English Witchcraft Trials

Name	*Date*	*Place*	*Primary Sources*	*Repository*
Mary Glover	1602	London	John Swan, 'A True and Brief Report of Mary Glover' (EEBO); Edward Jorden, 'A Brief Discourse of a Disease Called the Suffocation of the Mother' (EEBO); Bradwell, 'Mary Glovers Late Woeful Case'	British Library
Anne Gunter	1604	North Moreton Berkshire	PRO/STAC records 8/4/10	The National Archives, London
Thomas Harrison 'The Northwich Boy'	1604	Northwich	Very sparse references in: Drage, 'Daimonomageia a Small Treatise of Sickness and Disease' p. 9 (EEBO); Darrell, 'A Survey of Certain Dialogical Discourses' (EEBO); Anon, A Summarie Answer to All the Material Points…' (EEBO) pp. 70–79; A much fuller account in: W. Hinde, A Faithfull Remonstrance of the holy Life and happy death of John Bruen…' (EEBO) pp. 148–154	British Library
George Dell and daughter as Harrison	1606	Hartford or Hertford	'The Most Cruell and Bloody Murther Committed by an Inkeepers Wife, called Annis Dell and her Sonne George Dell…' (EBBO) and 'The Horrible Murther of a Young Boy of Three Years of Age..' (EEBO)	British Library
Anne Taylor	1609	Rye, Sussex	Contained within: Annabel Gregory, 'Witchcraft, Politics and "Good Neighbourhood" in Early Seventeenth-century Rye', *Past and Present*, vol. 133, 1991, pp. 31–66	East Sussex Record Office
Jennet Device	1612	Pendle Forest Area, Lancashire	Potts, 'The Wonderful Discovery of Witches in the County of Lancaster…' (EEBO)	British Library, University College (London), Bodleian Library

Grace Sowerbutts	1612	Samlesbury, Lancashire	Potts, 'The Wonderful Discovery of Witches in the County of Lancaster…' (EEBO),	British Library, University College (London), Bodleian Library and others
Joanne Vaughn and the murdering of children	1612	Northamptonshire	'The Witches of Northamptonshire' (EEBO); BL, Sloane MS 972, fol. 7	British Library and the Bodleian Library
Mary Sutton (daughter of Mother Sutton)	1613	Milton [Ernest], Bedford	'Witches Apprehended, Examined and Executed for Notable villainies…' (EEBO); Bernard, 'Guide', p. 189 (EEBO)	Bodleian Library
Son of Enger	1613	Bedfordshire	'Witches Apprehended, Examined and Executed for Notable Villainies…' (EEBO)	Bodleian Library
John Smith 'The Boy of Leicester'	1616	Husbands Boswcrth, Leicestershire	Heyrick letter found in Kittredge article, pp. 3–4; Osborne's 'On Such as Condemn All they Understand not a Reason For' contained in 'The works of Francis Osborne' (EEBO), p. 552–553 (EEBO); Letter from Secretary Chamberlain to Sir Dudley Carleton 12 October 1616 in Calendar	British Library and the Bodleian library
Francis Manner's (Earl of Rutland's) Children	1619	Rutland	'The Wonderful Discovery of the Witch-Crafts of Margaret and Philip Flower…' (EEBO); 'Damnable Practices of Three Lincoln-Shire Witches, J. Flower, and Her Two Daughters, Margaret and Phillip Flower, against Henry Lord Rosse' [Ballad]	British Library; Ballad found in Pepys Library, Magdalene College
William Perry 'The Boy of Bilson'	1620	Bilson (now known as Bilson Brook) in Staffordshire	'The Boy of Bilson or A True Discovery of the Late Notorious Impostures…' (EEBO); Richard Bernard, 'A Guide to Grand Jury Men' pp. 30–32 (EEBO)	British Library and the Bodleian library
Katherine Malpas	1622	Upton, Essex	PRO/STAC 8/32/13 (f. 18r). See also ASSI 35/63/7 with regards to Anne Godfrey's fate	The National Archives, London

(*Continued*)

Catalogue of Children in English Witchcraft Trials

Name	*Date*	*Place*	*Primary Sources*	*Repository*
Elizabeth and Helen Fairfax	1622	Fewston/York	'A Discourse of Witchcraft as it was Acted in the Family of Mr. Edward Fairfax…', BL, Western Manuscripts, Add MS 32496	British Library
Elizabeth Jennings	1622	Thistleworth [Isleworth, Middlesex]	British Library: 'Collection Relating to Magic and Witchcraft from the Papers of Various 16th and 17th Century Astrologers…' Add. MS., 36674, ff. 134–137	British Library
Thomas Paman	1629	Suffolk	Calendar of State Papers Domestic, 1629–1631, pp. 198–199; The National Archives reference SP 16/161 f. 89	The National Archives, London
10-year-old Boy	1629	Hertfordshire	GRO, D3549/6/2/4	Gloucester Record Office
A Child's Sickness	1632	Yorkshire	Borthwick Institute of Historical Research, York, Cause Papers, CP. H 1961	Borthwick Institute of Historical Research,
Edmund Robinson	1634	Lancashire	Webster, 'The Displaying of Supposed Witchcraft…' (EEBO); Dodsworth MS 61, fol. 45–47, Rawlinson D MS 399, fols. 211–212 both in the Bodleian library; Harleian MS 6854, fols. 22–29 and Add MS 36674, fols. 195–196 both in the British Library; MS 36674, fol. 193, 196 in the British Library; *An History of the Original Parish of Whalley*, p. 213	British Library and the Bodleian Library
Child of Thomas Baxter	1636	Lancashire	Lancashire Record Office, Quarter Session Records, QSB 1/170/55	Lancashire Record Office
Jane Maxie	1638	Devon	Devonshire Record Office, Quarter Session Rolls, Box 41, Bapt 1638/52, 56–57	Devonshire Record Office

Many inclusions of children	1645	Essex	'A True and Exact Relation of the Several Informations, Examinations and Confessions of the Late Witches, Arraigned and Executed in the County of Essex.' (EBBO)	British Library
Joseph Buxford	1645	Bow, Devon	'A True and Strange Relation of a Boy, Who Was Entertained by the Devil to Be a Servant to Him…' (EEBO)	British Library
The Children of George Muschamp (mostly Margaret Muschamp)	1645	Northumberland	M. Moore, 'Wonderful News from the North Or A True Relation…' (EEBO); BL Wing M2581; Ewen, WD, pp. 317–319	British Library
Children of Henry Cockcrofte	1646	West Riding, Yorkshire	PRO, ASSI, 45/1/5/38	The National Archives, London
Many inclusions of children	1646	Huntingdon	'The Witches of Huntingdon, Their Examinations and Confessions…' (EEBO)	British Library
Joyce Dovey	1646	Bewdley, Worcestershire	'A Strange and True Relation of a Young Woman Possessed with the Devil…' (EEBO)	Thomas Collection, British Library
Child of Alice Wade	1647	Isle of Ely	Cambridge University Library, Isle of Ely Gaol Delivery Records, Michaelmas 1647, EDR 12 1647/15	Cambridge University Library
Apparitions of Margaret Moore's Children	1647	Isle of Ely	John Stearne, A Confirmation and Discovery of Witchcraft, 1648, pp. 21–22 (EEBO); Cambridge UL, EDR [Ely Diocesan Records] E 12 1647/14	Stearne can be found at: British library; Cambridge University Library
Yorkshire Boy	1648	Yorkshire	PRO, ASSI, 45/3/1/242	The National Archives, London
A young boy	1649	Droitwich, Worcester	'A Collection of Modern Relations of Matter of Fact Concerning Witches and Witchcraft Upon the Persons of People' Part One, London, 1693, pp. 50–51 (EEBO)	Yale University Library

(*Continued*)

Catalogue of Children in English Witchcraft Trials

Name	*Date*	*Place*	*Primary Sources*	*Repository*
Child of Joan Booth	1650	Warmfield, Yorkshire	PRO, ASSI, 45/4/1/131	The National Archives, London
Sarah Rodes	1650	Yorkshire	PRO, ASSI, 45/ 3/2/129	The National Archives, London
Elizabeth Parkson	1650	Ilkstone, Derbyshire	J. C. Cox, *Three Centuries of Derbyshire* Annals, vol. 2, pp. 88–90; Ewen, WD, 319–320	N/A
Child of Anne Allen	1651	Scarborough	Baker, *The History of Scarborough*, pp. 481–483	N/A
Maid-servant and son of Joan Peterson	1652	London (?) Hanged at Tyburn Tree	'The Witch of Wapping…' (EEBO)	British Library
The children of Peter Gale	1653	Whitechapel	*The Grand Politique Post*, pp. 1256–1257 [17–24 January 1654] (EEBO); *The Weekly Intelligencer*, pp. 135–136, [1–24 January 1654] (EEBO); *Middlesex County Records* vol. 3, 1625–1667 [1 August 1653]	British Library
Elizabeth Mallory	1656	Yorkshire	PRO ASSI 45/5/3/ pp. 132–133	The National Archives, London
A Servant Girl	1658	Devon	Devonshire Record Office, Okehampton Borough Records, Quarter Sessions Minute Book, 1648–1658, 3248A/3/5, unfoliated, 7 June 1658	Devonshire Record Office,
Abraham Hartley	1658	Baildon, Yorkshire/ Lancashire border	PRO, ASSI, 45/5/5/1	The National Archives, London
The children of Jonas Cudworth	1660	Newcastle upon Tyne	ASSI 44/10	The National Archives, London
Edward Bright	1660	Devon	Devonshire Record Office, Exeter City Records, Quarter Sessions Minute Books, C1 65, f. 11	Devonshire Record Office

Margaret Lake	1660	Exeter, Devon	Devon Record Office, Minute Books of the Sessions of the Peace, Exeter City, C1/65 (1660–1672), f. 3v	Devon Record Office
Thomas Spatchet	1660	Dunwich, Suffolk	'A Faithful Narrative of the Wonderful and Extraordinary Fits…' (EEBO)	British Library
Faith Corbet	1660	Burton Agnes, Yorkshire	'A Collection of Modern Relations of Matter of Fact Concerning Witches and Witchcraft Upon the Persons of People' Part One, London, 1693, pp. 52–59 (EEBO); Ewen, *WH*, Gaol Book. Assize 42/1, p. 148 as his source	British Library and elsewhere
James Johnson	1661	Thorne, Yorkshire	PRO, ASSI, 45/6/1/69	The National Archives, London
Lucy Williams	1661	Cheshire	Cheshire Record Office, Consistory Court Papers, EDC 5 (1661) 38	Cheshire Record Office
James Barrow	1661	Southwark	'The Lord's Arm Stretched Out in an Answer of Prayer…' (EEBO)	British Library
Hannah Crump	1662	Warwick	'A True Relation of the Wonderful Deliverance of Hannah Crump…' which is contained within 'The Lord's Arm Stretched Out in an Answer of Prayer…' (EEBO)	British Library
Child of Ann Wright	1662	Cheshire	Cheshire Record Office, Chester Consistory Court Papers, EDC 5 (1662) 63.	Cheshire Record Office
Elizabeth and Deborah Pacy	1662	Bury St Edmunds	A Tryal of Witches at the Assizes Held at Bury St Edmunds…' (AEEBO); brief mention in 'A Faithful Narrative of the Wonderful and Extraordinary Fits…' (EEBO) in the preface	British Library
Thomas Sawdie	1663	Trebitian (?), Cornwall	'A Return of Prayer: Or A Faithful Relation…' (EEBO)	British Library
Mary Hall	1664	Little Gaddesden, Hertfordshire	William Drage, 'Daimonomageia: A Small Treatise of Sicknesses and Diseases from Witchcraft…' (EEBO)	British Library

(*Continued*)

Catalogue of Children in English Witchcraft Trials

Name	*Date*	*Place*	*Primary Sources*	*Repository*
Nathan Dodgson	1667	Wakefield, Yorkshire	Horsfall Turner (ed.), The Rev. Oliver Heywood, vol. 3, p. 100	N/A
Jane Stretton	1669	Ware, Hartford	'The Hartford-Shire Wonder: Or Strange News from Ware' (EEBO)	British Library and Bodleian Library
16-year-old Girl	1669	unknown	GRO, D3549/6/2/4	Gloucester Record Office
14-year-old Girl	1669	unknown	GRO, D3549/6/2/4	Gloucester Record Office
Child of Robert Webb	1670	Malmesbury, Wiltshire	ASSI 23/1	The National Archives, London
A Maid at Anthony Waterhouses	1672	Northowram, Yorkshire	J. Horsfall Turner, The Rev. Oliver Heywood, vol. 3, 1873, p. 111	N/A
Anne Armstrong	1673	Birchen Nook, Northumberland	PRO, ASSI 45/10/3/34, 36, 40, 43–54	The National Archives, London
Children from Great Bowden	1673	Great Bowden, Leicestershire	Sir G. Isham (ed.), The Diary of Thomas Isham of Lamport (1658–1681), Gregg International Publishers: Farnborough, 1971, 185–197	N/A
Mary Moor	1674	Woolley, Yorkshire	ASSI 44/17; ASSI 45/11/90–93	The National Archives, London
Children of Mr Merideth/Meredith	1675	Bristol	Richard Bovet, 'Pandaemonium' (AEEBO), p. 167–168	British Library
Twelve-year-old son of Mr Crook	1676	Leyland, Lancashire	Letter from Thomas Marsden to Zachary Taylor in 'The Devil Turned Casuist or the Cheats of Rome' (EEBO) in the Epistle Dedicatory c. p. 4 in (EEBO)	Bodleian Library

Alice Burt	1679	Leicester	Dublin University Magazine, vol. 26, 1845, pp. 26–29 seems to have the full primary source which is taken from 'some family papers'; Ewen, WD, p. 459 references the Dublin source	N/A
A Young Maid	1679	Orpington near Bexley in Kent	'Strange News from Arpington near Bexly in Kent…' (EEBO)	Houghton Library, Harvard
Thirteen-year-old Girl	1680	Taunton Dean (Somerset)	Roger North, *The Lives of the Right Hon. Francis North…*', vol. 1 (Google Books) pp. 168–169; Ewen, *WD*, p. 460	N/A
Elizabeth Burgiss/ Burridge	1681	Ewell, Surrey	'Strange and Wonderful News from Yowel in Surrey…' (EEBO)	Surrey Heritage in Working, Surrey.
Elizabeth Brooker	1681	Honiton, Devon	Richard Baxter, 'The Certainty of the Worlds of Spirits…' p. 65–69 (EEBO); BL, Add. MS 4460, fos 77v-78v	British Library
Margaret Gurr	1681	Tunbridge, Kent	'A Strange and Wonderful Relation of Margaret Gurr…' (EEBO)	National Library of Scotland
Mr Lutteril's child	1682	Exeter, Devon	'A True and Impartial Relation of the Informations against Three Witches…' (EEBO); 'The Tryal, Condemnation, and Execution of Three Witches…' (EEBO); 'The Life and Conversation of Temperance…' (EEBO)	British Library
Mary Farmer/ Farborough	1682	Borough of Southwark	'An Account of the Tryal and Examination of Joan Buts…' (EEBO)	British Library
Abraham Swift	1683	Yorkshire	Horsfall Turner (ed.)., *The Rev. Oliver Heywood*, vol. 4, pp. 53–54	N/A
John Tonken	1686	Penzance, Cornwall	'A True Account of a Strange and Wonderful Relation of John Tonken…' (EEBO)	Bodleian Library
Nathaniel Storch	1687	Lyme Regis, Dorset	ASSI 23/3, sub 4 July 1687	The National Archives, London

(Continued)

Catalogue of Children in English Witchcraft Trials

Name	*Date*	*Place*	*Primary Sources*	*Repository*
Elizabeth Tillman	1687	Lyme Regis, Dorset	ASSI 23/3, sub 4 July 1687	The National Archives, London
Peter Gleanes' daughter	1688	Norfolk	Bodleian Library Tanner MS 25, fol. 161v-162r and 162v-163r.	Bodleian Library
Richard Dugdale	1689	Surrey, Lancashire	Taylor, 'The Devil Turned Casuist…' (EEBO); Jolie, 'The Surey Demoniack…' (EEBO); Taylor, 'The Surey Imposter…' (EEBO); Jollie, 'A Vindication of the Surey Demoniack…' (EEBO); Taylor, 'Popery, Superstition, Ignorance and Knavery…' (EEBO); 'The Lancashire Levite Rebuked…' (EEBO); Taylor, 'Popery, Superstition, Ignorance and Knavery Confessed and Fully Proved…' (EBBO)	All in British Library except for 'A Vindication…' which is in the Oxford University Balliol College
Mary Hill	1691	Beckington, Frome, Somerset	Richard Baxter, 'The Certainty of the Worlds of Spirits…' pp. 74–82 (EEBO)	British Library
Sarah Bower	1693	Wapping, Middlesex	Richard Kirby, 'Dreadful News from Wapping…' (EEBO)	Bodleian Library
Mary Clarke	1698	Ashford, Kent	GRO, D3549/6/2/4 Y18	Gloucester Record Office
Elizabeth Noel	1698	Shipyard near Temple-Bar	GRO, D3549/6/2/4	Gloucester Record Office
8-year-old Girl	1699	Midlam [seems to be Middleham in North Yorkshire]	GRO, D3549/6/2/4	Gloucester Record Office

Richard Hathaway	1701	Southwark	'A Full and True Account of the Apprehending and Taking of Mrs. Sarah Moordike…' (EEBO); 'The Tryal of Richard Hathaway…' (NLA)	British Library
Children of John Baldwin	1701	Sarret, Hertfordshire	T. Aldridge, 'The Prevalency of Prayer, Set Forth in A Rustic, but Faithful Narrative…' (Google Books)	N/A
Margaret, Charlotte and Ellen Rawsthorne	1705	Ormskirk, Lancashire	GRO, D3549/6/2/4	Gloucester Record Office
Anne Thorne	1712	Hertfordshire	'A Full and Impartial Account of the Discovery of Sorcery and Witchcraft practis'd by Jane Wenham of Walkerne in Hertfordshire, upon the Bodies of Anne Thorne, Anne Street…' (Google Books)	Bodleian Library
Elizabeth Hicks	1716	Huntingdon	'The Whole Trial and Examination of Mrs Mary Hicks…' (NLA)	Bodleian Library

APPENDIX B

Catalogue of Children in New English Witchcraft Trials

Appendix B catalogues twenty-one New English witchcraft cases where children's involvement was deemed significant or influential. While seemingly like a relatively small number, the persistent inclusion of children in witchcraft cases is a testament to their tenacity in New England's witch-hunting narrative. As stated in the introduction, many of the sources of information for New English witchcraft cases come through secondary source documents, meaning archival repository information is non-applicable. Thankfully, most of the sources pertaining to New English witchcraft trials has either been digitised or survive in primary sourcebooks.

Catalogue of Children in New English Witchcraft Trials

Name	*Date*	*Place*	*Primary Sources*	*Repository*
A Girl in the Colony of Virginia	1626	Colony of Virginia	H. R. McIlwaine (ed.), *Minutes of the Council and General Court of Colonial Virginia, 1622-1632* (Richmond, Virginia, 1924), p. 111–112	N/A
Mention of a little child	1648	Charlestown, Massachusetts	*John Winthrop's Journal*, vol 2, pp. 344–345	N/A
Rev. MOxford's children	1651	Springfield, Massachusetts	Drake, *Annals of Witchcraft in New England...*, p. 219–258; Nathaniel B. Shrutkeff, eds., *Records of the Governor and Company of the Massachusetts Bay in New England*, vol. 4, part 1, 1650-1660, p. 47–48, 73; Edward Johnson, *Wonder-working Providence*, 1656, p. 237	N/A
Child of Goodman Jennings	1651	Cambridge, Massachusetts	Hale, 'A Modest Enquiry', p. 18–19	Massachusetts Historical Society, Boston
Sellevant and Hannah Goodyear and Desire Lamberton [names change depending on the document]	1653	New Haven, Connecticut	Frankling Bowditch Dexter, *New Haven Town Records 1649-1662*, vol. 1, p. 251–252 and pp. 256–257 for her fate; Records of the Colony or Jurisdiction of New Haven, from May 1653 to the Union, pp. 29–36 and 151–152; Hall, *Witch-Hunting in 17th C. NE*, pp. 61–73	N/A
Children of Sarah Birdgman	1656	Northampton, Massachusetts	James Russell Trumbull, *History of Northampton Massachusetts...*, vol. 1, p. 43–51 but esp. 47–48 and 51	N/A

(Continued)

Catalogue of Children in New English Witchcraft Trials

Name	*Date*	*Place*	*Primary Sources*	*Repository*
Child of Goody Davis	1658	Easthampton Long Island Connecticut	Drake, *Annals*, p. 110–112	N/A
Elizabeth Kelley	1662	Hartford, Connecticut	The Samuel Wyllys Papers; Tomlinson, *Witchcraft Trials of Connecticut*, pp. 27–40; Hall, *Witch-Hunting in 17th C. NE*, pp.152–156	The Annmary Brown Memorial Library, Brown University
Anne Cole	1662	Hartford, Connecticut	Letter from John Whiting to Increase Mather in 'The Mather Papers', p. 466–469; Increase Mather, 'An Essay for the Recording of Illustrious Providences,' p. 135 onwards	The Mather Papers, Boston Public Library
Mary Hale and Joan Francis's child	1669	Weathersfield, Connecticut	Taylor, *The Witchcraft Delusion in Colonial Connecticut*, p. 47	N/A
Elizabeth Knap	1671	Groton, Massachusetts	Samuel Willard, 'A Briefe Account of a Strange and Unusual Providence of God Befallen to Elizabeth Knap of Groton…'; Mather, 'An Essay for the Recording of Illustrious Providences', pp. 140–142	The Mather Papers, Boston Public Library
Ann Smith	1673	Hampton, present-day New Hampshire	Hall, *Witch-Hunting in 17th C. NE*, pp. 213–229	Massachusetts State Archives
Margaret Lord	1678	Beverly, Massachusetts	Records and Files of the Quarterly Courts of Essex County, vol. VII, pp. 43–55	Phillips Library Reading Room, Rowley, Massachusetts
Goodwin Children	1688	Boston, Massachusetts	Cotton Mather, 'Memorable Providences…'	The Mather Papers, Boston Public Library

The Salem Girls	1692	Salem Village, Massachusetts and elsewhere	Rosenthal, ed., *Records of the Salem Witch-Hunt*, New York: Cambridge University Press, 2009	Phillips Library Reading Room, Rowley, Massachusetts
Katherine Branch	May/June 1692–Trial in Sept 1692	Stamford-Fairfield, Connecticut	*The Samuel Wyllys Papers* [various]	The Annmary Brown Memorial Library, Brown University
Mercy Short	Nov 1692–March 1693	Boston, Massachusetts	Cotton Mather, 'A Brand Pluck'd Out Of The Burning', 1693 contained within Burr, *Narratives…*, pp. 253–285	American Antiquarian Society, Massachusetts
Eben Booth's 'Girl'	1693	Stratford, Connecticut	Taylor, *The Witchcraft Delusion in Colonial Connecticut*, p. 107	N/A
Margaret Rule	1693	Boston, Massachusetts	Calef, 'More Wonders of the Invisible World…', pp. 19–41	Boston Public Library
Winifred Benham Jr	1697	Wallingford, Connecticut	Calef, 'More Wonders of the Invisible World…', pp. 282–283	Boston Public Library
A Girl Called Norton	1768	Bristol, Connecticut	J. Hammond Trumbull ed., *The Memorial History of Hartford County* Connecticut…, vol. 2, p. 51	N/A

SELECT BIBLIOGRAPHY

Archive Repositories

The Bodleian Library.
The British Library.
.The Devonshire Record Office.
The Gloucestershire Record Office.
The National Archives, Kew

Primary Sources

Allison, K. J. 'An Elizabethan Village "Census"'. *Bulletin of the Institute of Historical Research* 93 (1963). Pp. 91–103.

Anon. *The Examination and Confession of Certain Witches at Chelmsford in the County of Essex…* . London: Printed by William Powell, 1566.

Anon. *The Disclosing of a Late Counterfeited Possession by the Devil in Two Maidens within the City of London…* . London: Printed by Richard Watkins, 1574.

Anon. *A Detection of Damnable Driftes, Practized by Three Witches Arraigned at Chelmisforde in Essex, at the Laste Assises There Holden, Whiche Were Executed in April, 1579*. London: Imprinted for Edward White, 1579.

Anon. *The Apprehension and Confession of Three Notorious Witches Arraigned and by Justice Condemned and Executed in Chelmsford in the County of Essex, the 5th Day of July, Last Past. 1589. With the Manner of Their Devilish Practices and Keeping of Their Spirits Whose Forms are Herein Truly Proportioned.* London: Imprinted for Edward Allde, 1589.

Anon. *The Most Strange and Admirable Discoverie of Three Witches of Warboys…* . London: Printed by the Widow Orwin for Thomas Man and John Winnington, 1593.

Anon. *A Brief Narration of the Possession, Dispossession and Repossession of William Sommers…* . Amsterdam: S.N, 1598.

Anon. *The Triall of Maist. Dorrell, or A Collection of Defences against Allegations Not Yet Suffered to Receive Convenient Answer. Tending to Clear Him from the*

Imputation of Teaching Sommers and Others to Counterfeit Possession of Devils. That the Mist of Pretended Counterfeiting Being Dispelled, the Glory of Christ His Royal Power in Casting Out Devils (At the Prayer and Fasting of His People) May Evidently Appear. Middelburg: Imprinted for R. Schilders, 1599.

Anon. *The Witches of Northamptonshire...* . London: Printed by Thomas Purfoot, 1612.

Anon. *A True and Strange Relation of a Boy Who Was Entertained by the Devil to be a Servant to Him...* . London: Printed by J. H, 1645.

Anon. *A Tryal of Witches, at the Assizes Held at Bury St. Edmunds for the County of Suffolk, on the Tenth Day of March, 1664, before Sir Matthew Hale Kt., then the Lord Chief Baron of His Majesties Court of Exchequer*. London: Printed for William Shrewsbury, 1682.

Anon. *A Collection of Modern Relations of Matter of Fact Concerning Witches and Witchcraft...* . London: Printed for John Harris, 1693.

Anon. *A Full and Impartial Account of the Discovery of Sorcery and Witchcraft, Practis'd by Jane Wenham....* Third edition. London: Printed for E. Curll, 1712.

Anon. *The Whole Trial and Examination of Mrs Mary Hicks and Her Daughter Elizabeth...* . London: Printed by W. Matthews, 1716.

Anon. *Vital Records of Andover, Massachusetts, to the End of the Year 1849*. Volume 2. Topsfield: Topsfield Historical Society, 1912.

Anon. 'Appendix No. I. Examination of Hugh Parsons of Springfield on a Charge of Witchcraft, and the Testimonies Given against Him, before Mr. William Pynchon, at Springfield, 1651'. In *Annals of Witchcraft in New England and Elsewhere in the United States from Their First Settlement*. Ed. Samuel G. Drake Boston: W. Elliot Woodward, 1869. Pp. 219–258.

Anon. '1563: Act against Conjurations, Enchantments and Witchcrafts, 5 Eliz. 1. c. 16'. In *Witchcraft and the Act of 1604*. Eds. John Newton and Jo Bath. Leiden and Boston: Brill, 2008. Pp. 233–237.

Anon. '1585: Act Against Jesuits and Seminarists, 27 Eliz. Cap. 2'. In *Documents Illustrative of English Church History*. Eds. Henry Gee and William John Harvey. New York: Macmillan, 1896. Pp. 485–492.

Barrow, John. *The Lord's Arm Stretched Out in an Answer of Prayer...* . London: Published by John Barrow, 1664.

Baxter, Richard. *The Certainty of the Worlds of Spirits*. London: Printed for T. Parkhurst, 1691.

Bernard, Richard. *A Guide to Grand-jury Men Divided into Two Books...* . London: Printed by Felix Kingston for Ed. Blackmore, 1627.

Bodin, Jean. *On the Demon-Mania of Witches*. Trans. Randy A. Scott, Toronto: Centre for Reformation and Renaissance Studies, 2001.

Bovet, Richard. *Pandemonium or the Devils Cloyster...* . London: Printed for Thomas Malthus, 1684.

Boyer, Paul and Nissenbaum, Stephen. *Salem-Village Witchcraft: A Documentary Record of Local Conflict in Colonial New England*. Belmont: Wadsworth, 1972.

Bradwell, Stephen. 'Mary Glovers Late Woeful Case, Together with Her Joyful Deliverance'. London, 1603. In *Witchcraft and Hysteria in Elizabethan London: Edward Jorden and the Mary Glover Case*. Ed. Michael MacDonald. London and New York: Routledge, 1991. Pp. 1–150.

Brattle, Thomas. 'Letter', Boston, 1692. In *Narratives of the Witchcraft Cases 1648-1706*. Ed. George Lincoln Burr. New York: Charles Scribner's, 1914.

Calef, Robert. *More Wonders of the Invisible World: Or the Wonders of the Invisible World Displayed in Five Parts*. Boston: Cushing & Appleton, 1700.

Calendar of State Papers, Domestic Series, of the Reign of Charles I 1634–1635, London: Great Britain Public Record Office, 1864.

Chamberlain, John. *Letters Written by John Chamberlain During the Reign of Queen Elizabeth*. Ed. Sarah Williams. Westminster: J. B. Nichols, 1861.

Cooper, Thomas. *The Mystery of Witchcraft: Discovering the Truth, Nature, Occasions, Growth and Power thereof…* . London: Printed by Nicholas Okes, 1617.

Cox, J. Charles. *Three Centuries of Derbyshire Annals as Illustrated by the Records of the Quarter Sessions of the County of Derby from Queen Elizabeth to Queen Victoria*. Second volume. London: Bemrose, 1890.

Dalton, Michael. *The Country Justice: Containing the Practice of the Justices of the Peace Out of Their Sessions…* .London: Printed by William Rawlins and Samuel Roycroft, 1690.

Anon. 'Danvers Church Records, August 25th 1706'. In *The New England Historical and Genealogical Register*. Ed. Samuel G. Drake. Vol. 12. Boston: H. W. Dutton, 1858.

Darrell, John. *A Detection of That Sinnful, Shamful, Lying and Ridiculous Discours of Samuel Harshnet…* . London: Imprinted by the English Secret Press, 1600.

Darrell, John. *A True Narration of the Strange and Grievous Vexation by the Devil of Seven Persons in Lancashire*. London: [publisher unknown], 1600.

Dasent, John Roche. Ed. *Acts of the Privy Council of England, vol. 12, 1580-1581*, London: Her Majesty's Stationery Office, 1896.

Dasent, John Roche. Ed. *Acts of the Privy Council of England, vol. 11, 1578-1580*, London: Her Majesty's Stationery Office, 1896.

Fairfax, Edward. 'A Discourse of Witchcraft as It Was Acted in the Family of Mr Edward Fairfax…, communicated by R. M. Milnes, 1621'. In *Miscellanies of the Philobiblon Society*, vol. 5. London: Printed by Charles Whittingham, 1858–9. Pp. 23–318.

Ffarington, Susan Maria. 'The Farington Papers. The Shrievalty of William Ffarington, Esq; a.d. 1636; Documents Relating to Civil War…'. In *Remains Historical and Literary Connected with the Palatine Counties of Lancaster and Chester*. The Chetham Society, vol. 39. Worden: Printed for the Chetham Society, 1856.

Fisher, John., Cawley, William and Hurleston, Richard. *The Copy of a Letter Describing the Wonderful Work of God in Delivering a Maiden with the City of Chester…* . London: Imprinted by John Awdely, 1564.

Fowler, Samuel. 'An Account of the Life and Character of the Rev. Samuel Parris, of Salem Village, and of his Connection with the Witchcraft Delusion of 1692'. In *The Witchcraft Delusion in New England*. Ed. Samuel G. Drake. Volume 3. Roxbury: Munsell, 1866. Pp. 195–222.

Foxe, John. *Acts and Monuments*. 1583 edition. See www.dhi.ac.uk/foxe/index.php. Accessed 23rd of February 2024.

Gifford, George. *A Discourse on the Subtil Practise of Devils by Witches…* . London: Imprinted for Toby Cooke, 1587.

Glanvill, Joseph. *Saducismus Triumphatus or a Full and Plain Evidence Concerning Witches and Apparitions*. London: Printed for J. Collins, 1681.
Green, Mary Anne Everett. Ed. *Calendar of State Papers, Domestic Series, of the Reign of James I 1611-1618*. Nendeln: Kraus Reprint Ltd, 1967.
Guazzo, Francesco Maria. *Compendium Maleficarum*. Trans. E. A. Ashwin. Ed. Montague Summers. New Jersey: University Books, 1974.
Hale, John. *A Modest Inquiry and How Persons Guilty of that Crime May Be Convicted…* . Boston: B. Green and J. Alten, 1702.
Hall, David D. *Witch-Hunting in Seventeenth-Century New England: A Documentary History 1638-1693*. Second edition. Boston: Northeastern University Press, 1999.
Harsnett, Samuel. *A Discovery of the Fraudulent Practices of John Darrell…* . London: Imprinted by John Wolfe, 1599.
Harsnett, Samuel. *A Declaration of Egregious Popish Impostures…* London: Printed by James Roberts, 1603.
Hinde, William. *A Faithful Remonstrance of the Holy Life and Happy Death of John Bruen…* . London: Printed by R.B, 1641.
Historical Manuscripts Commission. *Twelfth Report, Appendix, Part IV: The Manuscripts of His Grace the Duke of Rutland*, G.C.B., Volume 1. Preserved at Belvoir Castle. 1888.
Hoadly, Charles J. *Records of the Colony or Jurisdiction of New Haven from May 1653 to the Union*. Hartford: Printed by Case, Lockwood and Company, 1858.
Holinshed, Raphael. 'The Chronicles of England, Scotland and Ireland, 1684 edition'. In *The Witchcraft Papers: Contemporary Records of the Witchcraft Hysteria in Essex 1560-1700*. Ed. Peter Haining. London: Robert Hale and Company, 1974. Pp. 43–45.
Hopkins, Matthew. *The Discovery of Witches…* . Norfolk: Published by Matthew Hopkins, 1647.
Hosmer, James Kendal. Ed. *Winthrop's Journal 'History of New England: 1630-1649'*. Volume two. New York: Charles Scribner's Sons, 1908.
Huggarde, Miles. *The Displaying of the Protestants…* . London: Robert Caly, 1556.
Hutchinson, Francis. *An Historical Essay Concerning Witchcraft: With Observations Upon Matters of Fact…* . London: R. Knaplock, 1718.
Hutchinson, Thomas. *The History of the Province of Massachusetts-Bay*. Second edition. Boston: Thomas & John Fleet, 1768.
I. D. *The Most Wonderful and True Storie of a Certaine Witch Named Alse Gooderige…* London: Printed for I.O., 1597.
Inderwick, Frederick Andrew. *Side-Lights on the Stuarts*. Second edition. London: Sampson Low, Marston, Searle and Rivington, 1891.
James, Thomas. *A Faithful Narrative of the Strange Disturbances Which Now in Several Houses but Most Remarkable in Two Houses in Ashford in Kent With What Befell Mary Clarke…* . Ashford: T.J, 1698.
Jameson, J. Franklin. Ed. *Edward Johnson's Wonder-Working Providence: 1628-1651*. New York: Charles Scribner's Sons, 1910.
Jessey, Henry. *The Exceeding Riches of Grace Advanced by the Spirit of Grace, in an Empty Nothing Creature, viz. Mris. Sarah Wight…* . London: Printed by Matthew Simmons, 1648.

Jorden, Edward. *A Briefe Discourse of a Disease Called the Suffocation of the Mother*. London: Publisher unknown, 1603.

King James VI and I. *A Counterblaste to Tobacco*. London: R. Barker, 1604.

Lawson, Deodat. *A Brief and True Narrative of Some Remarkable Passages Relating to Sundry Persons Afflicted of Witchcraft…* . Boston: Benjamin Harris, 1692.

MacDonald, Michael. Ed., *Witchcraft and Hysteria in Elizabethan London: Edward Jorden and the Mary Glover Case*. Oxen: Routledge, 1991.

Mackay, Christopher S. *The Hammer of Witches: A Complete Translation of the Malleus Maleficarum*. Cambridge: Cambridge University Press, 2009.

Magomastix, Hieronymus. 'The Strange Witch at Greenwich…'. London. Printed by Thomas Harper, 1650.

Mather, Cotton. *Memorable Providences, Relating to Witchcrafts and Possessions…* . Boston: Sold by Joseph Brunning, 1689.

Mather, Cotton. *The Wonders of the Invisible World: Being an Account of the Tryals of Several Witches Lately Executed in New England…* . London: John Russell Smith, 1862 [originally published 1692.]

Mather, Cotton. *Diary of Cotton Mather 1681-1708*. Boston: The Plympton Press, 1708.

Mather, Cotton. 'A Brand Pluck'd Out of the Burning, 1693'. In *Narratives of the Witchcraft Cases 1648-1706*. Ed. George Lincoln Burr. New York: Charles Scribner's Sons, 1914. Pp. 253–285.

Mather, Increase. *A Call from Heaven to the Present and Succeeding Generations…* . Boston: Printed by John [?], 1679.

Mather, Increase. 'An Essay for the Recording of Illustrious Providences'. In *Narratives of the Witchcraft Cases 1648-1706*. Ed. George Lincoln Burr. New York: Charles Scribner's Sons, 1914. Pp. 1–37.

McIlwaine, H. R. Ed. *Minutes of the Council and General Court of Colonial Virginia, 1622-1632, 1670-1676 with Notes and Excerpts from Original Council and General Court Records into 1683, Now Lost*. Richmond: Publisher unknown, 1924.

Moor, Mary. *Wonderfull Newes from the North. Or, A True Relation of the Sad and Grievous Torments Inflicted Upon the Bodies of Three Children of Mr. George Muschamp…* . London: Printed by T.H, 1650.

More, Henry. *An Antidote against Antheisme, or, An Appeal to the Natural Faculties of the Minde of Man, Whether There Be Not a God…* . London: Printed by Roger Daniel, 1653.

Nichols, John. *The History and Antiquities of the County of Leicester*. Volume 2. Part 2. London: Printed by and for the author, 1798.

Nyndge [?], Edward. *A Book Declaring the Fearful Vexation of one Alexander Nyndge…* . London: Imprinted in London by Thomas Collwell, 1573.

Nyndge, Edward. *A True and Fearful Vexation of One Alexander Nyndge…* . London: Imprinted for W. B, 1615.

Osborne, Francis. *The Works of Francis Osborne…* . Seventh edition. London: Printed for R.D, 1673.

Parris, Samuel. 'Sermon from 19th November 1689'. In *The Sermon Notebook of Samuel Parris, 1689-1694*. Eds. James F. Cooper Jr and Kenneth P. Minkema. Boston: The Colonial Society of Massachusetts, 1993.

Philips, John. *The Wonderfull Worke of God Shewed upon a Chylde Whose Name Is William Withers…* . London: Printed by Robert Waldegrave, 1581.

Potts, Thomas. *The Wonderful Discoverie of Witches in the Countie of Lancaster…* . Second edition. London: Printed by W. Stansby, 1613.

R. B. *The Boy of Bilson: Or, A True Discovery of the Late Notorious Impostures of a Certain Romish Priests…* . London: Imprinted by Felix Kingston for William Barret, 1622.

Records of the Governor and Company of the Massachusetts Bay in New England, Ed. Nathaniel B. Shurtleff. Vol. 4. Part 1. Boston: From the Press of William White, 1854.

Rosen, Barbara. *Witchcraft in England 1558-1618*. Amherst: University of Massachusetts Press, 1991.

Rosenthal, Bernard. Ed. *Records of the Salem Witch-Hunt*. New York: Cambridge University Press, 2009.

Samuel Wyllys Papers, Box A, Series 1. Court Records, 1662–1757. Access via Brown University Library online. www.riamco.org/render?eadid=US-RPB-mswyllys&view=overview.

Scot, Reginald. *The Discoverie of Witchcraft*. 1691 edition. London: Publisher Unknown, 1691.

Sewall, Samuel. 'The Diary of Samuel Sewall: 1674–1729 Vol. I. 1674–1700'. In *Collections of the Massachusetts Historical Society*. Vol. 5, fifth series. Boston: Published by the Society, 1877.

Sharp, Jane. *The Midwives Book, or, The Whole Art of Midwifery Discovered….* London: Printed for Simon Miller, 1671.

Summers, Montague. *Malleus Maleficarum: Translated with an Introduction, Bibliography and Notes*. London: John Rodker, 1928.

Swan, John. *A True and Briefe Report of Mary Glovers Vexation, and of Her Deliverance by Fastings and Prayer*. London: Publisher Unknown, 1603.

Tapley, Harriet S. *Records and Files of the Quarterly Court of Essex County*. Ed. George Francis Dow. Volume 6. Essex Institute. Essex County: Published by the Institute, 1917.

The Bible, King James Version.

The Publications of the Surtees Society, *Depositions from The Castle of York relating to offenses Committed in the Northern Counties in the Seventeenth Century*. Vol. 40. London. 1840.

The Salem Witchcraft Papers: Verbatim Transcripts of the Legal Documents of the Salem Witchcraft Outbreak of 1692. Vol. 2. Eds. Paul Boyer Paul and Stephen Nissenbaum. New York: Da Capo Press, 1977.

Trumbull, J. Hammond. Ed. *The Memorial History of Hartford County Connecticut 1633–1884*, second volume. Boston: Edward L. Osgood Publisher, 1886.

Turner, J. Horsfall. Ed. *Rev. Oliver Heywood, 1630–1702: His Autobiography, Diaries, Anecdote and Event Books Illustrating the General and Family History of Yorkshire and Lancashire*, four Volume. Bingley: Printed for the Editor, 1885.

Webster, John. *The Displaying of Supposed Witchcraft…* . London: Printed by J.M, 1677.

Whitaker, Thomas Dunham. *An History of the Original Parish of Whalley, and Honor of Clitheroe, in the Counties of Lancaster and York*. London: Nichols and Son, 1818.

Whiting, John. 'Letter from John Whiting to Increase Mather'. In *Collections of the Massachusetts Historical Society*. Volume 8. Fourth series. Boston: Published for the Society, 1868. Pp. 466–469.

Willard, Samuel. *Useful Instructions for a Professing People in Times of Great Security and Degeneracy…* . Cambridge: Printed by Samuel Green, 1673.
Willard, Samuel. 'A Brief Account of a Strange and Unusual Providence of God Befallen to Elizabeth Knap of Groton'. In *Groton in The Witchcraft Times*. Ed. Samuel A. Green. Cambridge: John Wilson and Son, 1883. Pp. 7–21.
Winthrop, John. 'A Model of Christian Charity', *Winthrop Papers*. Volume 2. Ed. The Massachusetts Historical Society. Boston: The Massachusetts Historical Society, 1931. Pp. 282–295.
W. W. *A True and Just Recorde of the Information, Examination and Confession of All the Witches…* . London: Imprinted by Thomas Dawson, 1582.

Secondary Sources

Almond, Philip C. *Demonic Possession and Exorcism in Early Modern England: Contemporary Texts and Their Cultural Contexts*. Cambridge and New York: Cambridge University Press, 2004.
Almond, Philip C. *The Witches of Warboys: An Extraordinary Story of Sorcery, Sadism and Satanic Possession*. London and New York: I.B. Tauris, 2008.
Almond, Philip C. *The Lancashire Witches: A Chronicle of Sorcery and Death on Pendle Hill*. London and New York: Bloomsbury Academic, 2012.
Amussen, Susan Dwyer. '"Being Stirred to Much Unquietness": Violence and Domestic Violence in Early Modern England'. *Journal of Women's History* 6 (No. 2, 1994). Pp. 70–89.
Amussen, Susan Dwyer. 'Punishment, Discipline, and Power: The Social Meanings of Violence in Early Modern England'. *Journal of British Studies* 34 (No. 1995). Pp. 1–34.
Ankarloo, Bengt. 'Sweden: The Mass Burnings'. In *Early Modern European Witchcraft: Centres and Peripheries*. Eds. Bengt Ankarloo and Gustav Henningsen. New York: Oxford University Press, 1993. Pp. 285–318.
Apps, Lara. 'Motive Hunting in the Case of Richard Hathaway'. *Preternature: Critical and Historical Studies on the Preternatural* 1 (No. 1, 2012). Pp. 72–99.
Ariès, Philippe. *Centuries of Childhood: A Social History of Family Life*. Robert Baldick. Trans. New York: Alfred A. Knopf, 1962.
Bacon, Simon and Ruickbie, Leo. 'Introduction'. In *The Cultural Construction of Monstrous Children: Essays on Anomalous Children from 1595 to the Present Day*. Eds. Simon Bacon and Leo Ruickbie. London and New York: Anthem Press, 2020. Pp. 1–22.
Baker, Emerson W. *A Storm of Witchcraft: The Salem Trials and the American Experience*. New York and Oxford: University Press, 2015.
Barry, Jonathan and Davies, Owen. Eds., *Palgrave Advances in Witchcraft Historiography*. New York: Palgrave Macmillan, 2007.
Beales, A. C. F. *Education under Penalty: English Catholic Education from the Reformation to the Fall of James II*. London: Athlone Press, 1963.
Behringer, Wolfgang. 'KINDERHEXENPROZESSE: Zur Rolle von Kindern in der Geschichte der Hexenverfolgung', *Zeitschrift für Historische Forschung* 16 (No. 1, 1989). Pp. 31–47.
Behringer, Wolfgang. *Witchcraft Persecutions in Bavaria: Popular Magic, Religious Zealotry and Reason of State in Early Modern Europe*. Cambridge: Cambridge University Press, 1997.

Borman, Tracy. Witches: *A Tale of Sorcery, Scandal and Seduction*. London: Jonathan Cape, 2013.

Boyer, Paul and Nissenbaum, Stephen. *Salem Possessed: The Social Origins of Witchcraft*. Cambridge and London: Harvard University Press, 1974.

Briggs, Robin. *Witches and Neighbours: The Social and Cultural Context of European Witchcraft*. Second edition. Malden: Blackwell, 2002.

Ceppi, Elisabeth. 'Invisible Labor: Puritan Servitude and the Demonic Possession of Elizabeth Knapp'. *American Literature: A Journal of Literary History, Criticism, and Bibliography* 78 (No. 2, 2006). Pp. 263–292.

Cho, Nancy Jiwon. 'Extending Moral and Religious Verse for Children from Puritan Adults' Warnings to Romantic Children's Insights: Ann and Jane Taylor's Pedagogic Achievements in *Hymns for Infant Minds* (1810)'. *Feminist Studies in English Literature* 23 (No. 1, 2015). Pp. 5–42.

Clark, Michael. '"Like Images Made Black with the Lightning": Discourse and the Body in Colonial Witchcraft'. *The Eighteenth Century* 34 (No. 3, 1993). Pp. 199–220.

Clark, Stuart. *Thinking with Demons: The Idea of Witchcraft in Early Modern Europe*. Oxford: Oxford University Press, 1999.

Cockburn, J. S. 'Early Modern Assize Records as Historical Evidence'. *Journal of the Society of Archivists* 5 (No. 4, 1975). Pp. 215–231.

Coventry, William W. *Demonic Possession On Trial: Case Studies in Early Modern England and Colonial America, 1593–1692*. Lincoln: iUniverse, 2003.

Craker, Wendel D. 'Spectral Evidence, Non-Spectral Acts of Witchcraft, and Confession at Salem in 1692'. *The Historical Journal* 40 (No. 2, 1997). Pp. 331–358.

Cunningham, Hugh. *Children and Childhood in Western Society Since 1500*. Second edition. Harlow: Pearson, 2005.

Darr, Orna Alyagon. *Marks of an Absolute Witch: Evidentiary Dilemmas in Early Modern England*. Oxford and New York: Routledge, 2016.

Demos, John Putnam. *Entertaining Satan: Witchcraft and the Culture of Early New England*. New York: Oxford University Press, 2004.

Demos, John Putnam. *The Enemy Within: A Short History of Witch-Hunting*. New York: Penguin Group, 2008.

Eberle, Paul and Eberle, Shirley. *The Abuse of Innocence: The McMartin Preschool Trial*. New York: Notable Trials Library, 1993.

Eisenbichler, Konrad. Ed. *The Premodern Teenager: Youth in Society 1150-1650*. Toronto: Centre for Reformation and Renaissance Studies, 2002.

Eilola, Jari. 'Interpreting Children's Blåkulla Stories in Sweden (1675)'. In *Demonology and Witch-Hunting in Early Modern Europe*. Eds. Julian Goodare, Rita Voltmer and Live Helene Willumsen. Oxford and New York: Routledge, 2020. Pp. 327–244.

Elmer, Peter. *Witchcraft, Witch-Hunting, and Politics in Early Modern England*. Oxford: Oxford University Press, 2016.

Erikson, Kai T. *Wayward Puritans: A Study in the Sociology of Deviance*. New York: John Wiley, 1966.

Ewen, C. L'Estrange. *Witch Hunting and Witch Trials*. London: Kegan Paul, Trench, Trubner, 1929.

Ewen, C. L'Estrange. *Witchcraft and Demonism: A Concise Account Derived from Sworn Depositions and Confessions Obtained in the Courts of England and Wales*. London: Heath Cranton Limited, 1933.

Ferber, Sarah, *Demonic Possession and Exorcism in Early Modern France*. London and New York: Routledge, 2004.
Ferraro, Joanna M. 'Medieval and Early Childhood'. *In The Routledge History of Childhood in the Western World*. pp. 61–77. Ed. Paula Fass. New York: Routledge, 2013. Pp. 61–77.
French, Anna. *Children of Wrath: Possession, Prophecy and the Young in Early Modern England*. Oxford and New York: Routledge, 2016.
French, Anna. 'Locating the Early Modern Child'. In *Early Modern Childhood: An Introduction*. Ed Anna French. Oxford and New York: Routledge, 2020. Pp. 3–15.
Gibson, Marion. *Reading Witchcraft: Stories of Early English Witches*. Oxford: Routledge, 1999.
Gibson, Marion. *Early Modern Witches: Witchcraft Cases in Contemporary Writing*. London and New York: Routledge, 2000.
Gibson, Marion. *Possession, Puritanism and Print: Darrell, Harsnett, Shakespeare and the Elizabethan Exorcism Controversy*. London and New York: Routledge, 2006.
Gibson, Marion. *The Witches of St Osyth: Persecution, Betrayal and Murder in Elizabethan England*. Cambridge and New York: Cambridge University Press, 2022.
Godbeer, Richard. *Escaping Salem: The Other Witch Hunt of 1692*. Oxford and New York: Oxford University Press, 2005.
Greven, Philip. *The Protestant Temperament: Patterns of Child-Rearing, Religious Experience, and the Self in Early America*. New York: Alfred A. Knopf, 1977.
Hansen, Chadwick. *Witchcraft at Salem*. New York: George Braziller Inc., 1969.
Henningsen, Gustav. 'The Greatest Witch-Trial of All: Navarre, 1609–1614'. *History Today* 30 (No. 11, 1980). Pp. 36–39.
Henningsen, Gustav. *The Witches' Advocate: Basque Witchcraft and the Spanish Inquisition 1609-1614*. Reno: University of Nevada Press, 1980.
Hill, Christopher. *Society and Puritanism in Pre-Revolutionary England*. London: Secker & Warburg, 1964.
Hill, Francis. *A Delusion of Satan*. Cambridge: Da Capo Press, 1997.
Hoffer, Peter Charles. *The Devil's Disciples: Makers of the Salem witchcraft trials*. Baltimore: The John Hopkins University Press, 1996.
Hoffer, Peter Charles. *The Salem Witchcraft Trials: A Legal History*. Lawrence: University Press of Kansas, 1997.
Homza, Lu Ann. *Village Infernos and Witches' Advocates: Witch-Hunting in Navarre, 1608-1614*. University Park: The Pennsylvania State University Press, 2022.
Houlbrooke, Ralph A. *The English Family 1450–1750*. London and New York: Longman, 1984.
Hutton, Ronald. *The Witch: A History of Fear, from Ancient Times to the Present*. New Haven: Yale University Press, 2017.
Jackson, Louise. 'Witches, Wives and Mothers: Witchcraft Persecution and Women's Confessions in Seventeenth-Century England'. In *The Witchcraft Reader*. Ed. Darren Oldridge. Third edition. London and New York: Routledge, 2019. Pp. 347–360.
Karlsen, Carol. F. *The Devil in the Shape of a Woman: Witchcraft in Colonial New England*. New York: W. W. Norton, 1987.
Katajala-Peltomaa, Sari. 'Diabolical Rage? Children, Violence, and Demonic Possession in the Late Middle Ages'. *Journal of Family History* 41 (No. 3, 2016). Pp. 236–254.

Kent, E. J. 'Salem Girls (1692): Problems of Gender and Agency'. In *Religion, the Supernatural and Visual Culture in Early Modern Europe: An Album Amicorum for Charles Zika*. Eds. Jennifer Spinks and Dagmar Eichberger. Leiden: Brill, 2015. Pp. 68–82.

Kieckhefer, Richard. 'Avenging the Blood of Children: Anxiety over Child Victims and the Origins of the European Witch Trials'. In *The Devil, Heresy and Witchcraft in the Middle Ages: Essays in Honor of Jeffrey*. Ed. B. Russell. Alberto Ferreiro. Koninklijke: Brill, 1998. Pp. 91–109.

Kittredge, G. L. 'King James I and "The Devil Is an Ass"'. *Modern Philology* 9 (No. 2, 1911). Pp. 195–209.

Kittredge, G. L. *Witchcraft in Old and New England*. New York: Russell & Russell, 1929.

Kloepfer, Deborah Kelly. 'Cotton Mather's "Dora": The Case History of Mercy Short'. *Early American Literature* 44 (No. 1, 2009). Pp. 3–38.

Knight, Janice. 'Telling it Slant: The Testimony of Mercy Short'. *Early American Literature* 37 (No. 1, 2002). Pp. 39–69.

Krausman Ben-Amos, Ilana. *Adolescence and Youth in Early Modern England*. New Haven: Yale University, 1994.

La Fontaine, J. S. *Speak of the Devil: Tales of Satanic Abuse in Contemporary England* Cambridge: Cambridge University Press, 1998.

Laskaris, Isabelle. 'Agency and Emotion of Young Female Accusers in the Salem Witchcraft Trials'. *Cultural and Social History* 16 (No. 4, 2019). Pp. 1–17.

Levack, Brian P. *The Devil Within: Possession and Exorcism in the Christian West*. New Haven and London: Yale University Press, 2013.

Levack, Brian P. 'The Horrors of Witchcraft and Demonic Possession'. *Social Research* 81 (No. 4, 2014). Pp. 921–939.

Lyman Kittridge, George. *Witchcraft in Old and New England*. New York: Russell & Russell, 1929.

Macfarlane, Alan. 'Reviewed Work(s): The Family, Sex and Marriage in England 1500-1800 by Lawrence Stone'. *History and Theory* 18 (No. 1, 1979). Pp. 103–126.

Macfarlane, Alan. *Witchcraft in Tudor and Stuart England: A Regional and Comparative Study*. Second edition. London: Routledge, 1999.

Millar, Charlotte-Rose. *Witchcraft, the Devil, and Emotions in Early Modern England*. London and New York: Routledge, 2017.

Miller, Arthur. *The Crucible*. London: Penguin Group, 1953.

Morgan, John. *Godly Learning: Puritan Attitudes towards Reason, Learning and Education, 1560-1640*. Cambridge: Cambridge University Press, 1986.

Morison, Samuel Eliot. *The Intellectual Life of Colonial New England*. New York: New York University Press, 1956.

Norton, Mary Beth. *In the Devil's Snare: The Salem Witchcraft Crisis of 1692*. New York: Vintage Books, 2002.

Notestein, Wallace. *A History of Witchcraft in England, From 1558 to 1718*. Baltimore: The American Historical Association, 1911.

O'Malley, Thomas. 'Gallows Hill: The Ancient Place of Execution'. In *The Cambridge Historical Society: Publications XVII Proceedings for the Years 1923 and 1924*. Cambridge: Published by the Society, 1931. Pp. 46–53.

Ozment, Steven. 'Raising a Loving Child in Late Medieval and Early Modern Europe (1400-1700)'. In *The Best Love of the Child: Being Loved and Being Taught to*

Love as the First Human Right. Ed. Timothy P. Jackson. Grand Rapids: William B. Eredmans, 2011. Pp. 93–112.

Pollock, Linda A. *Forgotten Children: Parent-Child Relations from 1500 to 1900*. Cambridge and New York: Cambridge University Press, 1983.

Purkiss, Diane. 'Invasions: Prophecy and Bewitchment in the Case of Margaret Muschamp'. *Tulsa Studies in Women's Literature* 17 (No. 2, 1998). Pp. 235–253.

Rabinowitz, Dorothy. 'No Crueller Tyranny: The Sacrosanct Accusation'. *Opinion Journal from the Wall Street Journal*. April 28th 2003.

Raiswell, Richard. 'Faking It: A Case of Counterfeit Possession in the Reign of James I'. *Renaissance and Reformation* 23 (No. 3, 1999). Pp. 29–48.

Ray, Benjamin C. 'The Geography of Witchcraft Accusations in 1692 Salem Village'. *The William and Mary Quarterly* 65 third series (No. 3, 2008). Pp. 449–478.

Ray, Benjamin C. *Satan & Salem: The Witch-Hunt Crisis of 1692*. Charlottesville: University of Virginia Press, 2015.

Roach, Marilynne K. *The Salem Witch Trials: A Day-By-Day Chronicle of a Community Under Siege*. Lanham: Cooper Square Press, 2002.

Roach, Marilynne K. *Six Women of Salem: The Untold Story of the Accused and Their Accusers in the Salem Witch Trials*. Philadelphia: De Capo Press, 2013.

Robinson, Enders A. *The Devil Discovered: Salem Witchcraft of 1692*. New York: Hippocrene Books, 1991.

Roper, Lyndal. '"Evil Imaginings and Fantasies": Child-Witches and the End of the Witch Craze'. *Past & Present* (No. 167, 2000). Pp. 107–139.

Roper, Lyndal. *Witch Craze: Terror and Fantasy in Baroque Germany*. New Haven and London: Yale University Press, 2004.

Rosenthal, Bernard. *Salem Story: Reading the Witch Trials 1692*. Cambridge: Cambridge University Press, 1993.

Salter, Michael and Dagistanli, Selda. 'Cultures of Abuse: "Sex Grooming", Organised Abuse and Race in Rochdale, UK'. *International Journal for Crime, Justice and Social Democracy* 4 (No. 2, 2015). P. 2.

Sands, Kathleen R. *Demonic Possession in Elizabethan England*. Westport: Praeger, 2004.

Sebald, Hans. *Witch-Children from Salem Witch-Hunts to Modern Courtrooms*. New York: Prometheus Books, 1995.

Seth, Ronald. *Children against Witches*. London: Robert Hale, 1969.

Sharpe, J. A. 'Disruption in the Well-Ordered Household: Age, Authority and Possessed Young People'. In *The Experience of Authority in Early Modern Europe*. Eds. Paul Griffiths, Adam Fox and Steve Hindle. New York: St Martin's Press, 1996. Pp. 187–213.

Sharpe, J. A. *Instruments of Darkness: Witchcraft in Early Modern England*. Philadelphia: University of Pennsylvania Press, 1997.

Sharpe, J. A. *The Bewitching of Anne Gunter: A Horrible and True Story of Deception, Witchcraft, Murder, and the King of England*. New York: Routledge, 2001.

Starkey, Marion L. *The Devil in Massachusetts: A Modern Enquiry into the Salem Witch Trials*. New York: Doubleday, 1949.

Stone, Lawrence. *The Family, Sex and Marriage in England 1500-1800*. London: Weidenfeld and Nicolson, 1977.

Taylor, John M. *The Witchcraft Delusion in Colonial Connecticut 1647–1697*. Hartford: Corner House Publishers, 1908.

Thomas, Keith. *Religion and the Decline of Magic: Studies in Popular Beliefs in Sixteenth-and Seventeenth-Century England.* Harmondsworth: Penguin Books, 1973.

Thomas, Keith. 'Age and Authority in Early Modern England'. *Proceedings in the British Academy* 65 (1976). Pp. 205–248.

Thomas, Keith. 'Children in Early Modern England'. In *Children and Their books: A Celebration of the Work of Iona and Peter Opie.* Eds. Gillian Avery and Julia Briggs. Oxford: Clarendon Press, 1989. Pp. 45–78.

Tomlinson, R. G. *Witchcraft Trials of Connecticut: The First Comprehensive, Documented History of Witchcraft Trials in Colonial Connecticut.* Hartford: The Bond Press, 1978.

Trask, Richard B. *The Devil Hath Been Raised: A Documentary History of the Salem Village Witchcraft Outbreak of 1692.* Danvers: Phoenix Publishing, 1992.

Underwood, Lucy. *Childhood, Youth, and Religious Dissent in Post-Reformation England.* New York: Palgrave Macmillan, 2014.

Upham, Charles W. *Salem Witchcraft with an Account of Salem Village and a History of Opinions on Witchcraft and Kindred Subjects.* Boston: Wiggin & Lunt, 1867.

Waite, Gary K. *Heresy, Magic and Witchcraft in Early Modern Europe.* Basingstoke: Palgrave Macmillan, 2003.

Walinski-Kiehl, Robert S. 'The Devil's Children: Child Witch-Trials in Early Modern Germany'. *Continuity and Change* 11 (No. 2, 1996). Pp. 171–189.

Walker, Anita M. and Dickerman, Edmund H. '"A Woman under the Influence": A Case of Alleged Possession in Sixteenth-Century France'. *The Sixteenth Century Journal* 22 (No. 3, 1991). Pp. 534–554.

Walker, Anita M. and Dickerman, Edmund H. 'A Notorious Woman: Possession, Witchcraft and Sexuality in Seventeenth Century Provence'. *Historical Reflections* 27 (No. 1, 2001). Pp. 1–26.

Walker, D. P. *Unclean Spirits: Possession and Exorcism in France and England in the Late Sixteenth and Early Seventeenth Centuries.* Philadelphia: University of Pennsylvania Press, 1981.

Walsh, Brendan. *The English Exorcist: John Darrell and the Shaping of Early Modern English Protestant Demonology.* New York and London: Routledge, 2021.

Weisman, Richard. *Witchcraft, Magic, and Religion in 17th Century Massachusetts.* Amherst: The University of Massachusetts Press, 1984.

West, Kristina. *Reading the Salem Witch Child: The Guilt Innocent Blood.* Cham, Switzerland: Palgrave Macmillan, 2020.

Willis, Deborah. *Malevolent Nurture: Witch-Hunting and Maternal Power in Early Modern England.* Ithaca and London: Cornell University Press, 1995.

Young, Francis. *A History of Anglican Exorcism Deliverance and Demonology in Church Ritual.* New York: Bloomsbury, 2018.

INDEX

For Product Safety Concerns and Information please contact our EU representative GPSR@taylorandfrancis.com
Taylor & Francis Verlag GmbH, Kaufingerstraße 24, 80331 München, Germany

www.ingramcontent.com/pod-product-compliance
Ingram Content Group UK Ltd.
Pitfield, Milton Keynes, MK11 3LW, UK
UKHW020154200926
475702UK00016B/2697

9781041165781